OXFORD WORLD'S CLASSICS

THOMAS HARDY

The Mayor of Casterbridge

Edited with an Introduction and Notes by
DALE KRAMER

Oxford   New York
OXFORD UNIVERSITY PRESS

Oxford University Press, Great Clarendon Street, Oxford OX2 6DP

Oxford New York

Athens Auckland Bangkok Bogota Bombay Buenos Aires
Calcutta Cape Town Dar es Salaam Delhi Florence Hong Kong Istanbul
Karachi Kuala Lumpur Madras Madrid Melbourne Mexico City
Nairobi Paris Singapore Taipei Tokyo Toronto Warsaw

and associated companies in
Berlin Ibadan

Oxford is a trade mark of Oxford University Press

First published as a World's Classics paperback 1987
Reissued as an Oxford World's Classics paperback 1998

British Library Cataloguing in Publication Data

Data available

Library of Congress Cataloging in Publication Data
Hardy, Thomas, 1840–1928.
The mayor of Casterbridge.
(The World's classics)
I. Kramer, Dale, 1936– . II. Title.
PR4750 M25 1987 923'.8 86 23858
ISBN 0-19-283441-X

1 3 5 7 9 10 8 6 4 2

Printed in Great Britain by
Caledonian International Book Manufacturing Ltd.
Glasgow

CONTENTS

CONTENTS

GENERAL EDITOR'S PREFACE

THE first concern in The World's Classics editions of Hardy's works has been with the texts. Individual editors have compared every version of the novel or stories that Hardy might have revised, and have noted variant readings in words, punctuation, and styling in each of these substantive texts; they have thus been able to exclude much that their experience suggests that Hardy did not intend. In some cases this is the first time that the novel has appeared in a critical edition purged of errors and oversights; where possible Hardy's manuscript punctuation is used, rather than what his compositors thought he should have written.

Some account of the editors' discoveries will be found in the Note on the Text in each volume, while the most interesting revisions their work has revealed are included as an element of the Explanatory Notes. In some cases a Clarendon Press edition of the novel provides a wealth of further material for the reader interested in the way Hardy's writing developed from manuscript to final collected edition.

I should like to thank Shirley Tinkler for her help in drawing the maps that accompany each volume.

SIMON GATRELL

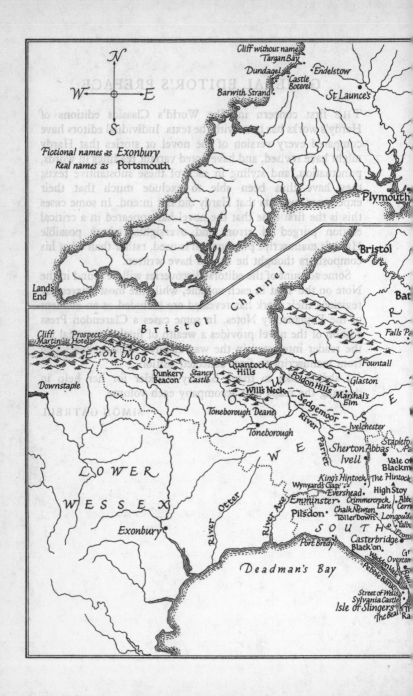

N
W — E
S

Fictional names as Exonbury
Real names as Portsmouth

Cliff without name
Targan Bay
Dundagel · Endelstow
Barwith Strand · Castle
Boterel
St Launce's

Plymouth

Bristol

Land's
End

Channel

Bristol

Bat

Cliff · Prospect
Martin · Hotel
Exon Moor

Falls Pa

R

Quantock
Hills

Dunkery
Beacon
Stancy
Castle
Will's Neck

Fountall

Downstaple

Poldon Hills · Glaston

Marshal's
Elm

Toneborough Deane

Sedgemoor

Ivelchester

Toneborough

Staplefo

River Parret

Sherton Abbas · Vale of
Blackm

Ivell

King's Hintock · The Hintock

LOWER

Wynards Gap · High Stoy

Evershead

Emminster · Crimmercrock
Lane
Abb
Cern

WESSEX

Pilsdon · Chalk Newton
Tollerdown
Longpudo
Yalbu

SOUTHE

River Otter

River Axe

Exonbury

Casterbridge

Port Bredy · Black'on · Overcom

Gr

Deadman's Bay

Weddon Val

Pebble

Street of Wells
Sylvania Castle
Isle of Slingers
The Beal

Th
Ra

HARDY'S WESSEX
OF THE NOVELS AND POEMS

0 ... 10 ... 20
Miles

The Channel

ACKNOWLEDGEMENTS

MARGARET DICKIE, former head of the Department of English at the University of Illinois at Urbana-Champaign, has during all the stages of preparation of this edition provided encouragement and, more practically, financial assistance at crucial times. Financial support has also come from the Research Board of the Graduate College of the University. Part of the financial assistance funded an early study based on a microfilm of the manuscript, by Suzanne Falck-Yi, whose careful work allowed my own research to proceed much more promptly than would otherwise have been possible. The American Philosophical Society and the National Endowment for the Humanities awarded travel grants for work at the British Library, the National Library of Scotland, and the Dorset County Museum. I am indebted to the governing boards and staffs of the above libraries and museums, in particular to Mr R. N. R. Peers and Mr P. C. Ensom of the Dorset County Museum and to Dr Iain Brown and Miss Margaret Deas of the National Library of Scotland, and also to Mr Michael Bott, Keeper of the Archives and Manuscripts at the Library of the University of Reading, to Richard Little Purdy, to the Interlibrary Loan Desk of the library of the University of Illinois, and to the Colby College Library, especially to J. Fraser Cocks III. Alan Manford generously loaned me his copy of Macmillan's Colonial Library Edition of *The Mayor of Casterbridge*. Nancy Marck helped correct the proofs.

INTRODUCTION

WRITTEN in 1884 and 1885, *The Mayor of Casterbridge* was the first of the four novels—the others being *The Woodlanders*, *Tess of the d'Urbervilles*, and *Jude the Obscure*—which capped Hardy's career in fiction. On 17 April 1885 he noted: 'Wrote the last page of "The Mayor of Casterbridge", begun at least a year ago, and frequently interrupted in the writing of each part' (*Life and Work*, p. 177).[1] Among other causes of the interruptions—which included trips to London and vacations—was the building of his permanent home, Max Gate. After nearly a decade of married life moving from one rented accommodation to another, Hardy had decided the country town of Dorchester, near his birthplace at Higher Bockhampton, was where he wanted to live when not in London 'for the season', rather than in a literary or major population centre, or in such a place as Winchester with its historical associations, or Devon, which his wife Emma would have preferred. Hardy once said that he liked to live amidst the scenes he was writing about. The novel he wrote while Max Gate was being planned and built not only celebrates the Dorchester of Hardy's youth (Robert Gittings notes that the opening chapters are set during the time of the youthful distresses of his mother, some of which formed the basis of stories she told him [*The Older Hardy*, p. 41, and see *Young Thomas Hardy*, pp. 8–9, 14–17]), but also the creative bond between place and Hardy's personality. Just before and during the writing of this novel the idea of 'Wessex' as a common setting for his novels became fixed, and his finest writings to the end of his life were based on West England scenes and lore.

Hardy was a literary person as much as a Dorsetman, and the shape his career took with *The Mayor of Casterbridge* may reflect not only an instinctive return to county heritage for a subject, or to the world of childhood for emotional sustenance, but also a

---

[1] Full documentation for most of the references and parenthetical citations in the introductory matter of this edition can be found in the Select Bibliography or at the beginning of the Explanatory Notes immediately following the text of the novel.

reaction to literary criticism. Hardy was sensitive to what was said about him and his works; and in the April 1883 issue of the *Westminster Review* appeared a retrospective by Havelock Ellis, the first extensive commentary his *œuvre* received, occasioned perhaps by the recent publication of *Two on a Tower*. What Ellis says about *Two on a Tower* and the novels preceding it may bear upon Hardy's concentrating subsequently on what he knew, using a setting familiar to him:

Mr. Hardy has given to each of his later novels a distinct and dominating background. In *The Return of the Native* the Dorset heathland formed a landscape in the manner of Old Crome which was visible throughout. The bustle of military preparation is used with admirable skill and reticence in *The Trumpet Major*. *A Laodicean* is an architectural novel, and *Two on a Tower* is astronomical. This method adds to the charm of freshness and variety which distinguishes Mr. Hardy's work; but on the whole is progressively unsatisfactory. The astronomical enthusiasm is wanting in spontaneity. We prefer Mr. Proctor [author of *Poetry of Astronomy* (1881)] for popular astronomy. [Reprinted in Cox, *Critical Heritage*, p. 125.]

That Ellis's essay in general strongly praised as well as discriminatingly evaluated Hardy's work would have made Hardy all the more receptive to this kind of observation. While Hardy's grateful letter to Ellis in response to the essay is non-committal it shows his sensitivity to the 'appearance' of his work in others' eyes (*Collected Letters*, I. 117–18), and while naturally he does not announce a programme for future works it is noticeable that none of the four great novels that followed this review employs protagonists or professions requiring arcane knowledge to portray—not even the knowledge of his own first profession, architecture.

Perhaps Ellis's review gives a clue also to certain somewhat marked qualities of *The Mayor of Casterbridge*. In addition to being sensitive to public statements, and eager to meet objections he felt fair, Hardy strongly objected to being 'typed'. After the success of *Far from the Madding Crowd* nearly ten years earlier he had put aside the story that later became *The Woodlanders* because of this objection, writing instead a novel of social comedy—*The Hand of Ethelberta*—

that was only the first of several failures in experimentation; and it is not unlikely that he was irritated (although his letter does not express this) with Ellis's emphasis on his skill as a portrayer of *women*. Only John Loveday among Hardy's men gains Ellis's clear approval, being called 'noble'. In *The Mayor of Casterbridge* Hardy may be attempting to show such as Ellis, first, what he can do with a male protagonist and, second, that he can write a story in which love does not drive the plot.

Of course Hardy's firm turning to tragic subjects within a rural and socially modest setting was not impelled by Ellis's essay alone. He was prepared for a development in his work. Michael Millgate sees the period between *Two on a Tower* (1882) and *The Mayor of Casterbridge* as a time of stock-taking, with 'The Dorsetshire Labourer' and the move to Max Gate indications of Hardy's dissatisfaction with his preceding experiments in fictional settings and with an unsettled residence. But Ellis's commentary came at a critical time during Hardy's self-assessment, and the impact of his prediction that in Hardy's future lay more works like the inferior *Two on a Tower* than like *Far from the Madding Crowd* (which he discusses as Hardy's most successful book to the time of the article) would at the least have urged upon Hardy added cause for his 'deliberate attempt', in Millgate's words, 'to pick up lost Wessex threads' (*Career as a Novelist*, p. 204) and 'virtually to reconstruct himself as a novelist upon a new basis' (p. 222).

In inaugurating his self-reconstruction, Hardy created in Henchard the most remarkable and dominant of all his characters, providing him with a surrounding group of fascinating if—in comparison with him—minor characters, and a rich historical and social scene. The mayor of Casterbridge is Michael Henchard; and Michael Henchard *is The Mayor of Casterbridge*. Thus put in tautological form is the principle of the novel's strength and the reason for its enduring appeal. Henchard—an inarticulate, selfish man, incapable of manifesting affection consistently—possesses a depth beyond the explicable. On the one hand, his ability to absorb punishment despite his often narrow perspective and aggressive and transitory passions justifies the simple but firm label 'tragedy'. Henchard lays fair claim to being the most Greek-like hero of the Victorian novel, bearing analogies at once with Oedipus, Creon, Agamemnon, and the Prometheus of Aeschylus (putting aside for the moment other analogies with such biblical and Elizabethan sufferers as Cain and Lear). He is the manifestation of elemental force, not a compilation of attributes that can be dissected and 'understood' separate from his own display. Similarly, to turn Henchard into an object of metaphysical abstraction is to erase his power. To put it inadequately, he simply exists—and those within his reach must accept him for what he is.

On the other hand, are all the indications of Henchard's contradictoriness and unknowableness on quite basic human levels of motivation. Most striking here is his attitude toward love. The point is established early on that he is a woman-hater 'by nature'; yet he simultaneously complains that he has gloomy fits because of 'the loneliness of my domestic life' that would cause him, like Job, to curse the day he was born; and the narrator soon after this marks him as needing someone for 'pouring out his heat upon'. The evidence is overwhelming that Henchard's needs do not include sexual or romantic love. His feeling at the sale of Susan is shame, not bereavement at loss of his wife (or daughter); he remarries Susan not for renewed love but because of a sense of permanent obligation and duty and 'rightness'; he is willing to marry Lucetta (before Susan returns) because it seems the right thing to do, and after the way is again clear to court and marry Lucetta he is slow, if dutiful, at taking up again the idea of marriage, whether for love or obligation. He is able to live in close quarters with Elizabeth-Jane after he knows she is not his daughter with nary a sexual feeling. The strongest loves he feels are of a brotherly nature (Farfrae resembles his long-dead brother) and fatherly ('the tenderest human tie' is what inspires the need for 'some human object for pouring out his heat upon'). There is no evident resolution to the question of Henchard and emotion, although many suggestions have been made.

A barely discernible but important common thread in his

affections is hinted at in the context of the passage 'He was the kind of man to whom some human object for pouring out his heat upon—were it emotive or were it choleric—was almost a necessity.' The suggestion is that the 'heat' needn't be returned. In the absence of human affection during his eighteen years in Casterbridge (apart from the evidently unique episode on the isle of Jersey with Lucetta) his 'heat' had been poured out upon business. Elaine Showalter calls this the 'commercialised energies of sexual sublimation' (in *Critical Approaches*, p. 106). Certainly some essential emotional need of Henchard's personality is being sublimated. This thread comes again to attention later, when the question is posed whether Henchard wants to marry Lucetta (after Susan's death) to fill the 'emotional void' caused by his discovery that Elizabeth-Jane is not his daughter, or to gain added wealth. One notes the element of ambivalence, the difficulty of pinning a motivation on Henchard; but more relevant is that the only love in the novel that Henchard clearly regrets losing is non-sexual, and one that goes *out* from him. Money, likewise, does not *return* affection. The thread tying together Henchard's affections, then, especially those related to females, is that perhaps Henchard, in self-contempt, doesn't want to *be* loved. In his characterizing postures toward love—rejection, indifference, abjection—Henchard seems unable to foster anything like a full relationship or communication, one of reciprocal responsibility.

In the context of Henchard's overall activities, this veering away from reciprocity may contribute to his grandeur and isolation, not to mention symbolic value. That is, it helps to emphasize that there may be more central problems than sex, or even one-to-one human relations. He is dissatisfied with *life*, a dissatisfaction masked for a good part of the novel by aggressiveness, competitiveness, and a will to conquer, but eventually laid bare when all the external trappings of success and then the internal compensations of affection are stripped from him. The similarities with Lear are neither accidental, nor mechanical; the parallels enrich the reader's perception of Henchard. Failure or refusal to quiz one's own motives can, again as with Lear, create a kind of grandeur in its self-isolating consequences, as is suggested by Henchard's existing on too large a scale to notice the minutiae of Lucetta's and Farfrae's courting.

Henchard gains and holds attention through the contrast between the way he is presented in comparison with the other characters and the novel's plot situations. While he is loomingly and indeed overbearingly present in the novel's texture, what one is to make of him evades precise definition; in contrast, other features of the book have much more restricted configurations, although the patterns of meaning may be complexly interwoven. That is, while there may be uncertainty in points of description and action, and in other characters' motivations, a straightforward acceptance of their evident meaning will not be far off the mark, but Henchard's actions form an opaque shield of his essential nature.

Although there may be a clinical diagnosis to be made of Henchard (and although my point is not that he is arcane or 'odd'), the main thrust appears to be that he is different from all others: his sexual urges, his familial bonds, his fraternal memories, his paternal and post-paternal feelings—all are either on the boundary or beyond the boundaries observed by everyone else within the novel's reach. He is, thus, set aside, marked, doomed, precisely because someone so exceptional and unique cannot exist in a society which endorses at every level (including Farfrae's when he arrives) conformity, especially conformity with what had gone before. Thus, Farfrae, although like Henchard an outsider and also a potential rider on the wheel of fortune (thus destined to be toppled), will not experience a fall as special as Henchard's, because he 'fits in': he loves a woman with protean charms but when those charms are revealed as perilously tawdry (by his conventional standards) he settles comfortably for someone wise. Henchard's uniqueness and his exclusion from normalcy give him an emotional status with the reader well beyond Farfrae's capabilities to repeat. What in Henchard's peculiarities accounts for his appeal? I—and I suspect most readers and critics—would say that it's his uncompromising, unflinching exertion toward goals he may not understand, and a similar stark willingness to suffer the consequences for being what he is—aspects of his asserted self-sufficiency, which of course has been at the core of his behaving as he has done and does. Thus he is of a piece. He stolidly suffers what comes rather than attempts to evade or excuse, and in this he is justified. Like Oedipus and Lear, Henchard is to blame for the disasters that bring about his fate.

The novel is a classic study of loneliness, all the more authoritative because it is not analytic or intellectual. Hardy writes of the aloneness of a human being who needs contact with another person but who, when such contact becomes available, cannot abide its constrictive impact. Inevitably, that other being's own sense of self impinges, interfering with the drive to self-realization that is primary in personality.

Henchard's behaviour is that of an 'isolate' who constantly realigns his affections towards people who, in a real sense, are different from him. He accurately calls himself a Cain— someone who learns by experience what is acceptable within a community and within a divine set of laws. He is also a Cain in that he is at home nowhere, seldom able to make and never able to maintain normal relationships with other people. It is significant that we never know where he was born and bred, from what part of England he gained his essential character: we know far less about the shaping forces in Henchard's background than about those of the other central actors in this drama, although like him none of them is a native of the town that gives the novel its name. To be termed the 'mayor *of* Casterbridge' is an almost entirely political status, then: it does not establish social or psychological kinship with the community, although Henchard shares more of the community's biases and superstitions than does Farfrae.

Henchard's isolation is intensified even by his massive persistence and strength, which instead of marshalling to forge stable human relationships he manifests mostly in business and in supporting his bare existence. He is able to hold to his oath of abstinence from alcohol for twenty-one years from sheer force of will, and to succeed in the corn-factoring business from 'energy'; but no more with Farfrae and Elizabeth-Jane than with the youthful Susan is he able to maintain his initial regard or affection. Envy and jealousy lead to impetuous outbreaks that exhaust Farfrae's patience; later, resentment and violence alternate with periods of affection and the acceptance of the seed-shop. His feelings toward Lucetta are shaded alternately with passion, pity, loneliness, greed, and jealousy, in such a way that it almost seems more a *series* of relationships he has with her than a single developing one. Towards Elizabeth-Jane there is an even more varied range of emotions, from acceptance when she and Susan arrive in Casterbridge to profound resentment upon the discovery of her true parentage, to a willingness to be served by her in his illness, to an overriding settling of all his affections, indeed will to live, upon her. (Apart from the fact that he allows this last mood to dominate him, and to kill him, there is no reason to expect that this last emotion towards her would be held to.) A comment recorded several years later may express part of Hardy's view of personality illustrated through Henchard: 'I am more than ever convinced that persons are successively various persons, according as each special strand in their characters is brought uppermost by circumstances' (*Life and Work*, p. 241). But Henchard has allowed this human trait to go out of control.

However, the novel is not all Henchard, and it is not just Henchard who moves through several relationships. And if Henchard exists alone on his extreme level of effort and suffering, the other characters are not one-dimensional foils. Much can be made of Farfrae's coldness and near-hypocritical (and, at the minimum, shallow) celebration in song of Scotland's appeal, and his penny-pinching wage policies are matched by his reluctance 'to make a hole in a sovereign' in his and Elizabeth-Jane's search for Henchard; but he is also honest and forthright in his affections for both Lucetta and Elizabeth-Jane (even if his manner of alternating between the two women suggests opportunism and an underlying instability), and he does all that is reasonable to maintain friendly relations toward Henchard both before and after their falling-out and Henchard's worldly decline. Farfrae parallels Henchard in many details of their imposing themselves upon the Casterbridge world; and if Henchard has flaws that bring him down within the novel, and which are disastrously brought into play in the trading world by his resentment of Farfrae, Farfrae clearly has flaws that can bring him down in time. (A question, of course, is whether Farfrae's fall would be tragic, or merely realistic: certainly the ease with which one can consider and balance up Farfrae's virtues and flaws suggests he lacks complexity and the tension of undefined internal forces that make Henchard's suffering so empathetic.)

Elizabeth-Jane is something of a prig; concerned with respectability from her first appearance, she is disturbed when she learns that Lucetta is newly rich (rather than someone from whom she can learn gentility). But she also has a very close relationship with the narrator. Chapter IX, for example, opens on Elizabeth-Jane's receptivity to the atmosphere of Casterbridge, presenting details about Casterbridge's city/country orientation that she could not possibly know at the time; and it is through her that the narrator channels the novel's concluding wisdom. Her common sense and insight into the value of things may be attractive and so admirable as to make her views a moral touchstone; but the energy of her wedding-day rejection of Henchard—containing false statements about the pain Henchard caused Newson by his lie—conveys, toward the novel's close, her self-protective passion and assertiveness that had been implicit in her earlier more muted anxiety about indecorum. Elizabeth-Jane's behaviour hints at an internal imbalance which a novel with a different overall conception might have encouraged Hardy to develop. While, as Hardy says, her mother is dominant in her personality, in an odd way she is more the daughter of Michael Henchard than of the bland and superficial Newson.

Elizabeth-Jane's mother Susan is also presented in a way to raise one's curiosity. She is treated with contempt by Henchard, and there are no direct indications from the narrator that Henchard is mistaken about her mental capacity. Still, her course through the novel is one of continued triumphs over circumstance: reading Newson's character at a glance she exchanges a carping and discontented husband for one who honours her self-concept; upon being made aware of the legal status of her relationship with Newson she manages to rid herself of him; she evaluates Henchard's position before making herself known to him, and succeeds in improving her worldly situation; most striking of all, she disguises the true age and situation of her surviving daughter so as to establish her in prosperity before her own death. And all of her points are gained while she seems to be wanly stupefied before others' greater energy. Is her portrayal the result of great skill, or of the author's using her only as an integer in others' equations?

This self-modifying aspect of the narrative has particular bearing for an understanding of Henchard. There can be little doubt but that Hardy conceived of Henchard as a tragic figure. Yet no character in this novel is so devastatingly exposed in his or her weaknesses, or has his or her standing queried by authorial irony, in a variety of contexts, as Henchard. In the most obvious instance, Henchard says his word is his bond, whereupon he immediately in effect breaks his bond to Jopp by hiring Farfrae before interviewing Jopp. His visit to the weather prophet is a reminder of his deep instinctual sense of the universal forces appealed to and tamed by superstition and folklore; but the narrator's commentary indicates that the forecasting methods of the intimidating 'Wide-oh' are little more mysterious than those of Gabriel Oak. This double perspective provides an assessment by realistic criteria of tragic or mythic pretension.

Irony also, of course, is employed in a fashion more conventional for tragedy. Henchard forces the churchgoers in the Three Mariners Inn to sing a Psalm as a curse against Farfrae, while in fact the force of the curse comes to be applied against Henchard himself, faintly but unmistakably echoed in his own deathbed will. What might have been a simple inversion of expectation is compacted by the ominous suggestion of forces greater than Henchard. Henchard exploits his chance notice of the Psalm, as he pages through the bandsman's psalter, to bring his feelings to the surface, and his dominating the crowd at the Three Mariners may immediately relieve his feelings; but the ultimate backlash from this gesture is suggestive of the threat to him of the universe, or moral system of poetic justice. Henchard himself has interpreted events according to this standard of judgement, suspecting that 'a sinister intelligence' is 'bent on punishing him' by revealing—via Susan's letter—Elizabeth-Jane's parentage. That the narrator rejects this interpretation further illustrates the way the text subverts Henchard's sense of his own significance, even as it steadily intensifies the sense of his isolation and loneliness as he fails repeatedly to get a grip on the changing situation.

As if in refutation of the occasional deflation of Henchard's stature, the setting in which his acts take place is a reminder of their resonance. 'Place' is scarcely invented by Hardy in this novel—Egdon Heath and the farms at Weatherbury are immediately obvious settings whose roles anticipate that of *The Mayor of Casterbridge*. But perhaps because *The Mayor of Casterbridge* was the first novel Hardy wrote following his decision to build a permanent home near Dorchester, from its inception the novel was deeply connected to the real Dorchester and the fields and streams near by, with historical associations and a precise archaeology. It comes as no surprise that some lines in the novel describing Roman burials closely resemble those in a paper Hardy gave to the Dorset County Antiquarian Group shortly after he finished the novel (see Explanatory Notes to p. 70). Drawing on so many sites and structures in and near the county town of Dorchester gives the impression that Hardy is attempting to freeze in his imagination the town near which he had been born in 1840 (about the time of the action of *The Mayor of Casterbridge*) and in which he had been educated, apprenticed, and employed until 1862. All of this points to the importance to Hardy's imagination of *real* scenes—not imaginary like Trollope's Barchester or Blackmore's Doone country in North Devon, and not fanciful and heightened like Dickens's London, but precise, closely observed, and accurate (allowing for such minor discrepancies brought about by the shifting of the location of certain objects in order to bring them into a more suggestive conjunction, such as Colliton House and its stone arch with the mask being moved nearer the market-place and renamed High-Place Hall). The consequence of Hardy's apparent need or desire to give attention to an actual setting is its natural, unstrained reinforcement of the novel's action.

Typically, this process depends upon the narrator's

establishment of the anthropology of a location before having a scene take place there, thereby explicitly relating the behaviour of present individuals to that of countless predecessors while implicitly indicating (through its interruption of the action to allow for the explanation of a place's previous relevance) that the dramatic personae are not specific persons only, but also representative of the range of possibilities of action and counter-action.

The contribution of physical background to the effectiveness of the scene being played out against it is clearly observable in Chapter XI, in which nearly as much space is given to the description of the Amphitheatre (Maumbury Ring) and to its evocations as to the presentation of the meeting between Henchard and the just-arrived Susan. Neither Henchard nor Susan is portrayed during the scene as conscious of the associations of the Amphitheatre, but this of itself only emphasizes that in this novel characters, at least in part, have an existence beyond that as individuals. Nor is the relevance of all the associations immediately seen. If the Amphitheatre had once been the site of the execution of a woman who had poisoned her spouse, it now serves as site of the initiation of restoration of marriage bonds by a man who had once got rid of *his* spouse—in a non-violent fashion but revealing a self-engrossment equal to that of the woman's, who killed her husband even though he had allowed her lovers. In addition, there is a parallel with Susan herself, who has brought about Newson's 'death' and who eventually, in contrast with Mary Channing, dies in worldly triumph as the mayor's wife rather than in public chastisement—but of course this recognition is retrospective. The narrator's dispassionate tone also accommodates a disquisition on the separateness of past and present that the novel overall rejects:

Imaginative inhabitants who would have felt an unpleasantness at the discovery of a comparatively modern skeleton in their gardens, were quite unmoved by these hoary shapes [newly uncovered Roman skeletons]. They had lived so long ago, their time was so unlike the present, their hopes and motives were so widely removed from ours, that between them and the living there seemed to stretch a gulf too wide for even a spirit to pass.

Numerous scenes in the novel take place in a similar context—particularities within a continuum. The beginning of Chapter XXXII, for instance, is a near duplication of that of Chapter XI: here it is the two bridges east of Dorchester/Casterbridge that are described as typifying different psychological reactions to worldly ruin, followed by an interchange between the novel's two characters most closely tied to the concepts of success and failure, Henchard, leaning over the coping of the farther bridge, and Farfrae, who has walked out to offer Henchard living quarters in his own house (the house that previously had been Henchard's). Similarly, the next chapter opens with a consideration of a 'convivial custom' in Casterbridge—the drinking, by the churchgoers and choir, of a half-pint of liquor at the Three Mariners Inn. It is the thing done 'at this date'; and the sociological portrait of the handling of liquor by conventional people forms an effective contrast to the succeeding scene, of Henchard drunkenly celebrating the completion of his vow of not drinking taken twenty-one years before.

Thus, scene after scene in this novel of specific locale takes place within the context of a past custom or an existing set of guidelines. Although none of the major characters participates consciously within this context (the closest any of them come are Farfrae's superficial 'It's the way o' the warrld!' and Henchard's scarcely more perceptive "Tis turn and turn about, isn't it?' as acknowledgements of their rise and fall in the world), the novel's presentation is an alternation between macrocosm and microcosm, between generalization and *exempla*. Thus arises the very tight and intimate relationship between context and character and event and 'meaning'. The bridges, for example, are structures that acquire their value from the way people perceive them, which in part is due exactly to their physical location in relation to the town and to each other and to the more distant countryside. Proximity is key, just as Henchard's proximity to people affects his feelings about them and himself. Mixen Lane is a locality that acquires moral significance because of typical activities there. It is a fester on the town, and like Tom-All-Alone's in *Bleak House*, or like Carlyle's typhoid carrier in *Past and Present*, it reveals its brotherhood to society by damaging members of the social order supposedly independent of such low existence. The actuality of place inspires Hardy to interpret all that is visible to his eye: the mask in the keystone arch might appear to offer only incidental symbolism, but as with Mixen Lane its meaning ('intrigue') is gained through its association with human activity, arching over the rear door to High-Place Hall—Lucetta's chosen residence in Casterbridge she has rented as part of her plan to have Henchard marry her, and in which building she manages to entice the affection of Farfrae away from Elizabeth-Jane.

Two of the most important associations stemming from Hardy's handling of place develop from remnants of the Roman era and the peculiarly close relationship of city and country. As the passage above suggests, the continued presence of the Romans offers the measure of timelessness, a consolation in our own fevered existence (which too will pass, giving rest). The portrayal of the rural in conjunction with the town forms the perfect image of an organic, complete society:

Casterbridge, as has been hinted, was a place deposited in the block upon a cornfield. There was no suburb in the modern sense, or transitional intermixture of town and down. It stood, with regard to the wide fertile land adjoining, clean-cut and distinct, like a chess board on a green table-cloth. The farmer's boy could sit under his barley-mow and pitch a stone into the office-window of the town-clerk; reapers at work among the sheaves nodded to acquaintances standing on the pavement-corner; the red-robed judge, when he condemned a sheep stealer, pronounced sentence to the tune of Baa, that floated in at the window from the remainder of the flock browsing hard by; and at executions the waiting crowd stood in a meadow immediately before the drop, out of which the cows had been temporarily driven to give the spectators room.

The bucolicism of this image of an interdependent society is subsequently much modified by the revelation that Mixen Lane also forms a part of it, but of course the awareness of corruption in the world is an inevitable and thus natural part of knowledge.

Consideration of place leads to two further observations about Hardy's concerns as he was rethinking his ambitions as a novelist, both of them clarifying the kind of tragedy he was writing. First, the commentaries on place I have referred to or quoted indicate that the narrator knows beforehand the import of the interrelationships of individual and society, of character and signifying role. This foreknowledge indicates an analogy between the narrator and the chorus of classical Greek drama, in providing a wisdom based on general standards. None the less, it is also true that the narrator of *The Mayor of Casterbridge*—again like the Greek tragic chorus—prevents certitude. That is, the narrator's participation is as a quality of drama, of situational tension. Just as a Greek chorus has a tendency to echo the feelings that have most recently been expressed by a major figure, as if to strengthen the sense of antithetical forces in a tragedy, so does Hardy's narrator in *The Mayor of Casterbridge* partake in the indeterminacies of the moment to heighten a transitory drama. These qualities of foreknowledge and indeterminacy combine to make the narrator's role in *The Mayor of Casterbridge* distinct. This novel's narrator is not, like that of *Tess of the d'Urbervilles*, a case of marked subjectivity, or, like that of *Jude the Obscure*, one of self-abandonment of control and detachment. Second, the emphasis on place in the novel inevitably calls to mind the concept of unity of place that has for centuries held a strong position in tragic theorizing, since this unity was elevated alongside that proposed by Aristotle, the unity of action. Both of these observations point up Hardy's ambitions in this novel of producing a tragedy.

The Mayor of Casterbridge is one of a handful of novels that justify being considered as tragedies in near-classical terms in all but its not being set on an actual stage—and its emphasis upon place can readily be seen as the compensating mode; the narrator's allusion to the market-place as the 'Open Place in spectacular dramas' only makes explicit what is implicit in the novel's deliberately confined setting. Hardy himself wrote other tragic novels, but not even *The Return of the Native* approaches *The Mayor of Casterbridge* in its adherence to traditional criteria of tragedy. Most novels that lay claim to tragic qualities are stiff and stilted, or pretentious; and *The Return of the Native* possesses some or all of these qualities.

But *The Mayor of Casterbridge* reaches these levels without the flaws that so often attend strenuous ambition or an inappropriate subject.

Different readers have thought of Henchard as a Sophoclean tragic hero because he is doomed in the present because of what he has done in the past, or as an Aeschylean or Euripidean tragic hero because he is made to suffer more than his deeds would seem to require; there are echoes of *King Lear* as well as of biblical conflicts between Saul and David. None of these possibilities is stressed in this novel about a market town and two ambitious men. But in his unostentatious way Hardy has made the novel a paradigm of Aristotle's description of a successful tragedy: it has of course a hero of elevated position; the pride of elevation creates resentment that contributes to one's fall, as is seen perhaps in Henchard but certainly in Lucetta at the visit of the Royal Personage; characters face reversals of expectation, and the plot contains 'recognition scenes' (for example at the end of the battle in the loft, and after Henchard flees Casterbridge).

Two of Hardy's comments about tragedy which frame the writing of *The Mayor of Casterbridge* suggest the primacy for him of the larger plot structure over sensitive recording of minute details of personality. In April 1878 he wrote: 'A Plot, or Tragedy, should arise from the gradual closing in of a situation that comes of ordinary human passions, prejudices, and ambitions, by reason of the characters taking no trouble to ward off the disastrous events produced by the said passions, prejudices, and ambitions' (*Life and Work*, p. 123), a comment which explicitly relates 'plot' and 'tragedy', and excludes fate or external force. Within months of finishing *The Mayor of Casterbridge*, he defines tragedy 'in brief': 'a tragedy exhibits a state of things in the life of an individual which unavoidably causes some natural aim or desire of his to end in a catastrophe when carried out' (*Life and Work*, p. 182).

If *The Mayor of Casterbridge* is successful from the action of the plot upon a character peculiarly fitted to suffer, that is not the only cause. Hardy founded his plot upon the universally-observed conflict between generations of a family, between ways of moral and economic activity, between different interpretations of nature's impact upon humanity. Such myth-like evocation must be simple at its heart, and so it is in *The Mayor of Casterbridge*. The opposition of Henchard and Farfrae is essentially a formal contrast of two different ways of dealing with the same elusive crop conditions, from planting to speculation based on harvest weather. This opposition can be expanded to two ways of dealing with conditions of life, with people, with the universe, as it is in Henchard and Farfrae: the friendly but shallow, and optimistic but withal cautious, man who recognizes that bankruptcy is a natural if avoidable feature of a business life, the intellectually limited and cruel egoist who can perceive no other's life but as circling around his own but who also perceives and accepts to the profoundest depths of his being that actions have consequences, and who while he can never move beyond the limitations of his self is able to understand the insignificance of both worthiness and worldly success.

The plot is as sound in detail as in conception. Hardy once complained that the serial publication of the novel forced him to create too many sensational incidents, weakening the structure of the book. But not only may this complaint be anachronistic, since it may refer only to the serial versions (see note 5 of the 'Note on the Text'), it is inaccurate, in that the plot forcefully traces Henchard's fall. However one describes Henchard's 'flaw'—impulsiveness, unwarranted concern for self, or a willingness to violate essential morality—the plot contains as least four crucial demonstrations of this flaw in action. The first is, of course, the sale of Susan, which reverberates more upon Henchard than upon Susan, who in her ignorance thinks initially that her being passed from one man to another is legitimate. This violation is central in the background of the major plot of the novel, providing an indication of Henchard's character behind the choices that justify his destruction.

When what can be called the novel proper begins (Chapter III), Henchard is at his high point, when he is mayor. During the banquet of the Corporation, Henchard turns aside human suffering in the form of the complaint about his 'growed wheat', thus marking himself as unworthy of his position, not to mention hinting at some degree of incompetence in his business. These are only matters of culpability; a more critical violation of humane assumptions occurs when in 'mortifying the flesh' of Abel Whittle he offends against another's self-respect and sense of decency (as well as taboos against nakedness) and against fairness, offences not offset by Henchard's kindnesses to Abel's mother. A third marked demonstration of Henchard's flaw stems from his jealousy of Farfrae, when he forces Lucetta to agree to marry him.

Immediately afterwards, the furmity woman appears to accuse him, and to remind him that he is morally no better than she. In one sense, this accusation is unjustified, since Henchard has both rectified his original offence and reformed in a way she has not. But not only do common-sense concepts of redeeming or compensatory acts play little part in the dynamism of tragic plot, this sketch of Henchard's serial violations of fundamental standards of conduct throughout the novel indicates that in the true sense she is right. The fall that had begun at the dinner accelerates through the reappearance of the furmity woman, for it brings into public scrutiny Henchard's basic worth, the first chink in which had been made visible at the dinner. His fall now becomes precipitous.

But Henchard's fall does not depend upon the furmity woman's accusation; nor, in reasonable extension, does it occur as a result of his sale of his wife—a point many readers of the novel have accepted as Hardy's intention, a sort of Victorian misreading. The novel is not a moral tract, nor a tracing of mythic cause-and-effect (as John Paterson and others have felt it to be). Rather, the novel's plot reveals the consequences on a non-moral level of a quality of character, a condition of existence Henchard cannot evade. This much is evident from the fact that toward the end of the novel Henchard has begun to recover his position, to have moved through a return bout with alcoholism and his back-biting at Farfrae, chastened by the death of Lucetta and his inability to alleviate her suffering because he has lost the residual confidence of Farfrae. But his character has not changed at the essential level: he is still subject to impulse, and still willing to sacrifice other people during an impulsive moment. Indeed, despite all the experience he has gone through in the novel, Henchard's fourth violation of human sanctity is prototypical. His impulsive lie to Newson leads to the separation of a parent and child, the identical result of his first violation, the sale of Susan. Trapped by his own character, and by his inability to compromise—which is, appropriately, also the sign of his tragic worth and stature—and fully aware of the heinousness and indefensibleness of his deed, and now aware of the chimerical quality of the success that another great expenditure of energy could win for him, Henchard withdraws in the face of his fear that he has forfeited Elizabeth-Jane's love, the last sole good he was able to acknowledge.

'There's a sort o' damage, sir, that can't be made up for,' says Adam Bede to Arthur Donnithorne in George Eliot's *Adam Bede*. This bitter truth is at the heart of the reader's dilemma in responding to Henchard. However much sympathy we may have for this erring and hopeful man, there is fittingness in the destruction that he himself, finally, must administer, being too robust to be destroyed by any of the forces that operate legally within his society. He has challenged the elements that operate within the self, the social body, and the universe of nature; as a consequence he recognizes there is no place for him in life as it is; there is no way he can become part of the Newson—Farfrae—Elizabeth-Jane family group. In one sense, perhaps, he dies unnecessarily defiant, but the only course tolerable to him is to allow the natural elemental operation of bodily needs and of spiritual deprivation to remove him from the pain of existence. The final tragic irony is that his death is both reward and self-punishment.

A few years after writing *The Mayor of Casterbridge*, Hardy copied into one of his notebooks a sentence from Schopenhauer expressing a sentiment that is perfectly illustrated by what he had done in the concluding pages of the novel: 'Only when intellect rises to the point where the vanity of all effort is manifest, & the will proceeds to an act of self-annulment, is the drama tragic in the true sense' (*Literary Notebooks*, II, Item 29). This may be the best evaluation yet made of the self-rejecting tragedy of Henchard's end.

NOTE ON THE TEXT

THIS critical text is based primarily on a study of the principal
versions of the novel listed at the head of the Explanatory Notes
(where are also located the sigla used in this note and elsewhere
in referring to the different versions). The novel's publishing
history, Hardy's general practice in composition and revision,
and the general conditions of publishing in late nineteenth- and
early twentieth-century England and America have also been
considered to establish the relationships among the versions.[1]
As with the text of *The Woodlanders*, which I also have

---

[1] Although this is the first critical edition of *The Mayor of Casterbridge* to
be published, previous scholars' work on the novel's differing texts has given
me much information (which I have independently verified), insight, and
guidance: Christine Winfield, 'The Manuscript of Hardy's *Mayor of
Casterbridge*', *Papers of the Bibliographical Society of America*, 67 (1973), 37–58,
and her 1971 University of London dissertation upon which the article is based
and which contains much further information; Dieter Riesner, 'Kunstprosa in
der Werkstatt: Hardys *The Mayor of Casterbridge* 1884–1912', *Festschrift für
Walter Hübner*, ed. Dieter Riesner and Helmut Gneuss (Berlin: Erich Schmidt
Verlag, 1964), pp. 267–326; and Mary Ellen Chase's *Thomas Hardy from Serial
to Novel* (Minneapolis: University of Minnesota Press, 1927). Chase's work
was the first extensive study of the novel's alterations, but is weakened by her
dealing primarily with only the serial and the 1895 text, despite her knowledge
that there were differences also in the first English book edition and the first
English one-volume edition; moreover, she seems unaware that the 1912 Wessex
Edition is a distinct version. None the less, her critical intelligence distinguishes
her observations about the differences among the versions. As far as I am able
to manage, limited by a poor command of German even with the use of a large
German-English dictionary, I take from Riesner's carefully researched and richly
detailed essay, without acknowledging each instance, several summary statements
about sorts of revisions Hardy made in different versions and supplement them
with further generalizations and detail. Riesner's and my counts of revisions
in several versions do not always coincide, but of course different people count
differently. For instance, some people will count several rewordings close together
or with common purpose as separate variants, while other people will lump
them all together as only one. Also, because Riesner does not study A1 as a
separate version, he includes variants which originated in A1 within his count
of E1 variants; and this also affects some of his comments about the duration
of revisions in HW as well as his comments about E1. I have accepted silently
Winfield's arguments in her dissertation for emending two substantives; all other
emendations are based on my own analyses of the evidence.

prepared for the World's Classics (1985), this edition is founded on dual authority: the last version revised by Hardy, the 1912 Wessex Edition, provides the words (in editing terminology, the 'substantives'); and the first version, the manuscript, is accepted in general as the most reliable source of such details as punctuation, paragraphing, spelling, and the like (the so-called 'accidentals'). Many scattered pages and sections of the manuscript, about a fifth of the whole, have not survived. For these portions of the novel, the accidentals are taken from the *Graphic*, the text nearest to the first typesetting. The decision to use the *Graphic* for this purpose followed a study of the changes in accidentals from the surviving parts of the manuscript to the Wessex Edition, which demonstrated that each new typesetting introduced sizeable numbers of variants scarcely likely to have been directed by Hardy himself. Following generally accepted modern editing practices, emendations of the conflated text are made when the surviving evidence, including the history of the transmission of the text, points to Hardy's intentions having been subverted or ignored. A few emendations, mostly involving commas and capitalization, are made for clarity. The following discussion describes the different versions of the novel and the history of the development of the text; the Explanatory Notes include some of the more interesting rejected passages, some of which are referred to in this textual discussion by page citations.

I

In accordance with his usual practice, Hardy sold the rights to *The Mayor of Casterbridge* to different publishers in England and America. His novels were usually printed first in monthly or weekly magazines and then brought out in book editions, resulting in the early versions being prepared to a lesser or, usually, greater degree of haste under pressure. This pressure was caused by printing deadlines, but also by the necessity to meet transatlantic shipping dates so that American publishers could begin to prepare the serial and book versions in advance of the arrival in America of copies

of the English magazine, from which (before the passage of
the International Copyright law of 1891) rival American
publishers could reprint without paying either author or
authorized publisher a fee or royalty. For several novels
Hardy revised separately for each of these versions, in keeping
with his customary anxious reluctance to let a set of proofs
pass through his hands without trying out fresh words, lines,
and images, and modifying characterizations and plot events.
The first versions of *The Mayor of Casterbridge*—the British
serial (*Graphic*), the American serial (*Harper's Weekly*), the
first American book edition (Henry Holt), and the first British
book edition (Smith, Elder)—all were published in 1886.[2]
Hardy received only £100 for the Smith, Elder edition,
perhaps reflecting the opinion of their reader, James Payn,
that in lacking gentry among its characters it also lacked
interest.

The next known distinct version of the novel was in the
format of the so-called cheap one-volume editions which were
published in England as soon as the substantially more costly
first editions had had their day. At this time in Hardy's career,
his cheap editions were being published by Sampson Low,
Marston; the cheap edition of *The Mayor of Casterbridge* was
brought out in 2,000 copies in late 1887.

A few years later Sampson Low's rights to the novels lapsed,
and Hardy turned them over to a new firm, Osgood,
McIlvaine & Co., which brought out a collected edition of
Hardy, the Wessex Novels (1895–6). Co-founder James Ripley
Osgood died before the Wessex Novels began to appear, and

---

[2] Also in 1886 he agreed to let the novel be published in Macmillan's
Colonial Library, which that firm had developed as a means of forestalling the
importation into India, Australia, and other British colonies of editions of
English books printed—i.e. pirated—by Americans taking advantage of the
lack of International Copyright. Hardy's role in this edition seems to have
been no more than to agree to it (see *Collected Letters*, I. 146–8). But as an
authorized resetting of the text of the novel it warrants scrutiny in the course
of preparing a critical edition. The conclusion of such a scrutiny is that its few
variants are almost certainly compositors' sophistications—that is, efforts to
'correct' Hardy's own choice of words and punctuation, thereby reminding us
that even a respected publisher and printer (R. & R. Clark, later the printer
of the 1912 Wessex Edition) were willing to make alterations, however trivial,
in the text of a writer already recognized as having special talents.

eventually the firm was absorbed into the English branch of Harper & Brothers. At this, Hardy decided he wanted a publisher whose head office was in England, and so his domestic publication rights joined his colonial at Macmillan.

Publishing elaborate de luxe editions, as memorials to living authors, became the thing to do around the turn of the century; Hardy was eager to have one, and he gave his fiction its last thorough revision for a projected de luxe edition. The de luxe aspect of the production was abandoned when the intended American co-publisher proved not to be up to the job; but Macmillan brought out the freshly revised texts anyway, in an attractively printed and serviceably bound edition that until recently has been judged to be Hardy's 'definitive' text: the Wessex Edition of 1912. (Clearly Hardy reconsidered the substantives carefully in preparing printer's copy for this edition, but he did not read the proofs of the Wessex Edition of this novel as carefully as he did those of other novels. The text of *The Mayor of Casterbridge* contains several erroneous accidentals—commas for periods are the most obvious—and some needed punctuation is missing, conditions that weaken this judgement.) The de luxe edition itself finally materialized in 1920 (the Mellstock Edition), but for this edition Hardy made a careful revision only of *A Pair of Blue Eyes*; as with the other novels, the text of *The Mayor of Casterbridge* in the Mellstock Edition represents a resetting of the Wessex Edition.

II

Modifications of the story during the writing of the manuscript itself suggests that its principal inspiration had been a large conception of the competition between members of different generations within a stable society. Hardy was flexible about details and about features of his story which some readers might not agree are minor but which clearly were not the controlling aspects of the story in Hardy's mind. He reconsidered such points as Henchard's occupation (p. 13 n.), and the period he and his wife had been married (p. 15 n.); and as customary in Hardy's manuscripts, the characters' names evolve steadily, so that Henchard's given name was Giles and then James before it became Michael. Farfrae's surname was first Stansbie, and his given name was Alan before it was Donald.

Potentially more problematic are such points among Hardy's earlier plot-lines (cancelled or altered within the manuscript itself) that Henchard and Susan originally had two daughters, one of whom he kept when he sold Susan (p. 15 n.); that the infant Elizabeth-Jane did not die, so that the adult Elizabeth-Jane actually *is* Henchard's daughter (pp. 34 n., 66 n.); and that the sailor Newson is indeed dead when Susan and Elizabeth-Jane come to Casterbridge (p. 28 n.). It is not at all clear how Hardy would have managed the plot with such circumstances as these present; but it is noticeable that none of these events affects in a significant fashion the concentration upon a conflict that develops between an older and a younger man. Nor does another major divergence from an early situation in the manuscript: detectable under cancellations and additions is evidence that Hardy originally intended Henchard and Lucetta to have had for six years a sexual liaison on Jersey (p. 118 n.), whereas in the final form of the manuscript Henchard proposes marriage out of gratitude when Lucetta saves him from drowning in a boating accident (p. 78 n.). Neither Hardy's early working notes, nor any subsequent comments about specific alterations in the plot and characters, survive; thus, all the differences I mention above cannot be ascribed to a single plot preceding the final manuscript draft, or be assigned to identifiable separate stages of the plot's development; evidently, sheets of previous drafts were retained whenever feasible, while sheets which had had to be newly copied or composed were inserted among those sheets of previous drafts.[3]

The first completed version of *The Mayor of Casterbridge* is not largely different from the story as we now have it. Hardy's revisions were evolutionary rather than revolutionary. But the first version bears the marks, naturally enough, of its intended

[3] This is one of Winfield's primary conclusions from a careful study of the different paper stocks in the manuscript, a conclusion confirmed by my own examination of the manuscript.

market—magazines whose readers shied away from recognizing the sexual component of human relations and who expected an eventful weekly instalment.

This final form of the manuscript portrays Henchard and Lucetta as having married only a fortnight before Susan's return. Lucetta has remained in Jersey, and is on her way to join him when Susan makes herself known. Henchard asks Farfrae to meet the boat at Budmouth to turn Lucetta back, but owing to Lucetta's seasickness from the 'breezy passage' she takes Henchard's letter from behind her cabin door (p. 80 n.), and Farfrae does not see her. When Henchard later attempts to return Lucetta's letters he gives them to Elizabeth-Jane and asks her to deliver them at the coach stop, and she in turn gives them to Farfrae—thus offering a second opportunity for Farfrae to see the woman of Henchard's tale, an opportunity unrealized, like the first, when Lucetta fails to be in the coach. Towards the end of the manuscript, the reappearance of Newson is unsurprising to Elizabeth-Jane, for she has been meeting him surreptitiously on a regular basis for some time.

To prompt reader interest in each week's portion of the serialization, the manuscript employs numerous attention-gathering scenes not strictly required to make the plot work. Two of these are a meeting between Lucetta and Susan that Henchard happens to observe, and an encounter in the dark Amphitheatre when Farfrae comes upon Henchard and the disguised Lucetta, by now Mrs Farfrae, and begins to josh Henchard about his planning to marry again. Such scenes as the encounter with the bull are presented at greater length and in a way to arouse apprehension and suspense. Another distinction of the manuscript is that Elizabeth-Jane is unreflective and simple, something of a priggish Fanny Robin.

These aspects of the manuscript are also those of the serializations. It was not uncommon in the latter part of his career as a novelist for Hardy to write his stories in the form he wanted for book publication, revise the plots for their appearance in a periodical (usually with an eye to mollifying readers or editors especially sensitive to sexual matters or unconventionality), and then print them as books with their original plots or with a plot only moderately altered beyond that of the manuscript. By contrast, the narrative of the manuscript of *The Mayor of Casterbridge* is nearly unchanged in the weekly serializations. Only with the first book editions did Hardy begin to reshape the plot.

The first two printed versions, the serializations, have essentially minor but cumulatively effective improvements and changes. The two serials are nearly identical, possessing in common nearly 300 differences from the manuscript. These concern small stylistic improvements—decrease of Latinisms and changes in adjectives, dialect, and descriptions of gestures and behaviour. What distinguish one serialization from the other result from an editor's queasiness and the impact of space restrictions upon serial publication. Arthur Locker, the editor of the *Graphic*, reduced the coarseness and frankness of several phrases or deleted the phrases altogether (e.g. p. 77 n.); perhaps Hardy made these alterations but in direct response to editorial pressure from the *Graphic*. Whatever the exact procedure, that these phrases appear in later versions (including the American versions) indicates that Hardy did not endorse their alterations to milder forms or their removal from the English serial. The most noticeable feature of the text in *Harper's Weekly* is that many passages were dropped from the American serialization, probably to fit weekly portions into available space. This obviously did not represent Hardy's wishes, because they appear in later versions. A few passages not in HW are also absent from AI: all but the very last of the concluding five paragraphs of Chapter XVII for instance, including the 'Character is Fate' passage; and the first conversation in Chapter XLIII and the following meditation.

While preparing printer's copy for the first (American) book edition, Hardy made over 500 revisions. None, however, were made in the last five chapters because Henry Holt had to print and bind the novel before the last instalment of the novel appeared on the stands in *Harper's Weekly*, enabling him to put his editions on sale before American pirates printing from the instalments in *Harper's Weekly* could take his market. It would seem that one of Hardy's main intentions while revising for the Holt book edition[4] was to consider which among the exciting events with which he felt he had crammed the narrative to enhance the serialization's need for striking occurrences were consequential. The ensuing alterations were not so much in large-scale shifts as in a significantly altered arrangement of events that affect some of the novel's points of strong interest. His general aims appear to have been greater plausibility, sharper characterization, and a reduction in the plot's arbitrariness or ironic coincidentalism, the probable source of which had been Hardy's awareness that in preparing the manuscript he had been shaping the story for weekly rather than monthly appeal. From this edition onward the narrative's neat and straightforward form refutes Hardy's own self-criticism that he had harmed the novel by loading it with plot-incident for the serialization.[5] He removed completely such striking but non-functional scenes as Lucetta's talking with Susan in the market one day and the accidental night meeting of Farfrae with Henchard and the disguised Lucetta in the Amphitheatre, and streamlined many others. Instances are the greater compactness of the presentation of the battle with the bull, the substitution of Henchard's writing a letter to Lucetta to tell her of Susan's return rather than have Farfrae deliver the letter to a boat at Budmouth, and the removal of the needless complexity in having Elizabeth-Jane give Lucetta's letters to Farfrae to return them to Lucetta; the last simplification is a particularly apt stroke in that it also results in the irony of the letters being in Farfrae's own possession because Henchard had left the letters in his safe during the collapse of his affairs

---

[4] By 11 May 1886 Holt had had in hand for 'some time' copy for the first forty chapters (according to a letter from Holt's editor Vogelius to *Harper's Weekly*; quoted by Seth Weiner, 'Thomas Hardy and His First American Publisher: A Chapter from the Henry Holt Archive', *Princeton University Library Chronicle*, 39 [1978], 154–5).

[5] *Life and Work*, p. 185. Although he is specifically referring to the book edition, from which he had removed so many of these incidents, he wrote the comment decades later, when probably the effort of creating the incidents came more readily to memory than the deletion of many of them for the edition to which he was referring.

(p. 243 n.). In the Holt book edition the novel has most of the plot by which it is now known, although it is still burdened with Elizabeth-Jane's conscious duplicity toward Henchard, which I shall discuss shortly.

An alteration in the plot for the Holt book edition that required Hardy to review carefully the many passages that bear upon it is the dispensing with the marriage of Henchard and Lucetta—the purpose of which had most likely been to give to magazine readers a respectable rationale for Lucetta's arrival in Casterbridge in pursuit of Henchard after Susan's death. In its place Hardy posits an 'acquaintance' (p. 117 n.) and 'a terrible scandal' brought about by Lucetta's nursing Henchard during one of his 'gloomy fits', a scandal based only on appearances but none the less destructive to Lucetta's standing on Jersey (pp. 78 n., 79 n.)—a consequence heightened by the social elevation (also made during the revision for the Holt edition) of Lucetta's family from the merchant to the professional class (p. 79 n.). It is perhaps the greater visibility attendant upon her new social class that makes her sensitive to the danger of speaking French (p. 153 n.), although during the same revision Hardy adds an occasional French word to her correspondence (p. 148 n.), as if to better render her background.

Clearly Hardy was aiming to bring to the book-buying audience and the lending libraries as well-prepared a novel as he was able. For the Holt edition Hardy gave close attention to matters of style, adding, for example, several allusions (cf. the Explanatory Notes to pp. 70, 96, 187, 205) and adjusting the wording of passages. The process of altering Elizabeth-Jane's character from one marked by basic simplicity to one more strongly motivated to improve her status receives several touches in the Holt edition: she goes from 'uninstructed' to 'unsophisticated' (p. 88), and Hardy attributes to her a knowledge resulting from 'great natural insight' (p. 87 n.) and a 'subtle soul' (p. 119 n.). A reduction in her dialect that had been begun in earlier revisions is continued (p. 138 n.). Most significantly, perhaps, he deletes her placid and simplistic Christian faith (p. 207 n.).

The most important plot-changes made for the English

two-volume edition (Smith, Elder, 1886) come within the chapters unaffected by the Holt revision. In previous versions Elizabeth-Jane not only had known for weeks or even months that Newson is alive but has been meeting him (pp. 306 n., 314 n.). The English first edition, in keeping with the novel's continually more favourable portrayal of Elizabeth-Jane, removes this knowledge from her—which of course had given her, in continuing to behave as a daughter toward Henchard, a touch of hypocrisy and calculation, out of character for a young woman so obsessed with respectability and with living according to honest feelings. Also, the penultimate chapter receives in the English first edition the novel's single most famous alteration, the cancellation of Henchard's return to Casterbridge for Elizabeth-Jane's marriage, including the deletion of his bringing a goldfinch as a wedding-gift. Hardy's motivation for removing this powerful image of Henchard's self-destructive impulsiveness and obsession with one idea at a time was probably, as he explained to persons who urged its reinstatement (see the Note to pp. 320-7), a concern that having Henchard go away twice weakened the story.

Hardy might have intended to make these changes in the Holt edition as well. But he was also working on *The Woodlanders* during the period when these changes were most likely to have been made and was having difficulty getting sufficiently ahead on that novel, which began to appear in monthly instalments in *Macmillan's Magazine* in the May 1886 issue.[6] He simply may not have been able to dispatch to America in time any improvements he had in mind for the final chapters of *The Mayor of Casterbridge*. This probably accounts for Holt's receiving only the first forty chapters.

But Hardy's failure to send Holt copy for the last five chapters may have been caused by a decision to give the entire novel further scrutiny. The first forty chapters of the English first edition contain 250 or so alterations in addition to those in the American edition—mostly small improvements in

[6] See my discussion of Hardy's timetable of delivering copy of *The Woodlanders* to the Macmillan firm, in the introduction to the Clarendon Edition of *The Woodlanders* (Oxford, 1981), pp. 7-8.

wording, additional reminders that Farfrae was a Scotchman, and again, as in the Holt edition, adjustments in Elizabeth-Jane's character. One completes a shift begun in the Holt edition: in the manuscript and serializations Elizabeth-Jane was concerned with a study of English only, presumably to fit her for her improved social situation as the mayor's daughter; in the Holt edition this is expanded to attribute to her an interest in the history of her country, and in the English first edition this was itself altered to a larger interest, the history of 'all the philosophies' (p. 97 n.). An accompanying revision alters her self-description from being an 'ignorant' girl to being an 'unfinished' girl (p. 97 n.). Elsewhere her simplicity becomes studiousness (p. 141 n.), and in one of Hardy's few unhappy revisions—which probably was intended to increase her beauty but when inserted resulted in a sentimental image—she gains 'peachy cheeks' which tears can 'glide down' (p. 133 n.).

Not many of the comparatively few changes made for the Sampson Low one-volume edition (1887) are of great matter, and some even could be compositors' errors. But among the significant variants is the addition to Farfrae's reluctance to spend a night away from home in looking for Henchard of his observation 'that would make a hole in a sovereign' (p. 331 n.). Also, for this edition Henchard identifies Farfrae in his caution with money to be 'just like a Scotchman!' (p. 104 n.), and Hardy removes the description of Elizabeth-Jane during her early days in Casterbridge as someone special and honoured (if not courted) in the eyes of Casterbridge's young men (see the Note to p. 96). A few other passages are deleted, and some words are altered in minor ways; but not only are such changes few, they are far between, as if Hardy either is preparing printer's copy in a random manner or is glancing through the proofs and giving close attention only occasionally.

Over 600 alterations were made for the Osgood, McIlvaine 'Wessex Novels' edition (1895), over two-thirds of them on proof; that is, following the initial revisions written in his revising copy (95rc). As in other novels revised for this edition, the emphasis was on bringing the novel more explicitly within the Wessex setting that was being established for all of the novels, but Hardy did not have to do a great deal of resituating to make the plot events of *The Mayor of Casterbridge* fit into the Wessex landscape, since he had from the beginning based the setting on Dorchester's buildings and streets. In other revisions, speech habits are made more consistent with education and class; descriptions of rural folk are changed, including making humour more robust; and in general, diction, syntax, and prose rhythms are worked on.

Among the 'Wessex' alterations are the adjustments of inns' names, from the Golden Crown to King's Arms, the King of Prussia to the Three Mariners, and the Stag to the Antelope; the change of High Street Hall as Lucetta's residence to High-Place Hall; the incorporation of names used in other Wessex novels for the landscape and areas surrounding Casterbridge, such as Dummerford Moor to Durnover Moor, and alterations in the names of towns to names used in other Wessex novels, such as Stickleford to Kingsbere. Also affected are directions, distances, and details of landscape. This edition more than any other single edition modifies dialect, particularly Farfrae's. (It was during the preparation for this edition that Hardy's friend Sir George Douglas [cf. Note to p. 4] advised Hardy on matters of the Scottish language. Many of the alterations of Farfrae's speech in 95rc are made in a hand other than Hardy's.) But it needs to be remembered that in all versions dialect and renderings of speech sounds are modified (some of them, particularly in the first type-setting, might be compositors' misreadings or sophistications [p. 55 n.: 'pirizes'], but it is difficult to distinguish these from Hardy's adjustments in his written representations of speech). Other important changes are the clarifying emphasis upon Lucetta's pregnancy as a contributory cause in her death (p. 288 n.), and the deletion of an early reference to a horse-drill (p. 31 n.) already on sale in Dorchester that contradicted the assertion later in the novel that Farfrae was supporting a revolutionary (for Wessex) method of agriculture (see Note to p. 167). The sincerity of Farfrae's love of Scotland is questioned (p. 324 n.); and among numerous changes in the reinstated return of Henchard are alterations in Elizabeth-Jane's reception of him that increases her condemnatory tone (p. 327 n.) in a manner, as Riesner points out (pp. 298–9), which ironically portrays this now 'subtle-souled' woman as lacking in intuitive understanding of her stepfather's behaviour.

A common feature of revisions of other novels made for the Osgood, McIlvaine edition is an increase in frankness concerning sexuality. For the Osgood, McIlvaine edition of *The Mayor of Casterbridge* Hardy again employed a sexual liaison between Lucetta and Henchard (which, as already mentioned, had been a six-years' affair in an early version of the manuscript), replacing the marriage (MS–HW) and the false scandal (A1–87) (p. 79 n.). It took this long, then, for the book version to return to Hardy's pre-serial conception in this aspect.

It was for this edition that Hardy responded to arguments in favour of Henchard's return for Elizabeth-Jane's wedding, restoring not only a sound justification for Elizabeth-Jane and Farfrae's search for Henchard but also for Henchard's abrupt movement toward death. Certainly the effect of Henchard's journey upon the novel's tragic force is entirely positive. With this journey—his final gesture toward reconciliation—forming part of the plot, Henchard's suicide is a reaction to the consequences of a characteristic if ill-thought-out gesture of sentiment and heedlessness rather than to a pining away from his general 'state of hopelessness' (p. 313 n.). (This general cause was added in E1; but the most forceful line in E1–Col [as well as in MS–A1, but there it is in the context of Henchard's return for the wedding] is: 'I . . . live on, and can't die if I try' [p. 320 n.].) The revisions I mention above involving Elizabeth-Jane's reception of Henchard at her wedding enhance the emotional impact of her denunciation; but by far the most powerful alteration is the restoration itself of the entire incident.

The revisions (over 150 by my count) for the Wessex Edition (1912) are mostly house-cleaning—continuations of patterns from earlier stages, particularly from the Osgood, McIlvaine edition, such as Wessex distances and dialect. For instance, 'ye' becomes ''ee' in considerable numbers, as also happened in the Wessex Editions of other novels. Another hint is given that Lucetta is pregnant (p. 249 n.); and several small changes affect the location and description of her house. There are several alterations in the duration of time since the wife-sale, seemingly intended to bear upon Elizabeth-Jane's age (Notes to pp. 21, 117, 235, 318); and it is ironic that while paying such close heed to this matter Hardy left in the text the error concerning the month of Newson's supposed death (cf. the Note to p. 22).

Although the text of the Mellstock Edition (1920) of *The Mayor of Casterbridge* exhibits only trivial differences from that of the Wessex Edition, this final edition, printed in Hardy's lifetime, has been taken into account here, particularly its readings of questionable passages in the Wessex Edition—that is, Wessex Edition passages which common sense or a reading of the context gives good reason to think are themselves typographical errors.

The impression of Hardy as creating artist one gains from looking at the texts of *The Mayor of Casterbridge* is, as with most of his other novels, that he begins with a core experience whose subtleties can be enhanced by prodding ungainly events into a greater degree of consistency and characterizations into portrayals bearing keener implications, but which is nearly exempt from change itself. In *The Mayor of Casterbridge*, that core experience is dramatized through Henchard and Farfrae, neither of whom is significantly altered by any of the changes this Note has been considering. That Elizabeth-Jane undergoes a major shift in conception only underscores the point that while she may serve as an index to wise conduct, as the novel's last lines suggest Hardy had in mind, she is only tangentially related to the energies that drive the narrative. The elemental Henchard, the trimming Farfrae—it is their dance which draws readers to the novel. Which is not to say that Hardy revised in vain. By hewing away the meretricious, by polishing the surface, Hardy allows the true vein to shine clear.

SELECT BIBLIOGRAPHY

A GREAT many excellent studies have been written about *The Mayor of Casterbridge*, both on its broad concerns and appeal and on various more limited topics. Any listing of secondary works on *The Mayor of Casterbridge*, then, must be extremely selective if it is to avoid being unusably long. A reading programme could begin with Jean Brooks, *Thomas Hardy: The Poetic Structure* (London, 1971); or Ian Gregor, *The Great Web: The Form of Hardy's Major Fiction* (London, 1974); or perhaps with Laurence Lerner, *Thomas Hardy's 'The Mayor of Casterbridge': Tragedy or Social History?* (London, 1975). Michael Millgate's *Thomas Hardy: His Career as a Novelist* (New York, 1971), like the above three books, applies intelligence and perceptiveness to the novel, and also presents, in an economical and straightforward fashion, a great deal of original research directed constantly toward clarifying the materials Hardy was working with and suggesting what he was trying to do with them. Recent books with germane approaches and intelligent comments are: J. B. Bullen, *The Expressive Eye: Fiction and Perception in the Work of Thomas Hardy* (Oxford, 1986); John Goode, *Thomas Hardy: The Offensive Truth* (Oxford, 1988); Peter Widdowson, *Hardy in History: A Study in Literary Sociology* (London, 1989); and Marjorie Garson, *Hardy's Fables of Integrity: Woman, Body, Text* (Oxford, 1991).

Among older essays on more-or-less special subjects (but which have implications for a general understanding of the novel) are Julian Moynahan, 'The Mayor of Casterbridge and the Old Testament's First Book of Samuel: A Study of Some Literary Relationships', *PMLA*, 71 (1956), 118–30; two by John Paterson: 'The Mayor of Casterbridge as Tragedy', *Victorian Studies*, 3 (1959), 151–72, and 'Hardy, Faulkner, and the Prosaics of Tragedy', *Centennial Review*, 5 (1961), 156–75; Frederick R. Karl, 'The Mayor of Casterbridge: A New Fiction Defined', *Modern Fiction Studies*, 6 (1960), 195–213; and two by Robert B. Heilman, 'Hardy's *Mayor* and the Problem of Intention', *Criticism*, 5 (1963), 199–213, and 'Hardy's *Mayor*: Notes on Style', *Nineteenth-Century Fiction*, 18 (1964), 307–29. Among somewhat later studies, standing well to the fore are two essays published in collections, both in 1979— Juliet M. Grindle, 'Compulsion and Choice in *The Mayor of Casterbridge*', *The Novels of Thomas Hardy*, ed. Anne Smith (London: Vision, 1979), pp. 91–106; and Elaine Showalter, 'The Unmanning of the Mayor of Casterbridge', *Critical Approaches to the Fic-*

tion of Thomas Hardy, ed. Dale Kramer (London: Macmillan, 1979), pp. 99–115—and an essay by R. P. Draper, '*The Mayor of Casterbridge*', *Critical Quarterly*, 25 (1983), 57–70. Simon Gatrell's 'The Fate of Michael Henchard's Character', in *Thomas Hardy and the Proper Study of Mankind* (London, 1993), considers its subject from a variety of productive angles; and Robert Langbaum's 'The Minimisation of Sexuality', in *Thomas Hardy in Our Time* (London, 1995), closely reads several passages to clarify the sexual drive of the novel's characters, especially Henchard's. A book specifically on tragedy which judges *The Mayor of Casterbridge* sensibly within a larger context is Jeannette King, *Tragedy in the Victorian Novel: Theory and Practice in the Novels of George Eliot, Thomas Hardy and Henry James* (Cambridge: Cambridge University Press, 1978). George Levine, *The Realistic Imagination: English Fiction from Frankenstein to Lady Chatterley* (Chicago, 1981), places Hardy, and *The Mayor of Casterbridge*, within the interrelated English traditions of realism, narrative myth, and romance. Ralph W. V. Elliott, *Thomas Hardy's English* (Oxford, 1984), offers masses of detail pertaining to Hardy's use of language; of interest for readers of this novel are explanations of many of its dialect usages.

Apart from criticism which pertains directly to this novel, a good deal of scholarly work has recently been making available information helpful to readers interested in developing their own insights into Hardy. Of central relevance are the biographies by Michael Millgate (*Thomas Hardy: A Biography*, Oxford, 1982) and by Robert Gittings (*Young Thomas Hardy*, London, 1975; *The Older Hardy*, London, 1978), which bring modern perspectives and research to bear on many features of Hardy's life which he had ignored or obscured in his own autobiography (published under the name of his second wife Florence), *The Early Life of Thomas Hardy* (London, 1928) and *The Later Years of Thomas Hardy* (London, 1930), combined as *The Life of Thomas Hardy* (London, 1962). A new edition of Hardy's autobiography, restoring passages written by Hardy that had been excised by Florence and her literary advisers, and removing passages that they had added to supplement the typescript left by Hardy, has been edited by Millgate (*The Life and Work of Thomas Hardy by Thomas Hardy*, London, 1985).

Hardy's non-fictional writing was collected by Harold Orel in *Thomas Hardy's Personal Writings* (London, 1966); and Millgate presently is preparing another, and somewhat fuller, edition of Hardy's prose and occasional non-fictional writings. Hardy's letters, interesting mostly for incidental information about his life

and his ideas about writing, have been edited by Richard Little
Purdy and Michael Millgate (*The Collected Letters of Thomas
Hardy*, Oxford, 1978–1988). Hardy's personal notebooks have
been edited by Richard H. Taylor (London, 1979), his literary
notebooks by Lennart A. Björk (Göteborg, Sweden, 1974; and,
more completely, London, 1985), and his architectural notebook
by C. J. P. Beatty (Philadelphia, 1966).

Further works which need to be known by readers closely interested in Hardy's career as well as in this novel in particular are
Richard Little Purdy's classic *Thomas Hardy: A Bibliographical
Study* (Oxford, 1954), for its details about the writing, editing, and
publication of Hardy's novels and poems; Simon Gatrell's *Hardy
the Creator: A Textual Biography* (Oxford, 1988), for its elegant
analyses of Hardy's responses to opportunities to revise his novels;
and R. B. Cox's *Thomas Hardy: The Critical Heritage* (London,
1970), which reprints many of the contemporary reviews of
Hardy's works.

A CHRONOLOGY OF
THOMAS HARDY

1840   2 June: Thomas Hardy born, first child of Thomas and Jemima (Hand) Hardy, five and a half months after their marriage. His father was a builder in a small but slowly developing way of business, thus setting the family apart socially from the 'work-folk' whom they clearly resembled in financial circumstances.

1848   Entered the newly opened Stinsford National School.

1849   Sent to Dorchester British School kept by Isaac Last.

1853   Last established an independent 'commercial academy', and Hardy became a pupil there. His education was practical and effective, including Latin, some French, theoretical and applied mathematics, and commercial studies.

1856   11 July: articled to Dorchester architect John Hicks. Soon after this he became friendly with Horace Moule, an important influence on his life.

1860   Summer: Hardy's articles, having been extended for a year, completed. Employed by Hicks as an assistant.

1862   17 April: without a position; travelled to London, but soon employed by Arthur Blomfield as a 'Gothic draughtsman'. November: Elected to the Architectural Association; began to find his feet in London.

1863   Won architectural prizes; began to consider some form of writing as a means of support.

1863–7 Possibly became engaged to Eliza Nicholls.

1865   March: 'How I Built Myself a House' published in *Chambers' Journal*. Began to write poetry.

1866   Hardy's commitment to the Church and his religious belief seem to have declined though he probably experienced no dramatic loss of faith.

1867   Returned to Dorset. Began his first unpublished novel.

1868   Sent MS of *The Poor Man and the Lady* to four publishers, where it was read by Morley and Meredith, amongst others, but finally rejected.

1869   Worked in Weymouth for the architect Crickmay; began
          writing *Desperate Remedies*.

1870   In order to take 'a plan and particulars' of the church,
          Hardy journeyed to St Juliot, near Boscastle in North
          Cornwall; there he met Emma Lavinia Gifford, who
          became his wife four years later.

1871   *Desperate Remedies* published after Hardy had ad-
          vanced £75.

1872   *Under the Greenwood Tree* published; the copyright sold to
          Tinsley for £30. Hardy moved temporarily to London to
          work in the offices of T. Roger Smith. Contracted to provide
          serial for *Tinsley's Magazine* for £200 (to include first edition
          rights). *A Pair of Blue Eyes* began to appear in September.
          Hardy decided to relinquish architecture and concentrate on
          writing. Leslie Stephen requested a serial for the *Cornhill
          Magazine*.

1873   *A Pair of Blue Eyes* published in three volumes; Horace
          Moule, his close adviser and friend, committed suicide in
          Cambridge.

1874   *Far From the Madding Crowd* begun as a serial in *Corn-
          hill* under Leslie Stephen's editorship and published later
          in the year in two volumes. Hardy married Emma Gifford
          on 17 September; they honeymooned in Paris and returned
          to live in London.

1875   *Cornhill* serialized *The Hand of Ethelberta*. The Hardys
          moved from London to Swanage in Dorset.

1876   Further moves to Yeovil and Sturminster Newton, where
          Hardy began writing *The Return of the Native*.

1878   Return to London (Tooting). *The Return of the Native*
          serialized in *Belgravia* and published in three volumes, to
          which Hardy affixed a map of the novel's environment.
          Made researches in the British Museum for the back-
          ground of *The Trumpet-Major*.

1879   With 'The Distracted Young Preacher', began regularly
          to publish short stories.

1880   *Good Words* serialized *The Trumpet-Major*, which was also
          published in three volumes with covers designed by
          Hardy. In October he became seriously ill and believed
          himself close to death; the cause of his illness uncertain,
          but led to five months' total inactivity.

1881   *A Laodicean,* mostly written from his bed, published as a serial in *Harper's New Monthly Magazine* (the first in the new European edition), and in three volumes. The Hardys returned to Dorset, living at Wimborne Minster.

1882   Controversy with Pinero over Hardy's adaptation of *Far From the Madding Crowd* and Pinero's use of the same material. Hardy's third novel in three years, *Two on a Tower,* serialized in the *Atlantic Monthly* and issued in three volumes.

1883   The final move of his life—from Wimborne to Dorchester, though into temporary accommodation while his own house was being built.

1884   Made a Justice of the Peace and began to receive invitations from aristocracy. Began writing *The Mayor of Casterbridge.*

1885   Max Gate, designed by Hardy and built by his brother Henry, completed; on the outskirts of Dorchester, it remained his home for the rest of his life.

1886   *The Mayor of Casterbridge* serialized in the *Graphic* and brought out in two volumes; in the same year *The Woodlanders* began its run in *Macmillan's Magazine.* William Barnes, the Dorset poet and friend of Hardy, died.

1887   *The Woodlanders* issued in three volumes. The Hardys visited France and Italy. Began work on *Tess of the d'Urbervilles.*

1888   Hardy's first collection of short stories, *Wessex Tales,* published in two volumes. Also published the first of three significant essays on the theory of fiction, *The Profitable Reading of Fiction.*

1889   The novel that was to become *Tess* rejected by Tillotson's Fiction Bureau, which had commissioned it; subsequent further rejections fuelled the bitterness behind a second essay, *Candour in English Fiction,* published in January of the following year.

1890   *A Group of Noble Dames* appeared in the *Graphic.*

1891   *Tess of the d'Urbervilles* serialized in the *Graphic* and published in three volumes; *A Group of Noble Dames* brought out in one volume. The third important essay,

The Science of Fiction, appeared. A Copyright Bill passed through the United States Congress in time for *Tess* to benefit from its provisions, a factor of considerable financial significance in Hardy's career.

1892   Father died 20 July. *The Pursuit of the Well-Beloved* serialized in the *Illustrated London News*.

1893   Met Florence Henniker, subject of the intensest of his romantic attachments to artistic ladies. Wrote *The Spectre of the Real* in collaboration with her. Began writing *Jude the Obscure*.

1894   Third volume of short stories, *Life's Little Ironies*, published in one volume.

1895   First collected edition of Hardy's work begun, published by Osgood, McIlvaine; it included the first edition of *Jude the Obscure*, previously serialized in *Harper's New Monthly Magazine*. Some reviews of *Jude* quite savage, a contributory factor to Hardy's writing no further novels. Hardy dramatized *Tess*.

1896   The first group of major poems with identifiable dates written since the 1860s; they included the three *In Tenebris* poems and *Wessex Heights*.

1897   *The Well-Beloved*, substantially revised from the 1892 serialization, published as part of the Osgood, McIlvaine edition. Visited Switzerland.

1898   Hardy's first collection of verse published, *Wessex Poems*; comprising mainly poems written in the 1860s and 1890s, and illustrated by himself.

1899   Boer War began, to which Hardy responded in verse. The gradual physical separation between Hardy and Emma intensified, following the mental separation that set in after the publication of *Jude the Obscure*.

1901   *Poems of the Past and the Present* published.

1902   Changed publishers for the last time, to Macmillan.

1904   First part of *The Dynasts* appeared. 3 April: Hardy's mother died, leaving a tremendous gap in his life.

1905   Met Florence Dugdale. Received LL D from Aberdeen University.

1906   Part Two of *The Dynasts* published.

1908   *The Dynasts* completed with the publication of the third part; it embodied Hardy's most complete statement of his philosophical outlook. Also published his *Select Poems of William Barnes*, undertaken as a memorial to his great predecessor. The first Dorchester dramatization of a Hardy novel, *The Trumpet-Major*. Meredith and Swinburne died, leaving Hardy as the greatest living English writer.

1909   Relationship with Florence Dugdale deepened. *Time's Laughingstocks*, Hardy's third volume of poems, published.

1910   Awarded the Order of Merit, having previously refused a knighthood. Received the freedom of Dorchester.

1912   Second collected edition of Hardy's works begun, the Wessex Edition. Received the gold medal of the Royal Society of Literature. 27 November: Emma Hardy died; as a direct result Hardy began writing the poems of 1912–13.

1913   Visited Cornwall in search of his and Emma's youth. Awarded Litt.D. at Cambridge and became an Honorary Fellow of Magdalene College—a partial fulfilment of an early aspiration. His final collection of short stories published, *A Changed Man*.

1914   10 February: married Florence Dugdale. *Satires of Circumstance* published. First World War began; Hardy's attitude to the future of humanity coloured by it in a profound way.

1915   At the age of 75 Hardy began to become reclusive. Frank George, his chosen heir, killed at Gallipoli. Hardy's sister Mary died 24 November.

1916   *Selected Poems of Thomas Hardy* published.

1917   Hardy's fifth collection of verse published, *Moments of Vision*. He and Florence began work on what was eventually to become *The Life of Thomas Hardy*.

1919–20   The de luxe edition of Hardy's work issued, the Mellstock Edition.

1922   *Late Lyrics and Earlier*, with its important Preface, published.

1923   Florence Henniker died. The Prince of Wales visited Max Gate. Friendship with T. E. Lawrence developed. *The Queen of Cornwall* published.

1924   Hardy's adaptation of *Tess* acted in Dorchester with the
            last of his romantic attachments, Gertrude Bugler, in the
            title role.

1925   *Tess* acted in London, but not by Miss Bugler. *Human
            Shows Far Phantasies Songs and Trifles*, Hardy's seventh
            volume of verse, published.

1928   11 January: Hardy died. His final book of poems, *Winter
            Words*, published posthumously.

THE LIFE AND DEATH

OF THE

MAYOR OF CASTERBRIDGE

A STORY OF A
MAN OF CHARACTER

PREFACE

READERS of the following story who have not yet arrived at middle age are asked to bear in mind that, in the days recalled by the tale, the home Corn Trade, on which so much of the action turns, had an importance that can hardly be realized by those accustomed to the sixpenny loaf of the present date, and to the present indifference of the public to harvest weather.

The incidents narrated arise mainly out of three events, which chanced to range themselves in the order and at or about the intervals of time here given, in the real history of the town called Casterbridge and the neighbouring country. They were the sale of a wife by her husband, the uncertain harvests which immediately preceded the repeal of the Corn Laws, and the visit of a Royal personage to the aforesaid part of England.

The present edition of the volume, like the previous one, contains nearly a chapter which did not at first appear in any English copy, though it was printed in the serial issue of the tale, and in the American edition. The restoration was made at the instance of some good judges across the Atlantic, who strongly represented that the home edition suffered from the omission. Some shorter passages and names, omitted or altered for reasons which no longer exist, in the original printing of both English and American editions, have also been replaced or inserted.

The story is more particularly a study of one man's deeds and character than, perhaps, any other of those included in my Exhibition of Wessex life. Objections have been raised to the Scotch language of Mr. Farfrae, the second character; and one of his fellow-countrymen went so far as to declare that men beyond the Tweed did not and never could say "warrld," "cannet," "advairrtisment," and so on. As this gentleman's pronunciation in correcting me seemed to my Southron ear an exact repetition of what my spelling implied, I was not struck with the truth of his remark, and somehow we did not get any forwarder in the matter. It must be remembered that the

Scotchman of the tale is represented not as he would appear
to other Scotchmen, but as he would appear to people of outer
regions. Moreover, no attempt is made herein to reproduce his
entire pronunciation phonetically, any more than that of the
Wessex speakers. I should add, however, that this new edition
of the book has had the accidental advantage of a critical
overlooking by a professor of the tongue in question—one of
undoubted authority:—in fact he is a gentleman who adopted
it for urgent personal reasons in the first year of his existence.

Furthermore, a charming non-Scottish lady, of strict
veracity and admitted penetration, the wife of a well-known
Caledonian, came to the writer shortly after the story was first
published, and inquired if Farfrae were not drawn from her
husband, for he seemed to her to be the living portrait of that
(doubtless) happy man. It happened that I had never thought
of her husband in constructing Farfrae. I trust therefore that
Farfrae may be allowed to pass, if not as a Scotchman to
Scotchmen, as a Scotchman to Southerners.

The novel was first published complete, in two volumes, in
May 1886.

T. H.

February 1895—*May* 1912.

I

ONE evening of late summer, before the nineteenth century had reached one-third of its span, a young man and woman, the latter carrying a child, were approaching the large village of Weydon-Priors, in Upper Wessex, on foot. They were plainly but not ill clad, though the thick hoar of dust which had accumulated on their shoes and garments from an obviously long journey lent a disadvantageous shabbiness to their appearance just now.

The man was of fine figure, swarthy, and stern in aspect; and he showed in profile a facial angle so slightly inclined as to be almost perpendicular. He wore a short jacket of brown corduroy, newer than the remainder of his suit, which was a fustian waistcoat with white horn buttons, breeches of the same, tanned leggings, and a straw hat overlaid with black glazed canvas. At his back he carried by a looped strap a rush basket from which protruded at one end the crutch of a hay-knife, a wimble for hay-bonds being also visible in the aperture. His measured springless walk was the walk of the skilled countryman as distinct from the desultory shamble of the general labourer;—while in the turn and plant of each foot there was, further, a dogged and cynical indifference, personal to himself, showing its presence even in the regularly interchanging fustian folds, now in the left leg, now in the right, as he paced along.

What was really peculiar, however, in this couple's progress, and would have attracted the attention of any casual observer otherwise disposed to overlook them, was the perfect silence they preserved. They walked side by side in such a way as to suggest afar off the low, easy, confidential chat of people full of reciprocity; but on closer view it could be discerned that the man was reading, or pretending to read, a ballad-sheet which he kept before his eyes with some difficulty by the hand that was passed through the basket-strap. Whether this apparent cause were the real cause, or whether it were an assumed one to escape an intercourse that would have been irksome to him, nobody but himself could have said precisely; but his taciturnity was unbroken, and the woman enjoyed no society whatever from his presence. Virtually she walked the highway alone, save for the child she bore. Sometimes the man's bent elbow almost touched her shoulder, for she kept as close to his side as was possible without actual contact; but she seemed to have no idea of taking his arm, nor he of offering it, and far from exhibiting surprise at his ignoring silence she appeared to receive it as a natural thing. If any word at all were uttered by the little group it was an occasional whisper of the woman to the child—a tiny girl in short clothes and blue boots of knitted yarn—and the murmured babble of the child in reply.

The chief—almost the only—attraction of the young woman's face was its mobility. When she looked down sideways to the girl she became pretty, and even handsome, particularly that in the action her features caught slantwise the rays of the strongly coloured sun, which made transparencies of her eyelids and nostrils, and set fire on her lips. When she plodded on in the shade of the hedge, silently thinking, she had the hard, half-apathetic expression of one who deems anything possible at the hands of Time and Chance except perhaps fair play. The first phase was the work of Nature, the second probably of civilization.

That the man and woman were husband and wife, and the parents of the girl in arms, there could be little doubt. No other than such relationship would have accounted for the atmosphere of stale familiarity which the trio carried along with them like a nimbus as they moved down the road.

The wife mostly kept her eyes fixed ahead, though with little interest—the scene for that matter being one that might have been matched at almost any spot in any county in England at this time of the year: a road neither straight nor crooked, neither level nor hilly, bordered by hedges, trees, and other vegetation, which had entered the blackened-green stage of colour that the doomed leaves pass through on their way to dingy, and yellow, and red. The grassy margin of the bank, and the nearest hedgerow boughs, were powdered by the dust that had been stirred over them by hasty vehicles, the same dust as it lay on the road deadening their footfalls like a carpet; and this, with the aforesaid total absence of conversation, allowed every extraneous sound to be heard.

For a long time there was none, beyond the voice of a weak bird singing a trite old evening song that might doubtless have been heard on the hill at the same hour, and with the self-same trills, quavers, and breves, at any sunset of that season for centuries untold. But as they approached the village sundry distant shouts and rattles reached their ears from some elevated spot in that direction, as yet screened from view by foliage. When the outlying houses of Weydon Priors could just be descried the family group was met by a turnip-hoer with his hoe on his shoulder and his dinner-bag suspended from it. The reader promptly glanced up.

"Any trade doing here?" he asked phlegmatically, designating the village in his van by a wave of the broadsheet. And thinking the labourer did not understand him he added, "Anything in the hay trussing line?"

The turnip-hoer had already begun shaking his head. "Why, save the man, what wisdom's in him that 'a should come to Weydon for a job of that sort this time o' year?"

"Then is there any house to let—a little small new cottage just a builded or such like?" asked the other.

The pessimist still maintained a negative: "Pulling down is more the nater of Weydon. There were five houses cleared away last year, and three this; and the volk nowhere to go—no, not so much as a thatched hurdle; that's the way o' Weydon Priors."

The hay-trusser, which he obviously was, nodded with some superciliousness. Looking towards the village, he continued, "There is something going on here, however, is there not?"

"Ay. 'Tis Fair Day. Though what you hear now is little more than the clatter and scurry of getting away the money o' children and fools, for the real business is done earlier than this. I've been working within sound o't all day, but I didn't go up—not I. 'Twas no business of mine."

The trusser and his family proceeded on their way, and soon entered the Fair field, which showed standing-places and pens where many hundreds of horses and sheep had been exhibited and sold in the forenoon, but were now in great part taken away. At present, as their informant had observed, but little real business remained on hand, the chief being the sale by auction of a few inferior animals, that could not otherwise be disposed of, and had been absolutely refused by the better class of traders, who came and went early. Yet the crowd was denser now than during the morning hours, the frivolous contingent of visitors, including journeymen out for a holiday, a stray soldier or two home on furlough, village shopkeepers, and the like, having latterly flocked in, persons whose activities found a congenial field among the peep-shows, toy-stands, wax-works, inspired monsters, disinterested medical men, who travelled for the public good, thimble-riggers, nick-nack vendors, and readers of Fate.

Neither of our pedestrians had much heart for these things, and they looked around for a refreshment tent among the many which dotted the down. Two, which stood nearest to them in the ochreous haze of expiring sunlight, seemed almost equally inviting. One was formed of new, milk-hued canvas, and bore red flags on its summit; it announced "Good Home-brewed Beer, Ale, and Cyder." The other was less new; a little iron stovepipe came out of it at the back, and in front appeared the placard, "Good Furmity Sold Hear." The man mentally weighed the two inscriptions, and inclined to the former tent.

"No—no—the other one," said the woman. "I always like furmity; and so does Elizabeth-Jane; and so will you. It is nourishing after a long hard day."

"I've never tasted it," said the man. However, he gave way to her representations, and they entered the furmity-booth forthwith.

A rather numerous company appeared within, seated at the long narrow tables that ran down the tent on each side. At the upper end stood a stove, containing a charcoal fire, over which hung a large three-legged crock, sufficiently polished round the rim to show that it was made of bell-metal. A haggish creature of about fifty presided, in a white apron, which, as it threw an air of respectability over her as far as it extended, was made so wide as to reach nearly round her waist. She slowly stirred the contents of the pot. The dull scrape of her large spoon was audible throughout the tent as she thus kept from burning the mixture of corn in the grain, flour, milk, raisins, currants, and what not, that composed the antiquated slop in which she dealt. Vessels holding the separate ingredients stood on a white-clothed table of boards and trestles close by.

The young man and woman ordered a basin each of the mixture, steaming hot, and sat down to consume it at leisure. This was very well so far, for furmity, as the woman had said, was nourishing, and as proper a food as could be obtained within the four seas; though, to those not accustomed to it, the grains of wheat, swollen as large as lemon-pips, which floated on its surface, might have a deterrent effect at first.

But there was more in that tent than met the cursory glance; and the man, with the instinct of a perverse character, scented it quickly. After a mincing attack on his bowl he watched the hag's proceedings from the corner of his eye, and saw the game she played. He winked to her, and passed up his basin in reply to her nod; when she took a bottle from under the table, slily measured out a quantity of its contents, and tipped the same into the man's furmity. The liquor poured in was rum. The man as slily sent back money in payment.

He found the concoction, thus strongly laced, much more to his satisfaction than it had been in its natural state. His wife had observed the proceeding with much uneasiness, but he persuaded her to have hers laced also, and she agreed to a milder allowance after some misgiving.

The man finished his basin, and called for another, the rum being signalled for in yet stronger proportion. The effect of it was soon apparent in his manner, and his wife but too sadly perceived that in strenuously steering off the rocks of the licensed liquor-tent she had only got into Maelstrom depths here amongst the smugglers.

The child began to prattle impatiently, and the wife more than once said to her husband, "Michael, how about our lodging? You know we may have trouble in getting it if we don't go soon."

But he turned a deaf ear to these bird-like chirpings. He talked loud to the company. The child's black eyes, after slow, round, ruminating gazes at the candles when they were lighted, fell together; then they opened, then shut again, and she slept.

At the end of the first basin the man had risen to serenity. At the second he was jovial; at the third, argumentative. At the fourth, the qualities signified by the shape of his face, the occasional clench of his mouth, and the fiery spark of his dark eye, began to tell in his conduct; he was overbearing—even brilliantly quarrelsome.

The conversation took a high turn, as it often does on such occasions. The ruin of good men by bad wives, and, more particularly the frustration of many a promising youth's high aims and hopes, and the extinction of his energies, by an early imprudent marriage, was the theme.

"I did for myself that way thoroughly," said the trusser, with a contemplative bitterness that was well-nigh resentful. "I married at eighteen, like the fool that I was; and this is the consequence o't." He pointed at himself and family with a wave of the hand intended to bring out the penuriousness of the exhibition.

The young woman his wife, who seemed accustomed to such remarks, acted as if she did not hear them, and continued her intermittent private words on tender trifles to the sleeping and waking child, who was just big enough to be placed for a moment on the bench beside her when she wished to ease her arms. The man continued:

"I haven't more than fifteen shillings in the world, and yet I am a good experienced hand in my line. I'd challenge England to beat me in the fodder business; and if I were a free man again I'd be worth a thousand pound before I'd done o't. But a fellow never knows these little things till all chance of acting upon 'em is past."

The auctioneer selling the old horses in the field outside could be heard saying, "Now this is the last lot—now who'll take the last lot for a song? Shall I say forty shillings? 'Tis a very promising brood-mare, a trifle over five years old, and nothing the matter with the hoss at all, except that she's a little holler in the back and had her left eye knocked out by the kick of another, her own sister, coming along the road."

"For my part I don't see why men who have got wives, and don't want 'em, shouldn't get rid of 'em as these gipsy fellows do their old horses," said the man in the tent. "Why shouldn't they put 'em up and sell 'em by auction to men who are in need of such articles? Hey? Why, begad, I'd sell mine this minute, if anybody would buy her!"

"There's them that would do that," some of the guests replied, looking at the woman, who was by no means ill-favoured.

"True," said a smoking gentleman, whose coat had the fine polish about the collar, elbows, seams, and shoulder blades that long-continued friction with grimy surfaces will produce, and which is usually more desired on furniture than on clothes. From his appearance he had possibly been in former time groom or coachman to some neighbouring county family. "I've had my breedings in as good circles, I may say, as any man," he added, "and I know true cultivation, or nobody do; and I can declare she's got it—in the bone, mind ye, I say—as much as any female in the fair—though it may want a little bringing out." Then, crossing his legs, he resumed his pipe with a nicely adjusted gaze at a point in the air.

The fuddled young husband stared for a few seconds at this unexpected praise of his wife, half in doubt of the wisdom of his own attitude towards the possessor of such qualities. But he speedily lapsed into his former conviction, and said harshly:

"Well, then, now is your chance; I am open to an offer for this gem o' creation."

She turned to her husband and murmured, "Michael, you have talked this nonsense in public places before. A joke is a joke, but you may make it once too often, mind!"

"I know I've said it before; I meant it. All I want is a buyer."

At the moment a swallow, one among the last of the season, which had by chance found its way through an opening into the upper part of the tent, flew to and fro in quick curves above their heads, causing all eyes to follow it absently. In watching the bird till it made its escape the assembled company neglected to respond to the workman's offer, and the subject dropped.

But a quarter of an hour later the man, who had gone on lacing his furmity more and more heavily, though he was either so strong-minded or such an intrepid toper that he still appeared fairly sober, recurred to the old strain, as in a musical fantasy the instrument fetches up the original theme. "Here—I am waiting to know about this offer of mine. The woman is no good to me. Who'll have her?"

The company had by this time decidedly degenerated, and the renewed inquiry was received with a laugh of appreciation. The woman whispered; she was imploring and anxious; "Come, come, it is getting dark, and this nonsense won't do. If you don't come along I shall go without you. Come!"

She waited and waited; yet he did not move. In ten minutes the man broke in upon the desultory conversation of the furmity drinkers with, "I asked this question, and nobody answered to 't. Will any Jack Rag or Tom Straw among ye buy my goods?"

The woman's manner changed, and her face assumed the grim shape and colour of which mention has been made.

"Mike, Mike," said she; "this is getting serious. Oh—too serious!"

"Will anybody buy her?" said the man.

"I wish somebody would," said she firmly. "Her present owner is not at all to her liking!'

"Nor you to mine," said he. "So we are agreed about that. Gentlemen, you hear? It's an agreement to part. She shall take the girl if she wants to, and go her ways. I'll take my tools and go my ways. 'Tis simple as Scripture history. Now then, stand up Susan, and show yourself."

"Don't my chiel," whispered a buxom staylace dealer in voluminous petticoats, who sat near the woman: "Yer good man don't know what he's saying."

The woman, however, did stand up. "Now who's auctioneer?" cried the hay trusser.

"I be," promptly answered a short man with a nose resembling a copper knob, a damp voice, and eyes like button-holes. "Who'll make an offer for this lady?"

The woman looked on the ground, as if she maintained her position by a supreme effort of will.

"Five shillings," said some one, at which there was a laugh.

"No insults," said the husband. "Who'll say a guinea?"

Nobody answered: and the female dealer in staylaces interposed. "Behave yerself moral, good man, for Heaven's love! Ah, what a cruelty is the poor soul married to! Bed and board is dear at some figures, 'pon my 'vation 'tis!"

"Set it higher, auctioneer," said the trusser.

"Two guineas," said the auctioneer: and no one replied.

"If they don't take her for that, in ten seconds they'll have to give more," said the husband. "Very well. Now auctioneer, add another."

"Three guineas—going for three guineas!" said the rheumy man.

"No bid?" said the husband. "Good Lord, why she's cost me fifty times the money, if a penny. Go on."

"Four guineas," cried the auctioneer.

"I'll tell ye what—I won't sell her for less than five," said the husband, bringing down his fist so that the basins danced. "I'll sell her for five guineas to any man that will pay me the money and treat her well; and he shall have her for ever, and never hear aught o' me. But she shan't go for less. Now then—five guineas—and she's yours. Susan you agree?"

She bowed her head with absolute indifference.

"Five guineas," said the auctioneer, "or she'll be withdrawn. Do anybody give it? The last time—Yes or no?"

"Yes," said a loud voice from the doorway.

All eyes were turned. Standing in the triangular opening which formed the door of the tent was a sailor, who unobserved by the rest had arrived there within the last two or three minutes. A dead silence followed his affirmation.

"You say you do?" asked the husband staring at him.

"I say so," replied the sailor.

"Saying is one thing, and paying is another. Where's the money?"

The sailor hesitated a moment, looked anew at the woman, came in, unfolded five crisp pieces of paper, and threw them down upon the tablecloth. They were Bank of England notes for five pounds. Upon the face of this he chinked down the shillings severally—one, two, three, four, five.

The sight of real money in full amount, in answer to a challenge for the same till then deemed slightly hypothetical, had a great effect upon the spectators. Their eyes became riveted upon the faces of the chief actors, and then upon the notes as they lay weighted by the shillings on the table.

Up to this moment it could not positively have been asserted that the man, in spite of his tantalizing declamation, was really in earnest. The spectators had indeed taken the proceedings throughout as a piece of mirthful irony carried to extremes; and had assumed that, being out of work, he was as a consequence out of temper with the world, and society, and his nearest kin. But with the demand and response of real cash the jovial frivolity of the scene departed. A lurid colour seemed to fill the tent, and change the aspect of all therein. The mirth-wrinkles left the listeners' faces, and they waited with parting lips.

"Now," said the woman, breaking the silence, so that her low dry voice sounded quite loud. "Before you go further Michael, listen to me. If you touch that money, I and this girl go with the man. Mind, it is a joke no longer."

"A joke—of course it is not a joke!" shouted her husband, his resentment rising at her suggestion. "I take the money: the sailor takes you. That's plain enough. It has been done elsewhere—and why not here?"

"'Tis quite on the understanding that the young woman is willing," said the sailor blandly. "I wouldn't hurt her feelings for the world."

"Faith, nor I," said her husband. "But she is willing provided she can have the child. She said so only the other day when I talked o't."

"That you swear?" said the sailor to her.

"I do," said she, after glancing at her husband's face and seeing no repentance there.

"Very well—she shall have the child, and the bargain's complete," said the trusser. He took the sailor's notes and deliberately folded them, and put them with the shillings in a high remote pocket, with an air of finality.

The sailor looked at the woman, and smiled. "Come along!" he said kindly. "The little one too—the more the merrier!"

She paused for an instant, with a close glance at him. Then dropping her eyes again, and saying nothing, she took up the child and followed him as he made towards the door. On reaching it she turned, and pulling off her wedding-ring flung it across the booth in the hay trusser's face.

"Mike," she said, "I've lived with thee a couple of years, and had nothing but temper. Now I'm no more to 'ee; I'll try my luck elsewhere. 'Twill be better for me and Elizabeth-Jane both. So good-bye." Seizing the sailor's arm with her right hand, and mounting the little girl on her left, she went out of the tent sobbing bitterly.

A stolid look of concern filled the husband's face, as if, after all, he had not quite anticipated this ending; and some of the guests laughed.

"Is she gone?" he said.

"Faith, aye; she's gone clane enough," said some rustics near the door.

He rose, and walked to the entrance with the careful tread of one conscious of his alcoholic load. Some others followed, and they stood looking into the twilight. The difference between the peacefulness of inferior nature and the wilful hostilities of mankind was very apparent at this place. In contrast with the harshness of the act just ended within the tent was the sight of several horses crossing their necks and rubbing each other lovingly as they waited in patience to be harnessed for the homeward journey. Outside the fair, in the valleys and woods, all was quiet. The sun had recently set, and the west heaven was hung with rosy cloud, which seemed permanent, yet slowly changed. To watch it was like looking at some grand feat of stagery from a darkened auditorium. In presence of this scene after the other there was a natural instinct to abjure man as the blot on an otherwise kindly universe; till it was remembered that all terrestrial conditions were intermittent, and that mankind might some night be innocently sleeping when these quiet objects were raging loud.

"Where do the sailor live?" asked a spectator, when they had vainly gazed around.

"God knows that," replied the man who had seen high life.

"He's without doubt a stranger here."

"He came in about five minutes ago," said the furmity-woman joining the rest with her hands on her hips. "And then 'a stepped back, and then 'a looked in again. I'm not a penny the better for him."

"Serves the husband well be-right," said the staylace vendor. "A comely respectable body like her—what can a man want more?—I glory in the woman's sperrit. I'd ha' done it myself—Od send if I wouldn't, if a husband had behaved so to me! I'd go, and 'a might call, and call, till his keacorn was raw; but I'd never come back—no, not till the great trumpet, would I."

"Well, the woman will be better off," said another of a more deliberative turn. "For sea-faring natures be very good shelter for shorn lambs, and the man do seem to have plenty of money, which is what she's not been used to lately, by all showings."

"Mark me—I'll not go after her!" said the trusser, returning doggedly to his seat. "Let her go. If she's up to such vagaries she must suffer for 'em. . . . She'd no business to take the maid—'tis my maid; and if it were the doing again she shouldn't have her!"

Perhaps from some little sense of having countenanced an indefensible proceeding, perhaps because it was late, the customers thinned away from the tent shortly after this episode. The man stretched his elbows forward on the table, leant his face upon his arms, and soon began to snore. The furmity-seller decided to close for the night, and after seeing the rum-bottles, milk, corn, raisins, etc., that remained on hand, loaded into the cart, came to where the man reclined. She shook him; but could not wake him. As the tent was not to be struck that night, the fair continuing for two or three days, she decided to let the sleeper, who was obviously no tramp, stay where he was and his basket with him. Extinguishing the last candle, and lowering the flap of the tent she left it, and drove away.

THE morning sun was streaming through the crevices of the canvas when the man awoke. A warm glow pervaded the whole atmosphere of the marquee, and a single big blue fly buzzed musically round and round in it. Besides the buzz of the fly there was not a sound. He looked about—at the benches—at the table supported by trestles—at his basket of tools—at the stove where the furmity had been boiled—at the empty basins—at some shed grains of wheat—at the corks which dotted the grassy floor. Among the odds and ends he discerned a little shining object, and picked it up. It was his wife's ring.

A confused picture of the events of the previous evening seemed to come back to him, and he thrust his hand into his breast-pocket. A rustling revealed the sailor's bank-notes thrust carelessly in.

This second verification of his dim memories was enough; he knew now they were not dreams. He remained seated, looking on the ground for some time. "I must get out of this as soon as I can," he said deliberately at last, with the air of one who could not catch his thoughts without pronouncing them. "She's gone—to be sure she is—gone with that sailor who bought her, and little Elizabeth-Jane. We walked here, and I had the furmity, and rum in it—and sold her. Yes, that's what's happened, and here am I. Now, what am I to do—am I sober enough to walk, I wonder?" He stood up, found that he was in fairly good condition for progress, unencumbered. Next he shouldered his tool basket, and found he could carry it. Then lifting the tent door he emerged into the open air.

Here the man looked around with gloomy curiosity. The freshness of the September morning inspired and braced him as he stood. He and his family had been weary when they arrived the night before, and they had observed but little of the place, so that he now beheld it as a new thing. It exhibited itself as the top of an open down, bounded on one extreme by a plantation, and approached by a winding road. At the bottom stood the village which lent its name to the upland, and the annual fair that was held thereon. The spot stretched downward into valleys, and onward to other uplands, dotted with barrows, and trenched with the remains of prehistoric forts. The whole scene lay under the rays of a newly-risen sun, which had not as yet dried a single blade of the heavily-dewed grass, whereon the shadows of the yellow and red vans were projected far away, those thrown by the felloe of each wheel being elongated in shape to the orbit of a comet. All the gipsies and showmen who had remained on the ground lay snug within their carts and tents, or wrapped in horse-cloths under them, and were silent and still as death, with the exception of an occasional snore that revealed their presence. But the Seven Sleepers had a dog; and dogs of the mysterious breeds that vagrants own, that are as much like cats as dogs, and as much like foxes as cats, also lay about here. A little one started up under one of the carts, barked as a matter of principle, and quickly lay down again. He was the only positive spectator of the hay-trusser's exit from the Weydon fair-field.

This seemed to accord with his desire. He went on in silent thought, unheeding the yellow-hammers which flitted about the hedges with straws in their bills, the crowns of the mushrooms, and the tinkling of local sheep-bells, whose wearers had had the good fortune not to be included in the fair. When he reached a lane, a good mile from the scene of the previous evening, the man pitched his basket, and leant upon a gate. A difficult problem or two occupied his mind.

"Did I tell my name to anybody last night, or didn't I tell my name?" he said to himself; and at last concluded that he did not. His general demeanour was enough to show how he was surprised and nettled that his wife had taken him so literally—as much could be seen in his face, and in the way he nibbled a straw which he pulled from the hedge. He knew that she must have been somewhat excited to do this; moreover, she must have believed that there was some sort of binding force in the transaction. On this latter point he felt almost certain, knowing her freedom from levity of character, and the extreme simplicity of her intellect. There may, too, have been enough recklessness and resentment beneath her ordinary placidity to make her stifle any momentary doubts. On a previous occasion when he had declared during a fuddle that he would dispose of her as he had done, she had replied that she would not hear him say that many times more before it happened, in the resigned tones of a fatalist. . . . "Yet she knows I am not in my senses when I do that!" he exclaimed. "Well, I must walk about till I find her. . . . Seize her! why didn't she know better, than bring me into this disgrace!" he roared out. "She wasn't queer if I was. 'Tis like Susan to show such idiotic simplicity. Meek—that meekness has done me more harm than the bitterest temper!"

When he was calmer, he turned to his original conviction that he must somehow find her and his little Elizabeth-Jane, and put up with the shame as best he could. It was of his own making, and he ought to bear it. But first he resolved to register an oath, a greater oath than he had ever sworn before; and to do it properly he required a fit place and imagery; for there was something fetichistic in this man's beliefs.

He shouldered his basket and moved on, casting his eyes inquisitively round upon the landscape as he walked, and at the distance of three or four miles perceived the roofs of a village and the tower of a church. He instantly made towards the latter object. The village was quite still, it being that motionless hour of rustic daily life which fills the interval between the departure of the field labourers to their work, and the rising of their wives and daughters to prepare the breakfast for their return. Hence he reached the church without observation, and the door being only latched he entered. The hay-trusser deposited his basket by the font, went up the nave till he reached the altar-rails, and opening the gate entered the sacrarium, where he seemed to feel a sense of the strangeness for a moment; then he knelt upon the foot-pace. Dropping his head upon the clamped book which lay on the Communion-table, he said aloud:

"I, Michael Henchard, on this morning of the sixteenth of September, do take an oath before God here in this solemn place that I will avoid all strong liquors for the space of twenty-one years to come, being a year for every year that I have lived. And this I swear upon the Book before me; and may I be strook dumb, blind, and helpless if I break this my oath."

When he had said it and kissed the big book, the hay-trusser arose, and seemed relieved at having made a start in a new direction. While standing in the porch a moment, he saw a thick jet of wood smoke suddenly start up from the red chimney of a cottage near, and knew that the occupant had just lit her fire. He went round to the door, and the housewife agreed to prepare him some breakfast for a trifling payment, which was done. Then he started on the search for his wife and child.

The perplexing nature of the undertaking became apparent soon enough. Though he examined and inquired, and walked hither and thither day after day, no such characters as those he described had anywhere been seen since the evening of the fair. To add to the difficulty he could gain no sound of the sailor's name. As money was short with him he decided, after some hesitation, to spend the sailor's money in the prosecution of this search; but it was equally in vain. The truth was that a certain shyness of revealing his conduct prevented Michael Henchard from following up the investigation with the loud hue-and-cry such a pursuit demanded to render it effectual; and it was probably for this reason that he obtained no clue, though everything was done by him that did not involve an explanation of the circumstances under which he had lost her.

Weeks counted up to months and still he searched on, maintaining himself by small jobs of work in the intervals. By this time he had arrived at a seaport, and there he derived intelligence that persons answering somewhat to his description had emigrated a little time before. Then he said he would search no longer, and that he would go and settle in the district which he had had for some time in his mind. Next day he started, journeying south-westward, and did not pause, except for nights' lodgings, till he reached the town of Casterbridge, in a far distant part of Wessex.

III

THE high-road into the village of Weydon Priors was again carpeted with dust. The trees had put on as of yore their aspect of dingy green, and where the Henchard family of three had once walked along, two persons not unconnected with that family walked now.

The scene in its broad aspect had so much of its previous character, even to the voices and rattle from the neighbouring village down, that it might for that matter have been the afternoon following the previously recorded episode. Change was only to be observed in details; but here it was obvious that a long procession of years had passed by. One of the two who walked the road was she who had figured as the young wife of Henchard on the previous occasion; now her face had lost much of its rotundity; her skin had undergone a textural change; and though her hair had not lost colour it was considerably thinner than heretofore. She was dressed in the mourning clothes of a widow. Her companion, also in black, appeared as a well-formed young woman about eighteen, completely possessed of that ephemeral precious essence youth, which is itself beauty, irrespective of complexion or contour. A glance was sufficient to inform the eye that this was Susan Henchard's grown-up daughter. While life's middle summer had set its hardening mark on the mother's face, her former spring-like specialities were transferred so dexterously by Time to the second figure her child that the absence of certain facts within her mother's knowledge from the girl's mind would have seemed for the moment, to one reflecting on those facts, to be a curious imperfection in Nature's powers of continuity.

They walked with joined hands, and it could be perceived that this was the act of simple affection. The daughter carried in her outer hand a withy basket of old-fashioned make; the mother a blue bundle, which contrasted oddly with her black stuff gown.

Reaching the outskirts of the village they pursued the same

track as formerly, and ascended to the fair. Here, too, it was evident that the years had told. Certain mechanical improvements might have been noticed in the roundabouts and highfliers, machines for testing rustic strength and weight, and in the erections devoted to shooting for nuts. But the real business of the fair had considerably dwindled. The new periodical great markets of neighbouring towns were beginning to interfere seriously with the trade carried on here for centuries. The pens for sheep, the tie-ropes for horses, were about half as long as they had been. The stalls of tailors, hosiers, coopers, linendrapers, and other such trades had almost disappeared, and the vehicles were far less numerous. The mother and daughter threaded the crowd for some little distance, and then stood still.

"Why did we hinder our time by coming in here? I thought you wished to get onward?" said the maiden.

"Yes, my dear Elizabeth-Jane," explained the other. "But I had a fancy for looking up here."

"Why?"

"It was here I first met with Newson—on such a day as this."

"First met with father here? Yes, you have told me so before. And now he's drowned and gone from us!" As she spoke the girl drew a card from her pocket and looked at it with a sigh. It was edged with black, and inscribed within a design resembling a mural tablet were the words, "In affectionate memory of Richard Newson, mariner, who was unfortunately lost at sea, in the month of November 184—, aged 41 years."

"And it was here," continued her mother, with more hesitation, "that I last saw the relation we are going to look for—Mr. Michael Henchard."

"What is his exact kin to us, mother? I have never clearly had it told me."

"He is, or was—for he may be dead—a connection by marriage," said her mother deliberately.

"That's exactly what you have said a score of times before!" replied the young woman looking about her inattentively. "He's not a near relation, I suppose?"

"Not by any means."

"He was a hay trusser, wasn't he, when you last heard of him?"

"He was."

"I suppose he never knew me?" the girl innocently continued.

Mrs. Henchard paused for a moment, and answered uneasily, "Of course not, Elizabeth-Jane. But come this way." She moved on to another part of the field.

"It is not much use inquiring here for anybody, I should think," the daughter observed, as she gazed round about. "People at fairs change like the leaves of trees; and I daresay you are the only one here to-day who was here all those years ago."

"I am not so sure of that," said Mrs. Newson, as she now called herself, keenly eyeing something under a green bank a little way off. "See there."

The daughter looked in the direction signified. The object pointed out was a tripod of sticks stuck into the earth, from which hung a three-legged crock, kept hot by a smouldering wood fire beneath. Over the pot stooped an old woman haggard, wrinkled, and almost in rags. She stirred the contents of the pot with a large spoon, and occasionally croaked in a broken voice "Good furmity sold here!"

It was indeed the former mistress of the furmity-tent—once thriving, cleanly, white-aproned, and chinking with money—now tentless, dirty, owning no tables or benches, and having scarce any customers except two small whitey-brown boys who came up and asked for "A ha'p'orth please—good measure," which she served in a couple of chipped yellow basins of commonest clay.

"She was here at that time," resumed Mrs. Newson, making a step as if to draw nearer.

"Don't speak to her—it isn't respectable!" urged the other.

"I will just say a word—you, Elizabeth-Jane, can stay here."

The girl was not loth, and turned to some stalls of coloured prints while her mother went forward. The old woman begged for the latter's custom as soon as she saw her, and responded to Mrs. Henchard-Newson's request for a pennyworth with more alacrity than she had shown in selling sixpennyworths in her younger days. When the *soi-disant* widow had taken the basin of thin poor slop that stood for the rich concoction of the former time the hag opened a little basket behind the fire, and looking up slily whispered, "Just a thought o' rum in it?—smuggled you know—say two penn'orth—'twill make it slip down like cordial."

Her customer smiled bitterly at this survival of the old trick, and shook her head with a meaning the old woman was far from translating. She pretended to eat a little of the furmity with the leaden spoon offered, and as she did so said blandly to the hag: "You've seen better days?"

"Ah, ma'am—well ye may say it!" responded the old woman opening the sluices of her heart forthwith. "I've stood in this fair-ground maid, wife, and widow, these nine and thirty year, and in that time have known what it was to do business with the richest stomachs in the land! Ma'am, you'd hardly believe that I was once the owner of a great pavilion tent that was the attraction of the fair. Nobody could come—nobody could go, without having a dish of Mrs. Goodenough's furmity. I knew the clergy's taste, the dandy-gent's taste; I knew the town's taste, the country's taste, I even knowed the taste of the coarse shameless females. But Lord's my life—the world's no memory; straightforward dealings don't bring profit—'tis the sly and the underhand that get on in these times!"

Mrs. Newson glanced round—her daughter was still bending over the distant stalls. "Can you call to mind," she said cautiously to the old woman, "the sale of a wife by her husband in your tent eighteen years ago to-day?"

The hag reflected, and half shook her head. "If it had been a big thing I should have minded it in a moment," she said. "I can mind every serious fight o' married parties, every murder, every manslaughter, even every pocket-picking—leastwise large ones—that 't has been my lot to witness. But a selling.—Was it done quiet-like?"

"Well yes—I think so."

The furmity woman half shook her head again. "And yet," she said, "I do. At any rate I can mind a man doing something o' the sort—a man in a cord jacket with a basket of tools: but Lord bless ye, we don't gie it head-room, we don't, such as that. The only reason why I can mind the man is that he came back here to the next year's fair, and told me quite private-like that if a woman ever asked for him I was to say he had gone to—where?—Casterbridge—yes—to Casterbridge, said he. But Lord's my life, I shouldn't ha' thought of it again!"

Mrs. Newson would have rewarded the old woman as far as her small means afforded, had she not discretely borne in mind that it was by that unscrupulous person's liquor her husband had been degraded. She briefly thanked her informant, and rejoined Elizabeth who greeted her with, "Mother, do let's go on—it was hardly respectable for you to buy refreshments there. I see none but the lowest do."

"I have learnt what I wanted, however," said her mother quietly. "The last time our relative visited this fair he said he was living at Casterbridge. It is a long, long way from here, and it was many years ago that he said it; but there I think we'll go."

With this they descended out of the fair, and went onward to the village, where they obtained a night's lodging.

IV

HENCHARD'S wife acted for the best, but she had involved herself in difficulties. A hundred times she had been upon the point of telling her daughter, Elizabeth-Jane, the true story of her life, the tragical crisis of which had been the transaction at Weydon Fair, when she was not much older than the girl now beside her. But she had refrained. An innocent maiden had thus grown up in the belief that the relations between the genial sailor and her mother were the ordinary ones that they had always appeared to be. The risk of endangering a child's strong affection by disturbing ideas which had grown with her growth was to Mrs. Henchard too fearful a thing to contemplate. It had seemed, indeed, folly to think of making Elizabeth-Jane wise.

But Susan Henchard's fear of losing her dearly loved daughter's heart by a revelation had little to do with any sense of wrong-doing on her own part. Her simplicity—the original ground of Henchard's contempt for her—had allowed her to live on in the conviction that Newson had acquired a morally real and justifiable right to her by his purchase—though the exact bearings and legal limits of that right were vague. It may seem strange to sophisticated minds that a sane young matron could believe in the seriousness of such a transfer; and were there not numerous other instances of the same belief the thing might scarcely be credited. But she was by no means the first or last peasant woman who had religiously adhered to her purchaser, as too many rural records show.

The history of Susan Henchard's adventures in the interim can be told in two or three sentences. Absolutely helpless she had been taken off to Canada, where they had lived several years without any great worldly success, though she worked as hard as any woman could to keep their cottage cheerful and well provided. When Elizabeth-Jane was about twelve years old the three returned to England, and settled at Falmouth, where Newson made a living for a few years as boatman and general handy shoreman.

He then engaged in the Newfoundland trade, and it was during this period that Susan had an awakening. A friend to whom she confided her history ridiculed her grave acceptance of her position; and all was over with her peace of mind. When Newson came home at the end of one winter he saw that the delusion he had so carefully sustained had vanished for ever.

There was then a time of sadness, in which she told him her doubts if she could live with him longer. Newson left home again on the Newfoundland trade when the season came round. The vague news of his loss at sea a little later on solved a problem which had become torture to her meek conscience. She saw him no more.

Of Henchard they heard nothing. To the liege subjects of Labour, the England of those days was a continent, and a mile a geographical degree.

Elizabeth-Jane developed early into womanliness. One day, a month or so after receiving intelligence of Newson's death off the Bank of Newfoundland, when the girl was about eighteen, she was sitting on a willow chair in the cottage they still occupied, working twine nets for the fishermen. Her mother was in a back corner of the same room, engaged in the same labour; and dropping the heavy wood needle she was filling she surveyed her daughter thoughtfully. The sun shone in at the door upon the young woman's head and hair, which was worn loose, so that the rays streamed into its depths as into a hazel copse. Her face, though somewhat wan and incomplete, possessed the raw materials of beauty in a promising degree. There was an under-handsomeness in it, struggling to reveal itself through the provisional curves of immaturity, and the casual disfigurements that resulted from the straitened circumstances of their lives. She was handsome in the bone, hardly as yet handsome in the flesh. She possibly might never be fully handsome, unless the carking accidents of her daily existence could be evaded before the mobile parts of her countenance had settled to their final mould.

The sight of the girl made her mother sad—not vaguely, but by logical inference. They both were still in that strait-waistcoat of poverty from which she had tried so many times to be delivered for the girl's sake. The woman had long perceived how zealously and constantly the young mind of her companion was struggling for enlargement; and yet now, in her eighteenth year, it still remained but little unfolded. The desire—sober and repressed—of Elizabeth-Jane's heart was indeed to see, to hear, and to understand. How could she become a woman of wider knowledge, higher repute— "better," as she termed it:—this was her constant inquiry of her mother. She sought further into things than other girls in her position ever did, and her mother groaned as she felt she could not aid in the search.

The sailor, drowned or no, was probably now lost to them: and Susan's staunch, religious adherence to him as her husband in principle, till her views had been disturbed by enlightenment, was demanded no more. She asked herself whether the present moment, now that she was a free woman again, were not as opportune a one as she would find, in a world where everything had been so inopportune, for making a desperate effort to advance Elizabeth. To pocket her pride and search for the first husband seemed, wisely or not, the best initiatory step. He had possibly drunk himself into his tomb. But he might, on the other hand, have had too much sense to do so; for in her time with him he had been given to bouts only, and was not a habitual drunkard.

At any rate the propriety of returning to him, if he lived, was unquestionable. The awkwardness of searching for him lay in enlightening Elizabeth, a proceeding which her mother could not endure to contemplate. She finally resolved to undertake the search without confiding to the girl her former relations with Henchard, leaving it to him if they found him to take what steps he might choose to that end. This will account for their conversation at the fair, and the half-informed state in which Elizabeth was led onward.

In this attitude they proceeded on their journey, trusting solely to the dim light afforded of Henchard's whereabouts by the furmity woman. The strictest economy was indispensable. Sometimes they might have been seen on foot, sometimes on farmers' waggons, sometimes in carriers' vans; and thus they drew near to Casterbridge. Elizabeth-Jane discovered to her alarm that her mother's health was not what it once had been, and there was ever and anon in her talk that renunciatory tone which showed that, but for the girl, she would not be very sorry to quit a life she was growing thoroughly weary of.

It was on a Friday evening, near the middle of September, and just before dusk, that they reached the summit of a hill within a mile of the place they sought. There were high-banked hedges to the coach-road here, and they mounted upon the green turf within, and sat down. The spot commanded a full view of the town and its environs.

"What an old-fashioned place it seems to be!" said Elizabeth-Jane, while her silent mother mused on other things than topography. "It is huddled all together; and it is shut in by a square wall of trees, like a plot of garden ground by a box-edging."

Its squareness was, indeed, the characteristic which most struck the eye in this antiquated borough, the borough of Casterbridge—at that time, recent as it was, untouched by the faintest sprinkle of modernism. It was compact as a box of dominoes. It had no suburbs—in the ordinary sense. Country and town met at a mathematical line.

To birds of the more soaring kind Casterbridge must have appeared on this fine evening as a mosaic-work of subdued reds, browns, greys, and crystals, held together by a rectangular frame of deep green. To the level eye of humanity it stood as an indistinct mass behind a dense stockade of limes and chestnuts, set in the midst of miles of rotund down and concave field. The mass became gradually dissected by the vision into towers, gables, chimneys, and casements, the highest glazings shining bleared and bloodshot with the coppery fire they caught from the belt of sun-lit cloud in the west.

From the centre of each side of this tree-bound square ran avenues east, west, and south into the wide expanse of corn-land and coomb, to the distance of a mile or so. It was by one of these avenues that the pedestrians were about to enter. Before they had risen to proceed two men passed outside the hedge, engaged in argumentative conversation.

"Why surely," said Elizabeth, as they receded; "those men mentioned the name of Henchard in their talk—the name of our relative?"

"I thought so too," said Mrs. Newson.

"That seems a hint to us that he is still here."

"Yes."

"Shall I run after them, and ask them about him——"

"No, no, no! Not for the world just yet. He may be in the workhouse or in the stocks for all we know."

"Dear me—why should you think that, mother?"

"'Twas just something to say—that's all. But we must make private inquiries."

Having sufficiently rested they proceeded on their way at evenfall. The dense trees of the avenue rendered the road dark as a tunnel, though the open land on each side was still under a faint daylight: in other words they passed down a midnight between two gloamings. The features of the town had a keen interest for Elizabeth's mother now that the human side came to the fore. As soon as they had wandered about they could see that the stockade of gnarled trees which framed in Casterbridge was itself an avenue, standing on a low green bank or escarpment with a ditch yet visible without. Within the avenue and bank was a wall more or less discontinuous, and within·the wall were packed the abodes of the burghers.

Though the two women did not know it, these external features were but the ancient defences of the town, planted as a promenade.

The lamplights now glimmered through the engirdling trees, conveying a sense of great snugness and comfort inside, and rendering at the same time the unlighted country without strangely solitary and vacant in aspect, considering its nearness to life. The difference between burgh and champaign was increased, too, by sounds which now reached them above others—the notes of a brass band. The travellers returned into the high street, where there were timber-houses with overhanging stories whose small paned lattices were screened by dimity curtains on a drawing-string and under whose barge-boards old cobwebs waved in the breeze. There were houses of brick-nogging which derived their chief support from those adjoining. There were slate roofs patched with tiles, and tile roofs patched with slate, with occasionally a roof of thatch.[1]

---

[1] Most of these old houses have now been pulled down (1912).

The agricultural and pastoral character of the people upon whom the town depended for its existence was shown by the class of objects displayed in the shop windows. Scythes, reap-hooks, sheep-shears, bill-hooks, spades, mattocks, and hoes, at the ironmonger's: bee-hives, butter-firkins, churns, milking-stools and pails, hay-rakes, field-flagons, and seed-lips, at the cooper's: cart-ropes and plough-harness at the saddler's; carts, wheel-barrows, and mill-gear at the wheelwright's and machinist's; horse-embrocations at the chemist's; at the glover's and leather-cutter's hedging-gloves, thatchers' knee-caps, ploughmen's leggings, villagers' pattens and clogs.

They came to a grizzled church, whose massive square tower rose unbroken into the darkening sky, the lower parts being illuminated by the nearest lamps sufficiently to show how completely the mortar from the joints of the stonework had been nibbled out by time and weather, which had planted in the crevices thus made little tufts of stonecrop and grass almost as far up as the very battlements. From this tower the clock struck eight, and thereupon a bell began to toll with a peremptory clang. The curfew was still rung in Casterbridge, and it was utilized by the inhabitants as a signal for shutting their shops. No sooner did the deep notes of the bell throb between the house-fronts than a clatter of shutters arose through the whole length of the high street. In a few minutes business at Casterbridge was ended for the day.

Other clocks struck eight from time to time—one gloomily from the gaol, another from the gable of an alms-house, with a preparative creak of machinery more audible than the note of the bell: a row of tall varnished case-clocks from the interior of a clockmaker's shop joined in one after another just as the shutters were enclosing them, like a row of actors delivering their final speeches before the fall of the curtain; then chimes were heard stammering out the Sicilian Mariners' Hymn;[1] so that chronologists of the advanced school were appreciably on their way to the next hour before the whole business of the old one was satisfactorily wound up.

In an open space before the church walked a woman with

[1] These chimes, like those of other country churches, have been silenced for many years.

her gown-sleeves rolled up so high that the edge of her under-linen was visible, and her skirt tucked up through her pocket-hole. She carried a loaf under her arm, from which she was pulling pieces of bread and handing them to some other women who walked with her; which pieces they nibbled critically. The sight reminded Mrs. Henchard-Newson and her daughter that they had an appetite; and they enquired of the woman for the nearest baker's.

"Ye may as well look for manna-food as good bread in Casterbridge just now," she said after directing them. "They can blare their trumpets and thump their drums, and have their roaring dinners"—(waving her hand towards a point further along the street, where the brass band could be seen standing in front of an illuminated building)—"but we must needs be put-to for want of a wholesome crust. There's less good bread than good beer in Casterbridge now."

"And less good beer than swipes," said a man with his hands in his pockets.

"How does it happen there's no good bread?" asked Mrs. Henchard.

"Oh, 'tis the corn-factor—he's the man that our millers and bakers all deal wi'—and he has sold 'em growed wheat, which they didn't know was growed, so they *say*, till the dough ran all over the ovens like quicksilver; so that the loaves be as flat as toads, and like suet pudden inside. I've been a wife, and I've been a mother, and I never see such unprincipled bread in Casterbridge as this before . . . . . . But you must be a real stranger here not to know what's made all the poor volks' insides plim like blowed bladders this week?"

"I am," said Elizabeth's mother, shyly. Not wishing to be observed further till she knew more of her future in this place, she withdrew with her daughter from the speaker's side. Getting a couple of biscuits at the shop indicated, as a temporary substitute for a meal, they next bent their steps instinctively to where the music was playing.

A FEW score yards brought them to the spot, where the town band was now shaking the window-panes with the strains of "The Roast Beef of Old England."

The building before whose doors they had pitched their music-stands was the chief hotel in Casterbridge, namely the King's Arms. A spacious bow-window projected into the street over the main portico, and from the open sashes came the babble of voices, the jingle of glasses, and the drawing of corks. The blinds moreover being left unclosed the whole interior of this room could be surveyed from the top of a flight of stone steps to the road-waggon office opposite, for which reason a knot of idlers had gathered there.

"We might, perhaps, after all, make a few inquiries about— our relation, Mr. Henchard," whispered Mrs. Newson, who since her entry into Casterbridge had seemed strangely weak and agitated, "And this I think would be a good place for trying it—just to ask, you know, how he stands in the town—if he is here, as I think he must be. You, Elizabeth-Jane, had better be the one to do it—I'm too worn out to do anything— pull down your fall first." She sat down upon the lowest step, and Elizabeth-Jane obeyed her directions and stood among the idlers.

"What's going on to-night?" asked the girl, after singling out an old man and standing by him long enough to acquire a neighbourly right of converse.

"Well—ye must be a stranger sure," said the old man without taking his eyes from the window. "Why 'tis a great public dinner of the gentlepeople and such like leading volk— wi' the mayor in the chair. As we plainer fellows baint invited they leave the winder-shutters open that we may get jist a sense o't out here. If you mount the steps you can see 'em. That's Mr. Henchard the mayor at the end of the table, a facing ye; and that's the councilmen right and left. . . . . . . Ah, lots of them, when they begun life, were no more than I be now!"

"Henchard?" said Elizabeth-Jane, surprised, but by no means suspecting the whole force of the revelation. She ascended to the top of the steps.

Her mother, though her head was bowed, had already caught from the inn-window tones that strangely riveted her attention, before the old man's words "Mr. Henchard the mayor" reached her ears. She arose, and stepped up to her daughter's side as soon as she could do so without showing exceptional eagerness.

The interior of the hotel dining room was spread out before her, with its tables, and glass, and plate, and inmates. Facing the window, in the chair of dignity, sat a man about forty years of age; of heavy frame, large features, and commanding voice, his general build being rather coarse than compact. He had a rich complexion which verged on swarthiness, a flashing black eye, and dark bushy brows and hair. When he indulged in an occasional loud laugh at some remark among the guests his large mouth parted so far back as to show to the rays of the chandelier a full score or more of the two-and-thirty sound white teeth that he obviously still could boast of.

That laugh was not encouraging to strangers; and hence it may have been well that it was rarely heard. Many theories might have been built upon it. It fell in well with conjectures of a temperament which would have no pity for weakness, but would be ready to yield ungrudging admiration to greatness and strength. Its producer's personal goodness, if he had any, would be of a very fitful cast—an occasional almost aggressive generosity rather than a mild and constant kindness.

Susan Henchard's husband, in law at least, sat before them, matured in shape, stiffened in line, exaggerated in traits; disciplined, thought-marked,—in a word, older. Elizabeth, encumbered with no recollections as her mother was, regarded him with nothing more than the keen curiosity and interest which the discovery of such unexpected social standing in the long sought relative naturally begot. He was dressed in an old-fashioned evening suit, an expanse of frilled shirt showing on his broad breast; jewelled studs, and a heavy gold chain. Three glasses stood at his right hand; but to his wife's surprise the two for wine were empty, while the third, a tumbler, was half full of water.

When last she had seen him he was sitting in a corduroy jacket, fustian waistcoat and breeches, and tanned leather leggings, with a basin of hot furmity before him. Time the magician had wrought much here. Watching him and thus thinking of past days, she became so moved that she shrank back against the jamb of the waggon-office doorway to which the steps gave access, the shadow from it conveniently hiding her features. She forgot her daughter, till a touch from Elizabeth-Jane aroused her. "Have you seen him, mother?" whispered the girl.

"Yes, yes," answered her companion hastily. "I have seen him, and it is enough for me! Now I only want to go—pass away—die."

"Why—O what?" She drew closer and whispered in her mother's ear: "Does he seem to you not likely to befriend us? I thought he looked a generous man. What a gentleman he is, isn't he? and how his diamond studs shine! How strange that you should have said he might be in the stocks, or in the workhouse, or dead! Did ever anything go more by contraries! Why do you feel so afraid of him? I am not at all: I'll call upon him—he can but say he don't own such remote kin."

"I don't know at all—I can't tell what to set about. I feel so down!"

"Don't be that, mother, now we have got here and all! Rest there where you be a little while—I will look on and find out more about him."

"I don't think I can ever meet Mr. Henchard. He is not how I thought he would be—he overpowers me. I don't wish to see him any more."

"But wait a little time and consider."

Elizabeth-Jane had never been so much interested in anything in her life as in their present position, partly from the natural elation she felt at discovering herself akin to a coach; and she gazed again at the scene. The younger guests were talking and eating with animation; their elders were searching for tit-bits, and sniffing and grunting over their plates like sows nuzzling for acorns. Three drinks seemed to be sacred to the company—port, sherry, and rum; outside which old-established trinity few or no palates ranged.

A row of ancient rummers with ground figures on their sides, and each primed with a spoon, was now placed down the table, and these were promptly filled with grog at such high temperatures as to raise serious considerations for the articles exposed to its vapours. But Elizabeth-Jane noticed that, though this filling went on with great promptness up and down the table, nobody filled the mayor's glass, who still drank large quantities of water from the tumbler behind the clump of crystal vessels intended for wine and spirits.

"They don't fill Mr. Henchard's wine-glasses," she ventured to say to her elbow acquaintance, the old man.

"Ah, no; don't ye know him to be the celebrated abstaining worthy of that name? He scorns all tempting liquors; never touches nothing. Oh yes, he've strong qualities that way. I have heard tell that he sware a gospel oath in bygone times, and has bode by it ever since. So they don't press him, knowing it would be unbecoming in the face of that; for yer gospel oath is a serious thing."

Another elderly man, hearing this discourse, now joined in by inquiring, "How much longer have he got to suffer from it, Solomon Longways?"

"Another two year, they say. I don't know the why and the wherefore of his fixing such a time, for 'a never has told anybody. But 'tis exactly two calendar years longer, they say. A powerful mind to hold out so long!"

"True. . . But there's great strength in hope. Knowing that in four-and-twenty months' time ye'll be out of your bondage, and able to make up for all you've suffered, by partaking without stint; why, it keeps a man up, no doubt."

"No doubt, Christopher Coney, no doubt. And 'a must need such reflections—a lonely widow man," said Longways.

"When did he lose his wife?" asked Elizabeth.

"I never knowed her. 'Twas afore he came to Caster-bridge," Solomon Longways replied with terminative emphasis, as if the fact of his ignorance of Mrs. Henchard were sufficient to deprive her history of all interest. "But I know that 'a's a banded teetotaller, and that if any of his men be ever so little overtook by a drop, he's down upon 'em as stern as the Lord upon the jovial Jews."

"Has he many men then?" said Elizabeth-Jane.

"Many? Why, my good maid, he's the powerfullest member of the town-council, and quite a principal man in the country round besides. Never a big dealing in wheat, barley, oats, hay, roots, and such-like but Henchard's got a hand in it. Ay, and he'll go into other things, too; and that's where he makes his mistake. He worked his way up from nothing when 'a came here; and now he's a pillar of the town. Not but what he's been shaken a little to-year about this bad corn he has supplied in his contracts. I've seen the sun rise over Durnover Moor these nine-and-sixty year, and though Mr. Henchard has never cussed me unfairly, ever since I've worked for'n, seeing I be but a little small man, I must say that I have never before tasted such rough bread as has been made from Henchard's wheat lately. 'Tis that growed out that ye could a'most call it malt, and there's a list at bottom o' the loaf as thick as the sole of one's shoe."

The band now struck up another melody, and by the time it was ended the dinner was over, and speeches began to be made. The evening being calm and the windows still open these orations could be distinctly heard. Henchard's voice arose above the rest: he was telling a story of his hay-dealing experiences, in which he had outwitted a sharper who had been bent upon outwitting him.

"Ha-ha-ha!" responded his audience at the upshot of the story; and hilarity was general till a new voice arose with "This is all very well; but how about the bad bread?"

It came from the lower end of the table, where there sat a group of minor tradesmen who, although part of the company, appeared to be a little below the social level of the others; and who seemed to nourish a certain independence of opinion, and carry on discussions not quite in harmony with those at the head; just as the west end of a church is sometimes persistently found to sing out of time and tune with the leading spirits in the chancel.

This interruption about the bad bread afforded infinite satisfaction to the loungers outside, several of whom were in the mood which finds its pleasure in others' discomfiture; and hence they echoed pretty freely, "Hey! How about the bad bread, Mr. Mayor?" Moreover, feeling none of the restraints of those who shared the feast, they could afford to add, "You rather ought to tell the story o' that, sir!"

The interruption was sufficient to compel the mayor to notice it.

"Well, I admit that the wheat turned out badly," he said. "But I was taken in in buying it as much as the bakers who bought it o' me."

"And the poor folk who had to eat it whether or no," said the inharmonious man outside the window.

Henchard's face darkened. There was temper under the thin bland surface—the temper which, artificially intensified, had banished a wife nearly a score of years before.

"You must make allowances for the accidents of a large business," he said. "You must bear in mind that the weather just at the harvest of that corn was worse than we have known it for years. However, I have mended my arrangements on account o't. Since I have found my business too large to be well looked after by myself alone, I have advertised for a thorough good man as manager of the corn department. When I've got him you will find these mistakes will no longer occur—matters will be better looked into."

"But what are you going to do to repay us for the past?" inquired the man who had before spoken, and who seemed to be a baker or miller. "Will you replace the grown flour we've still got by sound grain?"

Henchard's face had become still more stern at these interruptions, and he drank from his tumbler of water as if to calm himself or gain time. Instead of vouchsafing a direct reply, he stiffly observed,

"If anybody will tell me how to turn grown wheat into wholesome wheat, I'll take it back with pleasure. But it can't be done.'

Henchard was not to be drawn again. Having said this he sat down.

NOW the group outside the window had within the last few minutes been reinforced by new arrivals, some of them respectable shopkeepers and their assistants, who had come out for a whiff of air after putting up the shutters for the night; some of them of a lower class. Distinct from either there appeared a stranger—a young man of remarkably pleasant aspect, who carried in his hand a carpet-bag of the smart floral pattern prevalent in such articles at that time.

He was ruddy and of a fair countenance, bright-eyed, and slight in build. He might possibly have passed by without stopping at all, or at most for half a minute to glance in at the scene, had not his advent coincided with the discussion on corn and bread, in which event this history had never been enacted. But the subject seemed to arrest him, and he whispered some inquiries of the other bystanders, and remained listening.

When he heard Henchard's closing words, "It can't be done," he smiled, impulsively drew out his pocket-book, and wrote down a few words by the aid of the light in the window. He tore out the leaf, folded and directed it, and seemed about to throw it in through the open sash upon the dining-table, but, on second thoughts, edged himself through the loiterers, till he reached the door of the hotel, where one of the waiters who had been serving inside was now idly leaning against the doorpost.

"Give this to the mayor at once," he said, handing in his hasty note.

Elizabeth-Jane had seen his movements and heard the words, which attracted her both by their subject and by their accent—a strange one for those parts. It was quaint and northerly.

The waiter took the note, while the young stranger continued:

"And can ye tell me of a respectable hotel that's a little more moderate than this?"

The waiter glanced indifferently up and down the street.

"They say the Three Mariners, just below here, is a very good place," he languidly answered; "but I have never stayed there myself."

The Scotchman, as he seemed to be, thanked him, and strolled on in the direction of the Three Mariners aforesaid, apparently more concerned about the question of an inn than about the fate of his note now that the momentary impulse of writing it was over. While he was disappearing slowly down the street the waiter left the door, and Elizabeth-Jane saw with some interest the note brought into the dining-room and handed to the mayor.

Henchard looked at it carelessly, unfolded it with one hand, and glanced it through. Thereupon it was curious to note an unexpected effect. The nettled, clouded aspect which had held possession of his face since the subject of his corn-dealings had been broached, changed itself into one of arrested attention. He read the note slowly, and fell into thought, not moody but fitfully intense, as that of a man who has been captured by an idea.

By this time toasts and speeches had given place to songs, the wheat subject being quite forgotten. Men were putting their heads together in twos and threes, telling good stories, with pantomimic laughter, which reached convulsive grimace. Some were beginning to look as if they did not know how they had come there, what they had come for, or how they were going to get home again; and provisionally sat on with a dazed smile. Square-built men showed a tendency to become hunchbacks, men with a dignified presence lost it in a curious obliquity of figure, in which their features grew disarranged and one-sided; whilst the heads of a few who had dined with extreme thoroughness were somehow sinking into their shoulders, the corners of their mouth and eyes being bent upwards by the subsidence. Only Henchard did not conform to these flexuous changes; he remained stately and vertical, silently thinking.

The clock struck nine; Elizabeth-Jane turned to her companion. "The evening is drawing on, mother," she said. "What do you propose to do?"

She was surprised to find how irresolute her mother had become. "We must get a place to lie down in," she murmured. "I have seen—Mr. Henchard; and that's all I wanted to do."

"That's enough for to-night at any rate," Elizabeth-Jane replied soothingly. "We can think to-morrow what is best to do about him. The question now is—is it not?—how shall we find a lodging."

As her mother did not reply, Elizabeth-Jane's mind reverted to the words of the waiter, that the Three Mariners was an inn of moderate charges. A recommendation good for one person was probably good for another. "Let's go where the young man has gone to," she said. "He is respectable. What do you say?"

Her mother assented, and down the street they went.

In the mean-time the mayor's thoughtfulness, engendered by the note as stated, continued to hold him in abstraction; till, whispering to his neighbour to take his place, he found opportunity to leave the chair. This was just after the departure of his wife and Elizabeth.

Outside the door of the assembly-room he saw the waiter, and beckoning to him, asked who brought the note which had been handed in a quarter of an hour before.

"A young man, sir—a sort of traveller. He was a Scotchman seemingly."

"Did he say how he had got it?"

"He wrote it himself, sir, as he stood outside the window."

"Oh—wrote it himself. . . . . Is the young man in the hotel?"

"No, sir. He went to the Three Mariners, I believe."

The mayor walked up and down the vestibule of the hotel with his hands under his coat tails, as if he were merely seeking a cooler atmosphere than that of the room he had quitted. But there could be no doubt that he was in reality still possessed to the full by the new idea, whatever that might be. At length, he went back to the door of the dining-room, paused, and found that the songs, toasts, and conversation were proceeding quite satisfactorily without his presence. The corporation, private residents, and major and minor tradesmen had, in fact, gone in for comforting beverages to such an extent, that they had quite forgotten, not only the mayor, but all those vast political, religious, and social differences which they felt necessary to maintain in the day time, and which separated them like iron grills. Seeing this, the mayor took his hat, and, when the waiter had helped him on with a thin holland overcoat, went out and stood under the portico.

Very few persons were now in the street; and his eyes, by a sort of attraction, turned and dwelt upon a spot about a hundred yards further down. It was the house to which the writer of the note had gone—the Three Mariners—whose two prominent Elizabethan gables, bow window, and passage-light could be seen from where he stood. Having kept his eyes on it for a while, he strolled in that direction.

This ancient house of accommodation for man and beast, now, unfortunately, pulled down, was built of mellow sandstone, with mullioned windows of the same material, markedly out of perpendicular from the settlement of foundations. The bay window projecting into the street, whose interior was so popular among the frequenters of the inn, was closed with shutters, in each of which appeared a heart-shaped aperture, somewhat more attenuated in the right and left ventricles than is seen in nature. Inside these illuminated holes, at a distance of about three inches, were ranged at this hour, as every passer knew, the ruddy polls of Billy Wills the glazier, Smart the shoemaker, Buzzford the general dealer, and others of a secondary set of worthies, of a grade somewhat below that of the diners at the King's Arms, each with his yard of clay.

A four-centred Tudor arch was over the entrance, and over the arch the sign-board, now visible in the rays of an opposite lamp. Hereon, the Mariners, who had been represented by the artist as persons of two dimensions only—in other words, flat as a shadow—were standing in a row in paralyzed attitudes. Being on the sunny side of the street the three comrades had suffered largely from warping, splitting, fading, and shrinkage, so that they were but a half invisible film upon the reality of the grain, and knots, and nails, which composed the sign-board. As a matter of fact, this state of things was not so much owing to Stannidge, the landlord's, neglect, as from the lack of a painter in Casterbridge who would undertake to reproduce the features of men so traditional.

A long, narrow, dimly lit passage gave access to the inn, within which passage the horses going to their stalls at the back, and the coming and departing human guests, rubbed shoulders indiscriminately, the latter running no slight risk of having their toes trodden upon by the animals. The good stabling, and the good ale, of the Mariners, though somewhat difficult to reach on account of there being but this narrow way to both, were nevertheless perseveringly sought out by the sagacious old heads who knew what was what in Casterbridge.

Henchard stood without the inn for a few instants; then, lowering the dignity of his presence as much as possible by buttoning the brown-holland coat over his shirt-front, and in other ways toning himself down to his ordinary everyday appearance, he entered the inn door.

ELIZABETH-JANE and her mother had arrived some twenty minutes earlier. Outside the house they had stood and considered whether even this homely place, though recommended as moderate, might not be too serious in its prices for their light pockets. Finally however they had found courage to enter; and duly met Stannidge the landlord, a silent man, who drew and carried frothing measures to this room and to that shoulder to shoulder with his waiting-maids—a stately slowness however entering into his ministrations by contrast with theirs, as became one whose service was somewhat optional. It would have been altogether optional but for the orders of the landlady; a person who sat in the bar, corporeally motionless, but with a flitting eye and quick ear with which she observed and heard through the open door and hatchway the pressing needs of customers whom her husband overlooked though close at hand. Elizabeth and her mother were passively accepted as sojourners, and shown to a small bedroom under one of the gables, where they sat down.

The principle of the inn seemed to be to compensate for the antique awkwardness, crookedness, and obscurity of the passages, floors, and windows, by quantities of clean linen spread about everywhere, and this had a dazzling effect upon the travellers.

"'Tis too good for us—we can't meet it!" said the elder woman looking round the apartment with misgiving as soon as they were left alone.

"I fear it is too," said Elizabeth. "But we must be respectable."

"We must pay our way even before we must be respectable," replied her mother. "Mr. Henchard is too high for us to make ourselves known to him, I much fear; so we've only our own pockets to depend on."

"I know what I'll do," said Elizabeth-Jane after an interval of waiting, during which their needs seemed quite forgotten under the press of business below. And leaving the room she descended the stairs and penetrated to the bar.

If there was one good thing more than another which characterized this singlehearted girl, it was a willingness to sacrifice her personal comfort and dignity to the common weal. "As you seem busy here to-night, and mother's not well off, might I take out part of our accommodation by helping?" she asked of the landlady.

The latter, who remained as fixed in the arm-chair as if she had been melted into it when in a liquid state and could not now be unstuck, looked the girl up and down inquiringly with her hands on the chair-arms. Such arrangements as the one Elizabeth proposed were not uncommon in country villages; but though Casterbridge was old-fashioned the custom was well-nigh obsolete here. The mistress of the house, however, was an easy woman to strangers, and she made no objection. Thereupon Elizabeth, being instructed by nods and motions from the taciturn landlord as to where she could find the different things, trotted up and downstairs with materials for her own and her parent's meal.

While she was doing this the wood partition in the centre of the house thrilled to its centre with the tugging of a bell-pull upstairs. A bell below tinkled a note that was feebler in sound than the twanging of wires and cranks that had produced it.

"'Tis the Scotch gentleman," said the landlady omnisciently; and turning her eyes to Elizabeth: "Now then, can you go and see if his supper is on the tray? If it is you can take it up to him. The front room over this."

Elizabeth-Jane, though hungry, willingly postponed serving herself awhile, and applied to the cook in the kitchen, whence she brought forth the tray of supper viands, and proceeded with it upstairs to the apartment indicated. The accommodation of the Three Mariners was far from spacious, despite the fair area of ground it covered. The room demanded by intrusive beams and rafters, partitions, passages, staircases, disused ovens, settles, and four-posters, left comparatively small quarters for human beings. Moreover, this being at a time before home-brewing was abandoned by the smaller victuallers, and a house in which the twelve-bushel strength was still religiously adhered to by the landlord in his ale, the quality of the liquor was the chief attraction of the premises, so that everything had to make way for utensils and operations in connection therewith. Thus Elizabeth found that the Scotchman was located in a room quite close to the small one that had been allotted to herself and her mother.

When she entered nobody was present but the young man himself—the same whom she had seen lingering without the windows of the King's Arms Hotel. He was now idly reading a copy of the local paper, and was hardly conscious of her entry, so that she looked at him quite coolly, and saw how his forehead shone where the light caught it, and how nicely his hair was cut, and the sort of velvet-pile or down that was on the skin at the back of his neck, and how his cheek was so truly curved as to be part of a globe, and how clearly drawn were the lids and lashes which hid his bent eyes.

She set down the tray, spread his supper, and went away without a word. On her arrival below the landlady, who was as kind as she was fat and lazy, saw that Elizabeth-Jane was rather tired, though in her earnestness to be useful she was waiving her own needs altogether. Mrs. Stannidge thereupon said, with a considerate peremptoriness, that she and her mother had better take their own suppers if they meant to have any.

Elizabeth fetched their simple provisions, as she had fetched the Scotchman's, and went up to the little chamber where she had left her mother, noiselessly pushing open the door with the edge of the tray. To her surprise her mother, instead of being reclined on the bed where she had left her, was in an erect position, with lips parted. At Elizabeth's entry she lifted her finger.

The meaning of this was soon apparent. The room allotted to the two women had at one time served as a dressing-room to the Scotchman's chamber, as was evidenced by signs of a door of communication between them—now screwed up and pasted over with the wall paper. But, as is frequently the case with hotels of far higher pretensions than the Three Mariners, every word spoken in either of these rooms was distinctly audible in the other. Such sounds came through now.

Thus silently conjured Elizabeth deposited the tray, and her mother whispered as she drew near, "'Tis he."

"Who?" said the girl.

"The mayor." The tremors in Susan Henchard's tone might have led any person but one so perfectly unsuspicious of the truth as the girl was, to surmise some closer connection than the admitted simple kinship as a means of accounting for them.

Two men were indeed talking in the adjoining chamber, the young Scotchman, and Henchard, who, having entered the inn while Elizabeth-Jane was in the kitchen waiting for the supper, had been deferentially conducted upstairs by host Stannidge himself. The girl noiselessly laid out their little meal, and beckoned to her mother to join her, which Mrs. Henchard mechanically did, her attention being fixed on the conversation through the door.

"I merely strolled in on my way home, to ask you a question about something that has excited my curiosity," said the mayor with careless geniality. "But I see you have not finished supper."

"Ay, but I will be done in a little!—ye needn't go sir. Take a seat. I've almost done, and it makes no differrence at all?"

Henchard seemed to take the seat offered, and in a moment he resumed: "Well, first I should ask, did you write this?" A rustling of paper followed.

"Yes, I did," said the Scotchman.

"Then," said Henchard, "I am under the impression that we have met by accident while waiting for the morning to keep an appointment with each other? My name is Henchard; ha'n't you replied to an advertisement for a corn-factor's manager that I put into the paper—ha'n't you come here to see me about it?"

"No," said the Scotchman, with some surprise.

"Surely you are the man," went on Henchard, insistingly, "who arranged to come and see me? Joshua, Joshua, Jipp—Jopp—what was his name?"

"You're wrong," said the young man. "My name is Donald Farfrae. It is true I am in the corren trade—but I have replied to no advairrtisment, and arranged to see no one. I am on my way to Bristol—from there to the other side of the warrld to try my fortune in the great wheat-growing districts of the

West. I have some inventions useful to the trade, and there is no scope for developing them heere."

"To America—well, well," said Henchard, in a tone of disappointment, so strong as to make itself felt like a damp atmosphere. "And yet I could have sworn you were the man!"

The Scotchman murmured another negative, and there was a silence, till Henchard resumed: "Then I am truly and sincerely obliged to you for the few words you wrote on that paper."

"It was nothing, sir."

"Well, it has a great importance for me just now. This row about my grown wheat, which I declare to heaven I didn't know to be bad till the people came complaining, has put me to my wits' end. I've some hundreds of quarters of it on hand; and if your renovating process will make it wholesome, why you can see what a quag 'twould get me out of. I saw in a moment there might be truth in it. But I should like to have it proved; and of course you don't care to tell the steps of the process sufficiently for me to do that, without my paying ye well for't first."

The young man reflected a moment or two. "I don't know that I have any objection," he said. "I'm going to another country, and curing bad corn is not the line I'll take up there. Yes, I'll tell ye the whole of it—you'll make more out of it heere than I will in a foreign country. Just look heere a minute, sir. I can show ye by a sample in my carpet-bag."

The click of a lock followed, and there was a sifting and rustling; then a discussion about so many ounces to the bushel, and drying, and refrigerating, and so on.

"These few grains will be sufficient to show ye with," came in the young fellow's voice; and after a pause, during which some operation seemed to be intently watched by them both, he exclaimed, "There, now do you taste that."

"It's complete!—quite restored, or—well—nearly."

"Quite enough restored to make good seconds out of it," said the Scotchman. "To fetch it back entirely is impossible; Nature won't stand so much as that, but heere you go a great way towards it. Well, sir, that's the process; I don't value it, for it can be but of little use in countries where the weather is more settled than in ours; and I'll be only too glad if it's of service to you."

"But, hearken to me," pleaded Henchard. "My business, you know, is in corn and in hay; but I was brought up as a hay-trusser simply, and hay is what I understand best, though I now do more in corn than in the other. If you'll accept the place, you shall manage the corn branch entirely, and receive a commission in addition to salary."

"You're liberal—very liberal; but no, no—I cannet!" the young man still replied, with some distress in his accents.

"So be it!" said Henchard conclusively. "Now—to change the subject—one good turn deserves another; don't stay to finish that miserable supper. Come to my house; I can find something better for 'ee than cold ham and ale."

Donald Farfrae was grateful—said he feared he must decline—that he wished to leave early next day.

"Very well," said Henchard quickly, "please yourself. But I tell you, young man, if this holds good for the bulk, as it has done for the sample, you have saved my credit, stranger though you be. What shall I pay you for this knowledge?"

"Nothing at all, nothing at all. It may not prove necessary to ye to use it often, and I don't value it at all. I thought I might just as well let ye know, as you were in a difficulty, and they were harrd upon ye."

Henchard paused. "I shan't soon forget this," he said. "And from a stranger! . . . . I couldn't believe you were not the man I had engaged! Says I to myself 'He knows who I am, and recommends himself by this stroke.' And yet it turns out, after all, that you are not the man who answered my advertisement, but a stranger!"

"Ay, ay; that's so," said the young man.

Henchard again suspended his words, and then his voice came thoughtfully: "Your forehead, Farfrae, is something like my poor brother's—now dead and gone; and the nose, too, isn't unlike his. You must be, what—five foot nine, I reckon? I am six foot one and a half out of my shoes. But what of that? In my business, 'tis true that strength and bustle build up a firm. But judgment and knowledge are what keep it established. Unluckily, I am bad at science, Farfrae; bad at figures—a rule o' thumb sort of man. You are just the reverse—I can see that. I have been looking for such as you these two year, and yet you are not for me. Well, before I go, let me ask this: Though you are not the young man I thought you were, what's the difference? Can't ye stay just the same? Have you really made up your mind about this American notion? I won't mince matters. I feel you would be invaluable to me—that needn't be said—and if you will bide and be my manager I will make it worth your while."

"My plans are fixed," said the young man in negative tones, "I have formed a scheme, and so we need na say any more about it. But will you not drink with me, sir? I find this Casterbridge ale warreming to the stomach."

"No, no; I fain would, but I can't," said Henchard gravely, the scraping of his chair informing the listeners that he was rising to leave. "When I was a young man I went in for that sort of thing too strong—far too strong—and was well-nigh ruined by it! I did a deed on account of it which I shall be ashamed of to my dying day. It made such an impression on me that I swore, there and then, that I'd drink nothing stronger than tea for as many years as I was old that day. I have kept my oath; and though, Farfrae, I am sometimes that dry in the dog days that I could drink a quarter-barrel to the pitching, I think o' my oath, and touch no strong drink at all."

"I'll no' press ye, sir—I'll no' press ye. I respect your vow."

"Well, I shall get a manager somewhere, no doubt," said Henchard, with strong feeling in his tones. "But it will be long before I see one that would suit me so well!"

The young man appeared much moved by Henchard's warm convictions of his value. He was silent till they reached the door. "I wish I could stay—sincerely I would like to," he replied. "But no—it cannet be! it cannet! I want to see the warrld."

THUS they parted; and Elizabeth-Jane and her mother remained, each in her thoughts over their meal, the mother's face being strangely bright since Henchard's avowal of shame for a past action. The quivering of the partition to its core presently denoted that Donald Farfrae had again rung his bell, no doubt to have his supper removed; for humming a tune, and walking up and down, he seemed to be attracted by the lively bursts of conversation and melody from the general company below. He sauntered out upon the landing, and descended the staircase.

When Elizabeth-Jane had carried down his supper tray, and also that used by her mother and herself, she found the bustle of serving to be at its height below, as it always was at this hour. The young woman shrank from having anything to do with the ground-floor serving, and crept silently about observing the scene—so new to her, fresh from the seclusion of a sea-side cottage. In the general sitting-room, which was large, she remarked the two or three dozen strong-backed chairs that stood round against the wall, each fitted with its genial occupant—the sanded floor—the black settle which, projecting endwise from the wall within the door, permitted Elizabeth to be a spectator of all that went on, without herself being particularly seen.

The young Scotchman had just joined the guests. These, in addition to the respectable master tradesmen occupying the seats of privilege in the bow window and its neighbourhood, included an inferior set at the unlighted end, whose seats were mere benches against the wall, and who drank from cups instead of from glasses. Among the latter she noticed some of those personages who had stood outside the windows of the King's Arms.

Behind their backs was a small window, with a wheel ventilator in one of the panes, which would suddenly start off spinning with a jingling sound, as suddenly stop, and as suddenly start again.

While thus furtively making her survey, the opening words of a song greeted her ears from the front of the settle, in a melody and accent of peculiar charm. There had been some singing before she came down; and now the Scotchman had made himself so soon at home that at the request of some of the master-tradesmen, he too was favouring the room with a ditty.

Elizabeth-Jane was fond of music; she could not help pausing to listen; and the longer she listened the more she was enraptured. She had never heard any singing like this; and it was evident that the majority of the audience had not heard such frequently, for they were attentive to a much greater degree than usual. They neither whispered, nor drank, nor dipped their pipe-stems in their ale to moisten them, nor pushed the mug to their neighbours. The singer himself grew emotional, till she could imagine a tear in his eye as the words went on:—

> "It's hame, and it's hame, hame fain would I be,
>   O hame, hame, hame to my ain countree!
> There's an eye that ever weeps, and a fair face will be fain,
> As I pass through Annan Water with my bonnie bands again;
> When the flower is in the bud, and the leaf upon the tree,
>   The lark shall sing me hame to my ain countree!"

There was a burst of applause; and a deep silence which was even more eloquent than the applause. It was of such a kind that the snapping of a pipe-stem too long for him by old Solomon Longways, who was one of those gathered at the shady end of the room, seemed a harsh and irreverent act. Then the ventilator in the window-pane spasmodically started off for a new spin, and the pathos of Donald's song was temporarily effaced.

"'Twas not amiss—not at all amiss!" muttered Christopher Coney, who was also present. And removing his pipe a finger's breadth from his lips he said aloud, "Draw on with the next verse, young gentleman, please."

"Yes—let's have it again, stranger," said the glazier, a stout, bucket-headed man, with a white apron rolled up round his waist. "Folks don't lift up their hearts like that in this part of the world." And turning aside he said in undertones, "Who is the young man?—Scotch, d'ye say?"

"Yes, straight from the mountains of Scotland, I believe," replied Coney.

Young Farfrae repeated the last verse. It was plain that nothing so pathetic had been heard at the Three Mariners for a considerable time. The difference of accent, the excitability of the singer, the intense local feeling, and the seriousness with which he worked himself up to a climax, surprised this set of worthies, who were only too prone to shut up their emotions with caustic words.

"Danged if our country down here is worth singing about like that!" continued the glazier, as the Scotchman again melodized with a dying fall "my ain countree!"—"When you take away from among us the fools, and the rogues, and the lammigers, and the wanton hussies, and the slatterns, and such-like, there's cust few left to ornament a song with in Casterbridge, or the country round."

"True," said Buzzford the dealer, looking at the grain of the table. "Casterbridge is a old hoary place o' wickedness, by all account. 'Tis recorded in history that we rebelled against the king one or two hundred years ago in the time of the Romans, and that lots of us was hanged on Gallows-Hill, and quartered, and our different jints sent about the country like butcher's meat; and for my part I can well believe it."

"What did ye come away from yer own country for, young maister, if ye be so wownded about it?" inquired Christopher Coney from the background, with the tone of a man who preferred the original subject. "Faith, it wasn't worth your while on our account, for as Maister Billy Wills says, we be bruckle folk here—the best o' us hardly honest sometimes, what with hard winters, and so many mouths to fill, and Goda'mighty sending his little taties so terrible small to fill 'em with. We don't think about flowers and fair faces, not we—except in the shape o' cauliflowers and pigs' chaps."

"But no?" said Donald Farfrae gazing round into their faces with earnest concern. "The best of ye hardly honest—not that surely? None of ye has been stealing what didn't belong to him?"

"Lord! no, no!" said Solomon Longways, smiling grimly.

"That's only his random way o' speaking. 'A was always such a man of under-thoughts." (And reprovingly towards Christopher): "Don't ye be so over familiar with a gentleman that ye know nothing of—and that's travelled a'most from the North Pole."

Christopher Coney was silenced, and as he could get no public sympathy he mumbled his feelings to himself: "Be dazed if I loved my country half as well as the young feller do, I'd live by claning my neighbours' pigsties afore I'd go away! For my part I've no more love for my country than I have for Botany Bay."

"Come," said Longways; "let the young man draw onward with his ballet, or we shall be here all night."

"That's all of it," said the singer apologetically.

"Soul of my body, then we'll have another," said the general dealer.

"Can you turn a strain to the ladies, sir?" inquired a fat woman with a figured purple apron, the waist-string of which was overhung so far by her sides as to be invisible.

"Let him breathe—let him breathe, Mother Cuxsom. He haint got his second wind yet," said the master-glazier.

"Oh yes but I have," exclaimed the young man: and he at once rendered "Oh Nannie" with faultless modulations—and another or two of the like sentiment, winding up at their earnest request with "Auld Lang Syne."

By this time he had completely taken possession of the hearts of the Three Mariners' inmates, including even old Coney, notwithstanding an occasional odd gravity which awoke their sense of the ludicrous for the moment. They began to view him through a golden haze which the tone of his mind seemed to raise around him. Casterbridge had sentiment—Casterbridge had romance; but this stranger's sentiment was of differing quality. Or rather perhaps the difference was mainly superficial: He was to them like the poet of a new school who takes his contemporaries by storm; who is not really new, but is the first to articulate what all his listeners have felt, though but dumbly till then.

The silent landlord came and leant over the settle while the young man sang; and even Mrs. Stannidge managed to unstick herself from the framework of her chair in the bar, and get as far as the door-post, which movement she accomplished by rolling herself round, as a cask is trundled on the chine by a drayman without losing much of its perpendicular.

"And are you going to bide in Casterbridge, sir?" she asked.

"Ah—no!" said the Scotchman with melancholy fatality in his voice. "I'm only passing thirrough. I am on my way to Bristol, and on frae there to foreign parts."

"We be truly sorry to hear it," said Solomon Longways. "We can ill afford to lose tuneful wynd-pipes like yours, when they fall among us. And verily, to mak' acquaintance with a man a come from so far, from the land o' perpetual snow as we may say, where wolves and wild boars, and other dangerous animalcules be as common as blackbirds hereabout, why, 'tis a thing we can't do every day, and there's good sound information for bide-at-homes like we when such a man opens his mouth."

"Nay but ye mistake my country," said the young man, looking round upon them with tragic fixity, till his eye lighted up and his cheek kindled with a sudden enthusiasm to right their errors. "There are not perpetual snow and wolves at all in it!—except snow in winter, and—well—a little in summer just sometimes, and a gaberlunzie or two stalking about here and there, if ye may call them dangerous. Eh but you should take a summer jarreny to Edinboro', and Arthur's Seat, and all round there, and then go on to the Lochs, and all the Highland scenery—in May and June—and you would never say 'tis the land of wolves and perpetual snow!"

"Of course not—it stands to reason," said Buzzford. "'Tis barren ignorance that leads to such words. He's a simple homespun man, that never was fit for good company—think nothing of him, sir."

"And do ye carry your flock bed, and your quilt, and your crock, and your bit of chiney; or do ye go in bare bones, as I may say?" enquired Christopher Coney.

"I've sent on my luggage—though it isn't much; for the voyage is long." Donald's eyes dropped into a remote gaze as he added: "But I said to myself, 'never a one of the prizes of life will I come by unless I undertake it'; and I decided to go."

A general sense of regret, in which Elizabeth-Jane shared not least, made itself apparent in the company. As she looked at Farfrae from the back of the settle she decided that his statements showed him to be no less thoughtful than his fascinating melodies revealed him to be cordial and impassioned. She admired the serious light in which he looked at serious things. He had seen no jest in ambiguities and roguery, as the Casterbridge toss-pots had done; and rightly not—there was none. She disliked those wretched humours of Christopher Coney and his tribe; and he did not appreciate them. He seemed to feel exactly as she felt about life and its surroundings—that they were a tragical rather than a comical thing; that though one could be gay on occasion, moments of gaiety were interludes, and no part of the actual drama. It was extraordinary how similar their views were.

Though it was still early the young Scotchman expressed his wish to retire; whereupon the landlady whispered to Elizabeth to run upstairs and turn down his bed. She took a candlestick and proceeded on her mission, which was the act of a few moments only. When, candle in hand, she reached the top of the stairs on her way down again Mr. Farfrae was at the foot coming up. She could not very well retreat; they met and passed in the turn of the staircase.

She must have appeared interesting in some way—notwith-standing her plain dress—or rather, possibly, in consequence of it, for she was a girl characterised by earnestness and soberness of mien, with which simple drapery accorded well. Her face flushed, too, at the slight awkwardness of the meeting, and she passed him with her eyes bent on the candle flame that she carried just below her nose. Thus it happened that when confronting her he smiled; and then, with the manner of a temporarily light-hearted man who has started himself on a flight of song whose momentum he cannot readily check, he softly tuned an old ditty that she seemed to suggest:

> "As I came in by my bower door,
>   As day was waxin' wearie,
> Oh wha came tripping down the stair
>   But bonnie Peg my dearie."

Elizabeth-Jane, rather disconcerted, hastened on; and the Scotchman's voice died away humming more of the same within the closed door of his room.

Here the scene and sentiment ended for the present. When, soon after, the girl rejoined her mother, the latter was still in thought—on quite another matter than a young man's song.

"We've made a mistake," she whispered (that the Scotchman might not overhear). "On no account ought ye to have helped serve here to-night. Not because of ourselves, but for the sake of *him*. If he should befriend us, and take us up, and then find out what you did when staying here, 'twould grieve and wound his natural pride as mayor of the town."

Elizabeth, who would perhaps have been more alarmed at this than her mother had she known the real relationship, was not much disturbed about it as things stood. Her "he" was another man than her poor mother's. "For myself," she said, "I didn't at all mind waiting a little upon him. He's so respectable, and educated—far above the rest of 'em in the inn. They thought him very simple not to know their grim broad way of talking about themselves here. But of course he didn't know—he was too refined in his mind to know such things!" Thus she earnestly pleaded.

Meanwhile, the "he" of her mother was not so far away as even they thought. After leaving the Three Mariners he had sauntered up and down the empty high street, passing and repassing the inn in his promenade. When the Scotchman sang, his voice had reached Henchard's ears through the heart-shaped holes in the window-shutters, and had led him to pause outside them a long while.

"To be sure, to be sure how that fellow does draw me!" he had said to himself. "I suppose 'tis because I'm so lonely. I'd have given him a third share in the business to have stayed!"

IX

WHEN Elizabeth-Jane opened the hinged casement next morning the mellow air brought in the feel of imminent autumn almost as distinctly as if she had been in the remotest hamlet. Casterbridge was the complement of the rural life around; not its urban opposite. Bees and butterflies in the cornfields at the top of the town who desired to get to the meads at the bottom, took no circuitous course, but flew straight down High Street without any apparent consciousness that they were traversing strange latitudes. And in autumn airy spheres of thistledown floated into the same street, lodged upon the shop fronts, blew into drains; and innumerable tawny and yellow leaves skimmed along the pavement, and stole through people's doorways into their passages with a hesitating scratch on the floor, like the skirts of timid visitors.

Hearing voices, one of which was close at hand, she withdrew her head, and glanced from behind the window-curtains. Mr. Henchard—now habited no longer as a great personage, but as a thriving man of business—was pausing on his way up the middle of the street, and the Scotchman was looking from the window adjoining her own. Henchard, it appeared, had gone a little way past the inn before he had noticed his acquaintance of the previous evening. He came back a few steps, Donald Farfrae opening the window further.

"And you are off soon, I suppose?" said Henchard upwards.

"Yes—almost this moment sir," said the other. "Maybe I'll walk on till the coach makes up on me."

"Which way?"

"The way ye are going."

"Then shall we walk together to the top o' town?"

"If ye'll wait a minute," said the Scotchman.

In a few minutes the latter emerged, bag in hand. Henchard looked at the bag as at an enemy. It showed there was no mistake about the young man's departure. "Ah, my lad," he said; "you should have been a wise man, and have stayed with me."

"Yes, yes—it might have been wiser," said Donald looking microscopically at the houses that were furthest off. "It is only telling ye the truth when I say my plans are vague."

They had by this time passed on from the precincts of the inn, and Elizabeth-Jane heard no more. She saw that they continued in conversation, Henchard turning to the other occasionally, and emphasizing some remark with a gesture. Thus they passed the King's Arms Hotel, the market house, St. Peter's churchyard wall, ascending to the upper end of the long street till they were small as two grains of corn; when they bent suddenly to the right into the Bristol Road, and were out of view.

"He was a good man—and he's gone!" she said to herself. "I was nothing to him, and there was no reason why he should have wished me good-bye."

The simple thought, with its latent sense of slight, had moulded itself out of the following little fact: when the Scotchman came out at the door he had by accident glanced up at her; and then he had looked away again without nodding, or smiling, or saying a word.

"You are still thinking, mother," she said when she turned inwards.

"Yes—I am thinking of Mr. Henchard's sudden liking for that young man. He was always so. Now surely, if he takes so warmly to people who are not related to him at all, may he not take as warmly to his own kin?"

While they debated this question a procession of five large waggons went past, laden with hay up to the bedroom windows. They came in from the country, and the steaming horses had probably been travelling a great part of the night. To the shaft of each hung a little board on which was painted in white letters "Henchard, corn-factor and hay-merchant." The spectacle renewed his wife's conviction that for her daughter's sake she should strain a point to rejoin him.

The discussion was continued during breakfast, and the end of it was that Mrs. Henchard decided, for good or for ill, to send Elizabeth-Jane with a message to Henchard, to the effect that his relative Susan, a sailor's widow, was in the town; leaving it to him to say whether or not he would recognise her.

What had brought her to this determination were chiefly two things. He had been described as a lonely widower; and he had expressed shame for a past transaction of his life. There was promise in both.

"If he says no," she enjoined, as Elizabeth-Jane stood, bonnet on, ready to depart; "if he thinks it does not become the good position he has reached to in the town, to own—to let us call on him as—his distant kinsfolk, say, 'Then, sir, we would rather not intrude; we will leave Casterbridge as quietly as we have come, and go back to our own country.' . . . . I almost feel that I would rather he did say so, as I have not seen him for so many years, and we are so—little allied to him!"

"And if he say yes?" inquired the more sanguine one.

"In that case," answered Mrs. Henchard cautiously, "ask him to write me a note, saying when and how he will see us— or *me*."

Elizabeth-Jane went a few steps towards the landing. "And tell him," continued her mother, "that I fully know I have no claim upon him—that I am glad to find he is thriving; that I hope his life may be long and happy—there, go." Thus with a half-hearted willingness, a smothered reluctance, did the poor forgiving woman start her unconscious daughter on this errand.

It was about ten o'clock, and market-day, when Elizabeth paced up the high street, in no great hurry; for to herself her position was only that of a poor relation deputed to hunt up a rich one. The front doors of the private houses were mostly left open at this warm autumn time, no thought of umbrella stealers disturbing the minds of the placid burgesses. Hence, through the long, straight, entrance passages thus enclosed could be seen, as through tunnels, the mossy gardens at the back, glowing with nasturtiums, fuchsias, scarlet geraniums, "bloody warriors," snap-dragons, and dahlias, this floral blaze being backed by crusted grey stone-work remaining from a yet remoter Casterbridge than the venerable one visible in the street. The old-fashioned fronts of these houses, which had older than old-fashioned backs, rose sheer from the pavement, into which the bow-windows protruded like bastions, necessitating a pleasing *chassez-déchassez* movement to the time-pressed pedestrian at every few yards. He was bound also to evolve other Terpsichorean figures in respect of door-steps, scrapers, cellar-hatches, church buttresses, and the over-hanging angles of walls which, originally unobtrusive, had become bow-legged and knock-kneed.

In addition to these fixed obstacles which spoke so cheer-fully of individual unrestraint as to boundaries, movables occupied the path and roadway to a perplexing extent. First the vans of the carriers in and out of Casterbridge, who hailed from Mellstock, Weatherbury, the Hintocks, Sherton-Abbas, Kingsbere, Overcombe, and many other towns and villages round. Their owners were numerous enough to be regarded as a tribe, and had almost distinctiveness enough to be regarded as a race. Their vans had just arrived, and were drawn up on each side of the street in close file, so as to form at places a wall between the pavement and the roadway. Moreover every shop pitched out half its contents upon trestles and boxes on the kerb, extending the display each week a little further and further into the roadway, despite the expostulations of the two feeble old constables, until there remained but a tortuous defile for carriages down the centre of the street, which afforded fine opportunities for skill with the reins. Over the pavement on the sunny side of the way hung shop-blinds, so constructed as to give the passenger's hat a smart buffet off his head as from the unseen hands of Cranstoun's Goblin Page, celebrated in romantic lore.

Horses for sale were tied in rows, their forelegs on the pavement, their hind legs in the street, in which position they occasionally nipped little boys by the shoulder who were passing to school. And any inviting recess in front of a house that had been modestly kept back from the general line was utilised by pig-dealers as a pen for their stock.[1]

The yeomen, farmers, dairymen, and townsfolk, who came to transact business in these ancient streets, spoke in other ways than by articulation. Not to hear the words of your

[1] The reader will scarcely need to be reminded that time and progress have obliterated from the town that suggested these descriptions many or most of the old-fashioned features here enumerated.

interlocutor in metropolitan centres is to know nothing of
his meaning. Here the face, the arms, the hat, the stick, the
body throughout spoke equally with the tongue. To express
satisfaction the Casterbridge market-man added to his
utterance a broadening of the cheeks, a crevicing of the eyes,
a throwing back of the shoulders, which was intelligible from
the other end of the street. If he wondered, though all
Henchard's carts and waggons were rattling past him, you
knew it from perceiving the inside of his crimson mouth, and
a target-like circling of his eyes. Deliberation caused sundry
attacks on the moss of adjoining walls with the end of his stick,
a change of his hat from the horizontal to the less so; a sense
of tediousness announced itself in a lowering of the person by
spreading the knees to a lozenge-shaped aperture, and
contorting the arms. Chicanery, subterfuge, had hardly a
place in the streets of this honest borough to all appearance;
and it was said that the lawyers in the Court House hard by
occasionally threw in strong arguments for the other side out
of pure generosity (though apparently by mischance) when
advancing their own.

Thus Casterbridge was in most respects but the pole, focus,
or nerve-knot of the surrounding country life; differing from
the many manufacturing towns, which are as foreign bodies
set down, like boulders on a plain, in a green world with
which they have nothing in common. Casterbridge lived by
agriculture at one remove further from the fountain-head than
the adjoining villages—no more. The townsfolk understood
every fluctuation in the rustic's condition, for it affected their
receipts as much as the labourer's; they entered into the
troubles and joys which moved the aristocratic families ten
miles round—for the same reason. And even at the dinner
parties of the professional families the subjects of discussion
were corn, cattle disease, sowing and reaping, fencing and
planting; while politics were viewed by them less from their
own standpoint of burgesses with rights and privileges than
from the standpoint of their county neighbours.

All the venerable contrivances and confusions which
delighted the eye by their quaintness, and in a measure
reasonableness, in this rare old market town, were

metropolitan novelties to the unpractised eyes of Elizabeth-Jane, fresh from netting fish-seines in a sea-side cottage. Very little inquiry was necessary to guide her footsteps. Henchard's house was one of the best, faced with dull red-and-grey old brick. The front door was open, and, as in other houses, she could see through the passage to the end of the garden—nearly a quarter of a mile off.

Mr. Henchard was not in the house, but in the store-yard. She was conducted into the mossy garden, and through a door in the wall, which was studded with rusty nails speaking of generations of fruit trees that had been trained there. The door opened upon the yard, and here she was left to find him as she could. It was a place flanked by hay-barns, into which tons of fodder, all in trusses, were being packed from the waggons she had seen pass the inn that morning. On other sides of the yard were wooden granaries on stone-staddles, to which access was given by Flemish ladders, and a store-house several floors high. Wherever the doors of these places were open, a closely packed throng of bursting wheat sacks could be seen standing inside, with the air of awaiting a famine that would not come.

She wandered about this place, uncomfortably conscious of the impending interview, till she was quite weary of searching; she ventured to inquire of a boy in what quarter Mr. Henchard could be found. He directed her to an office which she had not seen before, and knocking at the door she was answered by a cry of "Come in."

Elizabeth turned the handle; and there stood before her, bending over some sample-bags on a table, not the corn merchant but the young Scotchman, Mr. Farfrae—in the act of pouring some grains of wheat from one hand to the other. His hat hung on a peg behind him, and the roses of his carpet bag glowed from the corner of the room.

Having toned her feelings and arranged words on her lips for Mr. Henchard, and for him alone, she was for the moment confounded.

"Yes, what is it?" said the Scotchman, like a man who permanently ruled there.

She said she wanted to see Mr. Henchard.

"Ah, yes; will you wait a minute? He's engaged just now," said the young man, apparently not recognizing her as the girl at the inn. He handed her a chair, bade her sit down, and turned to his sample-bags again. While Elizabeth-Jane sits waiting in great amaze at the young man's presence we may briefly explain how he came there.

When the two new acquaintances had passed out of sight that morning towards the Bath and Bristol road they went on silently, except for a few commonplaces, till they had gone down an avenue on the town walls called the Chalk Walk, leading to an angle where the North and West escarpments met. From this high corner of the square earthworks a vast extent of country could be seen. A footpath ran steeply down the green slope, conducting from the shady promenade on the walls to a road at the bottom of the scarp. It was by this path the Scotchman had to descend.

"Well, here's success to 'ee," said Henchard, holding out his right hand and leaning with his left upon the wicket which protected the descent. In the act there was the inelegance of one whose feelings are nipped and wishes defeated. "I shall often think of this time, and of how you came at the very moment to throw a light upon my difficulty."

Still holding the young man's hand he paused, and then added deliberately: "Now I am not the man to let a cause be lost for want of a word. And before ye are gone for ever I'll speak. Once more, will ye stay? There it is, flat and plain. You can see that it isn't all selfishness that makes me press 'ee; for my business is not quite so scientific as to require an intellect entirely out of the common. Others would do for the place without doubt. Some selfishness perhaps there is, but there is more; it isn't for me to repeat what. Come, bide with me—and name your own terms. I'll agree to 'em willingly and 'ithout a word of gainsaying; for, hang it, Farfrae, I like thee well!"

The young man's hand remained steady in Henchard's for a moment or two. He looked over the fertile country that stretched beneath them, then backward along the shaded walk reaching to the top of the town. His face flushed.

"I never expected this—I did not!" he said. "It's

Providence! Should any one go against it? No; I'll not go to America; I'll stay and be your man."

His hand, which had lain lifeless in Henchard's, returned the latter's grasp.

"Done," said Henchard.

"Done," said Donald Farfrae.

The face of Mr. Henchard beamed forth a satisfaction that was almost fierce in its strength. "Now you are my friend," he exclaimed. "Come back to my house; let's clinch it at once by clear terms, so as to be comfortable in our minds." Farfrae caught up his bag and retraced the North-West Avenue in Henchard's company as he had come. Henchard was all confidence now.

"I am the most distant fellow in the world when I don't care for a man," he said. "But when a man takes my fancy he takes it strong. Now I am sure you can eat another breakfast. You couldn't have eaten much so early even if they had anything at that place to gie thee, which they hadn't; so come to my house and we will have a solid, staunch tuck-in, and settle terms in black-and-white if you like; though my word's my bond. I can always make a good meal in the morning. I've got a splendid cold pigeon-pie going just now. You can have some home-brewed if you want to, you know."

"It is too airly in the morning for that," said Farfrae with a smile.

"Well, of course I didn't know. I don't drink it because of my oath; but I am obliged to brew for my work-people."

Thus talking they returned, and entered Henchard's premises by the back way or traffic entrance. Here the matter was settled over the breakfast, at which Henchard heaped the young Scotchman's plate to a prodigal fulness. He would not rest satisfied till Farfrae had written for his luggage from Bristol, and despatched the letter to the post-office. When it was done this man of strong impulses declared that his new friend should take up his abode in his house—at least till some suitable lodgings could be found.

He then took Farfrae round, and showed him the place, and the stores of grain, and other stock; and finally entered the offices where the younger of them has already been discovered by Elizabeth.

X

WHILE she still sat under the Scotchman's eyes a man came up to the door, reaching it as Henchard opened the door of the inner office to admit Elizabeth. The new-comer stepped forward like the quicker cripple at Bethesda, and entered in her stead. She could hear his words to Henchard: "Joshua Jopp, sir—by appointment—the new manager."

"The new manager!—he's in his office," said Henchard bluntly.

"In his office!" said the man with a stultified air.

"I mentioned Thursday," said Henchard; "and as you did not keep your appointment, I have engaged another manager. At first I thought he must be you. Do you think I can wait when business is in question?"

"You said Thursday or Saturday, sir," said the new-comer, pulling out a letter.

"Well, you are too late," said the corn-factor. "I can say no more."

"You as good as engaged me," murmured the man.

"Subject to an interview," said Henchard. "I am sorry for you—very sorry indeed. But it can't be helped."

There was no more to be said, and the man came out, encountering Elizabeth-Jane in his passage. She could see that his mouth twitched with anger, and that bitter disappointment was written in his face everywhere.

Elizabeth-Jane now entered, and stood before the master of the premises. His dark pupils—which always seemed to have a red spark of light in them, though this could hardly be a physical fact—turned indifferently round under his dark brows until they rested on her figure. "Now then, what is it, my young woman?" he said blandly.

"Can I speak to you—not on business, sir?" said she.

"Yes—I suppose." He looked at her more thoughtfully.

"I am sent to tell you, sir," she innocently went on, "that a distant relative of yours by marriage, Susan Newson, a sailor's widow, is in the town; and to ask whether you would wish to see her."

The rich *rouge et noir* of his countenance underwent a slight change. "Oh—Susan is—still alive?" he asked with difficulty.

"Yes sir."

"Are you her daughter?"

"Yes sir—her only daughter."

"What—do you call yourself—your Christian name?"

"Elizabeth-Jane, sir."

"Newson?"

"Elizabeth-Jane Newson."

This at once suggested to Henchard that the transaction of his early married life at Weydon Fair was unrecorded in the family history. It was more than he could have expected. His wife had behaved kindly to him in return for his unkindness, and had never proclaimed her wrong to her child or to the world.

"I am—a good deal interested in your news," he said. "And as this is not a matter of business, but pleasure, suppose we go indoors."

It was with a gentle delicacy of manner surprising to Elizabeth that he showed her out of the office, and through the outer room, where Donald Farfrae was overhauling bins and samples with the inquiring inspection of a beginner in charge. Henchard preceded her through the door in the wall to the suddenly changed scene of the garden and flowers, and onward into the house. The dining-room to which he introduced her still exhibited the remnants of the lavish breakfast laid for Farfrae. It was furnished to profusion with heavy mahogany furniture of the deepest red-Spanish hues. Pembroke tables, with leaves hanging so low that they well-nigh touched the floor, stood against the walls on legs and feet shaped like those of an elephant, and on one lay three huge folio volumes—a family Bible, a "Josephus," and a "Whole Duty of Man." In the chimney corner was a fire-grate with a fluted semicircular back having urns and festoons cast in relief thereon; and the chairs were of the kind which, since that day, has cast lustre upon the names of Chippendale and Sheraton, though in point of fact their patterns may have been such as those illustrious carpenters never saw or heard of.

"Sit down—Elizabeth-Jane—sit down," he said with a shake

in his voice as he uttered her name; and sitting down himself he allowed his hands to hang between his knees, while he looked upon the carpet. "Your mother, then, is quite well?"

"She is rather worn out, sir, with travelling."

"A sailor's widow—when did he die?"

"Father was lost last spring."

Henchard winced at the word "father," thus applied. "Do you and she come from abroad—America or Australia?" he asked.

"No. We have been in England some years. I was twelve when we came here from Canada."

"Ah—exactly." By such conversation he discovered the circumstances which had enveloped his wife and her child in such total obscurity that he had long ago believed them to be in their graves. These things being clear he returned to the present. "And where is your mother staying?"

"At the Three Mariners."

"And you are her daughter Elizabeth-Jane," repeated Henchard. He arose, came close to her, and glanced in her face. "I think," he said suddenly turning away with a wet eye, "you shall take a note from me to your mother. I should like to see her. . . . She is not left very well off by her late husband?" His eye fell on Elizabeth's clothes, which, though a respectable suit of black, and her very best, were decidedly old-fashioned even to Casterbridge eyes.

"Not very well," she said, glad that he had divined this without her being obliged to express it.

He sat down at the table and wrote a few lines; next taking from his pocket-book a five-pound note which he put in the envelope with the letter—adding to it, as by an afterthought, five shillings. Sealing the whole up carefully he directed it to "Mrs. Newson: Three Mariners Inn" and handed the packet to Elizabeth.

"Deliver it to her personally please," said Henchard. "Well—I am glad to see you here, Elizabeth-Jane—very glad. —We must have a long talk together—but not just now."

He took her hand at parting, and held it so warmly that she, who had known so little friendship, was much affected, and tears rose to her aerial-grey eyes. The instant that she was gone Henchard's state showed itself more distinctly; having shut the door he sat in his dining-room stiffly erect, gazing at the opposite wall as if he read his history there.

"Begad!" he suddenly exclaimed jumping up. "I didn't think of that. Perhaps these are impostors—and Susan and the child dead after all!"

However, a something in Elizabeth-Jane soon assured him that, as regarded her, at least, there could be little doubt. And a few hours would settle the question of her mother's identity; for he had arranged in his note to see her that evening.

"It never rains but it pours!" said Henchard. His keenly excited interest in his new friend the Scotchman was now eclipsed by this event: and Donald Farfrae saw so little of him during the rest of the day that he wondered at the suddenness of his employer's moods.

In the meantime Elizabeth had reached the inn. Her mother, instead of taking the note with the curiosity of a poor woman expecting assistance, was much moved at sight of it. She did not read it at once, asking Elizabeth to describe her reception, and the very words Mr. Henchard used. Elizabeth's back was turned when her mother opened the letter. It ran thus:

"Meet me at eight o'clock this evening, if you can, at the Ring on the Budmouth road. The place is easy to find. I can say no more now. The news upsets me almost. The girl seems to be in ignorance. Keep her so till I have seen you.   "M. H."

He said nothing about the enclosure of five guineas. The amount was significant; it may tacitly have said to her that he bought her back again. She waited restlessly for the close of the day, telling Elizabeth-Jane that she was invited to see Mr. Henchard; that she would go alone. But she said nothing to show that the place of meeting was not at his house, nor did she hand the note to Elizabeth.

THE Ring at Casterbridge was merely the local name of one of the finest Roman amphitheatres, if not the very finest, remaining in Britain.

Casterbridge announced old Rome in every street, alley, and precinct. It looked Roman, bespoke the art of Rome, concealed dead men of Rome. It was impossible to dig more than a foot or two deep about the town fields and gardens without coming upon some tall soldier or other of the Empire, who had lain there in his silent unobtrusive rest for a space of fifteen hundred years. He was mostly found lying on his side, in an oval scoop in the chalk, like a chicken in its shell; his knees drawn up to his chest; sometimes with the remains of his spear against his arm; a fibula or brooch of bronze on his breast or forehead; an urn at his knees, a jar at his throat, a bottle at his mouth; and mystified conjecture pouring down upon him from the eyes of Casterbridge street boys and men, who had turned a moment to gaze at the familiar spectacle as they passed by.

Imaginative inhabitants who would have felt an unpleasantness at the discovery of a comparatively modern skeleton in their gardens, were quite unmoved by these hoary shapes. They had lived so long ago, their time was so unlike the present, their hopes and motives were so widely removed from ours, that between them and the living there seemed to stretch a gulf too wide for even a spirit to pass.

The amphitheatre was a huge circular enclosure, with a notch at opposite extremities of its diameter north and south. From its sloping internal form it might have been called the spittoon of the Jötuns. It was to Casterbridge what the ruined Coliseum is to modern Rome, and was nearly of the same magnitude. The dusk of evening was the proper hour at which a true impression of this suggestive place could be received. Standing in the middle of the arena at that time there by degrees became apparent its real vastness, which a cursory view from the summit at noon day was apt to obscure.

Melancholy, impressive, lonely, yet accessible from every part of the town, the historic circle was the frequent spot for appointments of a furtive kind. Intrigues were arranged there; tentative meetings were there experimented after divisions and feuds. But one kind of appointment—in itself the most common of any—seldom had place in the amphitheatre; that of happy lovers.

Why, seeing that it was pre-eminently an airy, accessible, and sequestered spot for interviews, the cheerfullest form of those occurrences never took kindly to the soil of the ruin would be a curious inquiry. Perhaps it was because its associations had about them something sinister. Its history proved that. Apart from the sanguinary nature of the games originally played therein, such incidents attached to its past as these; that for scores of years the town gallows had stood at one corner; that in 1705 a woman who had murdered her husband was half strangled and then burnt there in the presence of ten thousand spectators. Tradition reports that at a certain stage of the burning her heart burst and leapt out of her body to the terror of them all, and that not one of those ten thousand people ever cared particularly for hot roast after that. In addition to these old tragedies pugilistic encounters almost to the death had come off down to recent dates in that secluded arena—entirely invisible to the outside world, save by climbing to the top of the enclosure, which few townspeople in the daily round of their lives ever took the trouble to do. So that though close to the turnpike-road crimes might be perpetrated there unseen at mid-day.

Some boys had latterly tried to impart gaiety to the ruin by using the central arena as a cricket-ground. But the game usually languished—for the aforesaid reason—the dismal privacy which the earthen circle enforced, shutting out every appreciative passer's vision, every commendatory remark from outsiders—everything except the sky; and to play at games in such circumstances was like acting to an empty house. Possibly too the boys were timid, for some old people said that at certain moments in the summer time, in broad daylight, persons sitting with a book or dozing in the arena had, on lifting their eyes, beheld the slopes lined with a gazing legion of Hadrian's soldiery as if watching the gladiatorial combat; and had heard the roar of their excited voices; that the scene would remain but a moment, like a lightning flash, and then disappear.

It was related that there still remained under the south entrance excavated cells for the reception of the wild animals and athletes who took part in the games. The arena was still smooth and circular, as if used for its original purpose not so very long ago. The sloping pathways by which spectators had ascended to their seats were pathways yet. But the whole was grown over with grass, which now, at the end of summer, was bearded with withered bents that formed waves under the brush of the wind, returning to the attentive ear Æolian modulations, and detaining for moments the flying globes of thistledown.

Henchard had chosen this spot as being the safest from observation which he could think of for meeting his long lost wife, and at the same time as one easily to be found by a stranger after nightfall. As mayor of the town with a reputation to keep up he could not invite her to come to his house till some definite course had been decided on.

Just before eight he approached the deserted earthwork, and entered by the south path which descended over the *débris* of the former dens. In a few moments he could discern a female figure creeping in by the great north gap or public gateway. They met in the middle of the arena. Neither spoke just at first—there was no necessity for speech—and the poor woman leant against Henchard, who supported her in his arms.

"I don't drink," he said in a low, halting, apologetic voice. "You hear, Susan?—I don't drink now—I haven't since that night." Those was his first words.

He felt her bow her head in acknowledgement that she understood. After a minute or two he again began:

"If I had known you were living, Susan! But there was every reason to suppose you and the child were dead and gone. I took every possible step to find you—travelled—advertised— my opinion at last was that you had started for some colony with that man, and had been drowned on your voyage out. Why did you keep silent like this?"

"O Michael—because of him—what other reason could there be? I thought I owed him faithfulness to the end of one of our lives—I foolishly believed there was something solemn and binding in the bargain; I thought that even in honour I dared not desert him when he had paid so much for me, in good faith. I meet you now only as his widow—I consider myself that, and that I have no claim upon you. Had he not died I should never have come—never. Of that you may be sure."

"Ts-s-s! How could you be so simple!"

"I don't know. Yet 't would have been very wicked—if I had not thought like that!" said Susan, almost crying.

"Yes—yes—so it would. It is only that which makes me feel 'ee an innocent woman. But—to lead me into this!"

"What, Michael?" she asked, alarmed.

"Why, this difficulty about our living together again, and Elizabeth-Jane. She cannot be told all—she would so despise us both that—I could not bear it!"

"That was why she was brought up in ignorance of you. I could not bear it, either."

"Well—we must talk of a plan for keeping her in her present belief, and getting matters straight in spite of it. You have heard I am in a large way of business here—that I am mayor of the town, and churchwarden, and I don't know what all?"

"Yes," she murmured.

"These things, as well as the dread of the girl discovering our disgrace, make it necessary to act with extreme caution. So that I don't see how you two can return openly to my house as the wife and daughter I once treated badly, and banished from me; and there's the rub o't."

"We'll go away at once. I only came to see——"

"No, no, Susan; you are not to go—you mistake me!" he said with kindly severity. "I have thought of this plan; that you and Elizabeth take a cottage in the town as the widow Mrs. Newson and her daughter; that I meet you, court you, and marry you, Elizabeth-Jane coming to my house as my stepdaughter. The thing is so natural and easy that it is half done in thinking o't. This would leave my shady, headstrong, disgraceful life as a young man absolutely unopened; the secret would be yours and mine only; and I should have the pleasure of seeing my own only child under my roof, as well as my wife."

"I am quite in your hands, Michael," she said meekly. "I came here for the sake of Elizabeth; for myself, if you tell me to leave again to-morrow morning, and never come near you more, I am content to go."

"Now, now; we don't want to hear that," said Henchard gently. "Of course you won't leave again. Think over the plan I have proposed for a few hours; and if you can't hit upon a better one we'll adopt it. I have to be away for a day or two on business, unfortunately; but during that time you can get lodgings—the only ones in the town fit for you are those over the china shop in High Street—and you can also look for a cottage."

"If the lodgings are in High Street they are dear, I suppose?"

"Never mind—you *must* start genteel, if our plan is to be carried out. Look to me for money. Have you enough till I come back?"

"Quite," said she.

"And are you comfortable at the inn."

"Oh yes."

"And the girl is quite safe from learning the shame of her case and ours?—that's what makes me most anxious of all."

"You would be surprised to find how unlikely she is to dream of the truth. How could she ever suppose such a thing!"

"True."

"I like the idea of repeating our marriage," said Mrs. Henchard after a pause. "It seems the only right course, after all this. Now I think I must go back to Elizabeth-Jane, and tell her that our kinsman Mr. Henchard kindly wishes us to stay in the town."

"Very well—arrange that yourself. I'll go some way with you."

"No, no. Don't run any risk!" said his wife anxiously. "I can find my way back—it is not late. Please let me go alone."

"Right," said Henchard. "But just one word. Do you forgive me, Susan?"

She murmured something; but seemed to find it difficult to frame her answer. "Never mind—all in good time," said he. "Judge me by my future works—good-bye."

He retreated, and stood at the upper side of the amphitheatre while his wife passed out through the lower way, and descended under the trees to the town. Then Henchard himself went homeward, going so fast that by the time he reached his door he was almost upon the heels of the unconscious woman from whom he had just parted. He watched her up the street, and turned into his house.

XII

ON entering his own door after watching his wife out of
sight, the mayor walked on through the tunnel-shaped passage
into the garden, and thence by the back door towards the
stores and granaries. A light shone from the office window,
and, there being no blind to screen the interior, Henchard
could see Donald Farfrae still seated where he had left him,
initiating himself into the managerial work of the house by
overhauling the books. Henchard entered, merely observing,
"Don't let me interrupt you, if ye will stay so late."

He stood behind Farfrae's chair, watching his dexterity
in clearing up the numerical fogs which had been allowed
to grow so thick in Henchard's books as almost to baffle
even the Scotchman's perspicacity. The corn-factor's mien
was half admiring, and yet it was not without a dash of pity
for the tastes of any one who could care to give his mind to
such finnikin details. Henchard himself was mentally and
physically unfit for grubbing subtleties from soiled paper; he
had in a modern sense received the education of Achilles, and
found penmanship a tantalizing art.

"You shall do no more to-night," he said at length,
spreading his great hand over the paper. "There's time
enough to-morrow. Come indoors with me and have some
supper. Now you shall! I am determind on't." He shut the
account-books with friendly force.

Donald had wished to get to his lodgings; but he already saw
that his friend and employer was a man who knew no
moderation in his requests and impulses, and he yielded
gracefully. He liked Henchard's warmth, even if it incon-
venienced him; the great difference in their characters adding
to the liking.

They locked up the office, and the young man followed his
companion through the private little door which, admitting
directly into Henchard's garden, permitted a passage from the
utilitarian to the beautiful at one step. The garden was silent,
dewy, and full of perfume. It extended a long way back from

the house, first as lawn and flower-beds, then as fruit-garden, where the long-tied espaliers, as old as the old house itself, had grown so stout, and cramped, and gnarled that they had pulled their stakes out of the ground, and stood distorted and writhing in vegetable agony, like leafy Laocoöns. The flowers which smelt so sweetly were not discernible; and they passed through them into the house.

The hospitalities of the morning were repeated, and when they were over Henchard said, "Pull your chair round to the fireplace, my dear fellow, and let's make a blaze—there's nothing I hate like a black grate, even in September." He applied a light to the laid-in fuel, and a cheerful radiance spread around.

"It is odd," said Henchard, "that two men should meet as we have done on a purely business ground, and that at the end of the first day I should wish to speak to 'ee on a family matter. But, damn it all, I am a lonely man, Farfrae; I have nobody else to speak to; and why shouldn't I tell it to 'ee?"

"I'll be glad to hear it, if I can be of any service," said Donald, allowing his eyes to travel over the intricate wood-carvings of the chimney-piece, representing garlanded lyres, shields, and quivers, on either side of a draped ox-skull, and flanked by heads of Apollo and Diana in low relief.

"I've not been always what I am now," continued Henchard, his firm deep voice being ever so little shaken. He was plainly under that strange influence which sometimes prompts men to confide to the new-found friend what they will not tell to the old. "I began life as a working hay-trusser, and when I was eighteen I married on the strength o' my calling. Would you think me a married man?"

"I heard in the town that you were a widower."

"Ah, yes—you would naturally have heard that. Well, I lost my wife nineteen years ago or so—by my own fault. . . . . This is how it came about. One summer evening I was travelling from employment, and she was walking at my side carrying the baby, our only child. We came to a booth in a country fair. I was a drinking man at that time."

Henchard paused a moment, threw himself back so that his elbow rested on the table, his forehead being shaded by his hand, which however did not hide the marks of introspective inflexibility on his features as he narrated in fullest detail the incidents of the transaction with the sailor. The tinge of indifference which had at first been visible in the Scotchman now disappeared.

Henchard went on to describe his attempts to find his wife; the oath he swore; the solitary life he led during the years which followed. "I have kept my oath for nineteen years," he went on; "I have risen to what you see me now."

"Ay!"

"Well—no wife could I hear of in all that time; and being by nature something of a woman-hater I have found it no hardship to keep mostly at a distance from the sex. No wife could I hear of, I say, till this very day. And now—she has come back."

"Come back, has she!"

"This morning—this very morning. And what's to be done?"

"Can ye no' take her and live with her, and make some amends?"

"That's what I've planned and proposed. But Farfrae," said Henchard gloomily, "by doing right with Susan I wrong another innocent woman."

"Ye don't say that!"

"In the nature of things, Farfrae, it is almost impossible that a man of my sort should have the good fortune to tide through twenty years o' life without making more blunders than one. It has been my custom for many years to run across to Jersey in the way of business, particularly in the potato and root season. I do a large trade wi' them in that line. Well, one autumn when stopping there I fell quite ill, and in my illness I sank into one of those gloomy fits I sometimes suffer from, on account o' the loneliness of my domestic life, when the world seems to have the blackness of hell, and, like Job, I could curse the day that gave me birth."

"Ah, now, I never feel like it," said Farfrae.

"Then pray to God that you never may, young man. While in this state I was taken pity on by a woman—a young lady I should call her, for she was of good family, well bred, and well educated—the daughter of some harum-scarum military officer who had got into difficulties, and had his pay sequestrated. He was dead now, and her mother, too, and she was as lonely as I. This young creature was staying at the boarding-house where I happened to have my lodging; and when I was pulled down she took upon herself to nurse me. From that she got to have a foolish liking for me. Heaven knows why, for I wasn't worth it. But, being together in the same house, and her feelings warm, we got naturally intimate. I won't go into particulars of what our relations were. It is enough to say that we honestly meant to marry. There arose a scandal, which did me no harm, but was of course ruin to her. Though Farfrae, between you and me, as man and man, I solemnly declare that philandering with womankind has neither been my vice nor my virtue. She was terribly careless of appearances, and I was perhaps more, because o' my dreary state; and it was through this that the scandal arose. At last I was well, and came away. When I was gone she suffered much on my account, and didn't forget to tell me so in letters one after another; till, latterly, I felt I owed her something, and thought that, as I had not heard of Susan for so long, I would make this other one the only return I could make, and ask her if she would run the risk of Susan being alive (very slight as I believed) and marry me, such as I was. She jumped for joy, and we should no doubt soon have been married—but, behold, Susan appears!"

Donald showed his deep concern at a complication so far beyond the degree of his simple experiences.

"Now see what injury a man may cause around him. Even after that wrong doing at the fair when I was young, if I had never been so selfish as to let this giddy girl devote herself to me over at Jersey, to the injury of her name, all might now be well. Yet, as it stands, I must bitterly disappoint one of these women; and it is the second. My first duty is to Susan— there's no doubt about that."

"They are both in a very melancholy position, and that's true!" murmured Donald.

"They are! For myself I don't care—'twill all end one way. But these two." Henchard paused in reverie. "I feel I should like to treat the second, no less than the first, as kindly as a man can in such a case."

"Ah, well, it cannet be helped!" said the other, with philosophic woefulness. "You mun write to the young lady, and in your letter you must put it plain and honest that it turns out she cannet be your wife, the first having come back; that ye cannet see her more; and that—ye wish her weel."

"That won't do. 'Od seize it, I must do a little more than that. I must send a useful sum of money to her, I suppose—just as a little recompense, poor girl—though she did always brag about her rich uncle or rich aunt, and her expectations from 'em. . . . Now, will you help me in this, and draw up an explanation to her of all I've told ye, breaking it as gently as you can?—I'm so bad at letters."

"And I will."

"Now I haven't told you quite all yet. My wife Susan has my daughter with her—the baby that was in her arms at the fair—and this girl knows nothing of me beyond that I am some sort of relation by marriage. She has grown up in the belief that the sailor to whom I made over her mother, and who is now dead, was her father, and her mother's husband. What her mother has always felt, she and I together feel now—that we can't proclaim our disgrace to the girl by letting her know the truth. Now what would you do—I want your advice?"

"I think I'd run the risk, and tell her the truth. She'll forgive ye both."

"Never!" said Henchard. "I am not going to let her know the truth. Her mother and I be going to marry again: and it will not only help us to keep our child's respect, but it will be more proper. Susan looks upon herself as the sailor's widow, and won't think o' living with me as formerly without another religious ceremony—and she's right."

Farfrae thereupon said no more. The letter to the young Jersey woman was carefully framed by him, and the interview ended, Henchard saying, as the Scotchman left: "I feel it a great relief, Farfrae, to tell some friend o' this! You see now that the mayor of Casterbridge is not so thriving in his mind as it seems he might be from the state of his pocket."

"I do. And I'm sorry for ye!" said Farfrae.

When he was gone, Henchard copied the letter, and, enclosing a cheque, took it to the post-office, from which he walked back thoughtfully.

"Can it be that it will go off so easily!" he said. "Poor thing—God knows! Now then, to make amends to Susan!"

XIII

THE cottage which Michael Henchard hired for his wife Susan under her name of Newson—in pursuance of their plan—was in the upper or western part of the town, near the Roman wall and the avenue which overshadowed it. The evening sun seemed to shine more yellowly there than anywhere else this autumn—stretching its rays, as the hours grew later, under the lowest sycamore boughs, and steeping the ground floor of the dwelling, with its green shutters, in a substratum of radiance which the foliage screened from the upper parts. Beneath these sycamores on the town walls could be seen from the sitting-room the tumuli and earth-forts of the distant uplands; making it altogether a pleasant spot, with the usual touch of melancholy that a past-marked prospect lends.

As soon as the mother and daughter were comfortably installed, with a white-aproned servant and all complete, Henchard paid them a visit, and remained to tea. During the entertainment Elizabeth was carefully hoodwinked by the very general tone of the conversation that prevailed—a proceeding which seemed to afford some humour to Henchard, though his wife was not particularly happy in it. The visit was repeated again and again with business-like determination by the mayor, who seemed to have schooled himself into a course of strict mechanical rightness towards this woman of prior claim, at any expense to the later one, and to his own sentiments.

One afternoon the daughter was not indoors when Henchard came, and he said drily, "This is a very good opportunity for me to ask you to name the happy day, Susan."

The poor woman smiled faintly; she did not enjoy pleasantries on a situation into which she had entered solely for the sake of her girl's reputation. She liked them so little, indeed, that there was room for wonder why she had countenanced deception at all, and had not bravely let the girl know her history. But the flesh is weak; and the true explanation came in due course.

"O Michael," she said, "I am afraid all this is taking up your time and giving trouble—when I did not expect any such thing!" And she looked at him and at his dress as a man of affluence, and at the furniture he had provided for the room—ornate and lavish, to her eyes.

"Not at all," said Henchard in rough benignity. "This is only a cottage—it costs me next to nothing. And as to taking up my time"—here his red and black visage kindled with satisfaction—"I've a splendid fellow to superintend my business now—a man whose like I've never been able to lay hands on before. I shall soon be able to leave everything to him, and have more time to call my own than I've had for these last twenty years."

Henchard's visits here grew so frequent and so regular that it soon became whispered, and then openly discussed in Casterbridge, that the masterful, coercive mayor of the town was captured and enervated by the genteel widow Mrs. Newson. His well-known haughty indifference to the society of womankind, his silent avoidance of converse with the sex, contributed a piquancy to what would otherwise have been an unromantic matter enough. That such a poor fragile woman should be his choice was inexplicable, except on the ground that the engagement was a family affair in which sentimental passion had no place; for it was known that they were related in some way. Mrs. Henchard was so pale that the boys called her "The Ghost." Sometimes Henchard overheard this epithet when they passed together along the Walks—as the avenues on the walls were named—at which his face would darken with an expression of destructiveness towards the speakers ominous to see; but he said nothing.

He pressed on the preparations for his union, or rather reunion, with this pale creature, in a dogged unflinching spirit which did credit to his conscientiousness. Nobody would have conceived from his outward demeanour that there was no amatory fire or pulse of romance acting as stimulant to the bustle going on in his gaunt great house, nothing but three large resolves; one to make amends to his neglected Susan, another to provide a comfortable home for Elizabeth-Jane under his paternal eye, and a third to castigate himself with the thorns which these restitutory acts brought in their train, among them the lowering of his dignity in public opinion by marrying so comparatively humble a woman.

Susan Henchard entered a carriage for the first time in her life when she stepped into the plain brougham which drew up at the door on the wedding day, to take her and Elizabeth-Jane to church. It was a windless morning of warm November rain, which floated down like meal, and lay in a powdery form on the nap of hats and coats. Few people had gathered round the church door, though they were well packed within. The Scotchman, who assisted as groomsman, was of course the only one present, beyond the chief actors, who knew the true situation of the contracting parties. He, however, was too inexperienced, too thoughtful, too judicial, too strongly conscious of the serious side of the business, to enter into the scene in its dramatic aspect. That required the special genius of Christopher Coney, Solomon Longways, Buzzford, and their fellows. But they knew nothing of the secret; though as the time for coming out of church drew on they gathered on the pavement adjoining, and expounded the subject according to their lights.

"'Tis five and forty years since I had my settlement in this here town," said Coney; "but daze me if ever I see a man wait so long before, to take so little. There's a chance even for thee after this, Nance Mockridge." The remark was addressed to a woman who stood behind his shoulder—the same who had exhibited Henchard's bad bread in public when Elizabeth and her mother entered Casterbridge.

"Be cust if I'd marry any such as he, or thee either," replied that lady. "As for thee, Christopher, we know what ye be, and the less said the better. And as for he—well there— [lowering her voice] 'tis said 'a was a poor parish 'prentice—I wouldn't say it for all the world—but 'a was a poor parish 'prentice that began life wi' no more belonging to en than a carrion crow."

"And now he's worth ever so much a minute," murmured Longways. "When a man is said to be worth so much a minute he's a man to be considered."—Turning he saw a circular disc reticulated with creases, and recognised the smiling countenance of the fat woman who had asked for another song at the Three Mariners. "Well, Mother Cuxsom," he said, "how's this? Here's Mrs. Newson, a mere skellinton, has got another husband to keep her, while a woman of your tonnage have not."

"I have not. Nor another to beat me. . . . Ah yes, Cuxsom's gone, and so shall leather breeches!"

"Yes; with the blessing of God leather breeches shall go."

"'Tisn't worth my old while to think of another husband," continued Mrs. Cuxsom. "And yet I'll lay my life I'm as respectable born as she."

"True; your mother was a very good woman—I can mind her. She were rewarded by the Agricultural Society for having begot the greatest number of healthy children without parish assistance, and other virtuous marvels."

"'Twas that that kept us so low upon ground—that great hungry family."

"Ay. Where the pigs be many the wash runs thin."

"And dostn't mind how mother would sing, Christopher?" continued Mrs. Cuxsom, kindling at the retrospection: "and how we went with her to the party at Mellstock, do ye mind;—at old Dame Ledlow's, farmer Shinar's aunt, do ye mind?—she we used to call Toadskin, because her face were so yaller and freckled, do ye mind?"

"I do, hee-hee, I do!" said Christopher Coney.

"And well do I—for I was getting up husband-high at that time—one half girl, and t'other half woman, as one may say.—And canst mind"—she prodded Solomon's shoulder with her finger-tip while her eyes twinkled between the crevices of their lids—"canst mind the sherry-wine, and the zilver snuffers, and how Joan Dummett was took bad when we were coming home, and Jack Griggs was forced to carry her through the mud; and how 'a let her fall in Dairyman Sweetapple's cow-barton and we had to clane her gown wi' grass—never such a mess as 'a were in?"

"Ay—that I do—hee-hee—such doggery as there was in them ancient days to be sure! Ah, the miles I used to walk then; and now I can hardly step over a furrow!"

Their reminiscences were cut short by the appearance of the re-united pair—Henchard looking round upon the idlers with that ambiguous gaze of his, which at one moment seemed to mean satisfaction, and at another fiery disdain.

"Well—there's a difference between 'em, though he do call himself a teetotaller," said Nance Mockridge. "She'll wish her cake dough afore she's done of him. There's a bluebeardy look about en; and 'twill out in time."

"Stuff—he's well enough. Some folk want their luck buttered. If I had a choice as wide as the ocean-sea I wouldn't wish for a better man. A poor twanking woman like her—'tis a godsend for her, and hardly a pair of jumps or night-rail to her name."

The plain little brougham drove off in the mist, and the idlers dispersed. "Well, we hardly know how to look at things in these times," said Solomon. "There was a man dropped down dead yesterday not so very many miles from here; and what wi' that, and this moist weather, 'tis scarce worth one's while to begin any work o' consequence to-day. I'm in such a low key with drinking nothing but small table ninepenny this last week or two that I shall call and warm up at the Mar'ners as I pass along."

"I don't know but that I may as well go with 'ee Solomon," said Christopher; "I'm as clammy as a cockle-snail."

XIV

A MARTINMAS summer of Mrs. Henchard's life set in with her entry into her husband's large house and respectable social orbit, and it was as bright as such summers well can be. Lest she should pine for deeper affection than he could give, he made a point of showing some semblance of it in external action. Among other things he had the iron railings, that had smiled sadly in dull rust for the last eighty years, painted a bright green, and the heavy-barred, small paned, Georgian sash windows enlivened with three coats of white. He was as kind to her as a man, mayor, and churchwarden could possibly be. The house was large, the rooms lofty, and the landings wide; and the two unassuming women scarcely made a perceptible addition to its contents.

To Elizabeth-Jane the time was a most triumphant one. The freedom she experienced, the indulgence with which she was treated, went beyond her expectations. The reposeful, easy, affluent life to which her mother's marriage had introduced her was, in truth, the beginning of a great change in Elizabeth. She found she could have nice personal possessions and ornaments for the asking, and, as the mediæval saying puts it, Take, have, and keep, are pleasant words. With peace of mind came development, and with development beauty. Knowledge—the result of great natural insight—she did not lack; learning, accomplishments—those, alas, she had not; but as the winter and spring passed by her thin face and figure filled out in rounder and softer curves; the lines and contractions upon her young brow went away; the muddiness of skin which she had looked upon as her lot by nature departed with a change to abundance of good things, and a bloom came upon her cheek. Perhaps too her grey thoughtful eyes revealed an arch gaiety sometimes; but this was infrequent; the sort of wisdom which looked from their pupils did not readily keep company with these lighter moods. Like all people who have known rough times, lightheartedness seemed to her too irrational and inconsequent to be indulged in except as a reckless dram now and then; for she had been too early habituated to anxious reasoning to drop the habit suddenly. She felt none of those ups and downs of spirit which beset so many people without cause; never—to paraphrase a recent poet—never a gloom in Elizabeth-Jane's soul but she well knew how it came there; and her present cheerfulness was fairly proportionate to her solid guarantees for the same.

It might have been supposed that, given a girl rapidly becoming good-looking, comfortably circumstanced, and for the first time in her life commanding ready money, she would go and make a fool of herself by dress. But no. The reasonableness of almost everything that Elizabeth did was nowhere more conspicuous than in this question of clothes. To keep in the rear of opportunity in matters of indulgence is as valuable a habit as to keep abreast of opportunity in matters of enterprise. This unsophisticated girl did it by an innate perceptiveness that was almost genius. Thus she refrained from bursting out like a water-flower that spring, and clothing herself in puffings and nick-nacks as most of the Casterbridge girls would have done in her circumstances. Her triumph was tempered by circumspection: she had still that field-mouse fear of the coulter of destiny despite fair promise, which is common among the thoughtful who have suffered early from poverty and oppression. "I won't be too gay on any account," she would say to herself. "It would be tempting Providence to hurl mother and me down, and afflict us again as he used to do."

We now see her in a black silk bonnet, velvet mantle or silk spencer, dark dress, and carrying a sunshade. In this latter article she drew the line at fringe, and had it plain edged, with a little ivory ring for keeping it closed. It was odd about the necessity for that sunshade. She discovered that with the clarification of her complexion and the birth of pink cheeks her skin had grown more sensitive to the sun's rays. She protected those cheeks forthwith, deeming spotlessness part of womanliness.

Henchard had become very fond of her, and she went out with him more frequently than with her mother now. Her appearance one day was so attractive that he looked at her critically.

"I happened to have a ribbon by me, so I made it up," she faltered, thinking him perhaps dissatisfied with some rather bright trimming she had donned for the first time.

"Ay—of course—to be sure," he replied in his leonine way. "Do as you like—or rather as your mother advises ye. 'Od send—I've nothing to say to't."

Indoors she appeared with her hair divided by a parting that arched like a white rainbow from ear to ear. All in front of this line was covered with a thick encampment of curls; all behind was dressed smoothly, and drawn to a knob.

The three members of the family were sitting at breakfast one day, and Henchard was looking silently, as he often did, at this head of hair, which in colour was brown—rather light than dark. "I thought Elizabeth-Jane's hair—didn't you tell me that Elizabeth-Jane's hair promised to be black when she was a baby," he said to his wife.

She looked startled, jerked his foot warningly, and murmured, "Did I?"

As soon as Elizabeth was gone to her own room Henchard resumed. "Begad, I nearly forgot myself just now! What I meant was that the girl's hair certainly looked as if it would be darker, when she was a baby?"

"It did; but they alter so," replied Susan.

"Their hair gets darker I know—but I wasn't aware it lightened ever?"

"Oh yes." And the same uneasy expression came out on her face, to which the future held the key. It passed as Henchard went on:

"Well, so much the better. Now Susan, I want to have her called Miss Henchard—not Miss Newson. Lots o' people do it already in carelessness—it is her legal name—so it may as well be made her usual name—I don't like t'other name at all for my own flesh and blood. I'll advertise it in the Casterbridge paper—that's the way they do it. She won't object."

"No—O no. But——"

"Well then, I shall do it," said he peremptorily. "Surely, if she's willing, you must wish it as much as I."

"O yes—if she agrees let us do it by all means," she replied.

Then Mrs. Henchard acted somewhat inconsistently; it might have been called falsely, but that her manner was emotional and full of the earnestness of one who wishes to do right at great hazard. She went to Elizabeth-Jane, whom she found sewing in her own sitting-room upstairs, and told her what had been proposed about her surname. "Can you agree—is it not a slight upon Newson—now he's dead and gone?"

Elizabeth reflected. "I'll think of it mother," she answered.

When, later in the day, she saw Henchard, she adverted to the matter at once, in a way which showed that the line of feeling started by her mother had been persevered in. "Do you wish this change so very much, sir?" she asked.

"Wish it? Why, my blessed fathers, what an ado you women make about a trifle! I proposed it—that's all. Now 'Lizabeth-Jane, just please yourself. Curse me if I care what you do. Now you understand, don't 'ee go agreeing to it to please me."

Here the subject dropped, and nothing more was said, and nothing was done, and Elizabeth still passed as Miss Newson, and not by her legal name.

Meanwhile the great corn and hay traffic conducted by Henchard throve under the management of Donald Farfrae as it had never thriven before. It had formerly moved in jolts; now it went on oiled castors. The old crude *vivâ voce* system of Henchard, in which everything depended upon his memory, and bargains were made by the tongue alone, was swept away. Letters and ledgers took the place of "I'll do't," and "you shall hae't"; and, as in all such cases of advance, the rugged picturesqueness of the old method disappeared with its inconveniences.

The position of Elizabeth-Jane's room—rather high in the house so that it commanded a view of the hay-stores and granaries across the garden—afforded her opportunity for accurate observation of what went on there. She saw that Donald and Mr. Henchard were inseparables. When walking together Henchard would lay his arm familiarly on his manager's shoulder, as if Farfrae were a younger brother, bearing so heavily that his slight figure bent under the weight. Occasionally she would hear a perfect cannonade of laughter from Henchard, arising from something Donald had said, the latter looking quite innocent and not laughing at all. In Henchard's somewhat lonely life, he evidently found the young man as desirable for comradeship as he was useful for consultations. Donald's brightness of intellect maintained in the corn-factor the admiration it had won at the first hour of their meeting. The poor opinion, and but ill-concealed, that he entertained of the slim Farfrae's physical girth, strength, and dash, was more than counterbalanced by the immense respect he had for his brains.

Her quiet eye discerned that Henchard's tigerish affection for the younger man, his constant liking to have Farfrae near him, now and then resulted in a tendency to domineer, which however was checked in a moment when Donald exhibited marks of real offence. One day looking down on their figures from on high, she heard the latter remark, as they stood in the doorway between the garden and yard, that their habit of walking and driving about together rather neutralized Farfrae's value as a second pair of eyes, which should be used in places where the principal was not. "'Od damn it," cried Henchard, "what's all the world! I like a fellow to talk to. Now come along and hae some supper, and don't take too much thought about things, or ye'll drive me crazy."

When she walked with her mother, on the other hand, she often beheld the Scotchman looking at them with a curious interest. The fact that he had met her at the Three Mariners was insufficient to account for it, since on the occasions on which she had entered his room he had never raised his eyes. Besides, it was at her mother more particularly than at herself that he looked, to Elizabeth-Jane's half unconscious, simple-minded, perhaps pardonable, disappointment. Thus she could not account for this interest by her own attractiveness and she decided that it might be apparent only—a way of turning his eyes that Mr. Farfrae had. She did not divine the ample explanation of his manner, without personal vanity, that was afforded by the fact of Donald being the depositary of Henchard's confidence in respect of his past treatment of the pale chastened mother who walked by her side. Her conjectures on that past never went further than faint ones based on things casually heard and seen—mere guesses that Henchard and her mother might have been lovers in their younger days, who had quarrelled and parted.

Casterbridge, as has been hinted, was a place deposited in the block upon a cornfield. There was no suburb in the modern sense, or transitional intermixture of town and down. It stood, with regard to the wide fertile land adjoining, clean-cut and distinct, like a chess board on a green table-cloth. The farmer's boy could sit under his barley-mow and pitch a stone into the office-window of the town-clerk; reapers at work among the sheaves nodded to acquaintances standing on the pavement-corner; the red-robed judge, when he condemned a sheep stealer, pronounced sentence to the tune of Baa, that floated in at the window from the remainder of the flock browsing hard by; and at executions the waiting crowd stood in a meadow immediately before the drop, out of which the cows had been temporarily driven to give the spectators room.

The corn grown on the upland side of the borough was garnered by farmers who lived in an eastern purlieu called Durnover. Here wheat ricks overhung the old Roman street, and thrust their eaves against the church tower; green-thatched barns with doorways as high as the gates of Solomon's temple opened directly upon the main thoroughfare. Barns indeed were so numerous as to alternate with every half-dozen houses along the way. Here lived burgesses who daily walked the fallow; shepherds in an intramural squeeze. A street of farmers' homesteads—a street ruled by a mayor and corporation, yet echoing with the thump of the flail, the flutter of the winnowing-fan, and the purr of the milk into the pails—a street which had nothing urban in it whatever—this was the Durnover end of Casterbridge.

Henchard, as was natural, dealt largely with this nursery or bed of small farmers close at hand—and his waggons were often down that way. One day, when arrangements were in progress for getting home corn from one of the aforesaid farms, Elizabeth-Jane received a note by hand, asking her to oblige the writer by coming at once to a granary on Durnover Hill. As this was the granary whose contents Henchard was removing, she thought the request had something to do with his business, and proceeded thither as soon as she had put on her bonnet. The granary was just within the farmyard, and stood on stone staddles, high enough for persons to walk under. The gates were open, but nobody was within. However she entered and waited. Presently she saw a figure approaching the gate—that of Donald Farfrae. He looked up at the church clock, and came in. By some unaccountable shyness, some wish not to meet him there alone, she quickly ascended the step-ladder leading to the granary door and entered it before he had seen her. Farfrae advanced, imagining himself in solitude; and a few drops of rain beginning to fall he moved and stood under the shelter where she had just been standing. Here he leant against one of the staddles, and gave himself up to patience. He too was plainly expecting some one; could it be herself? if so, why? In a few minutes he looked at his watch, and then pulled out a note, a duplicate of the one she had herself received.

The situation began to be very awkward, and the longer she waited the more awkward it became. To emerge from a door just above his head and descend the ladder, and show she had been in hiding there would look so very foolish that she still waited on. A winnowing-machine stood close beside her, and to relieve her suspense she gently moved the handle; whereupon a cloud of wheat-husks flew out into her face and covered her clothes and bonnet, and stuck into the fur of her victorine. He must have heard the slight movement, for he looked up, and then ascended the steps.

"Ah—it's Miss Newson," he said as soon as he could see into the granary, "I didn't know you were there. I have kept the appointment, and am at your service."

"O Mr. Farfrae," she faltered; "so have I. But I didn't know it was you who wished to see me, otherwise I——"

"I wished to see you? Oh no——at least, that is, I am afraid there may be a mistake?"

"Didn't you ask me to come here? Didn't you write this?" Elizabeth held out her note.

"No. Indeed at no hand would I have thought of it. And for you—didn't you ask me? This is not your writing?" And he held up his.

"By no means."

"And is that really so! Then it's somebody wanting to see us both. Perhaps we would do well to wait a little longer."

Acting on this consideration they lingered, Elizabeth-Jane's face being arranged to an expression of preternatural composure, and the young Scot, at every footstep in the street without, looking from under the granary to see if the passer were about to enter and declare himself their summoner. They watched individual drops of rain creeping down the thatch of the opposite rick—straw after straw, till they reached the bottom; but nobody came, and the granary roof began to drip.

"The person is not likely to be coming," said Farfrae. "It's a trick perhaps, and if so, it's a great pity to waste our time like this, and so much to be done."

"'Tis a great liberty," said Elizabeth.

"It's true, Miss Newson. We'll hear news of this some day, depend on't, and who it was that did it. I wouldn't stand for it hindering myself, but you, Miss Newson——"

"I don't mind—much," she replied.

"Neither do I."

They lapsed again into silence. "You are anxious to get back to Scotland, I suppose, Mr. Farfrae?" she inquired.

"Oh no, Miss Newson—why would I be?"

"I only supposed you might be—from the song you sang at the Three Mariners—about Scotland and home, I mean—which you seemed to feel so deep down in your heart; so that we all felt for you."

"Ay—and I did sing there—I did . . . . But Miss Newson"—and Donald's voice musically undulated between two semitones, as it always did when he became earnest—"it's well you feel a song for a few minutes, and your eyes they get quite tearful; but you finish it, and for all you felt you don't mind it or think of it again for a long while. Oh no—I don't want to go back! Yet I'll sing the song to you wi' pleasure whenever you like—I could sing it now, and not mind at all?"

"Thank you indeed. But I fear I must go—rain or no."

"Ay! Then, Miss Newson, ye had better say nothing about this hoax, and take no heed of it. And if the person should say anything to you be civil to him or her as if you did not mind it—so you'll take the clever person's laugh away." In speaking his eyes became fixed upon her dress, still sown with wheat husks. "There's husks and dust on you, perhaps you don't know it?" he said in tones of extreme delicacy. 'And it's very bad to let rain come upon clothes when there's chaff on them—it washes in and spoils them. Let me help you—blowing is the best."

As Elizabeth neither assented nor dissented Donald Farfrae began blowing her back hair, and her side hair, and her neck, and the crown of her bonnet, and the fur of her victorine, Elizabeth saying, "Oh thank you," at every puff. At last she was fairly clean, though Farfrae, having got over his first concern at the situation, seemed in no manner of hurry to be gone.

"Ah—now I'll go and get ye an umbrella!" he said.

She declined the offer, stepped out and was gone. Farfrae walked slowly after, looking thoughtfully at her diminishing figure, and whistling in undertones, "As I came down through Cannobie."

XV

AT first Miss Newson's budding beauty was not regarded with much interest by anybody in Casterbridge. Donald Farfrae's gaze, it is true, was now attracted by the mayor's so-called step-daughter, but he was only one. The truth is that she was but a poor illustrative instance of the prophet Baruch's sly definition: "The virgin that loveth to go gay."

When she walked abroad she seemed to be occupied with an inner chamber of ideas, and to have slight need for visible objects. She formed curious resolves on checking gay fancies in the matter of clothes, because it was inconsistent with her past life to blossom gaudily the moment she had become possessed of money. But nothing is more insidious than the evolution of wishes from mere fancies, and of wants from mere wishes. Henchard gave Elizabeth-Jane a box of delicately tinted gloves one spring day. She wanted to wear them, to show her appreciation of his kindness, but she had no bonnet that would harmonize. As an artistic indulgence she thought she would have such a bonnet. When she had a bonnet that would go with the gloves she had no dress that would go with the bonnet. It was now absolutely necessary to finish; she ordered the requisite article; and found that she had no sunshade to go with the dress. In for a penny in for a pound; she bought the sunshade; and the whole structure was at last complete.

Everybody was attracted, and some said that her bygone simplicity was the art that conceals art, the "delicate imposition" of Rochefoucauld; she had produced an effect, a contrast; and it had been done on purpose. As a matter of fact this was not true, but it had its result; for as soon as Casterbridge thought her artful it thought her worth notice. "It is the first time in my life that I have been so much admired!" she said to herself. "Though perhaps it is by those whose admiration is not worth having."

But Donald Farfrae admired her, too; and altogether the time was an exciting one; sex had never before asserted itself in her so strongly, for in former days she had perhaps been too impersonally human to be distinctively feminine. After an unprecedented success one day she came indoors, went upstairs, and leant upon her bed face downwards, quite forgetting the possible creasing and damage. "Good heaven," she whispered, "Can it be? Here am I setting up as the town beauty!"

When she had thought it over, her usual fear of exaggerating appearances engendered a deep sadness. "There is something wrong in all this," she mused. "If they only knew what an unfinished girl I am—that I can't talk Italian, or use globes, or show any of the accomplishments they learn at boarding schools—how they would despise me! Better sell all this finery and buy myself grammar-books, and dictionaries, and a history of all the philosophies!"

She looked from the window, and saw Henchard and Farfrae in the hay-yard talking, with that impetuous cordiality on the mayor's part, and genial modesty on the younger man's, that was now so generally observable in their intercourse. Friendship between man and man; what a rugged strength there was in it, as evinced by these two. And yet the seed that was to lift the foundation of this friendship was at that moment taking root in a chink of its structure.

It was about six o'clock: the men were dropping off homeward one by one. The last to leave was a round shouldered blinking young man of nineteen or twenty, whose mouth fell ajar on the slightest provocation, seemingly because there was no chin to support it. Henchard called aloud to him as he went out of the gate. "Here—Abel Whittle!"

Whittle turned and ran back a few steps. "Yes, sir," he said in breathless deprecation, as if he knew what was coming next.

"Once more—be in time to-morrow morning. You see what's to be done, and you hear what I say, and you know I'm not going to be trifled with any longer."

"Yes sir." Then Abel Whittle left, and Henchard, and Farfrae; and Elizabeth saw no more of them.

Now there was good reason for this command on Henchard's

part. Poor Abel, as he was called, had an inveterate habit of oversleeping himself and coming late to his work. His anxious will was to be among the earliest; but if his comrades omitted to pull the string that he always tied round his great toe and left hanging out of the window for that purpose, his will was as wind. He did not arrive in time.

As he was often second hand at the hay-weighing, or at the crane which lifted the sacks, or was one of those who had to accompany the waggons into the country to fetch away stacks that had been purchased, this affliction of Abel's was productive of much inconvenience. For two mornings in the present week he had kept the others waiting nearly an hour: hence Henchard's threat. It now remained to be seen what would happen to-morrow.

Six o'clock struck, and there was no Whittle. At half past six Henchard entered the yard: the waggon was horsed that Abel was to accompany; and the other man had been waiting twenty minutes. Then Henchard swore, and Whittle coming up breathless at that instant, the corn-factor turned on him, and declared with an oath that this was the last time; that if he were behind once more by God he would come and drag him out o' bed.

"There is sommit wrong in my make, your worshipful," said Abel, "especially in the inside, whereas my poor dumb brain gets as dead as a clot afore I've said my few scrags of prayers. Yes—it came on as a stripling, just afore I'd got man's wages, whereas I never enjoy my bed at all, for no sooner do I lie down than I be asleep, and afore I be awake I be up. I've fretted my gizzard green about it, maister, but what can I do? Now last night afore I went to bed I only had a scantling o' cheese and——"

"I don't want to hear it!" roared Henchard. "To-morrow the waggons must start at four, and if you're not here, stand clear. I'll mortify thy flesh for thee!"

"But let me clear up my points, your worshipful——"

Henchard turned away.

"He asked me and he questioned me, and then 'a wouldn't hear my points!" said Abel to the yard in general. "Now I shall twitch like a moment-hand all night to-night for fear o' him!"

The journey to be taken by the waggons next day was a long one, into Blackmoor Vale, and at four o'clock lanterns were moving about the yard. But Abel was missing. Before either of the other men could run to Abel's and warn him Henchard appeared in the garden doorway. "Where's Abel Whittle? Not come after all I've said? Now I'll carry out my word—by my blessed fathers—nothing else will do him any good! I'm going up that way."

Henchard went off, entered Abel's house, a little cottage in Back Street, the door of which was never locked because the inmates had nothing to lose. Reaching Whittle's bedside the corn-factor shouted a bass note so vigorously that Abel started up instantly, and beholding Henchard standing over him was galvanized into spasmodic movements which had not much relation to getting on his clothes.

"Out of bed, sir; and off to the granary, or you leave my employ to-day! 'Tis to teach ye a lesson. March on; never mind your breeches!"

The unhappy Whittle threw on his sleeve waistcoat, and managed to get into his boots at the bottom of the stairs, while Henchard thrust his hat over his head. Whittle then trotted on down Back Street, Henchard walking sternly behind.

Just at this time Farfrae, who had been to Henchard's house to look for him, came out of the back gate, and saw something white fluttering in the morning gloom, which he soon perceived to be the part of Abel's shirt that showed below his waistcoat.

"For maircy's sake, what object's this?" said Farfrae, following Abel into the yard, Henchard being some way in the rear by this time.

"Ye see, Mr. Farfrae," gibbered Abel with a resigned smile of terror. "He said he'd mortify my flesh if so be I didn't get up sooner, and now he's a doing on't. Ye see it can't be helped, Mr. Farfrae; things do happen queer sometimes. Yes—I'll go to Blackmoor Vale half-naked as I be, since he do command it; but I shall kill myself afterwards; I can't outlive the disgrace; for the women-folk will be looking out of their winders at my mortification all the way along, and laughing me to scorn as a man 'ithout breeches! You know how I feel such things, maister Farfrae, and how forlorn thoughts get hold upon me. Yes—I shall do myself harm—I feel it coming on!"

"Get back home, and slip on your breeches, and come to wark like a man. If ye go not you'll hae your death standing there."

"I'm afeard I mustn't! Mr. Henchard said——"

"I don't care what Mr. Henchard said, nor anybody else! 'Tis simple foolishness to do this. Go and dress yourself instantly, Whittle."

"Hullo, hullo!" said Henchard coming up behind. "Who's sending him back?"

All the men looked towards Farfrae.

"I am," said Donald. "I say this joke has been carried far enough."

"And I say it hasn't. Get up in the waggon, Whittle."

"Not if I am manager," said Farfrae. "He either goes home, or I march out of this yard for good."

Henchard looked at him with a face stern and red. But he paused for a moment, and their eyes met. Donald went up to him, for he saw in Henchard's look that he began to regret this.

"Come," said Donald quietly, "a man o' your position should ken better, sir! It is tyrannical, and no worthy of you."

"'Tis not tyrannical!" murmured Henchard like a sullen boy. "It is to make him remember!" He presently added, in a tone of one bitterly hurt: "Why did you speak to me before them like that, Farfrae! You might have stopped till we were alone. Ah—I know why! I've told ye the secret o' my life—fool that I was to do't—and you take advantage of me."

"I had forgot it," said Farfrae simply.

Henchard looked on the ground, said nothing more, and turned away. During the day Farfrae learnt from the men that Henchard had kept Abel's old mother in coals and snuff all the previous winter, which made him less antagonistic to the corn-factor. But Henchard continued moody and silent, and when one of the men enquired of him if some oats should be hoisted to an upper floor or not, he said shortly, "Ask Mr. Farfrae. He's master here!"

Morally he was; there could be no doubt of it. Henchard, who had hitherto been the most admired man in his circle, was the most admired no longer. One day the daughters of a deceased farmer in Durnover wanted an opinion on the value of their haystack, and sent a messenger to ask Mr. Farfrae to oblige them with one. The messenger, who was a child, met in the yard not Farfrae but Henchard.

"Very well," he said. "I'll come."

"But please will Mr. Farfrae come?" said the child.

"I am going that way. . . . . . Why Mr. Farfrae?" said Henchard with the fixed look of thought. "Why do people always want Mr. Farfrae?"

"I suppose because they like him so—that's what they say."

"Oh—I see—that's what they say—hey? They like him because he's cleverer than Mr. Henchard, and because he knows more; and in short Mr. Henchard can't hold a candle to him—hey?"

"Yes—that's just it, sir—some of it."

"Oh there's more. Of course there's more. What besides? Come, here's sixpence for a fairing."

"And he's better tempered, and Henchard's a fool to him, they say. And when some of the women were a walking home they said 'He's a diment—he's a chap o' wax—he's the best— he's the horse for my money' says they. And they said, 'He's the most understanding man o' them two by long chalks. I wish he was the master instead of Henchard,' they said."

"They'll talk any nonsense," Henchard replied with covered gloom. "Well, you can go now. And *I* am coming to value the hay, d'ye hear—I." The boy departed, and Henchard murmured, "Wish he were master here, do they."

He went towards Durnover. On his way he overtook Farfrae. They walked on together, Henchard looking mostly on the ground.

"You're no yoursel' the day?" Donald inquired.

"Yes—I am very well," said Henchard.

"But ye are a bit down—surely ye are down? Why, there's nothing to be angry about—'Tis splendid stuff that we've got from Blackmoor Vale. By the by, the people in Durnover want their hay valued."

"Yes—I am going there."

"I'll go with ye." As Henchard did not reply Donald practised a piece of music *sotto voce* till, getting near the bereaved people's door he stopped himself with, "Ah—as their father is dead I won't go on with such as that. How could I forget!"

"Do you care so very much about hurting folks' feelings!" observed Henchard with a half sneer. "You do, I know—especially mine!"

"I am sorry if I have hurt yours, sir," replied Donald standing still, with a second expression of the same sentiment in the regretfulness of his face. "Why should you say it—think it?"

The cloud lifted from Henchard's brow, and as Donald finished, the corn-merchant turned to him, regarding his breast rather than his face. "I have been hearing things that vexed me," he said. "'Twas that made me short in my manner—made me overlook what you really are. Now—I don't want to go in here about this hay, Farfrae—you can do it better than I,—they sent for 'ee, too. I have to attend a meeting of the Town Council at eleven, and 'tis drawing on for't."

They parted thus in renewed friendship, Donald forbearing to ask Henchard for meanings that were not very plain to him. On Henchard's part there was now again repose; and yet, whenever he thought of Farfrae it was with a dim dread; and he often regretted that he had told the young man his whole heart, and confided to him the secrets of his life.

XVI

ON this account Henchard's manner towards Farfrae insensibly became more reserved. He was courteous—too courteous—and Farfrae was quite surprised at the good-breeding which now for the first time showed itself among the qualities of a man he had hitherto thought undisciplined, if warm and sincere. The corn-factor seldom or never again put his arm upon the young man's shoulder so as to nearly weigh him down with the pressure of mechanized friendship. He left off coming to Donald's lodgings and shouting into the passage, "Hoy—Farfrae, boy—come and have some dinner with us—don't sit here in solitary confinement!" But in the daily routine of their business there was little change.

Thus their lives rolled on till a day of public rejoicing was suggested to the country at large, in celebration of a national event that had recently taken place.

For some time Casterbridge, by nature slow, made no response. Then one day Donald Farfrae broached the subject to Henchard by asking if he would have any objection to lend some rick-cloths to himself and a few others, who contemplated getting up an entertainment of some sort on the day named, and required a shelter for the same, to which they might charge admission at the rate of so much a head.

'Have as many cloths as you like," Henchard replied.

When his manager had gone about the business Henchard was fired with emulation. It certainly had been very remiss of him, as mayor, he thought, to call no meeting ere this, to discuss what should be done on this holiday. But Farfrae had been so cursed quick in his movements as to give old-fashioned people in authority no chance of the initiative. However, it was not too late; and on second thoughts he determined to take upon his own shoulders the responsibility of organizing some amusements, if the other councilmen would leave the matter in his hands. To this they quite readily agreed, the majority being fine old crusted characters who had a decided taste for living without worry.

So Henchard set about his preparations for a really brilliant thing—such as should be worthy of the venerable town. As for Farfrae's little affair, Henchard nearly forgot it, except once now and then when, on it coming into his mind, he said to himself "Charge admission at so much a head—just like a Scotchman!—who is going to pay anything a head?" The diversions which the mayor intended to provide were to be entirely free.

He had grown so dependent upon Donald that he could scarcely resist calling him in to consult. But by sheer self-coercion he refrained. No, he thought, Farfrae would be suggesting such improvements in his damned luminous way, that in spite of himself he, Henchard, would sink to the position of second fiddle, and only scrape harmonies to his manager's talents.

Everybody applauded the mayor's proposed entertainment, especially when it became known that he meant to pay for it all himself.

Close to the town was an elevated green spot surrounded by an ancient square earthwork—earthworks square and not square were as common as blackberries hereabout—a spot whereon the Casterbridge people usually held any kind of merry-making, meeting, or sheep-fair that required more space than the streets would afford. On one side it sloped to the river Froom, and from any point a view was obtained of the country round for many miles. This pleasant upland was to be the scene of Henchard's exploit.

He advertised about the town, in long posters of a pink colour, that games of all sorts would take place here; and set to work a little battalion of men under his own eye. They erected greasy-poles for climbing, with smoked hams and local cheeses at the top. They placed hurdles in rows for jumping over; across the river they laid a slippery pole, with a live pig of the neighbourhood tied at the other end, to become the property of the man who could walk over and get it. There were also provided wheelbarrows for racing, donkeys for the same, a stage for boxing, wrestling, and drawing blood generally; sacks for jumping in. Moreover, not forgetting his principles, Henchard provided a mammoth tea, of which everybody who lived in the borough was invited to partake without payment. The tables were laid parallel with the inner slope of the rampart, and awnings were stretched overhead.

Passing to and fro the mayor beheld the unattractive exterior of Farfrae's erection in the West Walk, rick-cloths of different sizes and colours being hung up to the arching trees without any regard to appearance. He was easy in his mind now, for his own preparations far transcended these.

The morning came. The sky, which had been remarkably clear down to within a day or two, was overcast, and the weather threatening, the wind having an unmistakable hint of water in it. Henchard wished he had not been quite so sure about the continuance of a fair season. But it was too late to modify or postpone, and the proceedings went on. At twelve o'clock the rain began to fall, small and steady, commencing and increasing so insensibly that it was difficult to state exactly when dry weather ended or wet established itself. In an hour the slight moisture resolved itself into a monotonous smiting of earth by heaven, in torrents to which no end could be prognosticated.

A number of people had heroically gathered in the field, but by three o'clock Henchard discerned that his project was doomed to end in failure. The hams at the top of the poles dripped watered smoke in the form of a brown liquor, the pig shivered in the wind, the grain of the deal tables showed through the sticking tablecloths, for the awning allowed the rain to drift under at its will, and to enclose the sides at this hour seemed a useless undertaking. The landscape over the river disappeared; the wind played on the tent-cords in Æolian improvisations; and at length rose to such a pitch that the whole erection slanted to the ground, those who had taken shelter within it having to crawl out on their hands and knees.

But towards six the storm abated, and a drier breeze shook the moisture from the grass bents. It seemed possible to carry out the programme after all. The awning was set up again; the band was called out from its shelter, and ordered to begin, and where the tables had stood a place was cleared for dancing.

"But where are the folk?" said Henchard after the lapse of half an hour during which time only two men and a woman had stood up to dance. "The shops are all shut. Why don't they come?"

"They are at Farfrae's affair in the West Walk," answered a councilman who stood in the field with the mayor.

"A few I suppose. But where are the body o'em?"

"All out of doors are there."

"Then the more fools they!"

Henchard walked away moodily. One or two young fellows gallantly came to climb the poles, to save the hams from being wasted; but as there were no spectators, and the whole scene presented the most melancholy appearance, Henchard gave orders that the proceedings were to be suspended, and the entertainment closed, the food to be distributed among the poor people of the town. In a short time nothing was left in the field but a few hurdles, the tents, and the poles.

Henchard returned to his house, had tea with his wife and daughter, and then walked out. It was now dusk. He soon saw that the tendency of all promenaders was towards a particular spot in the Walks; and eventually proceeded thither himself. The notes of a stringed band came from the enclosure that Farfrae had erected—the pavilion, as he called it—and when the mayor reached it he perceived that a gigantic tent had been ingeniously constructed without poles or ropes. The densest point of the avenue of sycamores had been selected, where the boughs made a closely interlaced vault overhead; to these boughs the canvas had been hung, and a barrel roof was the result. The end towards the wind was enclosed, the other end was open. Henchard went round and saw the interior.

In form it was like the nave of a cathedral with one gable removed, but the scene within was anything but devotional. A reel or fling of some sort was in progress; and the usually sedate Farfrae was in the midst of the other dancers in the costume of a wild Highlander, flinging himself about and spinning to the tune. For a moment Henchard could not help laughing. Then he perceived the immense admiration for the Scotchman that revealed itself in the women's faces; and when this exhibition was over, and a new dance proposed, and Donald had disappeared for a time to return in his natural garments, he had an unlimited choice of partners, every girl being in a coming-on disposition towards one who so thoroughly understood the poetry of motion as he.

All the town crowded to the Walk, such a delightful idea of a ball-room never having occurred to the inhabitants before. Among the rest of the onlookers were Elizabeth and her mother—the former thoughtful yet much interested, her eyes beaming with a longing lingering light, as if Nature had been advised by Correggio in their creation. The dancing progressed with unabated spirit, and Henchard walked and waited till his wife should be disposed to go home. He did not care to keep in the light, and when he went into the dark it was worse for there he heard remarks of a kind which were becoming too frequent:

"Mr. Henchard's rejoicings couldn't say Good-morning to this," said one. "A man must be a headstrong stunpoll to think folk would go up to that bleak place to-day."

The other answered that people said it was not only in such things as those that the mayor was wanting. "Where would his business be if it were not for this young fellow. 'Twas verily Fortune sent him to Henchard. His accounts were like a bramble-wood when Mr. Farfrae came. He used to reckon his sacks by chalk strokes all in a row like garden-palings, measure his ricks by stretching with his arms, weigh his trusses by a lift, judge his hay by a chaw, and settle the price with a curse. But now this accomplished young man does it all by ciphering and mensuration. Then the wheat—that sometimes used to taste so strong o' mice when made into bread that people could fairly tell the breed—Farfrae has a plan for purifying, so that nobody would dream the smallest four-legged beast had walked over it once. Oh yes, everybody is full of him, and the care Mr. Henchard has to keep him, to be sure!" concluded this gentlemen.

"But he won't do it for long, good-now," said the other.

"No!" said Henchard to himself behind the tree. "Or if he do, he'll be honeycombed clean out of all the character and standing that he's built up in these eighteen year!"

He went back to the dancing pavilion. Farfrae was footing a quaint little dance with Elizabeth-Jane—an old country thing, the only one she knew, and though he considerately toned down his movements to suit her demurer gait, the pattern of the shining little nails in the soles of his boots became familiar to the eyes of every bystander. The tune had enticed her into it; being a tune of a busy, vaulting-leaping sort—some low notes on the silver string of each fiddle, then a skipping on the small, like running up and down ladders— "Miss M'Leod of Ayr" was its name, so Mr. Farfrae had said, and that it was very popular in his own country.

It was soon over, and the girl looked at Henchard for approval; but he did not give it. He seemed not to see her. "Look here, Farfrae," he said like one whose mind was elsewhere; "I'll go to Port-Bredy great market to-morrow myself. You can stay and put things right in your clothes-box, and recover strength to your knees after your vagaries." He planted on Donald an antagonistic glare that had begun as a smile.

Some other townsmen came up, and Donald drew aside. "What's this, Henchard—" said Alderman Tubber, applying his thumb to the corn-factor like a cheese-taster. "An opposition randy to yours—eh? Jack's as good as his master, eh? Cut ye out quite, hasn't he?"

"You see, Mr. Henchard," said the lawyer, another goodnatured friend, "where you made the mistake was in going so far afield. You should have taken a leaf out of his book, and have had your sports in a sheltered place like this. But you didn't think of it, you see; and he did, and that's where he's beat you."

"He'll be top sawyer, soon, of you two, and carry all afore him," added jocular Mr. Tubber.

"No," said Henchard gloomily. "He won't be that, because he's shortly going to leave me." He looked towards Donald, who had again come near. "Mr. Farfrae's time as my manager is drawing to a close—isn't it, Farfrae?"

The young man, who could now read the lines and folds of Henchard's strongly traced face as if they were clear verbal inscriptions, quietly assented; and when people deplored the fact and asked why it was, he simply replied that Mr. Henchard no longer required his help.

Henchard went home, apparently satisfied. But in the

morning when his jealous temper had passed away his heart sank within him at what he had said and done. He was the more disturbed when he found that this time Farfrae was determined to take him at his word.

XVII

ELIZABETH-JANE had perceived from Henchard's manner that in assenting to dance she had made a mistake of some kind. In her simplicity she did not know what it was, till a hint from a nodding acquaintance enlightened her. As the mayor's step-daughter, she learnt, she had not been quite in her place in treading a measure amid such a mixed throng as filled the dancing pavilion.

Thereupon her ears, cheeks and chin glowed like live coals at the dawning of the idea that her tastes were not good enough for her position, and would bring her into disgrace.

This made her very miserable, and she looked about for her mother; but Mrs. Henchard, who had less idea of conventionality than Elizabeth herself, had gone away, leaving her daughter to return at her own pleasure. The latter moved on into the dark dense old avenues, or rather vaults of living woodwork, which ran along the town boundary, and stood reflecting.

A man followed in a few minutes, and her face being towards the shine from the tent he recognised her. It was Farfrae—just come from the dialogue with Henchard which had signified his dismissal.

"And it's you, Miss Newson?—and I've been looking for ye everywhere!" he said overcoming a sadness imparted by the estrangement with the corn-merchant. "May I walk on with you as far as your street-corner?"

She thought there might be something wrong in this; but did not utter any objection. So together they went on, first down the West Walk, and then into the Bowling Walk, till Farfrae said "It's like that I'm going to leave you soon."

She faltered "Why?"

"Oh—as a mere matter of business—nothing more. But we'll not concern ourselves about it—it is for the best. I hoped to have another dance with you."

She said she could not dance—in any proper way.

"Nay but you do. It's the feeling for it rather than the

learning of steps that makes pleasant dancers. . . . I fear I offended your father by getting up this! And now, perhaps, I'll have to go to another part o' the warrld altogether!"

This seemed such a melancholy prospect that Elizabeth-Jane breathed a sigh—letting it off in fragments that he might not hear her. But darkness makes people truthful, and the Scotchman went on impulsively—perhaps he had heard her after all:

"I wish I was richer, Miss Newson; and your step-father had not been offended; I would ask you something in a short time—yes, I would ask you to-night. But that's not for me!"

What he would have asked her he did not say; and instead of encouraging him she remained incompetently silent. Thus afraid one of another they continued their promenade along the walls till they got near the bottom of the Bowling-Walk: twenty steps further and the trees would end, and the street corner and lamps appear. In consciousness of this they stopped.

"I never found out who it was that sent us to Durnover granary on a fool's errand that day," said Donald in his undulating tones. "Did ye ever know yourself, Miss Newson?"

"Never," said she.

"I wonder why they did it?"

"For fun, perhaps."

"Perhaps it was not for fun. It might have been that they thought they would like us to stay waiting there, talking to one another. Ay, well!—I hope you Casterbridge folk will no forget me if I go."

"That I'm sure we won't!" she said earnestly. "I—wish you wouldn't go at all."

They had got into the lamplight. "Now I'll think over that," said Donald Farfrae. "And I'll not come up to your door; but part from you here; lest it make your father more angry still."

They parted, Farfrae returning into the dark Bowling Walk, and Elizabeth-Jane going up the street. Without any consciousness of what she was doing she started running with all her might till she reached her father's door. "O dear me—what am I at!" she thought as she pulled up, breathless.

Indoors she fell to conjecturing the meaning of Farfrae's enigmatic words about not daring to ask her what he fain would. Elizabeth, that silent observing woman, had long noted how he was rising in favour among the townspeople; and, knowing Henchard's nature now, she had feared that Farfrae's days as manager were numbered; so that the announcement gave her little surprise. Would Mr. Farfrae stay in Casterbridge, despite his words and her father's dismissal? His occult breathings to her might be solvable by his course in that respect.

The next day was windy—so windy that walking in the garden she picked up a portion of the draft of a letter on business in Donald Farfrae's writing, which had flown over the wall from the office. The useless scrap she took indoors, and began to copy the caligraphy, which she much admired. The letter began "Dear Sir," and presently writing on a loose slip "Elizabeth-Jane," she laid the latter over "Sir," making the phrase "Dear Elizabeth-Jane." When she saw the effect a quick red ran up her face and warmed her through, though nobody was there to see what she had done. She quickly tore up the slip, and threw it away. After this she grew cool and laughed at herself, walked about the room and laughed again; not joyfully, but distressfully rather.

It was quickly known in Casterbridge that Farfrae and Henchard had decided to dispense with each other. Elizabeth-Jane's anxiety to know if Farfrae were going away from the town reached a pitch that disturbed her, for she could no longer conceal from herself the cause. At length the news reached her that he was not going to leave the place. A man following the same trade as Henchard, but on a very small scale, had sold his business to Farfrae, who was forthwith about to start as corn and hay merchant on his own account.

Her heart fluttered when she heard of this step of Donald's, proving that he meant to remain—and yet—would a man who cared one little bit for her have endangered his suit by setting up a business in opposition to Mr. Henchard's? Surely not; and it must have been a passing impulse only which had led him to address her so softly.

To solve the problem whether her appearance on the evening of the dance were such as to inspire a fleeting love at first sight, she dressed herself up exactly as she had dressed then—the muslin, the spencer, the sandals, the parasol—and looked in the mirror. The picture glassed back was, in her opinion, precisely of such a kind as to inspire that fleeting regard, and no more;—"just enough to make him silly, and not enough to keep him so," she said luminously; and Elizabeth thought, in a much lower key, that by this time he had discovered how plain and homely was the informing spirit of that pretty outside.

Hence, when she felt her heart going out to him she would say to herself with a mock pleasantry that carried an ache with it, "No, no, Elizabeth-Jane—such dreams are not for you!" She tried to prevent herself from seeing him, and thinking of him; succeeding fairly well in the former attempt, in the latter not so completely.

Henchard, who had been hurt at finding that Farfrae did not mean to put up with his temper any longer, was incensed beyond measure when he learnt what the young man had done as an alternative. It was in the town-hall, after a council-meeting, that he first became aware of Farfrae's *coup* for establishing himself independently in the town; and his voice might have been heard as far as the town-pump expressing his feelings to his fellow councilmen. Those tones showed that, though under a long reign of self-control he had become mayor, and churchwarden, and what-not, there was still the same unruly volcanic stuff beneath the rind of Michael Henchard as when he had sold his wife at Weydon Fair.

"Well he's a friend of mine, and I'm a friend of his—or if we are not, what are we? 'Od send, if I've not been his friend, who has, I should like to know? Didn't he come here without a sound shoe to his voot?—didn't I keep him here—help him to a living—didn't I help him to money, or whatever he wanted? I stuck out for no terms—I said, name your own price. I'd have shared my last crust with that young fellow at one time, I liked him so well! And now he's defied me! But damn him, I'll have a tussle with him now—at fair buying and selling mind—at fair buying and selling—and if I can't overbid such a stripling as he then I'm not wo'th a varden. We'll show that we know our business as well as one here and there."

His friends of the corporation did not specially respond. Henchard was less popular now than he had been when, nearly two years before, they had voted him to the chief magistracy on account of his amazing energy. While they had collectively profited by this quality of the corn-factor's, they had been made to wince individually on more than one occasion. So he went out of the hall and down the street alone.

Reaching home he seemed to recollect something with a sour satisfaction. He called Elizabeth-Jane. Seeing how he looked when she entered she appeared alarmed.

"Nothing to find fault with!" he said, observing her concern. "Only I want to caution you, my dear. That man Farfrae—it is about him. I've seen him talking to you two or three times—he danced with 'ee at the rejoicings, and came home with 'ee. Now, now—no blame to you. But just hearken: Have you made him any foolish promise—gone the least bit beyond sniff and snaff at all?"

"No. I have promised him nothing."

"Good. All's well that ends well. I particularly wish you not to see him again."

"Very well sir."

"You promise?"

She hesitated for a moment and then said "Yes—if you much wish it."

"I do. He's an enemy to our house."

When she had gone he sat down and wrote in a heavy hand to Farfrae thus:

"Sir,

"I make request that henceforth you and my stepdaughter be as strangers to each other. She on her part has promised to welcome no more addresses from you; and I trust therefore you will not attempt to force them upon her.

"M. Henchard."

One would almost have supposed Henchard to have had policy to see that no better *modus vivendi* could be arrived at with Farfrae than by encouraging him to become his son-in-law. But such a scheme for buying over a rival had nothing to recommend it to the mayor's headstrong faculties. With all domestic *finesse* of that kind he was hopelessly at variance. Loving a man or hating him, his diplomacy was as wrong-headed as a buffalo's; and his wife had not ventured to suggest the course which she, for many reasons, would have welcomed gladly.

Meanwhile Donald Farfrae had opened the gates of commerce on his own account at a spot on Durnover Hill—as far as possible from Henchard's stores, and with every intention of keeping clear of his former friend and employer's customers. There was, it seemed to the younger man, room for both of them and to spare. The town was small, but the corn and hay trade was proportionately large, and with his native sagacity he saw opportunity for a share of it. So determined was he to do nothing which should seem like trade-antagonism to the mayor that he refused his first customer—a large farmer of good repute—because Henchard and this man had dealt together within the preceding three months.

"He was once my friend," said Farfrae, "and it's not for me to take business from him. I am sorry to disappoint you, but I cannot hurt the trade of a man who's been so kind to me."

In spite of this praiseworthy course the Scotchman's trade increased. Whether it were that his northern energy was an over-mastering force among the easy-going Wessex worthies, or whether it was sheer luck, the fact remained that whatever he touched he prospered in. Like Jacob in Padan-Aram, he would no sooner humbly limit himself to the ring-straked and spotted exceptions of trade, than the ring-straked and spotted would multiply and prevail.

But most probably luck had little to do with it. Character is Fate, said Novalis, and Farfrae's character was just the reverse of Henchard's, who might not inaptly be described as Faust has been described—as a vehement, gloomy being, who had quitted the ways of vulgar men without light to guide him on a better way.

Farfrae duly received the request to discontinue attentions to Elizabeth-Jane. His acts of that kind had been so slight that the request was almost superfluous. Yet he had felt a considerable interest in her, and after some cogitation he decided that it would be as well to enact no Romeo part just then—for the young girl's sake no less than his own. Thus the incipient attachment was stifled down.

A time came when, avoid collision with his former friend as he might, Farfrae was compelled, in sheer self-defence, to close with Henchard in mortal commercial combat. He could no longer parry the fierce attacks of the latter by simple avoidance. As soon as their war of prices began everybody was interested, and some few guessed the end. It was, in some degree, Northern insight matched against Southron doggedness—the dirk against the cudgel—and Henchard's weapon was one which, if it did not deal ruin at the first or second stroke, left him afterwards well-nigh at his antagonist's mercy.

Almost every Saturday they encountered each other amid the crowd of farmers which thronged about the market-place in the weekly course of their business. Donald was always ready, and even anxious, to say a few friendly words; but the mayor invariably gazed stormfully past him, like one who had endured and lost on his account, and could in no sense forgive the wrong; nor did Farfrae's snubbed manner of perplexity at all appease him. The large farmers, corn-merchants, millers, auctioneers, and others, had each an official stall in the corn-market room, with their names painted thereon; and when to the familiar series of "Henchard," "Everdene," "Shiner," "Darton," and so on, was added one inscribed "Farfrae," in staring new letters, Henchard was stung into bitterness: like Bellerophon, he wandered away from the crowd, cankered in soul.

From that day Donald Farfrae's name was seldom mentioned in Henchard's house. If at breakfast or dinner Elizabeth-Jane's mother inadvertently alluded to her favourite's movements the girl would implore her by a look to be silent; and her husband would say, "What—are you, too, my enemy?"

XVIII

THERE came a shock which had been foreseen for some time by Elizabeth, as the box passenger foresees the approaching jerk from some channel across the highway.

Her mother was ill—too unwell to leave her room. Henchard, who treated her kindly except in moments of irritation, sent at once for the richest busiest doctor, whom he supposed to be the best. Bedtime came, and they burnt a light all night. In a day or two she rallied.

Elizabeth, who had been staying up, did not appear at breakfast on the second morning, and Henchard sat down alone. He was startled to see a letter for him from Jersey in a writing he knew too well and had expected least to behold again. He took it up in his hands and looked at it as at a picture, a vision, a vista of past enactments; and then he read it as an unimportant finale to conjecture.

The writer said that she at length perceived how impossible it would be for any further communications to proceed between them, now that his re-marriage had taken place. That such re-union had been the only straightforward course open to him she was bound to admit. "On calm reflection therefore," she went on, "I quite forgive you for landing me in such a dilemma, remembering that you concealed nothing before our ill-advised acquaintance; and that you really did set before me in your grim way the fact of there being a certain risk in intimacy with you, slight as it seemed to be after fifteen or sixteen years of silence on your wife's part. I thus look upon the whole as a misfortune of mine, and not a fault of yours.

"So that, Michael, I must ask you to overlook those letters with which I pestered you day after day in the heat of my feelings. They were written whilst I thought your conduct to me cruel; but now I know more particulars of the position you were in I see how inconsiderate my reproaches were.

"Now you will, I am sure, perceive that the one condition which will make any future happiness possible for me is that the past connection between our lives be kept secret outside this isle. Speak of it I know you will not; and I can trust you not to write of it. One safeguard more remains to be mentioned—that no writings of mine, or trifling articles belonging to me, should be left in your possession through neglect or forgetfulness. To this end may I request you to return to me any such you may have, particularly the letters written in the first abandonment of feeling.

"For the handsome sum you forwarded to me as a plaster to the wound I heartily thank you.

"I am now on my way to Bristol to see my only relative. She is rich, and I hope will do something for me. I shall return through Casterbridge, and Budmouth, where I shall take the packet-boat. Can you meet me with the letters and other trifles? I shall be in the coach which changes horses at the Antelope Hotel at half past five Wednesday evening; I shall be wearing a Paisley shawl with a red centre, and thus may easily be found. I should prefer this plan of receiving them to having them sent.

I remain still,
Yours ever,
"Lucetta."

Henchard breathed heavily. "Poor thing—better you had not known me! Upon my heart and soul, if ever I should be left in a position to carry out that marriage with thee, I *ought* to do it—I ought to do it, indeed!"

The contingency that he had in his mind was of course the death of Mrs. Henchard.

As requested, he sealed up Lucetta's letters, and put the parcel aside till the day she had appointed; this plan of returning them by hand being apparently a little *ruse* of the young lady for exchanging a word or two with him on past times. He would have preferred not to see her; but deeming that there could be no great harm in acquiescing thus far, he went at dusk and stood opposite the coach-office.

The evening was chilly, and the coach was late. Henchard crossed over to it while the horses were being changed; but there was no Lucetta inside or out. Concluding that something had happened to modify her arrangements he gave the matter up and went home, not without a sense of relief.

Meanwhile Mrs. Henchard was weakening visibly. She could not go out of doors any more. One day, after much thinking which seemed to distress her, she said she wanted to write something. A desk was put upon her bed with pen and paper, and at her request she was left alone. She remained writing for a short time, folded her paper carefully, called Elizabeth-Jane to bring a taper and wax, and then, still refusing assistance, sealed up the sheet, directed it, and locked it in her desk. She had directed it in these words:

"Mr. Michael Henchard. Not to be opened till Elizabeth-Jane's wedding-day."

The latter sat up with her mother to the utmost of her strength, night after night. To learn to take the universe seriously there is no quicker way than to watch—to be a "waker," as the country people call it. Between the hours at which the last toss-pot went by and the first sparrow shook himself the silence in Casterbridge—barring the rare sound of the watchman—was broken in Elizabeth's ear only by the time piece in the bedroom ticking frantically against the clock on the stairs; ticking harder and harder till it seemed to clang like a gong; and all this while the subtle-souled girl asking herself why she was born, why sitting in a room, and blinking at the candle; why things around her had taken the shape they wore in preference to every other possible shape; why they stared at her so helplessly, as if waiting for the touch of some wand that should release them from terrestrial constraint; what that chaos called consciousness, which spun in her at this moment like a top, tended to, and began in. Her eyes fell together; she was awake, yet she was asleep.

A word from her mother roused her. Without preface, and as the continuation of a scene already progressing in her mind, Mrs. Henchard said: "You remember the note sent to you and Mr. Farfrae—asking you to meet some one in Durnover Barton—and that you thought it was a trick to make fools of you?"

"Yes."

"It was not to make fools of you—it was done to bring you together. 'Twas I did it——"

"Why?" said Elizabeth with a start.

"I—wanted—you to marry Mr. Farfrae."

"Oh mother!" Elizabeth-Jane bent down her head so much that she looked quite into her own lap. But as her mother did not go on she said, "What reason?"

"Well—I had a reason. 'Twill out one day. I wish it could have been in my time! But there—nothing is as you wish it. Henchard hates him."

"Perhaps they'll be friends again," murmured the girl.

"I don't know—I don't know." After this her mother was silent, and dozed; and she spoke on the subject no more.

Some little time later on, Farfrae was passing Henchard's house on a Sunday morning, when he observed that the blinds were all down. He rang the bell so softly that it only sounded a single full note and a small one; and then he was informed that Mrs. Henchard was dead—just dead—that very hour.

At the town-pump there were gathered when he passed a few old inhabitants who came there for water whenever they had, as at present, spare time to fetch it, because it was purer from that original fount than from their own wells. Mrs. Cuxsom, who had been standing there for an indefinite time with her pitcher, was describing the incidents of Mrs. Henchard's death, as she had learnt them from the nurse.

"And she was as white as marble-stone," said Mrs. Cuxsom. "And likewise such a thoughtful woman too—ah, poor soul!—that 'a minded every little thing that wanted tending. 'Yes,' says she, 'when I'm gone, and my last breath's blowed, look in the top drawer o' the chest in the back room by the window, and you'll find all my coffin-clothes; a piece of flannel—that's to put under me, and the little piece is to put under my head; and my new stockings for my feet—they are folded alongside, and all my other things. And there's four ounce pennies, the heaviest I could find, a-tied up in bits of linen, for weights—two for my right eye and two for my left,' she said. 'And when you've used 'em, and my eyes don't open no more, bury the pennies, good souls, and don't ye go spending 'em, for I shouldn't like it. And open the windows as soon as I am carried out, and make it as cheerful as you can for Elizabeth-Jane.' "

"Ah, poor heart!"

"Well, and Martha did it, and buried the ounce pennies in the garden. But if ye'll believe words, that man Christopher Coney went and dug 'em up, and spent 'em at the Three Mariners.—'Faith,' he said, 'Why should death rob life o' fourpence? Death's not of such good report that we should respect en to that extent,' says he."

"'Twas a cannibal deed," deprecated her listeners.

"Gad, then, I won't quite hae it," said Solomon Longways. "I say it to-day, and 'tis a Sunday morning, and I wouldn't speak wrongfully for a zilver zixpence at such a time. I don't see noo harm in it. To respect the dead is sound doxology; and I wouldn't sell skellintons—leastwise respectable skellintons—to be varnished for natomies, except I were out o' work. But money is scarce, and throats get dry. Why *should* death rob life o' fourpence?—I say there was no treason in it."

"Well, poor soul; she's helpless to hinder that or anything now," answered Mother Cuxsom. "And all her shining keys will be took from her, and her cupboards opened; and little things 'a didn't wish seen, anybody will see; and her wishes and ways will all be as nothing!"

XIX

HENCHARD and Elizabeth sat conversing by the fire. It was three weeks after Mrs. Henchard's funeral; the candles were not lighted, and a restless, acrobatic flame, poised on a coal, called from the shady walls the smiles of all shapes that could respond—the old pier-glass, with gilt columns and huge entablature, the picture-frames, sundry knobs and handles, and the brass rosette at the bottom of each riband bell-pull on either side of the chimney-piece.

"Elizabeth, do you think much of old times?" said Henchard.

"Yes, sir; often," said she.

"Who do you put in your pictures of 'em?"

"Mother and father—nobody else hardly."

Henchard always looked like one bent on resisting pain when Elizabeth-Jane spoke of Richard Newson as "father." "Ah! I am out of all that, am I not," he said. . . . . . "Was Newson a kind father?"

"Yes, sir; very."

Henchard's face settled into an expression of stolid loneliness which gradually modulated into something softer. "Suppose I had been your real father?" he said. "Would you have cared for me as much as you cared for Richard Newson?"

"I can't think it," she said quickly. "I can think of no other as my father except my father."

Henchard's wife was dissevered from him by death; his friend and helper Farfrae by estrangement; Elizabeth-Jane by ignorance. It seemed to him that only one of them could possibly be recalled, and that was the girl. His mind began vibrating between the wish to reveal himself to her, and the policy of leaving well alone, till he could no longer sit still. He walked up and down, and then he came and stood behind her chair, looking down upon the top of her head. He could no longer restrain his impulse. "What did your mother tell you about me—my history?" he asked.

"That you were related by marriage."

"She should have told more—before you knew me. Then my task would not have been such a hard one . . . . . Elizabeth, it is I who am your father, and not Richard Newson. Shame alone prevented your wretched parents from owning this to you while both of 'em were alive."

The back of Elizabeth's head remained still, and her shoulders did not denote even the movements of breathing. Henchard went on: "I'd rather have your scorn, your fear, anything, than your ignorance; 'tis that I hate. Your mother and I were man and wife when we were young. What you saw was our second marriage. Your mother was too honest. We had thought each other dead—and—Newson became her husband."

This was the nearest approach Henchard could make to the full truth. As far as he personally was concerned he would have screened nothing; but he showed a respect for the young girl's sex and years worthy of a better man.

When he had gone on to give details which a whole series of slight and unregarded incidents in her past life strangely corroborated; when, in short, she believed his story to be true, she became greatly agitated, and turning round to the table, flung her face upon it weeping.

"Don't cry—don't cry," said Henchard, with vehement pathos, "I can't bear it, I won't bear it. I am your father; why should you cry? Am I so dreadful, so hateful to 'ee? Don't take against me, Elizabeth-Jane!" he cried, grasping her wet hand. "Don't take against me—though I was a drinking man once, and used your mother roughly—I'll be kinder to you than *he* was! I'll do anything, if you will only look upon me as your father!"

She tried to stand up and confront him trustfully; but she could not; she was troubled at his presence, like the brethren at the avowal of Joseph.

"I don't want you to come to me all of a sudden," said Henchard, in jerks, and moving like a great tree in a wind. "No, Elizabeth, I don't. I'll go away and not see you till to-morrow, or when you like; and then I'll show 'ee papers to prove my words. There, I am gone and won't disturb you any more. . . . 'Twas I that chose your name, my daughter; your mother wanted it Susan. There, don't forget 'twas I gave you your name." He went out at the door and shut her softly in, and she heard him go away into the garden. But he had not done. Before she had moved, or in any way recovered from the effect of his disclosure, he reappeared.

"One word more, Elizabeth," he said. "You'll take my surname now—hey? Your mother was against it; but it will be much more pleasant to me. 'Tis legally yours, you know. But nobody need know that. You shall take it as if by choice. I'll talk to my lawyer—I don't know the law of it exactly; but will you do this—let me put a few lines into the newspaper that such is to be your name?"

"If it is my name I must have it, mustn't I?" she asked.

"Well, well; usage is everything in these matters."

"I wonder why mother didn't wish it?"

"Oh, some whim of the poor soul's. Now get a bit of paper and draw up a paragraph as I shall tell you. But let's have a light."

"I can see by the firelight," she answered. "Yes—I'd rather."

"Very well."

She got a piece of paper, and bending over the fender, wrote at his dictation words which he had evidently got by heart from some advertisement or other—words to the effect that she, the writer, hitherto known as Elizabeth-Jane Newson, was going to call herself Elizabeth-Jane Henchard forthwith. It was done, and fastened up, and directed to the office of the *Casterbridge Chronicle.*

"Now," said Henchard, with the blaze of satisfaction that he always emitted when he had carried his point—though tenderness softened it this time—"I'll go upstairs, and hunt for some documents that will prove it all to you. But I won't trouble you with them till to-morrow. Good-night, my Elizabeth-Jane."

He was gone before the bewildered girl could realise what it all meant, or adjust her filial sense to the new centre of gravity. She was thankful that he had left her to herself for the evening, and sat down over the fire. Here she remained in silence, and wept—not for her mother now, but for the genial sailor Richard Newson, to whom she seemed doing a wrong.

Henchard, in the mean time, had gone upstairs. Papers of a domestic nature he kept in a drawer in his bedroom, and this he unlocked. Before turning them over he leant back and indulged in reposeful thought. Elizabeth was his at last, and she was a girl of such good sense and kind heart that she would be sure to like him. He was the kind of man to whom some human object for pouring out his heat upon—were it emotive or were it choleric—was almost a necessity. The craving of his heart for the re-establishment of this tenderest human tie had been great during his wife's lifetime, and now he had submitted to its mastery without reluctance and without fear. He bent over the drawer again, and proceeded in his search.

Among the other papers had been placed the contents of his wife's little desk, the keys of which had been handed to him at her request. Here was the letter addressed to him with the restriction, '*Not to be opened till Elizabeth-Jane's wedding-day.*'

Mrs. Henchard, though more patient than her husband, had been no practical hand at anything. In sealing up the sheet, which was folded and tucked in without an envelope in the old-fashioned way, she had overlaid the junction with a large mass of wax without the requisite under-touch of the same. The seal had cracked, and the letter was open. Henchard had no reason to suppose the restriction one of serious weight, and his feeling for his late wife had not been of the nature of deep respect. "Some trifling fancy or other of poor Susan's, I suppose," he said; and without curiosity he allowed his eyes to scan the letter:

"My Dear Michael,

"For the good of all three of us, I have kept one thing a secret from you till now. I hope you will understand why; I think you will; though perhaps you may not forgive me. But, dear Michael, I have done it for the best. I shall be in my grave when you read this, and Elizabeth-Jane will have a home. Don't curse me Mike—think of how I was situated. I can hardly write it, but here it is. Elizabeth-Jane is not your Elizabeth-Jane—the child who was in my arms when you sold me. No: she died three months after that, and this living one is my other husband's. I christened her by the same name we had given to the first, and she filled up the ache I felt at the other's loss.

Michael, I am dying, and I might have held my tongue; but I could not. Tell her husband of this, or not, as you may judge; and forgive, if you can, a woman you once deeply wronged; as she forgives you.

"Susan Henchard."

Her husband regarded the paper—— as if it were a window pane through which he saw for miles. His lip twitched, and he seemed to compress his frame, as if to bear better. His usual habit was not to consider whether destiny were hard upon him or not—the shape of his ideas in cases of affliction being simply a moody "I am to suffer I perceive,"—"This much scourging, then, is it, for me." But now through his passionate head there stormed this thought—that the blasting disclosure was what he had deserved.

His wife's extreme reluctance to have the girl's name altered from Newson to Henchard was now accounted for fully. It furnished another illustration of that honesty in dishonesty which had characterized her in other things.

He remained unnerved and purposeless for near a couple of hours; till he suddenly said, "Ah—I wonder if it is true!"

He jumped up in an impulse, kicked off his slippers and went with a candle to the door of Elizabeth-Jane's room, where he put his ear to the keyhole and listened. She was breathing profoundly. Henchard softly turned the handle, entered, and shading the light approached the bedside. Gradually bringing the light from behind a screening curtain he held it in such a manner that it fell slantwise on her face without shining on her eyes. He steadfastly regarded her features.

They were fair; his were dark. But this was an unimportant preliminary. In sleep there come to the surface buried genealogical facts, ancestral curves, dead men's traits, which the mobility of daytime animation screens and overwhelms. In the present statuesque repose of the young girl's countenance Richard Newson's was unmistakably reflected. He could not endure the sight of her, and hastened away.

Misery taught him nothing more than defiant endurance of it. His wife was dead, and the first impulse for revenge died with the thought that she was beyond him. He looked out at the night as at a fiend. Henchard, like all his kind, was superstitious, and he could not help thinking that the concatenation of events this evening had produced was the scheme of some sinister intelligence bent on punishing him. Yet they had developed naturally. If he had not revealed his past history to Elizabeth he would not have searched the drawer for papers, and so on. The mockery was, that he should have no sooner taught a girl to claim the shelter of his paternity than he discovered her to have no kinship with him.

This ironical sequence of things angered him like an impish trick from a fellow-creature. Like Prester John's his table had been spread, and infernal harpies had snatched up the food. He went out of the house, and moved sullenly onward down the pavement till he came to the bridge at the bottom of the high-street. Here he turned in upon a byepath on the river bank, skirting the north-eastern limits of the town.

These precincts embodied the mournful phases of Casterbridge life, as the south avenues embodied its cheerful moods. The whole way along here was sunless, even in summer time; in spring white frosts lingered here when other places were steaming with warmth; while in winter it was the seed-field of all the aches, rheumatisms, and torturing cramps of the year. The Casterbridge doctors must have pined away for want of sufficient nourishment but for the configuration of the landscape on the north-eastern side.

The river—slow, noiseless and dark—the Schwarzwasser of Casterbridge—ran beneath a low cliff, the two together forming a defence which had rendered walls and artificial earthworks on this side unnecessary. Here were ruins of a Franciscan priory, and a mill attached to the same, the water of which roared down a back-hatch like the voice of desolation. Above the cliff, and behind the river, rose a pile of buildings, and in the front of the pile a square mass cut into the sky. It was like a pedestal lacking its statue. This missing feature, without which the design remained incomplete, was, in truth, the corpse of a man; for the square mass formed the base of the gallows, the extensive buildings at the back being the county gaol. In the meadow where Henchard now walked the mob were wont to gather whenever an execution took place, and there to the tune of the roaring weir they stood and watched the spectacle.

The exaggeration which darkness imparted to the glooms of this region impressed Henchard more than he had expected. The lugubrious harmony of the spot with his domestic situation was too perfect for him, impatient of effects, scenes, and adumbrations. It reduced his heartburning to melancholy, and he exclaimed "Why the deuce did I come here!" He went on past the cottage in which the old local hangman had lived and died, in times before that calling was monopolized over all England by a single gentleman; and climbed up by a steep back lane into the town.

For the sufferings of that night, engendered by his bitter disappointment, he might well have been pitied. He was like one who half-fainted, and could neither recover nor complete the swoon. In words he could blame his wife, but not in his heart; and, had he obeyed the wise directions outside her letter this pain would have been spared him for long—possibly for ever, Elizabeth-Jane seeming to show no ambition to quit her safe and secluded maiden courses for the speculative path of matrimony.

The morning came after this night of unrest, and with it the necessity for a plan. He was far too self-willed to recede from a position, especially as it would involve humiliation. His daughter he had asserted her to be, and his daughter she should always think herself, no matter what hypocrisy it involved. But he was ill-prepared for the first step in this new situation. The moment he came into the breakfast-room Elizabeth advanced with open confidence to him and took him by the arm:

"I have thought and thought all night of it," she said frankly. "And I see that everything must be as you say. And I am going to look upon you as the father that you are, and not to call you Mr. Henchard any more. It is so plain to me now—indeed, father, it is; for of course you would not have done half the things you have done for me, and let me have my own way so entirely, and bought me presents, if I had only been your step-daughter. He—Mr. Newson—whom my poor mother married by such a strange mistake—[Henchard was glad that he had disguised matters here] was very kind—O so kind!"—she spoke with tears in her eyes—"but that is not the same thing as being one's real father after all . . . Now father, breakfast is ready," said she cheerfully.

Henchard bent and kissed her cheek. The moment and the act he had prefigured for weeks with a thrill of pleasure; yet it was no less than a miserable insipidity to him now that it had come. His reinstation of her mother had been chiefly for the girl's sake; and the fruition of the whole scheme was such dust and ashes as this.

XX

OF all the enigmas which ever confronted a girl there can have been seldom one like that which followed Henchard's announcement of himself to Elizabeth as her father. He had done it in an ardour and an agitation which had half carried the point of affection with her; yet, behold, from the next morning onwards his manner was constrained as she had never seen it before.

The coldness soon broke out into open chiding. One grievous failing of Elizabeth's was her occasional pretty and picturesque use of dialect words—those terrible marks of the beast to the truly genteel.

It was dinner-time—they never met except at meals—and she happened to say when he was rising from table, wishing to show him something, "If you'll bide where you be a minute, father, I'll get it."

" 'Bide where you be!' " he echoed sharply. "Good God, are you only fit to carry wash to a pig-trough, that ye use such words as those?"

She reddened with shame and sadness.

"I meant 'Stay where you are,' father," she said, in a low, humble voice. "I ought to have been more careful."

He made no reply, and went out of the room.

The sharp reprimand was not lost upon her, and in time it came to pass that for "fay" she said "succeed"; that she no longer spoke of "dumbledores" but of "humble bees"; no longer said of young men and women that they "walked together," but that they were "engaged"; that she grew to talk of "greggles" as "wild hyacinths"; that when she had not slept she did not quaintly tell the servants next morning that she had been "hag-rid," but that she had "suffered from indigestion."

These improvements, however, are somewhat in advance of the story. Henchard, being uncultivated himself, was the bitterest critic the fair girl could possibly have had of her own lapses—really slight now, for she read omnivorously. A gratuitous ordeal was in store for her in the matter of her handwriting. She was passing the dining-room door one evening, and had occasion to go in for something. It was not till she had opened the door that she knew the mayor was there in the company of a man with whom he transacted business.

"Here, Elizabeth-Jane," he said, looking round at her, "just write down what I tell you—a few words of an agreement for me and this gentleman to sign. I am a poor tool with a pen."

"Be jowned, and so be I," said the gentleman.

She brought forward blotting-book, paper, and ink, and sat down.

"Now then—'An agreement entered into this sixteenth day of October'—write that first."

She started the pen in an elephantine march across the sheet. It was a splendid round bold hand of her own conception, a style that would have stamped a woman as Minerva's own in more recent days. But other ideas reigned then: Henchard's creed was that proper young girls wrote ladies'-hand—nay, he believed that bristling characters were as innate and inseparable a part of refined womanhood as sex itself. Hence when, instead of scribbling, like the Princess Ida,

> In such a hand as when a field of corn
> Bows all its ears before the roaring East,

Elizabeth-Jane produced a line of chain-shot and sand-bags, he reddened in angry shame for her, and peremptorily saying "Never mind—I'll finish it," dismissed her there and then.

Her considerate disposition became a pitfall to her now. She was, it must be admitted, sometimes provokingly and unnecessarily willing to saddle herself with manual labours. She would go to the kitchen instead of ringing, "not to make Phœbe come up twice"; she went down on her knees, shovel in hand, when the cat overturned the coal-scuttle; moreover she would persistently thank the parlour maid for everything, till one day, as soon as the girl was gone from the room, Henchard broke out with, "Good God, why dostn't leave off thanking that girl as if she were a goddess-born! Don't I pay her a dozen pound a year to do things for 'ee?" Elizabeth shrank so visibly at the exclamation that he became sorry a few minutes after, and said that he did not mean to be rough.

These domestic exhibitions were the small protruding needle-rocks which suggested rather than revealed what was underneath. But his passion had less terror for her than his coldness. The increasing frequency of the latter mood told her the sad news that he disliked her with a growing dislike. The more interesting that her appearance and manners became under the softening influences which she could now command, and in her wisdom did command, the more she seemed to estrange him. Sometimes she caught him looking at her with a louring invidiousness that she could hardly bear. Not knowing his secret, it was a cruel mockery that she should for the first time excite his animosity when she had taken his surname.

But the most terrible ordeal was to come. Elizabeth had latterly been accustomed of an afternoon to present a cup of cider or ale and bread-and-cheese to Nance Mockridge, who worked in the yard, wimbling hay-bonds. Nance accepted this offering thankfully at first; afterwards as a matter of course. On a day when Henchard was on the premises he saw his stepdaughter enter the hay-barn on this errand; and, as there was no clear spot on which to deposit the provisions, she at once set to work arranging two trusses of hay as a table, Mockridge meanwhile standing with her hands on her hips, easefully looking at the preparations on her behalf.

"Elizabeth, come here!" said Henchard; and she obeyed.

"Why do you lower yourself so confoundedly?" he said with suppressed passion. "Haven't I told you o't fifty times? Hey? Making yourself a drudge for a common workwoman of such a character as hers! Why, ye'll disgrace me to the dust!"

Now these words were uttered loud enough to reach Nance inside the barn door, who fired up immediately at the slur upon her personal character. Coming to the door, she cried, regardless of consequences, "Come to that, Mr. Michael Henchard, I can let 'ee know she've waited on worse!"

"Then she must have had more charity than sense," said Henchard.

"Oh no, she hadn't. 'Twere not for charity but for hire; and at a public-house in this town."

"It is not true," cried Henchard indignantly.

"Just ask her," said Nance, folding her naked arms in such a manner that she could comfortably scratch her elbows.

Henchard glanced at Elizabeth-Jane, whose complexion, now pink and white from confinement, lost nearly all of the former colour. "What does this mean?" he said to her. "Anything, or nothing?"

"It is true," said Elizabeth-Jane. "But it was only——"

"Did you do it, or didn't you? Where was it?"

"At the Three Mariners; one evening for a little while, when we were staying there."

Nance glanced triumphantly at Henchard, and sailed into the barn; for, assuming that she was to be discharged on the instant, she had resolved to make the most of her victory. Henchard, however, said nothing about discharging her. Unduly sensitive on such points by reason of his own past, he had the look of one completely ground down to the last indignity. Elizabeth followed him to the house like a culprit; but when she got inside she could not see him. Nor did she see him again that day.

Convinced of the scathing damage to his local repute and position that must have been caused by such a fact, though it had never before reached his own ears, Henchard showed a positive distaste for the presence of this girl not his own, whenever he encountered her. He mostly dined with the farmers at the market-room of one of the two chief hotels, leaving her in utter solitude. Could he have seen how she made use of those silent hours he might have found reason to reverse his judgment on her quality. She read and took notes incessantly, mastering facts with painful laboriousness, but never flinching from her self-imposed task. She began the study of Latin, incited by the Roman characteristics of the town she lived in. "If I am not well-informed it shall be by no fault of my own!" she would say to herself through the tears that would occasionally glide down her peachy cheeks when she was fairly baffled by the portentous obscurity of many of these educational works.

Thus she lived on, a dumb, deep-feeling, great-eyed creature, construed by not a single contiguous being;

quenching with patient fortitude her incipient interest in Farfrae because it seemed to be one-sided, unmaidenly, and unwise. True that, for reasons best known to herself, she had, since Farfrae's dismissal, shifted her quarters from the back room affording a view of the yard (which she had occupied with such zest) to a front chamber overlooking the street; but as for the young man, whenever he passed the house he seldom or never turned his head.

Winter had almost come, and unsettled weather made her still more dependent upon indoor resources. But there were certain early winter days in Casterbridge—days of firmamental exhaustion which followed angry south-westerly tempests—when, if the sun shone, the air was like velvet. She seized on these days for her periodical visits to the spot where her mother lay buried—the still-used burial-ground of the old Roman-British city, whose curious feature was this its continuity as a place of sepulture. Mrs. Henchard's dust mingled with the dust of women who lay ornamented with glass hairpins and amber necklaces, and men who held in their mouths coins of Hadrian, Posthumus, and the Constantines.

Half past ten in the morning was about her hour for seeking this spot—a time when the town avenues were deserted as the avenues of Karnac. Business had long since passed down them into its daily cells, and Leisure had not arrived there. So Elizabeth-Jane walked and read, or looked over the edge of the book to think, and thus reached the churchyard.

There approaching her mother's grave she saw a solitary dark figure, in the middle of the gravel walk. This figure, too, was reading; but not from a book: the words which engrossed it being the inscription on Mrs. Henchard's tombstone. The personage was in mourning like herself, was about her age and size, and might have been her wraith or double, but for the fact that it was a lady much more beautifully dressed than she. Indeed, comparatively indifferent as Elizabeth-Jane was to dress, unless for some temporary whim or purpose, her eyes were arrested by the artistic perfection of the lady's appearance. Her gait, too, had a flexuousness about it, which seemed to avoid angularity of movement less from choice than from predisposition. It was a revelation to Elizabeth that human beings could reach this stage of external development —she had never suspected it. She felt all the freshness and grace to be stolen from herself on the instant by the neighbourhood of such a stranger. And this was in face of the fact that Elizabeth could now have been writ handsome, while the young lady was simply pretty.

Had she been envious she might have hated the woman; but she did not do that—she allowed herself the pleasure of feeling fascinated. She wondered where the lady had come from. The stumpy and practical walk of honest homeliness which mostly prevailed there, the two styles of dress thereabout, the simple and the mistaken, equally avouched that this figure was no Casterbridge woman's, even if a book in her hand resembling a guide-book had not also suggested it.

The stranger presently moved from the tombstone of Mrs. Henchard, and vanished behind the corner of the wall. Elizabeth went to the tomb herself; beside it were two footprints distinct in the soil, signifying that the lady had stood there a long time. She returned homeward, musing on what she had seen, as she might have mused on a rainbow or the Northern Lights, a rare butterfly or a cameo.

Interesting as things had been out of doors, at home it turned out to be one of her bad days. Henchard, whose two years' mayoralty was ending, had been made aware that he was not to be chosen to fill a vacancy in the list of aldermen; and that Farfrae was likely to become one of the Council. This caused the unfortunate discovery that she had played the waiting-maid in the town of which he was mayor to rankle in his mind yet more poisonously. He had learnt by personal inquiry at the time that it was to Donald Farfrae—that treacherous upstart—that she had thus humiliated herself. And though Mrs. Stannidge seemed to attach no great importance to the incident—the cheerful souls at the Three Mariners having exhausted its aspects long ago—such was Henchard's haughty spirit that the simple thrifty deed was regarded as little less than a social catastrophe by him.

Ever since the evening of his wife's arrival with her daughter there had been something in the air which had changed his luck. That dinner at the King's Arms with his friends had been Henchard's Austerlitz: he had had his successes since, but his course had not been upward. He was not to be numbered among the aldermen—that Peerage of burghers—as he had expected to be, and the consciousness of this soured him to-day.

"Well, where have you been?" he said to her, with off-hand laconism.

"I've been strolling in the Walks and churchyard, father, till I feel quite leery." She clapped her hand to her mouth, but too late.

This was just enough to incense Henchard after the other crosses of the day. "I *won't* have you talk like that!" he thundered. " 'Leery,' indeed. One would think you worked upon a farm. One day I learn that you lend a hand in public-houses. Then I hear you talk like a clodhopper. I'm burned, if it goes on, this house can't hold us two."

The only way of getting a single pleasant thought to go to sleep upon after this was by recalling the lady she had seen that day, and hoping she might see her again.

Meanwhile Henchard was sitting up, thinking over his jealous folly in forbidding Farfrae to pay his addresses to this girl who did not belong to him, when if he had allowed them to go on he might not have been encumbered with her. At last he said to himself with satisfaction as he jumped up and went to the writing-table: "Ah!—he'll think it means peace, and a marriage portion—not that I don't want my house to be troubled with her, and no portion at all." He wrote as follows:—

"Sir,—On consideration, I don't wish to interfere with your courtship of Elizabeth-Jane, if you care for her. I therefore withdraw my objection; excepting in this—that the business be not carried on in my house.—Yours,

"M. Henchard.

"Mr. Farfrae."

The morrow, being fairly fine, found Elizabeth-Jane again in the churchyard; but while looking for the lady she was startled by the apparition of Farfrae, who passed outside the gate. He glanced up for a moment from a pocket-book in which he appeared to be making figures as he went; whether or not he saw her he took no notice, and disappeared.

Unduly depressed by a sense of her own superfluity she thought he probably scorned her; and quite broken in spirit sat down on a bench. She fell into painful thought on her position, which ended with her saying quite loud, "Oh, I wish I was dead with dear mother!"

Behind the bench was a little promenade under the wall where people sometimes walked instead of on the gravel. The bench seemed to be touched by something; she looked round, and a face was bending over her, veiled, but still distinct—the face of the young woman she had seen yesterday.

Elizabeth-Jane looked confounded for a moment, knowing she had been overheard, though there was pleasure in her confusion. "Yes, I heard you," said the lady, in a vivacious voice, answering her look. "What can have happened?"

"I don't—I can't tell you," said Elizabeth, putting her hand to her face to hide a quick flush that had come.

There was no movement or word for a few seconds; then the girl felt that the young lady was sitting down beside her.

"I guess how it is with you," said the latter. "That was your mother." She waved her hand towards the tombstone. Elizabeth looked up at her as if inquiring of herself whether there should be confidence. The lady's manner was so desirous, so anxious, that the girl decided there should be confidence. "It was my mother," she said, "my only friend."

"But your father, Mr. Henchard. He is living?"

"Yes, he is living," said Elizabeth-Jane.

"Is he not kind to you!"

"I've no wish to complain of him."

"There has been a disagreement?"

"A little."

"Perhaps you were to blame?" suggested the stranger.

"I was—in many ways," sighed the meek Elizabeth. "I swept up the coals when the servant ought to have done it, and I said I was leery; and he was angry with me."

The lady seemed to warm towards her for that reply. "Do you know the impression your words give me?" she said ingenuously. "That he is a hot-tempered man—a little proud—perhaps ambitious; but not a bad man." Her anxiety not to condemn Henchard, while siding with Elizabeth, was curious.

"Oh no—certainly not *bad*," agreed the honest girl. "And he has not even been unkind to me till lately—since mother died. But it has been very much to bear while it has lasted! All is owing to my defects, I dare say; and my defects are owing to my history."

"What is your history?"

Elizabeth-Jane looked wistfully at her questioner. She found that her questioner was looking at her; turned her eyes down; and then seemed compelled to look back again. "My history is not gay or attractive," she said. "And yet I can tell it, if you really want to know."

The lady assured her that she did want to know; whereupon Elizabeth-Jane told the tale of her life as she understood it, which was in general the true one, except that the sale at the fair had no part therein.

Contrary to the girl's expectation her new friend was not shocked. This cheered her; and it was not till she thought of returning to that home in which she had been treated so roughly of late that her spirits fell.

"I don't know how to return!" she murmured. "I think of going away. But what can I do? Where can I go?"

"Perhaps it will be better soon," said her friend gently. "So I would not go far. Now what do you think of this—I shall soon want somebody to live in my house—partly as housekeeper, partly as companion—would you mind coming to me? But perhaps——"

"Oh yes!" cried Elizabeth with tears in her eyes. "I would indeed—I would do anything to be independent; for then perhaps my father might get to love me. But—ah!"

"What?"

"I am no accomplished person. And a companion to *you* must be that."

"Oh—not necessarily."

"Not? But I can't help using rural words sometimes, when I don't mean to."

"Never mind—I shall like to know them."

"And—oh, I know I shan't do!"—she cried with a distressful laugh. "I accidentally learned to write round-hand instead of ladies'-hand. And of course you want some one who can write that?"

"Well no."

"What—not necessary to write ladies'-hand?" cried the joyous Elizabeth.

"Not at all."

"But where do you live?"

"In Casterbridge—or rather I shall be living here, after twelve o'clock to-day."

Elizabeth expressed her astonishment.

"I have been staying at Budmouth for a few days while my house was getting ready. The house I am going into is that one they call High-Place Hall—the old stone one looking down the lane to the Market. Two or three rooms are fit for occupation, though not all; I sleep there to-night for the first time. Now will you think over my proposal, and meet me here the first fine day next week, and say if you are still in the same mind?"

Elizabeth, her eyes shining at this prospect of a change from an unbearable position, joyfully assented; and the two parted at the gate of the churchyard.

As a maxim glibly repeated from childhood remains practically unmarked till some mature experience enforces it, so did this High-Place Hall now for the first time really show itself to Elizabeth-Jane, though her ears had heard its name on a hundred occasions.

Her mind dwelt upon nothing else but the stranger, and the house, and her own chance of living there, all the rest of the day. In the afternoon she had occasion to pay a few bills in the town and do a little shopping; when she learnt that what was a new discovery to herself had become a common topic about the streets. High-Place Hall was undergoing repair; a lady was coming there to live shortly; all the shop-people knew it, and had already discounted the chance of her being a customer.

Elizabeth-Jane could, however, add a capping touch to information so new to her in the bulk. The lady, she said, had arrived that day.

When the lamps were lighted, and it was yet not so dark as to render chimneys, attics and roofs invisible, Elizabeth, almost with a lover's feeling, thought she would like to look at the outside of High-Place Hall. She went up the street in that direction.

The Hall, with its grey *façade* and parapet, was the only residence of its sort so near the centre of the town. It had, in the first place, the characteristics of a country mansion—birds'-nests in its chimneys, damp nooks where fungi grew, and irregularities of surface direct from Nature's trowel. At night the forms of passengers were patterned by the lamps in black shadows upon the pale walls.

This evening motes of straw lay around, and other signs of the premises having been in that lawless condition which accompanies the entry of a new tenant. The house was entirely of stone, and formed an example of dignity without great size. It was not altogether aristocratic, still less consequential, yet the old-fashioned stranger instinctively said, "Blood built it, and Wealth enjoys it," however vague his opinions of those accessories might be.

Yet as regards the enjoying it, the stranger would have been wrong, for until this very evening, when the new lady had arrived, the house had been empty for a year or two, while before that interval its occupancy had been irregular. The reason of its unpopularity was soon made manifest. Some of its rooms overlooked the market-place; and such a prospect from such a house was not considered desirable or seemly by its would-be occupiers.

Elizabeth's eyes sought the upper rooms, and saw lights there. The lady had obviously arrived. The impression that this woman of comparatively practised manner had made upon the studious girl's mind was so deep that she enjoyed standing under an opposite archway merely to think that the charming lady was inside the confronting walls, and to wonder what she was doing. Her admiration for the architecture of that front was entirely on account of the inmate it screened. Though for that matter the architecture deserved admiration, or at least study, on its own account. It was Palladian, and, like most architecture erected since the Gothic age, was a compilation rather than a design. But its reasonableness made it impressive. It was not rich, but rich enough. A timely consciousness of the ultimate vanity of human architecture, no less than of other human things, had prevented artistic superfluity.

Men had till quite recently been going in and out with parcels and packing-cases, rendering the door and hall within like a public thoroughfare. Elizabeth trotted through the open door in the dusk, but becoming alarmed at her own temerity, she went quickly out again by another which stood open in the lofty wall of the back court. To her surprise she found herself in one of the little-used alleys of the town. Looking round at the door which had given her egress, by the light of the solitary lamp fixed in the alley, she saw that it was arched and old—older even than the house itself. The door was studded, and the keystone of the arch was a mask. Originally the mask had exhibited a comic leer, as could still be discerned; but generations of Casterbridge boys had thrown stones at the mask, aiming at its open mouth; and the blows thereon had chipped off the lips and jaws as if they had been eaten away by disease. The appearance was so ghastly by the weakly lamp glimmer that she could not bear to look at it—the first unpleasant feature of her visit.

The position of the queer old door and the odd presence of the leering mask suggested one thing above all others as appertaining to the mansion's past history—intrigue. By the alley it had been possible to come unseen from all sorts of quarters in the town—the old play-house, the old bull-stake, the old cock-pit, the pool, wherein nameless infants had been used to disappear. High-Place Hall could boast of its conveniences undoubtedly.

She turned to come away in the nearest direction homeward, which was down the alley, but hearing footsteps approaching in that quarter, and having no great wish to be found in such a place at such a time, she quickly retreated. There being no other way out, she stood behind a brick pier till the intruder should have gone his ways.

Had she watched she would have been surprised. She would have seen that the pedestrian on coming up made straight for the arched doorway: that as he paused with his hand upon the latch the lamplight fell upon the face of Henchard.

But Elizabeth-Jane clung so closely to her nook that she discerned nothing of this. Henchard passed in as ignorant of her presence as she was ignorant of his identity, and disappeared in the darkness. Elizabeth came out a second time into the alley, and made the best of her way home.

Henchard's chiding, by begetting in her a nervous fear of doing anything definable as unlady-like, had operated thus curiously in keeping them unknown to each other at a critical moment. Much might have resulted from recognition—at the least a query on either side in one and the self-same form: What could he or she possibly be doing there?

Henchard, whatever his business at the lady's house, reached his own home only a few minutes later than Elizabeth-Jane. Her plan was to broach the question of leaving his roof this evening; the events of the day had urged her to the course. But its execution depended upon his mood, and she anxiously awaited his manner towards her. She found that it had changed. He showed no further tendency to be angry; he showed something worse. Absolute indifference had taken the place of irritability; and his coldness was such that it encouraged her to departure even more than hot temper could have done.

"Father, have you any objection to my going away?" she asked.

"Going away? No—none whatever. Where are you going?"

She thought it undesirable, and unnecessary, to say anything at present about her destination, to one who took so little interest in her. He would know that soon enough. "I have heard of an opportunity of getting more cultivated and finished, and being less idle," she answered with hesitation. "A chance of a place in a household where I can have advantages of study, and seeing refined life."

"Then make the best of it, in Heaven's name—if you can't get cultivated where you are."

"You don't object?"

"Object—I? Ho—no! Not at all." After a pause he said "But you won't have enough money for this lively scheme without help, you know? If you like I should be willing to make you an allowance, so that you be not bound to live upon the starvation wages refined folk are likely to pay 'ee."

She thanked him for this offer.

"It had better be done properly," he added, after a pause. "A small annuity is what I should like you to have—so as to be independent of me—and so that I may be independent of you. Would that please ye?"

"Certainly."

"Then I'll see about it this very day." He seemed relieved to get her off his hands by this arrangement, and as far as they were concerned the matter was settled. She now simply waited to see the lady again.

The day and the hour came; but a drizzling rain fell. Elizabeth-Jane, having now changed her orbit from one of gay independence to laborious self-help, thought the weather good enough for such declined glory as hers, if her friend would only face it—a matter of doubt. She went to the boot-room where her pattens had hung ever since her apotheosis; took them down, had their mildewed leathers blacked, and put them on as she had done in old times. Thus mounted, and with cloak and umbrella, she went off to the place of appointment—intending if the lady were not there, to call at the house.

One side of the churchyard—the side towards the weather—was sheltered by an ancient thatched mud wall, whose eaves overhung as much as one or two feet. At the back of the wall was a corn yard with its granary, and barns—the place wherein she had met Farfrae many months earlier. Under the projection of the thatch she saw a figure. The young lady had come.

Her presence so exceptionally substantiated the girl's utmost hopes that she almost feared her good fortune. Fancies find room in the strongest minds. Here in a churchyard old as civilization, in the worst of weathers, was a strange woman of curious fascinations never seen elsewhere: there might be some devilry about her presence. However, Elizabeth went on to the church tower, on whose summit the rope of a flag-staff rattled in the wind; and thus she came to the wall.

The lady had such a cheerful aspect in the drizzle that Elizabeth forgot her fancy. "Well?" said the lady, a little of the whiteness of her teeth appearing with the word through the black fleece that protected her face, "have you decided?"

"Yes, quite," said the other, eagerly.

"Your father is willing?"

"Yes."

"Then come along."

"When?"

"Now—as soon as you like. I had a good mind to send to you to come to my house, thinking you might not venture up here in the wind. But, as I like getting out of doors I thought I would come and see first."

"It was my own thought."

"That shows we shall agree. Then can you come to-day? My house is so hollow and dismal that I want some living thing there."

"I think I might be able to," said the girl reflecting.

Voices were borne over to them at that instant on the wind and raindrops from the other side of the wall. There came such words as "sacks," "quarters," "threshing," "tailing," "next Saturday's market," each sentence being disorganized by the gusts like a face in a cracked mirror. Both the women listened. "Who are those?" said the lady.

"One is my father. He rents that yard and barn."

The lady seemed to forget the immediate business in listening to the technicalities of the corn trade. At last she said suddenly, "Did you tell him where you were going to?"

"No."

"Oh—how was that?"

"I thought it safer to get away first—as he is so uncertain in his temper."

"Perhaps you are right . . . Besides I have never told you my name. It is Miss Templeman. . . . Are they gone—on the other side?"

"No. They have only gone up into the granary."

"Well—it is getting damp here. I shall expect you to-day—this evening say, at six."

"Which way shall I come, ma'am?"

"The front way—round by the gate. There is no other that I have noticed."

Elizabeth-Jane had been thinking of the door in the alley.

"Perhaps, as you have not mentioned your destination, you may as well keep silent upon it till you are clear off. Who knows but that he may alter his mind?"

Elizabeth-Jane shook her head. "On consideration I don't fear it," she said sadly. "He has grown quite cold to me."

"Very well. Six o'clock then."

When they had emerged upon the open road, and parted, they found enough to do in holding their bowed umbrellas to the wind. Nevertheless the lady looked in at the corn-yard gates as she passed them, and paused on one foot for a moment. But nothing was visible there save the ricks, and the hump-backed barn cushioned with moss, and the granary, rising against the church tower behind, where the smacking of the rope against the flag-staff still went on.

Now Henchard had not the slightest suspicion that

Elizabeth-Jane's movement was to be so prompt. Hence when, just before six, he reached home and saw a fly at the door from the King's Arms, and his step-daughter with all her little bags and boxes getting into it, he was taken by surprise.

"But you said I might go, father?" she explained through the carriage window.

"Said!—yes. But I thought you meant next month, or next year. 'Od seize it—you take time by the forelock. This, then, is how you be going to treat me for all my trouble about ye?"

"Oh, father—how can you speak like that? It is unjust of you!" she said with spirit.

"Well, well. Have your own way," he replied. He entered the house, and, seeing that all her things had not yet been brought down, went up to her room to look on. He had never been there since she had occupied it. Evidences of her care, of her endeavours for improvement, were visible all around, in the form of books, sketches, maps, and little arrangements for tasteful effects. Henchard had known nothing of these efforts. He gazed at them, turned suddenly about, and came down to the door.

"Look here," he said in an altered voice—he never called her by name now—"Don't 'ee go away from me. It may be I've spoke roughly to you—but I've been grieved beyond everything by you—there's something that caused it."

"By me?" she said with deep concern. "What have I done."

"I can't tell you now. But if you'll stop, and go on living as my daughter I'll tell you all in time."

But the proposal had come ten minutes too late. She was in the fly—was already, in imagination, at the house of the lady whose manner had such charms for her. "Father," she said as considerately as she could, "I think it best for us that I go on now. I need not stay long; I shall not be far away; and if you want me badly, I can soon come back again."

He nodded ever so slightly, as a receipt of her decision and no more. "You are not going far, you say. What will be your address, in case I wish to write to you. Or am I not to know?"

"O yes—certainly. It is only in the town—High-Place Hall."

"Where?" said Henchard, his face stilling.

She repeated the words. He neither moved nor spoke, and waving her hand to him in utmost friendliness she signified to the flyman to drive up the street.

XXII

WE go back for a moment to the preceding night, to account for Henchard's attitude.

At the hour when Elizabeth-Jane was contemplating her stealthy reconnoitring excursion to the abode of the lady of her fancy, he had been not a little amazed at receiving a letter by hand in Lucetta's well-known charactery. The self-repression, the resignation, of her previous communication had vanished from her mood: she wrote with some of the natural lightness which had marked her in their early acquaintance:

High-Place Hall.

"My Dear Mr. Henchard,

"Don't be surprised. It is for your good and mine, as I hope, that I have come to live at Casterbridge—for how long I cannot tell. That depends upon another; and he is a man, and a merchant, and a mayor, and one who has the first right to my affections.

"Seriously, *mon ami*, I am not so light-hearted as I may seem to be from this. I have come here in consequence of hearing of the death of your wife—whom you used to think of as dead so many years before! Poor woman, she seems to have been a sufferer, though uncomplaining, and though weak in intellect not an imbecile. I am glad you acted fairly by her. As soon as I knew she was no more, it was brought home to me very forcibly by my conscience that I ought to endeavour to disperse the shade which my *étourderie* flung over my name, by asking you to carry out your promise to me. I hope you are of the same mind, and that you will take steps to this end. As however I did not know how you were situated, or what had happened since our separation I decided to come and establish myself here before communicating with you.

"You probably feel as I do about this. I shall be able to see you in a day or two. Till then farewell. Yours,

"Lucetta.

"*P.S.*—I was unable to keep my appointment to meet you for a moment or two in passing through Casterbridge the other day. My plans were altered by a family event, which it will surprise you to hear of."

Henchard had already heard that High-Place Hall was being prepared for a tenant. He said with a puzzled air to the first person he encountered: "Who is coming to live at the Hall?"

"A lady of the name of Templeman, I believe sir," said his informant.

Henchard thought it over. "Lucetta is related to her, I suppose," he said to himself. "Yes—I must put her in her proper position, undoubtedly."

It was by no means with the oppression that would once have accompanied the thought that he regarded the moral necessity now: it was, indeed, with interest, if not warmth. His bitter disappointment at finding Elizabeth-Jane to be none of his, and himself a childless man, had left an emotional void in Henchard that he unconsciously craved to fill. In this frame of mind, though without strong feeling, he had strolled up the alley and into High-Place Hall by the postern at which Elizabeth had so nearly encountered him. He had gone on thence into the court, and inquired of a man whom he saw unpacking china from a crate, if Miss Le Sueur was living there. Miss Le Sueur had been the name under which he had known Lucetta—or "Lucette" as she had called herself at that time.

The man replied in the negative that that—Miss Templeman only had come. Henchard went away, concluding that Lucetta had not as yet settled in.

He was in this interested stage of the inquiry when he witnessed Elizabeth-Jane's departure the next day. On hearing her announce the address there suddenly took possession of him the strange thought that Lucetta and Miss Templeman were one and the same person, for he could recall that in her season of intimacy with him the name of the rich relative whom he had deemed somewhat a mythical personage had been given as Templeman. Though he was not a fortune-hunter, the possibility that Lucetta had been sublimed into a lady of means by some munificent testament on the part of this relative lent a charm to her image which it might not otherwise have acquired. He was getting on towards the dead level of middle age, when material things increasingly possess the mind.

But Henchard was not left long in suspense. Lucetta was

rather addicted to scribbling, as had been shown by the torrent of letters after the *fiasco* in their marriage arrangements, and hardly had Elizabeth gone away when another note came to the mayor's house from High-Place Hall.

"I am in residence," she said, "and comfortable, though getting here has been a wearisome undertaking. You probably know what I am going to tell you, or do you not? My good Aunt Templeman, the banker's widow, whose very existence you used to doubt, much more her affluence, has lately died; and bequeathed some of her property to me. I will not enter into details except to say that I have taken her name—as a means of escape from mine, and its wrongs.

"I am now my own mistress, and have chosen to reside in Casterbridge—to be tenant of High-Place Hall that at least you may be put to no trouble if you wish to see me. My first intention was to keep you in ignorance of the changes in my life till you should meet me in the street; but I have thought better of this.

"You probably are aware of my arrangement with your daughter, and have doubtless laughed at the—what shall I call it?—practical joke (in all affection) of my getting her to live with me. But my first meeting with her was purely an accident. Do you see, Michael, partly why I have done it?—why, to give you an excuse for coming here as if to visit *her*, and thus to form my acquaintance naturally. She is a dear good girl, and she thinks you have treated her with undue severity. You may have done so in your haste, but not deliberately, I am sure. As the result has been to bring her to me I am not disposed to upbraid you. In haste, yours always,

Lucetta."

The excitement which these announcements produced in Henchard's gloomy soul was to him most pleasurable. He sat over his dining-table long and dreamily, and by an almost mechanical transfer the sentiments which had run to waste since his estrangement from Elizabeth-Jane and Donald Farfrae gathered around Lucetta before they had grown dry. She was plainly in a very coming-on disposition for marriage. But what else could a poor woman be who had given her time and heart to him so thoughtlessly, at that former time, as to lose her credit by it? Probably conscience no less than affection had brought her here. On the whole he did not blame her.

"The artful little woman!" he said smiling (with reference

to Lucetta's adroit and pleasant manœuvre with Elizabeth-Jane).

To feel that he would like to see Lucetta was with Henchard to start for her house. He put on his hat and went. It was between eight and nine o'clock when he reached her door. The answer brought him was that Miss Templeman was engaged for that evening; but that she would be happy to see him the next day.

"That's rather like giving herself airs!" he thought. "And considering what we——" But, after all, she plainly had not expected him, and he took the refusal quietly. Nevertheless he resolved not to go next day. "These cursed women—there's not an inch of straight grain in 'em!" he said.

Let us follow the track of Mr. Henchard's thought as if it were a clue line, and view the interior of High-Place Hall on this particular evening.

On Elizabeth-Jane's arrival she had been phlegmatically asked by an elderly woman to go upstairs and take off her things. She had replied with great earnestness that she would not think of giving that trouble, and on the instant divested herself of her bonnet and cloak in the passage. She was then conducted to the first door on the landing, and left to find her way further alone.

The room disclosed was prettily furnished as a boudoir or small drawing-room, and on a sofa with two cylindrical pillows reclined a dark-haired, large-eyed, pretty woman, of unmistakably French extraction on one side or the other. She was probably some years older than Elizabeth, and had a sparkling light in her eye. In front of the sofa was a small table, with a pack of cards scattered upon it faces upward.

The attitude had been so full of abandonment that she bounded up like a spring on hearing the door open.

Perceiving that it was Elizabeth she lapsed into ease, and came across to her with a reckless skip that innate grace only prevented from being boisterous.

"Why, you are late," she said, taking hold of Elizabeth-Jane's hands.

"There were so many little things to put up."

"And you seem dead-alive and tired. Let me try to enliven you by some wonderful tricks I have learnt, to kill time. Sit there and don't move." She gathered up the pack of cards, pulled the table in front of her, and began to deal them rapidly, telling Elizabeth to choose some.

"Well, have you chosen?" she asked, flinging down the last card.

"No," stammered Elizabeth, arousing herself from a reverie. "I quite forgot, I was thinking of—you, and me—and how strange it is that I am here."

Miss Templeman looked at Elizabeth-Jane with interest, and laid down the cards. "Ah! never mind," she said. 'I'll lie here while you sit by me; and we'll talk."

Elizabeth drew up silently to the head of the sofa, but with obvious pleasure. It could be seen that though in years she was younger than her entertainer in manner and general vision she seemed more of the sage. Miss Templeman deposited herself on the sofa in her former flexuous position, and throwing her arm above her brow—somewhat in the pose of a well-known conception of Titian's—talked up at Elizabeth-Jane invertedly across her forehead and arm.

"I must tell you something," she said. "I wonder if you have suspected it. I have only been mistress of a large house and fortune a little while."

"Oh! only a little while?" murmured Elizabeth-Jane, her countenance slightly falling.

"As a girl I lived about in garrison towns and elsewhere with my father, till I was quite flighty and unsettled. He was an officer in the army. I should not have mentioned this had I not thought it best you should know the truth."

"Yes, yes." She looked thoughtfully round the room—at the little square piano with brass inlayings, at the window-curtains, at the lamp, at the fair and dark kings and queens on the card-table, and finally at the inverted face of Lucetta Templeman, whose large lustrous eyes had such an odd effect upside down.

Elizabeth's mind ran on acquirements to an almost morbid degree. "You speak French and Italian fluently, no doubt," she said. "I have not been able to get beyond a wretched bit of Latin yet."

"Well, for that matter, in my native isle speaking French does not go for much. It is rather the other way."

"Where is your native isle?"

It was with rather more reluctance that Miss Templeman said, "Jersey. There they speak French on one side of the street and English on the other, and a mixed tongue in the middle of the road. But it is a long time since I was there. Bath is where my people really belong to—though my ancestors in Jersey were as good as anybody in England. They were the Le Sueurs—an old family who have done great things in their time. I went back and lived there after my father's death. But I don't value such past matters, and am quite an English person in my feelings and tastes."

Lucetta's tongue had for a moment outrun her discretion. She had arrived at Casterbridge as a Bath lady, and there were obvious reasons why Jersey should drop out of her life. But Elizabeth had tempted her to make free, and a deliberately formed resolve had been broken.

It could not, however, have been broken in safer company. Lucetta's words went no further, and after this day she was so much upon her guard that there appeared no chance of her identification with the young Jersey woman who had been Henchard's dear comrade at a critical time. Not the least amusing of her safeguards was her resolute avoidance of a French word if one by accident came to her tongue more readily than its English equivalent. She shirked it with the suddenness of the weak Apostle at the accusation, "Thy speech bewrayeth thee!"

Expectancy sat visibly upon Lucetta the next morning. She dressed herself for Mr. Henchard, and restlessly awaited his call before mid-day: as he did not come she waited on through the afternoon. But she did not tell Elizabeth that the person expected was the girl's stepfather.

They sat in adjoining windows of the same room in Lucetta's great stone mansion, netting, and looking out upon the market, which formed an animated scene. Elizabeth could see the crown of her stepfather's hat among the rest beneath, and was not aware that Lucetta watched the same object with yet intenser interest. He moved about amid the throng, at this point lively as an anthill, elsewhere more reposeful, and broken up by stalls of fruit and vegetables. The farmers as a rule preferred the open *carrefour* for their transactions, despite its inconvenient jostlings and the danger from crossing vehicles, to the gloomy sheltered market-room provided for them. Here they surged on this one day of the week forming a little world of leggings, switches, and sample-bags; men of extensive stomachs, sloping like mountain sides; men whose heads in walking swayed as the trees in November gales; who in conversing varied their attitudes much, lowering themselves by spreading their knees, and thrusting their hands into the pockets of remote inner jackets. Their faces radiated tropical warmth; for though when at home their countenances varied with the seasons, their market-faces all the year round were glowing little fires.

All over-clothes here were worn as if they were an inconvenience, a hampering necessity. Some men were well-dressed; but the majority were careless in that respect, appearing in suits which were historical records of their wearer's deeds, sun-scorchings, and daily struggles for many years past. Yet many carried ruffled cheque-books in their pockets which regulated at the bank hard by a balance of never less than four figures. In fact, what these gibbous human shapes specially represented was ready money—money insistently ready—not ready next year like a nobleman's—often not merely ready at the bank like a professional man's—but ready in their large plump hands.

It happened that to-day there rose in the midst of them all two or three tall apple trees standing as if they grew on the spot; till it was perceived that they were held by men from the cider districts who came here to sell them, bringing the clay of their county on their boots. Elizabeth-Jane, who had often observed them, said, "I wonder if the same trees come every week?"

"What trees?" said Lucetta, absorbed in watching for Henchard.

Elizabeth replied vaguely, for an incident checked her. Behind one of the trees stood Farfrae, briskly discussing a sample-bag with a farmer. Henchard had come up, accidentally encountering the young man, whose face seemed to inquire, "Do we speak to each other?"

She saw her step father throw a shine into his eye which answered "No!" Elizabeth-Jane sighed.

"Are you particularly interested in anybody out there?" said Lucetta.

"Oh no," said her companion a quick red shooting over her face. Luckily Farfrae's figure was immediately covered by the appletree. Lucetta looked hard at her. "Quite sure?" she said.

"Oh yes," said Elizabeth-Jane.

Again Lucetta looked out. "They are all farmers I suppose?" she said.

"No. There's Mr. Bulge; he's a wine merchant: there's Benjamin Brownlet—a horse-dealer; and Kitson the pig-breeder; and Yopper the auctioneer; besides maltsters; and millers—and so on." Farfrae stood out quite distinctly now; but she did not mention him.

The Saturday afternoon slipped on thus desultorily. The market changed from the sample-showing hour to the idle hour before starting homewards, when tales were told. Henchard had not called on Lucetta, though he had stood so near. He must have been too busy, she thought. He would come on Sunday or Monday.

The days came, but not the visitor, though Lucetta repeated her dressing with scrupulous care. She was disheartened. It may at once be declared that Lucetta no longer bore towards Henchard all that warm allegiance which had characterized her in their first acquaintance: the then unfortunate issue of things had chilled pure love considerably. But there remained a conscientious wish to bring about her union with him, now that there was nothing to hinder it—to right her position, which in itself was a happiness to sigh for. With strong social reasons on her side why their marriage should take place, there had ceased to be any worldly reason on his why it should be postponed, since she had succeeded to fortune.

Tuesday was the great Candlemas fair. At breakfast she said to Elizabeth-Jane quite coolly: "I imagine your father may call to see you to-day? I suppose he stands close by in the market-place with the rest of the corn dealers?"

She shook her head. "He won't come."

"Why?"

"He has taken against me," she said in a husky voice.

"You have quarrelled more deeply than I know of?"

Elizabeth, wishing to shield the man she believed to be her father from any charge of unnatural dislike, said "Yes."

"Then where you are is, of all places, the one he will avoid?"

Elizabeth nodded sadly.

Lucetta looked blank, twitched up her lovely eyebrows and lip and burst into hysterical sobs. Here was a disaster—her ingenious scheme completely stultified!

"Oh, my dear Miss Templeman—what's the matter!" cried her companion.

"I like your company much!" said Lucetta, as soon as she could speak.

"Yes, yes—and so do I yours!" Elizabeth chimed in soothingly.

"But—but——" She could not finish the sentence which was, naturally, that if Henchard had such a rooted dislike for the girl as now seemed to be the case, Elizabeth-Jane would have to be got rid of—a disagreeable necessity.

A provisional resource suggested itself. "Miss Henchard—will you go on an errand for me as soon as breakfast is over?—Ah, that's very good of you. Will you go and order——" Here she enumerated several commissions at sundry shops, which would occupy Elizabeth's time for the next hour or two at least.

"And have you ever seen the Museum?"

Elizabeth-Jane had not.

"Then you should do so at once. You can finish the morning by going there. It is an old house in a back street—I forget where—but you'll find out—and there are crowds of interesting things—skeletons—teeth—old pots and pans—ancient boots and shoes—birds' eggs—all charmingly instructive. You'll be sure to stay till you get quite hungry."

Elizabeth hastily put on her things and departed. "I wonder why she wants to get rid of me to-day!" she said sorrowfully as she went. That her absence rather than her services or instruction was in request had been readily apparent to Elizabeth-Jane, simple as she seemed, and difficult as it was to attribute a motive for the desire.

She had not been gone ten minutes when one of Lucetta's servants was sent to Henchard's with a note. The contents were briefly

"Dear Michael,

"You will be standing in view of my house to-day for two or three hours in the course of your business, so do please call and see me. I am sadly disappointed that you have not come before, for can I help anxiety about my own equivocal relation to you—especially now my aunt's fortune has brought me more prominently before society? Your daughter's presence here may be the cause of your neglect; and I have therefore sent her away for the morning. Say you come on business—I shall be quite alone.   "Lucetta."

When the messenger returned her mistress gave directions that if a gentleman called he was to be admitted at once; and sat down to await results.

Sentimentally she did not much care to see him, his delays had wearied her; but it was necessary; and with a sigh she arranged herself picturesquely in the chair; first this way, then that; next so that the light fell over her head. Next she flung herself on the couch in the cyma-recta curve which so became her, and with her arm over her brow looked towards the door. This, she decided, was the best position after all; and thus she remained till a man's step was heard on the stairs. Whereupon Lucetta, forgetting her curve (for Nature was too strong for Art as yet) jumped up, and ran and hid herself behind one of the window curtains in a freak of timidity. In spite of the waning of passion the situation was an agitating one; she had not seen Henchard since his (supposed) temporary parting from her in Jersey.

She could hear the servant showing the visitor into the room, shutting the door upon him, and leaving as if to go and look for her mistress. Lucetta flung back the curtain with a nervous greeting. The man before her was not Henchard.

XXIII

A CONJECTURE that her visitor might be some other
person had, indeed, flashed through Lucetta's mind when she
was on the point of bursting out; but it was just too late to
recede.

He was years younger than the mayor of Casterbridge; fair,
fresh, and slenderly handsome. He wore genteel cloth leggings
with white buttons, polished boots with infinite lace-holes,
light cord breeches under a black velveteen coat and waistcoat;
and he had a silver-topped switch in his hand. Lucetta
blushed, and said with a curious mixture of pout and laugh on
her face—"Oh—I've made a mistake!"

The visitor, on the contrary, did not laugh half a wrinkle.
"But I'm very sorry!" he said in deprecating tones. "I came
and I inquired for Miss Henchard and they showed me up
heere, and in no case would I have caught ye so unmannerly
if I had known!"

"I was the unmannerly one," said she.

"But is it that I have come to the wrong house, madam?"
said Mr. Farfrae, blinking a little in his bewilderment and
nervously tapping his legging with his switch.

"Oh no sir—sit down. You must come and sit down now
you are here," replied Lucetta kindly, to relieve his embarrassment. "Miss Henchard will be here directly."

Now, this was not strictly true; but that something about
the young man—that Hyperborean crispness, stringency, and
charm as of a well braced musical instrument which had
awakened the interest of Henchard, and of Elizabeth-Jane, and
of the Three Mariners' jovial crew, at sight, made his
unexpected presence here attractive to Lucetta. He hesitated,
looked at the chair, thought there was no danger in it (though
there was), and sat down.

Farfrae's sudden entry was simply the result of Henchard's
permission to him to see Elizabeth, if he were minded to woo
her. At first he had taken no notice of Henchard's brusque
letter; but an exceptionally fortunate business transaction put

him on good terms with everybody and revealed to him that he could undeniably marry if he chose. Then who so pleasing, thrifty, and satisfactory in every way as Elizabeth-Jane? Apart from her personal recommendations, a reconciliation with his former friend Henchard would in the natural course of things flow from such a union. He therefore forgave the mayor his curtness; and this morning on his way to the fair he had called at her house, where he learnt that she was staying at Miss Templeman's. A little stimulated at not finding her ready and waiting—so fanciful are men—he hastened on to High-Place Hall, to encounter no Elizabeth but its mistress herself.

"The fair to-day seems a large one," she said when, by a natural deviation, their eyes sought the busy scene without. "Your numerous fairs and markets keep me interested. How many things I think of while I watch from here!"

He seemed in doubt how to answer, and the babble without reached them as they sat—voices as of wavelets on a lopping sea, one ever and anon rising above the rest. "Do you look out often?" he asked.

"Yes—very often."

"Do you look for any one you know?"

Why should she have answered as she did? "I look as at a picture merely. But," she went on, turning pleasantly to him, "I may do so now—I may look for you. You are always there, are you not? Ah—I don't mean it seriously! But it is amusing to look for somebody one knows in a crowd, even if one does not want him. It takes off the terrible oppressiveness of being surrounded by a throng and having no point of junction with it through a single individual."

"Ay—maybe you'll be very lonely, ma'am?"

"Nobody knows how lonely."

"But you are rich, they say?"

"If so, I don't know how to enjoy my riches. I came to Casterbridge thinking I should like to live here. But—I wonder if I shall."

"Where did ye come from, ma'am?"

"The neighbourhood of Bath."

"And I from near Edinboro'," he murmured. "It's better to stay at home, and that's true; but a man must live where his money is made. It is a great pity, but it's always so! . . . Yet I've done very well this year.—Oh yes," he went on with ingenuous enthusiasm, "You see that man with the drab kerseymere coat? I bought largely of him in the autumn when wheat was down, and then afterwards when it rose a little I sold off all I had. It brought only a small profit to me; while the farmers kept theirs, expecting higher figures, yes, though the rats were gnawing the ricks hollow. Just when I sold the markets went lower, and I bought up the corn of those who had been holding back, at less price than my first purchases. And then," cried Farfrae, impetuously, his face alight, "I sold it a few weeks after when it happened to go up again! And so, by contenting mysel' with small profits frequently repeated I soon made five hundred pounds—yes!—[bringing down his hand upon the table, and quite forgetting where he was]—while the others by keeping theirs in hand made nothing at all!"

Lucetta regarded him with a critical interest. He was quite a new type of person to her. At last his eye fell upon the lady's, and their glances met. "Ay now—I'm wearying you!" he exclaimed.

She said "No indeed," colouring a shade.

"What then?"

"Quite otherwise—you are most interesting."

It was now Farfrae who showed the modest pink.

"I mean all you Scotchmen," she added in hasty correction. "So free from Southern extremes. We common people are all one way or the other—warm or cold, passionate or frigid. You have both temperatures going on in you at the same time."

"But—how do you mean that? Ye were best to explain clearly ma'am."

"You are animated—then you are thinking of getting on. You are sad the next moment—then you are thinking of Scotland and friends."

"Yes—I think of home sometimes!" he said simply.

"So do I—as far as I can. But it was an old house where I was born, and they pulled it down for improvements, so I seem hardly to have any home to think of now." Lucetta did not add, as she might have done, that the house was in St. Helier, and not in Bath.

"But the mountains, and the mists, and the rocks, they are there? And don't they seem like home?"

She shook her head.

"They do to me—they do to me!" he murmured. And his mind could be seen flying away northwards. Whether its origin were national or personal it was quite true what Lucetta had said, that the curious double strands in Farfrae's thread of life—the commercial and the romantic—were very distinct at times. Like the colours in a variegated cord those contrasts could be seen intertwisted, yet not mingling.

"You are wishing you were back again," said she.

"Ah no, ma'am!" said Farfrae, suddenly recalling himself.

The fair without the windows was now raging thick and loud. It was the chief hiring-fair of the year, and differed quite from the market of a few days earlier. In substance it was a whitey-brown crowd flecked with white—this being the body of labourers waiting for places. The long bonnets of the women, like waggon-tilts, their cotton gowns and checked shawls, mixed with the carters' smockfrocks, for they too entered into the hiring. Among the rest, at the corner of the pavement, stood an old shepherd, who attracted the eyes of Lucetta and Farfrae by his stillness. He was evidently a chastened man. The battle of life had been a sharp one with him, for to begin with, he was a man of small frame. He was now so bowed by hard work and years that, approaching from behind, a person could hardly see his head. He had planted the stem of his crook in the gutter and was resting upon the bow, which was polished to silver brightness by the long friction of his hands. He had quite forgotten where he was, and what he had come for, his eyes being bent on the ground. A little way off negociations were proceeding which had reference to him, but he did not hear them, and there seemed to be passing through his mind pleasant visions of the hiring successes of his prime—when his skill laid open to him any farm for the asking.

The negociations were between a farmer from a distant county and the old man's son. In these there was a difficulty. The farmer would not take the crust without the crumb of the bargain, in other words, the old man without the younger; and the son had a sweetheart on his present farm; who stood by, waiting the issue with pale lips.

"I'm sorry to leave ye, Nelly," said the young man with emotion. "But, you see, I can't starve father, and he's out o' work at Lady Day. 'Tis only thirty-five mile."

The girl's lips quivered. "Thirty-five mile!" she murmured. "Ah—'tis enough! I shall never see 'ee again!" It was indeed a hopeless length of traction for Dan Cupid's magnet; for young men were young men at Casterbridge as elsewhere.

"Oh no, no—I never shall,' she insisted, when he pressed her hand; and she turned her face to Lucetta's wall to hide her weeping. The farmer said he would give the young man half an hour for his answer, and went away, leaving the group sorrowing.

Lucetta's eyes, full of tears, met Farfrae's. His too, to her surprise, were moist at the scene.

"It is very hard!" she said with strong feelings. "Lovers ought not to be parted like that; Oh, if I had my wish I'd let people live and love at their pleasure!"

"Maybe I can manage that they'll not be parted!" said Farfrae. "I want a young carter. And perhaps I'll take the old man too—yes, he'll not be very expensive, and doubtless he will answer ma pairrpose somehow!"

"Oh you are so good!" she cried, delighted. "Go and tell them—and let me know if you have succeeded."

Farfrae went out, and she saw him speak to the group. The eyes of all brightened—the bargain was soon struck. Farfrae returned to her immediately it was concluded.

"It is kind-hearted of you, indeed," said Lucetta. "For my part, I have resolved that all my servants shall have lovers if they want them. Do make the same resolve."

Farfrae looked more serious, waving his head a half-turn. "I must be a little stricter than that," he said.

"Why?"

"You are a—a thriving woman; and I am a struggling hay and corn merchant."

"I am a very unambitious woman."

"Ah well, I cannet explain!—I don't know how to talk to

ladies, ambitious or no, and that's true!" said Donald, with grave regret. "I try to be civil to a' folk—no more."

"I see you are as you say," replied she, sensibly getting the upper hand in these exchanges of sentiment. Under this revelation of insight Farfrae again looked out of the window into the thick of the fair.

Two farmers met and shook hands, and being quite near the window their remarks could be heard as others' had been.

"Have you seen young Mr. Farfrae this morning?" asked one. "He promised to meet me here at the stroke of twelve; but I've gone athwart and about the fair half a dozen times, and never a sign of him; though he's mostly a man to his word."

"I quite forgot the engagement!" murmured Farfrae.

"Now you must go," said she; "must you not?"

"Yes," he replied. But he still remained.

"You had better go," she urged. "You will lose a customer."

"Now, Miss Templeman, you will make me angry!" exclaimed Farfrae.

"Then suppose you don't go, but stay a little longer?"

He looked anxiously at the farmer who was seeking him, and who just then ominously walked across to where Henchard was standing, and he looked into the room and at her. "I like staying, but I fear I must go!" he said. "Business ought not to be neglected, ought it?"

"Not for a single minute."

"It's true! I'll come another time—if I may, ma'am?"

"Certainly," she said. "What has happened to us to-day is very curious."

"Something to think over when we are alone, it's like to be."

"Oh—I don't know that. It is commonplace, after all."

"No—I'll not say that! Oh no!"

"Well whatever it has been it is now over, and the market calls you to be gone."

"Yes—yes. Market—business! I wish there were no business in the warrld!"

Lucetta almost laughed—she would quite have laughed, but

that there was a little emotion going in her at the time. "How you change!" she said. "You should not change like this."

"I have never wished such things before," said the Scotchman with a simple, shamed, apologetic look for his weakness. "It is only since coming heere—and seeing you!"

"If that's the case you had better not look at me any longer. Dear me, I feel I have quite demoralized you!"

"But look or look not, I will see you in my thoughts? . . . Well—I'll go—thank you for the pleasure of this visit."

"Thank you for staying."

"Maybe I'll get into my market-mind when I've been out a few minutes," he murmured. "But I don't know—I don't know!"

As he went she said eagerly: "You may hear them speak of me in Casterbridge as time goes on. If they tell you I'm a coquette—which some may, because of the incidents of my life, don't believe it, for I am not."

"I swear I will not," he said fervidly.

Thus the two. She had enkindled the young man's enthusiasm till he was quite brimming with sentiment, while he, from merely affording her a new form of idleness, had gone on to wake her serious solicitude. Why was this? They could not have told.

Lucetta as a young girl would hardly have looked at a tradesman. But her ups-and-downs, capped by her indiscretions with Henchard, had made her uncritical as to station. In her poverty she had met with repulse from the society to which she had belonged, and she had no great zest for renewing an attempt upon it now. Her heart longed for some ark into which it could fly and be at rest. Rough or smooth she did not care, so long as it was warm.

Farfrae was shown out, it having entirely escaped him that he had called to see Elizabeth. Lucetta at the window watched him threading the maze of farmers and farmers' men. She could see by his gait that he was conscious of her eyes, and her heart went out to him for his modesty—pleaded with her sense of his unfitness that he might be allowed to come again. He entered the market-house, and she could see him no more.

Three minutes later, when she had left the window, knocks,

not of multitude but of strength, sounded through the house, and the waiting maid tripped up.

"The mayor," she said.

Lucetta had reclined herself and was looking dreamily through her fingers. She did not answer at once and the maid repeated the information with the addition, "And he's afraid he hasn't much time to spare, he says."

"Oh. Then tell him that as I have a headache I won't detain him to-day." The message was taken down, and she heard the door close.

Lucetta had come to Casterbridge to quicken Henchard's feelings with regard to her. She had quickened them, and now she was indifferent to the achievement.

Her morning view of Elizabeth-Jane as a disturbing element changed, and she no longer felt strongly the necessity of getting rid of the girl for her step-father's sake. When the young woman came in, sweetly unconscious of the turn in the tide, Lucetta went up to her, and said quite sincerely, "I'm so glad you've come. You'll live with me a long time, won't you?"

Elizabeth as a watch-dog to keep her father off—what a new idea. Yet it was not unpleasing. Henchard had neglected her all these days, after compromising her indescribably in the past. The least he could have done when he found himself free, and herself affluent, would have been to respond heartily and promptly to her invitation.

Her emotions rose, fell, undulated, filled her with wild surmise at their suddenness; and so passed Lucetta's experiences of that day.

XXIV

POOR Elizabeth-Jane, little thinking what her malignant star had done to blast the budding attentions she had won from Donald Farfrae, was glad to hear Lucetta's words about remaining.

For in addition to Lucetta's house being a home, that raking view of the market-place which it afforded had as much attraction for her as for Lucetta. The *carrefour* was like the regulation Open Place in spectacular dramas, where the incidents that occur always happen to bear on the lives of the adjoining residents. Farmers, merchants, dairymen, quacks, hawkers, appeared there from week to week, and disappeared as the afternoon wasted away. It was the node of all orbits.

From Saturday to Saturday was as from day to day with the two young women now. In an emotional sense they did not live at all during the intervals. Wherever they might go wandering on other days, on market day they were sure to be at home. Both stole sly glances out of the window at Farfrae's shoulders and poll. His face they seldom saw, for, either through shyness, or not to disturb his mercantile mood, he avoided looking towards their quarters.

Thus things went on, till a certain market morning brought a new sensation. Elizabeth and Lucetta were sitting at breakfast when a parcel containing two dresses arrived for the latter from London. She called Elizabeth from her breakfast, and entering her friend's bedroom Elizabeth saw the gowns spread out on the bed, one of a deep cherry colour, the other lighter—a glove lying at the end of each sleeve, a bonnet at the top of each neck, and parasols across the gloves, Lucetta standing beside the suggested human figure in an attitude of contemplation.

"I wouldn't think so hard about it," said Elizabeth, marking the intensity with which Lucetta was alternating the question whether this or that would suit best.

"But settling upon new clothes is so trying," said Lucetta. "You are that person" (pointing to one of the arrangements), "or you are *that* totally different person" (pointing to the other) "for the whole of the coming spring; and one of the two, you don't know which, may turn out to be very objectionable."

It was finally decided by Miss Templeman that she would be the cherry-coloured person at all hazards. The dress was pronounced to be a fit, and Lucetta walked with it into the front room, Elizabeth following her.

The morning was exceptionally bright for the time of year. The sun fell so flat on the houses and pavement opposite Lucetta's residence that they poured their brightness into her rooms. Suddenly after a rumbling of wheels there were added to this steady light a fantastic series of circling irradiations upon the ceiling, and the companions turned to the window. Immediately opposite a vehicle of strange description had come to a standstill, as if it had been placed there for exhibition.

It was the new-fashioned agricultural implement called a horse-drill, till then unknown, in its modern shape, in this part of the country, where the venerable seed-lip was still used for sowing as in the days of the Heptarchy. Its arrival created about as much sensation in the corn-market as a flying machine would create at Charing Cross. The farmers crowded round it, women drew near it, children crept under and into it. The machine was painted in bright hues of green, yellow, and red, and it resembled as a whole a compound of hornet, grasshopper, and shrimp, magnified enormously. Or it might have been likened to an upright musical instrument with the front gone. That was how it struck Lucetta. "Why, it is a sort of agricultural piano," she said.

"It has something to do with corn," said Elizabeth.

"I wonder who thought of introducing it here?"

Donald Farfrae was in the minds of both as the innovator, for though not a farmer he was closely leagued with farming operations. And as if in response to their thought he came up at that moment, looked at the machine, walked round it, and handled it as if he knew something about its make. The two watchers had inwardly started at his coming, and Elizabeth left the window, went to the back of the room, and stood as if absorbed in the panelling of the wall. She hardly knew that she had done this till Lucetta, animated by the conjunction of her new attire with the sight of Farfrae, spoke out: "Let us go and look at the instrument, whatever it is."

Elizabeth-Jane's bonnet and shawl were pitchforked on in a moment, and they went out. Among all the agriculturists gathering round the only appropriate possessor of the new machine seemed to be Lucetta, because she alone rivalled it in colour.

They examined it curiously; observing the rows of trumpet-shaped tubes one within the other, the little scoops, like revolving salt-spoons, which tossed the seed into the upper ends of the tubes that conducted it to the ground; till somebody said "Good morning Elizabeth-Jane." She looked up and there was her stepfather.

His greeting had been somewhat dry and thunderous, and Elizabeth-Jane, embarrassed out of her equanimity, stammered at random, "This is the lady I live with, father—Miss Templeman."

Henchard put his hand to his hat, which he brought down with a great wave till it met his body at the knee. Miss Templeman bowed. "I am happy to become acquainted with you, Mr. Henchard," she said. "This is a curious machine."

"Yes," Henchard replied; and he proceeded to explain it, and still more forcibly to ridicule it.

"Who brought it here?" said Lucetta.

"Oh, don't ask me, ma'am!" said Henchard. "The thing—why 'tis impossible it should act. 'Twas brought here by one of our machinists on the recommendation of a jumped-up jackanapes of a fellow who thinks——" His eye caught Elizabeth-Jane's imploring face, and he stopped, probably thinking that the suit might be progressing.

He turned to go away. Then something seemed to occur which his stepdaughter fancied must really be a hallucination of hers. A murmur apparently came from Henchard's lips in which she detected the words, "You refused to see me!" reproachfully addressed to Lucetta. She could not believe that they had been uttered by her stepfather; unless, indeed, they might have been spoken to one of the yellow-gaitered farmers near them. Yet Lucetta seemed silent; and then all thought of the incident was dissipated by the humming of a song, which sounded as though from the interior of the machine. Henchard had by this time vanished into the market-house, and both the women glanced towards the corn-drill. They could see behind it the bent back of a man who was pushing his head into the internal works to master their simple secrets. The hummed song went on:

> "'Tw—s on a s—m—r aftern—n
> A wee bef—re the s—n w—nt d—n,
> When Kitty wi' a braw n—w g—wn
> C—me ow're the h—lls to Gowrie."

Elizabeth-Jane had apprehended the singer in a moment, and looked guilty of she did not know what. Lucetta next recognised him, and, more mistress of herself, said archly, "The 'Lass of Gowrie' from the inside of a seed-drill—what a phenomenon!"

Satisfied at last with his investigation, the young man stood upright, and met their eyes across the summit.

"We are looking at the wonderful new drill," Miss Templeman said. "But practically it is a stupid thing—is it not?" she added, on the strength of Henchard's information.

"Stupid? Oh no!" said Farfrae, gravely. "It will revolutionise sowing heerabout. No more sowers flinging their seed about broadcast, so that some falls by the wayside, and some among thorns, and all that. Each grain will go straight to its intended place, and nowhere else whatever!"

"Then the romance of the sower is gone for good," observed Elizabeth-Jane, who felt herself at one with Farfrae in Bible reading at least. " 'He that observeth the wind shall not sow,'—so the Preacher said; but his words will not be to the point any more. How things change!"

"Ay—ay. . . . . . It must be so!" Donald admitted, his gaze fixing itself on a blank point far away. "But the machines are already very common in the east and north of England," he added apologetically.

Lucetta seemed to be outside this train of sentiment, her acquaintance with the Scriptures being somewhat limited. "Is the machine yours?" she asked of Farfrae.

"Oh no, ma'am," said he becoming embarrassed and deferential at the sound of her voice, though with Elizabeth-Jane he was quite at his ease. "No, no—I merely recommended that it should be got.'

In the silence which followed Farfrae appeared only conscious of her; to have passed from perception of Elizabeth into a brighter sphere of existence than she appertained to. Lucetta, discerning that he was much mixed that day—partly in his mercantile mood and partly in his romantic one, said gaily to him, "Well, don't forsake the machine for us," and went indoors with her companion.

The latter felt that she had been in the way, though why was unaccountable to her. Lucetta explained the matter somewhat by saying when they were again in the sitting room, "I had occasion to speak to Mr. Farfrae the other day, and so I knew him this morning."

Lucetta was very kind towards Elizabeth that day. Together they saw the market thicken, and in course of time thin away with the slow decline of the sun towards the upper end of the town, its rays taking the street endways and enfilading the long thoroughfare from top to bottom. The gigs and vans disappeared one by one till there was not a vehicle in the street. The time of the riding world was over; the pedestrian world held sway. Field labourers and their wives and children trooped in from the villages for their weekly shopping, and instead of a rattle of wheels and a tramp of horses ruling the sounds as earlier, there was nothing but the shuffle of many feet. All the implements were gone; all the farmers; all the moneyed class. The character of the town's trading had changed from bulk to multiplicity, and pence were handled now as pounds had been handled earlier in the day.

Lucetta and Elizabeth looked out upon this, for though it was night, and the street lamps were lighted, they had kept their shutters unclosed. In the faint blink of the fire they spoke more freely.

"Your father was distant with you," said Lucetta.

"Yes"; and having forgotten the momentary mystery of Henchard's seeming speech to Lucetta she continued, "It is because he does not think I am respectable. I have tried to be so more than you can imagine, but in vain! My mother's separation from my father was unfortunate for me. You don't know what it is to have shadows like that upon your life."

Lucetta seemed to wince. "I do not—of that kind precisely," she said; "but you may feel a—sense of disgrace—shame—in other ways."

"Have you ever had any such feeling?" said the younger innocently.

"Oh no," said Lucetta quickly. "I was thinking of—what happens sometimes when women get themselves in strange positions in the eyes of the world from no fault of their own."

"It must make them very unhappy afterwards."

"It makes them anxious; for might not other women despise them?"

"Not altogether despise them. Yet not quite like or respect them."

Lucetta winced again. Her past was by no means secure from investigation, even in Casterbridge. For one thing, Henchard had never returned to her the cloud of letters she had written and sent him in her first excitement. Possibly they were destroyed; but she could have wished that they had never been written.

The rencounter with Farfrae and his bearing towards Lucetta had made the reflective Elizabeth more observant of her brilliant and amiable companion. A few days afterwards, when her eyes met Lucetta's as the latter was going out, she somehow knew that Miss Templeman was nourishing a hope of seeing the attractive Scotchman. The fact was printed large all over Lucetta's cheeks and eyes to any one who could read her as Elizabeth-Jane was beginning to do. Lucetta passed on and closed the street door.

A seer's spirit took possession of Elizabeth, impelling her to sit down by the fire, and divine events so surely from data already her own that they could be held as witnessed. She followed Lucetta thus mentally—saw her encounter Donald somewhere as if by chance—saw him wear his special look when meeting women, with an added intensity because this one was Lucetta. She depicted his impassioned manner; beheld the indecision of both between their lothness to separate and their desire not to be observed; depicted their shaking of hands; how they probably parted with frigidity in their general contour and movements, only in the smaller features showing the spark of passion, thus invisible to all but themselves. This discerning silent witch had not done thinking of these things when Lucetta came noiselessly behind her, and made her start.

It was all true as she had pictured—she could have sworn it. Lucetta had a heightened luminousness in her eye over and above the advanced colour of her cheeks.

"You've seen Mr. Farfrae," said Elizabeth, demurely.

"Yes," said Lucetta. "How did you know?"

She knelt down on the hearth and took her friend's hands excitedly in her own. But after all she did not say when or how she had seen him or what he had said.

That night she became restless; in the morning she was feverish; and at breakfast time she told her companion that she had something on her mind—something which concerned a person in whom she was interested much. Elizabeth was earnest to listen and sympathise.

"This person—a lady—once admired a man much—very much," she said, tentatively.

"Ah," said Elizabeth-Jane.

"They were intimate—rather. He did not think so deeply of her as she did of him. But in an impulsive moment, purely out of reparation, he proposed to make her his wife. She agreed. But there was an unexpected hitch in the proceedings; though she had been so far compromised with him that she felt she could never belong to another man, as a pure matter of conscience, even if she should wish to. After that they were much apart, heard nothing of each other for a long time, and she felt her life quite closed up for her."

"Ah—poor girl!"

"She suffered much on account of him; though I should add that he could not altogether be blamed for what had happened. At last the obstacle which separated them was providentially removed; and he came to marry her."

"How delightful!"

"But in the interval she—my poor friend—had seen a man

she liked better than him. Now comes the point: Could she in honour dismiss the first?"

"A new man she liked better—that's bad!"

"Yes," said Lucetta, looking pained at a boy who was swinging the town-pump handle. "It is bad! Though you must remember that she was forced into an equivocal position with the first man by an accident—that he was not so well educated or refined as the second, and that she had discovered some qualities in the first that rendered him less desirable as a husband than she had at first thought him to be."

"I cannot answer," said Elizabeth-Jane, thoughtfully. "It is so difficult. It wants a Pope to settle that."

"You prefer not to, perhaps?" Lucetta showed in her appealing tone how much she leant on Elizabeth's judgment.

"Yes, Miss Templeman," admitted Elizabeth. "I would rather not say."

Nevertheless, Lucetta seemed relieved by the simple fact of having opened out the situation a little, and was slowly convalescent of her headache. "Bring me a looking-glass. How do I appear to people?" she said languidly.

"Well—a little worn," answered Elizabeth, eyeing her as a critic eyes a doubtful painting; fetching the glass she enabled Lucetta to survey herself in it, which Lucetta anxiously did.

"I wonder if I wear well, as times go," she observed after a while.

"Yes—fairly."

"Where am I worst?"

"Under your eyes—I notice a little brownness there."

"Yes. That is my worst place, I know.. How many years more do you think I shall last before I get hopelessly plain?"

There was something curious in the way in which Elizabeth, though the younger, had come to play the part of experienced sage in these discussions. "It may be five years," she said judicially. "Or, with a quiet life, as many as ten. With no love you might calculate on ten."

Lucetta seemed to reflect on this as on an unalterable, impartial verdict. She told Elizabeth-Jane no more of the past attachment she had roughly adumbrated as the experiences of a third person; and Elizabeth, who in spite of her philosophy was very tender-hearted, sighed that night in bed at the thought that her pretty, rich Lucetta did not treat her to the full confidence of names and dates in her confessions. For by the "she" of Lucetta's story Elizabeth had not been beguiled.

XXV

THE next phase of the supersession of Henchard in Lucetta's heart was an experiment in calling on her, performed by Farfrae with some apparent trepidation. Conventionally speaking he conversed with both Miss Templeman and her companion; but in fact it was rather that Elizabeth sat invisible in the room. Donald appeared not to see her at all, and answered her wise little remarks with civilly indifferent monosyllables, his looks and faculties hanging on the woman who could boast of a more Protean variety in her phases, moods, opinions and, alas, principles than could Elizabeth. Lucetta had persisted in dragging her into the circle; but she had remained like an awkward third point which that circle would not touch.

Susan Henchard's daughter bore up against the frosty ache of the treatment, as she had borne up under worse things, and contrived as soon as possible to get out of the inharmonious room without being missed. The Scotchman seemed hardly the same Farfrae who had danced with her, and walked with her, in a delicate poise between love and friendship—that period in the history of a love when alone it can be said to be unalloyed with pain.

She stoically looked from her bedroom window, and contemplated her fate as if it were written on the top of the church tower hard by. "Yes," she said at last bringing down her palm upon the sill with a pat: '*He* is the second man of that story she told me!"

All this time Henchard's smouldering sentiments towards Lucetta had been fanned into higher and higher inflammation by the circumstances of the case. He was discovering that the young woman, for whom he once felt a pitying warmth, which had been almost chilled out of him by reflection, was, when now qualified with a slight inaccessibility and a more matured beauty, the very being to make him satisfied with life. Day after day proved to him, by her silence, that it was no use to think of bringing her round by holding aloof; so he gave in, and called upon her again, Elizabeth-Jane being absent.

He crossed the room to her with a heavy tread of some awkwardness, his strong warm gaze upon her—like the sun beside the moon in comparison with Farfrae's modest look—and with something of a hail-fellow bearing, as indeed was not unnatural. But she seemed so transubstantiated by her change of position, and held out her hand to him in such cool friendship, that he became deferential, and sat down with a perceptible loss of power. He understood but little of fashion in dress, yet enough to feel himself inadequate in appearance beside her whom he had hitherto been dreaming of as almost his property. She said something very polite about his being good enough to call. This caused him to recover balance. He looked her oddly in the face, losing his awe.

"Why, of course I have called, Lucetta," he said. "What does that nonsense mean? You know I couldn't have helped myself if I had wished—that is, if I had any kindness at all. I've called to say that I am ready, as soon as custom will permit, to give you my name in return for your devotion, and what you lost by it, in thinking too little of yourself and too much of me; to say that you can fix the day or month, with my full consent, whenever in your opinion it would be seemly: you know more of these things than I."

"It is full early yet," she said evasively.

"Yes, yes—I suppose it is. But you know, Lucetta, I felt directly my poor ill-used Susan died, and when I could not bear the idea of marrying again, that after what had happened between us it was my duty not to let any unnecessary delay occur before putting things to rights. Still, I wouldn't call in a hurry, because—well you can guess how this money you've come into made me feel." His voice slowly fell; he was conscious that in this room his accents and manner wore a roughness not observable in the street. He looked about the room at the novel hangings and ingenious furniture with which she had surrounded herself. "Upon my life I didn't know such furniture as this could be bought in Casterbridge," he said.

"Nor can it," said she. "Nor will it till fifty years more of civilization have passed over the town. It took a waggon and four horses to get it here."

"H'm. It looks as if you were living on capital."

"Oh no, I am not."

"So much the better. But the fact is, your setting up like this makes my bearing towards you rather awkward."

"Why?"

An answer was not really needed, and he did not furnish one. "Well," he went on, "there's nobody in the world I would have wished to see enter into this wealth before you, Lucetta; and nobody, I am sure, who will become it more." He turned to her with congratulatory admiration so fervid that she shrank somewhat, notwithstanding that she knew him so well.

"I am greatly obliged to you for all that," said she, rather with an air of speaking ritual. The stint of reciprocal feeling was perceived, and Henchard showed chagrin at once—nobody was more quick to show that than he.

"You may be obliged or not for't. Though the things I say may not have the polish of what you've lately learnt to expect for the first time in your life, they are real, my lady Lucetta."

"That's rather a rude way of speaking to me," pouted Lucetta, with stormy eyes.

"Not at all!" replied Henchard hotly. "But there, there, I don't wish to quarrel with 'ee. I come with an honest proposal for silencing your Jersey enemies, and you ought to be thankful."

"How can you speak so!" she answered, firing quickly. "Knowing that my only crime was the indulging in a foolish girl's passion for you with too little regard for correctness, and that I was what *I* call innocent all the time they called me guilty, you ought not to be so cutting! I suffered enough at that worrying time, when you wrote to tell me of your wife's return, and my consequent dismissal, and if I am a little independent now, surely the privilege is due to me?"

"Yes, it is," he said. "But it is not by what is, in this life, but by what appears, that you are judged; and I therefore think you ought to accept me—for your own good name's sake. What is known in your native Jersey may get known here."

"How you keep on about Jersey. I am English."

"Yes, yes. Well, what do you say to my proposal?"

For the first time in their acquaintance Lucetta had the move; and yet she was backward. "For the present let things be," she said with some embarrassment. "Treat me as an acquaintance; and I'll treat you as one. Time will——" she stopped; and he said nothing to fill the gap for a while, there being no pressure of half-acquaintance to drive them into speech if they were not minded for it.

"That's the way the wind blows, is it?" he said at last grimly, nodding an affirmative to his own thoughts.

A yellow flood of reflected sunlight filled the room for a few instants. It was produced by the passing of a load of newly-trussed hay from the country in a waggon marked with Farfrae's name. Beside it rode Farfrae himself on horseback. Lucetta's face became—as a woman's face becomes when the man she loves rises upon her gaze like an apparition.

A turn of the eye by Henchard, a glance from the window, and the secret of her inaccessibility would have been revealed. But Henchard in estimating her tone was looking down so plumb-straight that he did not note the warm consciousness upon Lucetta's face.

"I shouldn't have thought it—I shouldn't have thought it of women!" he said emphatically by-and-by, rising and shaking himself into activity; while Lucetta was so anxious to divert him from any suspicion of the truth, that she asked him to be in no hurry. Bringing him some apples, she insisted upon paring one for him.

He would not take it. "No, no; such is not for me," he said drily, and moved to the door. At going out he turned his eye upon her.

"You came to live in Casterbridge entirely on my account," he said. "Yet now you are here you won't have anything to say to my offer!"

He had hardly gone down the staircase when she dropped upon the sofa, and jumped up again in a fit of desperation. 'I *will* love him!" she cried passionately; "as for *him*—he's hot-tempered and stern, and it would be madness to bind myself to him, knowing that. I won't be a slave to the past—I'll love where I choose!"

Yet having decided to break away from Henchard, one might have supposed her capable of aiming higher than Farfrae. But Lucetta reasoned nothing: she feared hard words from the people with whom she had been earlier associated; she had no relatives left; and with native lightness of heart took kindly to what fate offered.

Elizabeth-Jane, surveying the position of Lucetta between her two lovers from the crystalline sphere of a straightforward mind, did not fail to perceive that her father, as she called him, and Donald Farfrae became more desperately enamoured of her friend every day. On Farfrae's side it was the unforced passion of youth; on Henchard's the artificially stimulated coveting of maturer age.

The pain she experienced from the almost absolute obliviousness to her existence that was shown by the pair of them became at times half dissipated by her sense of its humorousness. When Lucetta had pricked her finger they were as deeply concerned as if she were dying: when she herself had been seriously sick or in danger they uttered a conventional word of sympathy at the news, and forgot all about it immediately. But, as regarded Henchard, this perception of hers also caused her some filial grief; she could not help asking what she had done to be neglected so, after the professions of solicitude he had made. As regarded Farfrae she thought, after honest reflection, that it was quite natural. What was she beside Lucetta?—as one of the "meaner beauties of the night" when the moon had risen in the skies.

She had learnt the lesson of renunciation, and was as familiar with the wreck of each day's wishes as with the diurnal setting of the sun. If her earthly career had taught her few book philosophies it had at least well-practised her in this. Yet her experience had consisted less in a series of pure disappointments than in a series of substitutions. Continually it had happened that what she had desired had not been granted her, and that what had been granted her she had not desired. So she viewed with an approach to equanimity the now cancelled days when Donald had been her undeclared lover, and wondered what unwished for thing Heaven might send her in place of him.

XXVI

IT chanced that on a fine spring morning Henchard and
Farfrae met in the chestnut walk which ran along the south
wall of the town. Each had just come out from his early
breakfast, and there was not another soul near. Henchard was
reading a letter from Lucetta, sent in answer to a note from
him, in which she made some excuse for not immediately
granting him a second interview that he had desired.

Donald had no wish to enter into conversation with his
former friend on their present constrained terms; neither
would he pass him in scowling silence. He nodded, and
Henchard did the same. They had receded from each other
several paces when a voice cried "Farfrae!" It was
Henchard's, who stood regarding him.

"Do you remember," said Henchard, as if it were the
presence of the thought and not of the man which made him
speak: "do you remember my story of that second woman—
who suffered for her thoughtless intimacy with me?"

"I do," said Farfrae.

"Do you remember my telling 'ee how it all began, and how
it ended?"

"Yes."

"Well: I have offered to marry her, now that I can; but she
won't marry me. Now what would you think of her—I put it
to you?"

"Well—ye owe her nothing more now," said Farfrae
heartily.

"It is true," said Henchard, and went on.

That he had looked up from a letter to ask his questions
completely shut out from Farfrae's mind all vision of Lucetta
as the culprit. Indeed, her present position was so different
from that of the young woman of Henchard's story as of itself
to be sufficient to blind him absolutely to her identity. As for
Henchard, he was reassured by Farfrae's words and manner
against a suspicion which had crossed his mind. They were
not those of a conscious rival.

Yet that there was rivalry by some one he was firmly persuaded. He could feel it in the air around Lucetta, see it in the turn of her pen. There was an antagonistic force in exercise, so that when he had tried to hang near her he seemed standing in a refluent current. That it was not innate caprice he was more and more certain. Her windows gleamed as if they did not want him; her curtains seemed to hang slily, as if they screened an ousting presence. To discover whose presence that was—whether really Farfrae's after all, or another's—he exerted himself to the utmost to see her again; and at length succeeded.

At the interview, when she offered him tea, he made it a point to launch a cautious inquiry if she knew Mr. Farfrae.

Oh yes, she knew him, she declared: she could not help knowing almost everybody in Casterbridge, living in such a gazebo over the centre and arena of the town.

"Pleasant young fellow," said Henchard.

"Yes," said Lucetta.

"We both know him," said kind Elizabeth-Jane, to relieve her companion's divined embarrassment.

There was a knock at the door; literally, three full knocks and a little one at the end.

"That kind of knock means half-and-half—somebody between gentle and simple," said the corn-merchant to himself. "I shouldn't wonder therefore if it is he." In a few seconds surely enough Donald walked in.

Lucetta was full of little fidgets and flutters which increased Henchard's suspicions without affording any special proof of their correctness. He was well-nigh ferocious at the sense of the queer situation in which he stood towards this woman. One who had reproached him for deserting her when calumniated, who had urged claims upon his consideration on that account, who had lived waiting for him, who at the first decent moment had come to ask him to rectify, by making her his, the false position into which she had placed herself for his sake: such she had been. And now he sat at her tea-table eager to gain her attention, and in his amatory rage feeling the other man present to be a villain, just as any young fool of a lover might feel.

They sat stiffly side by side at the darkening table, like some Tuscan painting of the two disciples supping at Emmaus. Lucetta, forming the third and haloed figure, was opposite them. Elizabeth-Jane, being out of the game, and out of the group, could observe all from afar, like the evangelist who had to write it down: that there were long spaces of taciturnity, when all exterior circumstance was subdued to the touch of spoons and china, the click of a heel on the pavement under the window, the passing of a wheelbarrow or cart and the whistling of the carter, the gush of water into householders' buckets at the town-pump opposite; the exchange of greetings among these neighbours, and the rattle of the yokes by which they carried off their evening supply.

"More bread and butter?" said Lucetta to Henchard and Farfrae equally, holding out between them a plateful of long slices. Henchard took a slice by one end and Donald by the other; each feeling certain he was the man meant, neither let go, and the slice came in two.

"Oh—I am so sorry!" cried Lucetta with a nervous titter. Farfrae tried to laugh; but he was too much in love to see the incident in any but a tragic light.

"How ridiculous of all three of them!" said Elizabeth to herself.

Henchard left the house with a ton of conjecture though without a grain of proof that the counter-attraction was Farfrae; and therefore he would not make up his mind. Yet to Elizabeth-Jane it was plain as the town-pump that Donald and Lucetta were incipient lovers. More than once, in spite of her care Lucetta had been unable to restrain her glance from flitting across into Farfrae's eyes like a bird to its nest. But Henchard was constructed upon too large a scale to discern such minutiæ as these by an evening light, which to him were as the notes of an insect that lie above the compass of the human ear.

But he was disturbed. And the sense of occult rivalry in suitorship was so much superadded to the palpable rivalry of their business lives. To the coarse materiality of that rivalry it added an inflaming soul.

The thus vitalized antagonism took the form of action by

Henchard sending for Jopp, the manager originally displaced by Farfrae's arrival. Henchard had frequently met this man about the streets, observed that his clothing spoke of neediness, heard that he lived in Mixen Lane—a back slum of the town, the *pis aller* of Casterbridge domiciliation—itself almost a proof that a man had reached a stage when he would not stick at trifles.

Jopp came after dark, by the gates of the store-yard, and felt his way through the hay and straw to the office where Henchard sat in solitude awaiting him.

"I am again out of a foreman," said the corn-factor. "Are you in a place?"

"Not so much as a beggar's, sir."

"How much do you ask?"

Jopp named his price, which was very moderate.

"When can you come?"

"At this hour and moment, sir," said Jopp, who, standing hands-pocketed at the street corner till the sun had faded the shoulders of his coat to scarecrow green, had regularly watched Henchard in the marketplace, measured him, and learnt him, by virtue of the power which the still man has in his stillness of knowing the busy one better than he knows himself. Jopp, too, had had a convenient experience; he was the only one in Casterbridge besides Henchard and the close-lipped Elizabeth who knew that Lucetta came truly from Jersey, and but proximately from Bath. "I know Jersey, too, sir," he said. "Was living there when you used to do business that way. Oh yes—have often seen ye there."

"Indeed! . . . . Very good. Then the thing is settled. The testimonials you showed me when you first tried for't are sufficient." That characters deteriorate in time of need possibly did not occur to Henchard. Jopp said Thank you, and stood more firmly, in the consciousness that at last he officially belonged to that spot.

"Now," said Henchard, digging his strong eyes into Jopp's face, "one thing is necessary to me, as the biggest corn and hay dealer in these parts. The Scotchman who's taking the town trade so bold into his hands must be cut out. D'ye hear? We two can't live side by side—that's clear and certain."

"I've seen it all," said Jopp.

"By fair competition I mean, of course," Henchard continued. "But as hard, keen, and unflinching as fair—rather more so. By such a desperate bid against him for the farmers' custom as will grind him into the ground—starve him out. I've capital, mind ye, and I can do it."

"I'm all that way of thinking," said the new foreman. Jopp's dislike of Farfrae as the man who had once usurped his place, while it made him a willing tool, made him, at the same time, commercially as unsafe a colleague as Henchard could have chosen.

"I sometimes think," he added, "that he must have some glass that he sees next year in. He has such a knack of making everything bring him fortune."

"He's deep beyond all honest men's discerning; but we must make him shallower. We'll under-sell him, and over-buy him, and so snuff him out."

They then entered into specific details of the process by which this would be accomplished, and parted at a late hour.

Elizabeth-Jane heard by accident that Jopp had been engaged by her step-father. She was so fully convinced that he was not the right man for the place that at the risk of making Henchard angry she expressed her apprehension to him when they met. But it was done to no purpose: Henchard shut up her argument with a sharp rebuff.

The season's weather seemed to favour their scheme. The time was in the years immediately before foreign competition had revolutionized the trade in grain, when still, as from the earliest ages, the wheat quotations from month to month depended entirely upon the home harvest. A bad harvest, or the prospect of one, would double the price of corn in a few weeks; and the promise of a good yield would lower it as rapidly. Prices were like the roads of the period, steep in gradient, reflecting in their phases the local conditions, without engineering, levellings, or averages.

The farmer's income was ruled by the wheat-crop within his own horizon, and the wheat-crop by the weather. Thus in person he became a sort of flesh-barometer, with feelers always directed to the sky and wind around him. The local atmosphere was everything to him; the atmospheres of other countries a matter of indifference. The people, too, who were not farmers, the rural multitude, saw in the god of the weather a more important personage than they do now. Indeed the feeling of the peasantry in this matter was so intense as to be almost unrealizable in these equable days. Their impulse was well-nigh to prostrate themselves in lamentation before untimely rains and tempests, which came as the Alastor of those households whose crime it was to be poor.

After Midsummer they watched the weather-cocks as men waiting in ante-chambers watch the lackey. Sun elated them; quiet rain sobered them; weeks of watery tempest stupefied them. That aspect of the sky which they now regard as disagreeable they then beheld as maleficent.

It was June, and the weather was very unfavourable. Casterbridge, being as it were the bell-board on which all the adjacent hamlets and villages sounded their notes, was decidedly dull. Instead of new articles in the shop windows those that had been rejected in the foregoing summer were brought out again; superseded reap-hooks, badly shaped rakes, shop-worn leggings, and time-stiffened water-tights reappeared, furbished up as near to new as possible.

Henchard, backed by Jopp, read a disastrous garnering and resolved to base his strategy against Farfrae upon that reading. But before acting he wished—what so many have wished—that he could know for certain what was at present only strong probability. He was superstitious—as such headstrong natures often are—and he nourished in his mind an idea bearing on the matter; an idea he shrank from disclosing even to Jopp.

In a lonely hamlet a few miles from the town—so lonely that what are called lonely villages were teeming by comparison—there lived a man of curious repute as a forecaster or weather-prophet. The way to his house was crooked and miry—even difficult in the present unpropitious season. One evening when it was raining so heavily that ivy and laurel resounded like distant musketry, and an out-door man could be excused for shrouding himself to his ears and eyes, such a shrouded figure on foot might have been perceived travelling in the direction of the hazel copse which dripped over the prophet's cot. The turnpike-road became a lane, the lane a cart-track; the cart-track a bridle-path, the bridle-path a footway, the footway overgrown. The solitary walker slipped here and there, and stumbled over the natural springes formed by the brambles, till at length he reached the house, which, with its garden was surrounded with a high dense hedge. The cottage, comparatively a large one, had been built of mud by the occupier's own hands, and thatched also by himself. Here he had always lived, and here it was assumed he would die.

He existed on unseen supplies; for it was an anomalous thing that while there was hardly a soul in the neighbourhood but affected to laugh at this man's assertions, uttering the formula "There's nothing in 'em," with full assurance on the surface of their faces, very few of them were unbelievers in their secret hearts. Whenever they consulted him they did it, "for a fancy." When they paid him they said, "Just a trifle for Christmas," or "Candlemas," as the case might be.

He would have preferred more honesty in his clients, and less sham ridicule; but fundamental belief consoled him for superficial irony. As stated, he was enabled to live: people supported him with their backs turned. He was sometimes astonished that men could profess so little and believe so much at his house when at church they professed so much and believed so little.

Behind his back he was called "Wide-oh," on account of his reputation: to his face "Mr." Fall.

The hedge of his garden formed an arch over the entrance, and a door was inserted as in a wall. Outside the door the tall traveller stopped, bandaged his face with a handkerchief as if he were suffering from toothache, and went up the path. The window-shutters were not closed, and he could see the prophet within, preparing his supper.

In answer to the knock Fall came to the door, candle in hand. The visitor stepped back a little from the light, and said, "Can I speak to 'ee?" in significant tones. The other's invitation to come in, was responded to by the country formula, "This will do, thank 'ee," after which the householder has no alternative but to come out. He placed the candle on the corner of the dresser, took his hat from a nail, and joined the stranger in the porch, shutting the door behind him.

"I've long heard that you can—do things of a sort?" began the other, repressing his individuality as much as he could.

"Maybe so, Mr. Henchard," said the weather-caster.

"Ah—why do you call me that?" asked the visitor with a start.

"Because it's your name. Feeling you'd come, I've waited for 'ee; and thinking you might be leery from your walk I laid two supper-plates: look ye here." He threw open the door and disclosed the supper-table, at which appeared a second chair, knife and fork, plate, and mug, as he had declared.

Henchard felt like Saul at his reception by Samuel; he remained in silence for a few moments, then throwing off the disguise of frigidity which he had hitherto preserved he said, "Then I have not come in vain. . . . Now, for instance, can ye charm away warts?"

"Without trouble."

"Cure the evil?"

"That I've done—with consideration—if they will wear the toad-bag by night as well as by day."

"Forecast the weather?"

"With labour and time."

"Then take this," said Henchard. " 'Tis a crown piece. Now, what is the harvest fortnight to be? When can I know?"

"I've worked it out already, and you can know at once." (The fact was that five farmers had already been there on the same errand from different parts of the country.) "By the sun, moon and stars, by the clouds, the winds, the trees and grass, the candle flame and swallows, the smell of the herbs; likewise by the cats' eyes, the ravens, the leeches, the spiders, and the dung-mixen, the last fortnight in August will be—rain and tempest."

"You are not certain, of course."

"As one can be in a world where all's unsure. 'Twill be more like living in Revelations this autumn than in England. Shall I sketch it out for 'ee in a scheme?"

"Oh no, no," said Henchard. "I don't altogether believe in forecasts, come to second thoughts on such. But I—'

"You don't—you don't—'tis quite understood," said Wide-oh, without a sound of scorn. "You have given me a crown because you've one too many. But won't you join me at supper, now 'tis waiting and all?"

Henchard would gladly have joined; for the savour of the stew had floated from the cottage into the porch with such appetizing distinctness that the meat, the onions, the pepper, and the herbs, could be severally recognized by his nose. But as sitting down to hob-and-nob there would have seemed to mark him too implicitly as the weathercaster's apostle he declined, and went his way.

The next Saturday Henchard bought grain to such an enormous extent that there was quite a talk about his purchases among his neighbours, the lawyer, the wine merchant, and the doctor; also on the next, and on all available days. When his granaries were full to choking, all the weathercocks of Casterbridge creaked and set their faces in another direction, as if tired of the south-west. The weather changed; the sunlight which had been like tin for weeks assumed the hues of topaz. The temperament of the welkin passed from the phlegmatic to the sanguine: an excellent harvest was almost a certainty; and as a consequence prices rushed down.

All these transformations, lovely to the outsider, to the wrong-headed corn-dealer were terrible. He was reminded of what he had well-known before, that a man might gamble upon the square green areas of fields as readily as upon those of a card-room.

Henchard had backed bad weather, and apparently lost. He had mistaken the turn of the flood for the turn of the ebb. His dealings had been so extensive that settlement could not long be postponed, and to settle he was obliged to sell off corn that he had bought only a few weeks before at figures higher by many shillings a quarter. Much of the corn he had never seen; it had not even been moved from the ricks in which it lay stacked miles away. Thus he lost heavily.

In the blaze of an early August day he met Farfrae in the market-place. Farfrae knew of his dealings (though he did not guess their intended bearing on himself) and commiserated him; for since their exchange of words in the South Walk they had been on stiffly speaking terms. Henchard, for the moment, appeared to resent the sympathy; but he suddenly took a careless turn.

"Ho, no, no!—nothing serious, man!" he cried with fierce gaiety. "These things always happen, don't they? I know it has been said that figures have touched me tight lately; but is that anything rare? The case is not so bad as folk make out perhaps. And dammy, a man must be a fool to mind the common hazards of trade!"

But he had to enter the Casterbridge Bank that day for reasons which had never before sent him there—and to sit a long time in the partners' room with a constrained bearing. It was rumoured soon after that much real property, as well as vast stores of produce, which had stood in Henchard's name in the town and neighbourhood, was actually the possession of his bankers.

Coming down the steps of the Bank he encountered Jopp. The gloomy transactions just completed within had added fever to the original sting of Farfrae's sympathy that morning, which Henchard fancied might be satire disguised. So that Jopp met with anything but a bland reception. The latter was in the act of taking off his hat to wipe his forehead, and saying "A fine hot day," to an acquaintance.

"You can wipe and wipe, and say 'A fine hot day' can ye!" cried Henchard in a savage undertone, imprisoning Jopp between himself and the bank wall. "If it hadn't been for your blasted advice it might have been a fine day enough. Why did ye let me go on, hey?—when a word of doubt from you or anybody would have made me think twice! For you can never be sure of weather till 'tis past."

"My advice, sir, was to do what you thought best."

"A useful fellow: and the sooner you help somebody else in that way the better!" Henchard continued his address to Jopp in similar terms till it ended in Jopp's dismissal there and then, Henchard turning upon his heel and leaving him.

"You shall be sorry for this sir; sorry as a man can be!" said Jopp, standing pale, and looking after the corn-merchant as he disappeared in the crowd of market-men hard by.

XXVII

IT was the eve of harvest. Prices being low Farfrae was buying. As was usual, after reckoning too surely on famine weather the local farmers had flown to the other extreme, and (in Farfrae's opinion) were selling off too recklessly—calculating with just a trifle too much certainty upon an abundant yield. So he went on buying old corn at its comparatively ridiculous price; for the produce of the previous year, though not large, had been of excellent quality.

When Henchard had squared his affairs in a disastrous way, and got rid of his burdensome purchases at a monstrous loss, the harvest began. There were three days of excellent weather, and then—"What if that curst conjuror should be right after all!" said Henchard.

The fact was that no sooner had the sickles begun to play than the atmosphere suddenly felt as if cress would grow in it without other nourishment. It rubbed people's cheeks like damp flannel when they walked abroad. There was a gusty high warm wind; isolated rain drops starred the window panes at remote distances; the sunlight would flap out like a quickly opened fan, throw the pattern of the window upon the floor of the room in a milky colourless shine, and withdraw as suddenly as it had appeared.

From that day and hour it was clear that there was not to be so successful an ingathering after all. If Henchard had only waited long enough he might at least have avoided loss though he had not made a profit. But the momentum of his character knew no patience. At this turn of the scales he remained silent. The movements of his mind seemed to tend to the thought that some power was working against him.

"I wonder," he asked himself with eerie misgiving; "I wonder if it can be that somebody has been roasting a waxen image of me, or stirring an unholy brew to confound me! I don't believe in such power; and yet—what if they should ha' been doing it!" Even he could not admit that the perpetrator, if any, might be Farfrae. These isolated hours of superstition came to Henchard in time of moody depression, when all his practical largeness of view had oozed out of him.

Meanwhile Donald Farfrae prospered. He had purchased in so depressed a market that the present moderate stiffness of prices was sufficient to pile for him a large heap of gold where a little one had been.

"Why—he'll soon be mayor!" said Henchard. It was indeed hard that the speaker should of all others have to follow the triumphal chariot of this man to the Capitol.

The rivalry of the masters was taken up by the men.

September night shades had fallen upon Casterbridge; the clocks had struck half-past eight, and the moon had risen. The streets of the town were curiously silent for such a comparatively early hour. A sound of jangling horse-bells and heavy wheels passed up the street. These were followed by angry voices outside Lucetta's house, which led her and Elizabeth-Jane to run to the windows and pull up the blinds.

The neighbouring market-house and Town-hall abutted against its next neighbour the church except in the lower story, where an arched thoroughfare gave admittance to a large square called Bull-Stake. A stone post rose in the midst, to which the oxen had formerly been tied for baiting with dogs to make them tender before they were killed in the adjoining shambles. In a corner stood the stocks.

The thoroughfare leading to this spot was now blocked by two four-horse waggons and horses, one laden with hay-trusses, the leaders having already passed each other and become entangled head to tail. The passage of the vehicles might have been practicable if empty; but built up with hay to the bedroom-windows as one was it was impossible.

"You must have done it a' purpose!" said Farfrae's waggoner. "You can hear my horses' bells half a mile such a night as this."

"If ye'd been minding your business instead of zwailing along in such a gawkhammer way, you would have zeed me!" retorted the wroth representative of Henchard.

However, according to the strict rule of the road it appeared that Henchard's man was most in the wrong; he therefore attempted to back into the High Street. In doing this the near hind-wheel rose against the churchyard wall, and the whole mountainous load went over, two of the four wheels rising in the air, and the legs of the thill horse.

Instead of considering how to gather up the load the two men closed in a fight with their fists. Before the first round was quite over Henchard came upon the spot, somebody having run for him.

Henchard sent the two staggering in contrary directions by collaring one with each hand, turned to the horse that was down, and extricated him after some trouble. He then enquired into the circumstances; and seeing the state of his waggon and its load began hotly rating Farfrae's man.

Lucetta and Elizabeth-Jane had by this time run down to the street corner, whence they watched the bright heap of new hay lying in the moon's rays, and passed and re-passed by the forms of Henchard and the waggoners. The women had witnessed what nobody else had seen—the origin of the mishap, and Lucetta spoke.

"I saw it all, Mr. Henchard," she cried; "and your man was most in the wrong!"

Henchard paused in his harangue and turned. "Oh—I didn't notice you Miss Templeman," said he. "My man in the wrong? Ah—to be sure; to be sure! But I beg your pardon notwithstanding. The other's is the empty waggon, and he must have been most to blame for coming on."

"No—I saw it too," said Elizabeth-Jane. "And I can assure you he couldn't help it."

"You can't trust *their* senses!" murmured Henchard's man.

"Why not?" asked Henchard sharply.

"Why, you see, sir, all the women side with Farfrae—being a damn young dand—of the sort that he is—one that creeps into a maid's heart like the giddying worm into a sheep's brain—making crooked seem straight to their eyes."

"But—do you know who that lady is you talk about in such a fashion? Do you know that I pay my attentions to her, and have for some time? Just be careful."

"Not I. I know nothing sir, outside eight shillings a week."

"And that Mr. Farfrae is well aware of it? He's sharp in trade, but he wouldn't do anything so underhand as what you hint at."

Whether because Lucetta heard this low dialogue, or not, her white figure disappeared from her doorway inward, and the door was shut before Henchard could reach it to converse with her further. This disappointed him, for he had been sufficiently disturbed by what the man had said to wish to speak to her more closely. While pausing the old constable came up.

"Just see that nobody drives against that hay and waggon to-night, Stubberd," said the corn-merchant. "It must bide till morning, for all hands are in the fields still. And if any coach or road-waggon wants to come along, tell 'em they must go round by the back street, and be hanged to 'em. . . . Any case to-morrow up in Hall?"

"Yes sir. One in number, sir."

"Oh—what's that?"

"A old flagrant female, sir, swearing and committing a nuisance in a horrible profane manner against the church wall, sir, as if 'twere no more than a pot-house! That's all, sir."

"Oh. The mayor's out o' town, isn't he?"

"He is, sir."

"Very well, then I'll be there. Don't forget to keep an eye on that hay. Good night t' 'ee."

During those moments Henchard had determined to follow up Lucetta, notwithstanding her elusiveness, and he knocked for admission.

The answer he received was an expression of Miss Templeman's sorrow at being unable to see him again that evening, because she had an engagement to go out.

Henchard walked away from the door to the opposite side of the street, and stood by his hay in a lonely reverie, the constable having strolled elsewhere, and the horses being removed. Though the moon was not bright as yet there were no lamps lighted, and he entered the shadow of one of the projecting jambs which formed the thoroughfare to Bull-stake; here he watched Lucetta's door.

Candlelights were flitting in and out of her bedroom, and it was obvious that she was dressing for the appointment, whatever the nature of that might be at such an hour. The lights disappeared; the clocks struck nine; and almost at the moment Farfrae came round the opposite corner and knocked. That she had been waiting just inside for him was certain, for she instantly opened the door herself. They went together by the way of a back lane westward, avoiding the front street; guessing where they were going, he determined to follow.

The harvest had been so delayed by the capricious weather that whenever a fine day occurred all sinews were strained to save what could be saved of the damaged crops. On account of the rapid shortening of the days the harvesters worked by moonlight. Hence to-night the wheat-fields abutting on two sides of the square formed by Casterbridge town were animated by the gathering hands. Their shouts and laughter had reached Henchard at the market-house while he stood there waiting, and he had little doubt from the turn which Farfrae and Lucetta had taken that they were bound for the spot.

Nearly the whole town had gone into the fields. The Casterbridge populace still retained the primitive habit of helping one another in time of need; and thus though the corn belonged to the farming section of the little community—that inhabiting the Durnover quarter—the remainder was no less interested in the labour of getting it home.

Reaching the top of the lane Henchard crossed the shaded avenue on the walls, slid down the green rampart, and stood amongst the stubble. The "stitches" or shocks rose like tents about the yellow expanse, those in the distance becoming lost in the moonlit hazes. He had entered at a point removed from the scene of immediate operations; but two others had entered at that place, and he could see them winding among the shocks. They were paying no regard to the direction of their walk, whose vague serpentining soon began to bear down towards Henchard. A meeting promised to be awkward, and he therefore stepped into the hollow of the nearest shock and sat down.

"You have my leave," Lucetta was saying gaily. "Speak what you like."

"Well then," replied Farfrae with the unmistakable inflection of the lover pure, which Henchard had never heard in full resonance on his lips before; "you are sure to be much sought after, for your position, wealth, talents, and beauty. But will ye resist the temptation to be one of those ladies with lots of admirers—aye—and be content to have only a homely one?"

"And he the speaker," said she laughing. "Very well, sir; what next?"

"Ah—I'm afraid that what I feel will make me forget my manners!"

"Then I hope you'll never have any, if you lack them only for that cause." . . . After some broken words which Henchard lost she added "Are you sure you won't be jealous?"

Farfrae seemed to assure her that he would not by taking her hand.

"You are convinced, Donald, that I love nobody else," she presently said. "But I should wish to have my own way in some things."

"In everything! What special thing did you mean?"

"If I wished not to live always in Casterbridge, for instance, upon finding that I should not be happy here?"

Henchard did not hear the reply; he might have done so and much more, but he did not care to play the eavesdropper. They went on towards the scene of activity, where the sheaves were being handed, a dozen a minute, upon the carts and waggons which carried them away.

Lucetta insisted on parting from Farfrae when they drew near the workpeople. He had some business with them, and though he entreated her to wait a few minutes she was inexorable and tripped off homeward alone.

Henchard thereupon left the field and followed her. His state of mind was such that on reaching Lucetta's door he did not knock, but opened it, and walked straight up to her sitting-room, expecting to find her there. But the room was empty, and he perceived that in his haste he had somehow passed her on the way hither. He had not to wait many minutes however, for he soon heard her dress rustling in the hall, followed by a soft closing of the door. In a moment she appeared.

The light was so low that she did not notice Henchard at first. As soon as she saw him she uttered a little cry, almost of terror.

"How can you frighten me so!" she exclaimed with a flushed face. "It is past ten o'clock, and you have no right to surprise me here at such a time."

"I don't know that I've not the right. At any rate I have the excuse. Is it so necessary that I should stop to think of manners and customs?"

"It is too late for propriety—and might injure me."

"I called an hour ago, and you would not see me, and I thought you were in when I called now. It is you, Lucetta, who are doing wrong. It is not proper in 'ee to throw me over like this. I have a little matter to remind you of, which you seem to forget."

She sank into a chair, and turned pale. "I don't want to hear it—I don't want to hear it!" she said through her hands, as he, standing close to the edge of her gown, began to allude to the Jersey days.

"But you ought to hear it," said he.

"It came to nothing; and through you. Then why not leave me the freedom that I gained with such sorrow! Had I found that you proposed to marry me for pure love I might have felt bound now. But I soon learnt that you had planned it out of mere charity—almost as an unpleasant duty—because I had nursed you, and compromised myself, and you thought you must repay me. After that I did not care for you so deeply as before."

"Why did you come here to find me, then?"

"I thought I ought to marry you for conscience' sake, since you were free, even though I—did not like you so well."

"And why then don't you think so now?"

She was silent. It was only too obvious that conscience had ruled well enough till new love had intervened, and usurped that rule. In feeling this she herself forgot for the moment her partially justifying argument—that having discovered Henchard's infirmities of temper, she had some excuse for not risking her happiness in his hands after once escaping them. The only thing she could say was "I was a poor girl then; and now my circumstances have altered so I am hardly the same person."

"That's true. And it makes the case awkward for me. But

I don't want to touch your money. I am quite willing that every penny of your property shall remain to your personal use. Besides, that argument has nothing in it. The man you are thinking of is no better than I."

"If you were as good as he you would leave me!" she cried passionately.

This unluckily aroused Henchard. "You cannot in honour refuse me," he said. "And unless you give me your promise this very night to be my wife, before a witness, I'll reveal our intimacy—in common fairness to other men!"

A look of resignation settled upon her. Henchard saw its bitterness; and had Lucetta's heart been given to any other man in the world than Farfrae he would probably have had pity upon her at that moment. But the supplanter was the upstart (as Henchard called him) who had mounted into prominence upon his shoulders, and he could bring himself to show no mercy.

Without another word she rang the bell, and directed that Elizabeth-Jane should be fetched from her room. The latter appeared, surprised in the midst of her lucubrations. As soon as she saw Henchard she went across to him dutifully.

"Elizabeth-Jane," he said taking her hand, "I want you to hear this." And turning to Lucetta: "Will you, or will you not, marry me?"

"If you—wish it, I must agree!"

"You say yes?"

"I do."

No sooner had she given the promise than she fell back in a fainting state.

"What dreadful thing drives her to say this, father, when it is such a pain to her?" asked Elizabeth, kneeling down by Lucetta. "Don't compel her to do anything against her will. I have lived with her, and know that she cannot bear much."

"Don't be a no'thern simpleton!" said Henchard drily. "This promise will leave him free for you, if you want him, won't it?"

At this Lucetta seemed to wake from her swoon with a start. "Him? Who are you talking about?" she said wildly.

"Nobody, as far as I am concerned," said Elizabeth firmly

"Oh—well. Then it is my mistake," said Henchard. "But the business is between me and Miss Templeman. She agrees to be my wife."

"But don't dwell on it just now," entreated Elizabeth, holding Lucetta's hand.

"I don't wish to, if she promises," said Henchard.

"I have, I have," groaned Lucetta, her limbs hanging like flails, from very misery and faintness. "Michael, please don't argue it any more!"

"I will not," he said. And taking up his hat he went away.

Elizabeth-Jane continued to kneel by Lucetta. "What is this?" she said. "You called my father Michael as if you knew him well? And how is it he has got this power over you that you promise to marry him against your will. Ah—you have many many secrets from me!"

"Perhaps you have some from me," Lucetta murmured with closed eyes, little thinking however, so unsuspicious was she, that the secret of Elizabeth's heart concerned the young man who had caused this damage to her own.

"I would not—do anything against you at all!" stammered Elizabeth, keeping in all signs of emotion till she was ready to burst. "I cannot understand how my father can command you so; I don't sympathize with him in it at all. I'll go to him and ask him to release you."

"No, no," said Lucetta. "Let it all be."

XXVIII

THE next morning Henchard went to the Town-hall below Lucetta's house, to attend petty sessions, being still a magistrate for the year by virtue of his late position as mayor. In passing he looked up at her windows, but nothing of her was to be seen.

Henchard as a Justice of the Peace may at first seem to be an even greater incongruity than Shallow and Silence themselves. But his rough and ready perceptions, his sledge-hammer directness, had often served him better than nice legal knowledge in dispatching such simple business as fell to his hands in this court. To-day, Dr. Chalkfield, the mayor for the year, being absent, the corn-merchant took the big chair, his eyes still abstractedly stretching out of the window to the ashlar front of High-Place Hall.

There was one case only, and the offender stood before him. She was an old woman of mottled countenance, attired in a shawl of that nameless tertiary hue which comes, but cannot be made—a hue neither tawny, russet, hazel, nor ash; a sticky black bonnet that seemed to have been worn in the country of the Psalmist where the clouds drop fatness, and an apron that had been white in times so comparatively recent as still to contrast visibly with the rest of her clothes. The steeped aspect of the woman as a whole showed her to be no native of the country-side, or even of a country-town.

She looked cursorily at Henchard and the second magistrate, and Henchard looked at her, with a momentary pause, as if she had reminded him indistinctly of somebody or something which passed from his mind as quickly as it had come. "Well, and what has she been doing?" he said, looking down at the charge-sheet.

"She is charged, sir, with the offence of disorderly female and nuisance," whispered Stubberd.

"Where did she do that?" said the other magistrate.

"By the church sir, of all the horrible places in the world!—I caught her in the act, your worship."

"Stand back then," said Henchard, "and let's hear what you've got to say."

Stubberd was sworn, the magistrate's clerk dipped his pen, Henchard being no note-taker himself, and the constable began:

"Hearing a illegal noise I went down the street at twenty five minutes past eleven, b. m., on the night of the fifth instinct, Hannah Dominy. When I had——"

"Don't go on so fast, Stubberd," said the clerk.

The constable waited, with his eyes on the clerk's pen, till the latter stopped scratching and said "yes." Stubberd continued: "When I had proceeded to the spot, I saw defendant at another spot, namely the gutter." He paused watching the point of the clerk's pen again.

"Gutter—yes Stubberd."

"Spot measuring twelve feet nine inches or thereabouts, from where I——" Still careful not to outrun the clerk's penmanship Stubberd pulled up again, for having got his evidence by heart it was immaterial to him whereabouts he broke off.

"I object to that!" spoke up the old woman. "'Spot measuring twelve feet nine or thereabouts from where I,' is not sound testimony."

The magistrates consulted, and the second one said that the bench was of opinion that twelve feet nine inches from a man on his oath was admissible. Stubberd with a suppressed gaze of victorious rectitude at the old woman, continued: "Was standing myself. She was wambling about quite dangerous to the thoroughfare, and when I approached to draw near she committed the nuisance, and insulted me."

"'Insulted me.' . . . . yes, what did she say?"

"She said, 'put away that dee lantern,' she says."

"Yes."

"Says she, 'Dost hear, old turmit-head? Put away that dee lantern. I have floored fellows a dee sight finer-looking than a dee fool like thee, you son of a bee, dee me if I haint,' she says."

"I object to that conversation!" interposed the old woman. "I was not capable enough to hear what I said, and what is said out of my hearing is not evidence."

There was another stoppage for consultation, a book was referred to, and finally Stubberd was allowed to go on again. The truth was that the old woman had appeared in court so many more times than the magistrates themselves, that they were obliged to keep a sharp look out upon their procedure. However, when Stubberd had rambled on a little further Henchard broke out impatiently "Come—we don't want to hear any more of them cust dees and bees! Say the words out like a man, and don't be so modest, Stubberd: or else leave it alone!" Turning to the woman, "Now then, have you any questions to ask him or anything to say?"

"Yes," she replied with a twinkle in her eye; and the clerk dipped his pen.

"Twenty years ago or thereabout I was selling furmity in a tent at Weydon Fair——"

" 'Twenty years ago.'—well, that's beginning at the beginning—suppose you go back to the Creation?" said the clerk, not without satire.

But Henchard stared, and quite forgot what was evidence and what was not.

"A man, and a woman with a little child came into my tent," the woman continued. "They sat down and had a basin apiece. Ah, Lord's my life! I was of a more respectable station in the world then than I am now, being a land-smuggler in a large way of business; and I used to season my furmity with rum for them who asked for't. I did it for the man; and then he had more, and more; till at last he quarrelled with his wife, and offered to sell her to the highest bidder. A sailor came in, and bid five guineas, and paid the money, and led her away. And the man who sold his wife in that fashion is the man sitting there in the great big chair." The speaker concluded by nodding her head at Henchard and folding her arms.

Everybody looked at Henchard. His face seemed strange, and in tint as if it had been powdered over with ashes. "We don't want to hear your life and adventures," said the second magistrate sharply, filling the pause which followed. "You've been asked if you've anything to say bearing on the case."

"That bears on the case. It proves that he's no better than I, and has no right to sit there in judgment upon me."

"'Tis a concocted story," said the clerk. "So hold your tongue."

"No—'tis true." The words came from Henchard. "'Tis as true as the light," he said slowly. "And upon my soul it does prove that I'm no better than she! And to keep out of any temptation to treat her hard for her revenge I'll leave her to you."

The sensation in the court was indescribably great. Henchard left the chair, and came out, passing through a group of people on the steps and outside that was much larger than usual; for it seemed that the old furmity dealer had mysteriously hinted to the denizens of the lane in which she had been lodging since her arrival, that she knew a queer thing or two about their great local man Mr. Henchard, if she chose to tell it. This had brought them hither.

"Why are there so many idlers round the Town-hall to-day?" said Lucetta to her servant when the case was over. She had risen late, and had just looked out of the window.

"Oh, please ma'am, 'tis this larry about Mr. Henchard. A woman has proved that before he became a gentleman he sold his wife for five guineas in a booth at a fair."

In all the accounts which Henchard had given her of the separation from his wife Susan for so many years, of his belief in her death, and so on, he had never clearly explained the actual and immediate cause of that separation. The story she now heard for the first time.

A gradual misery overspread Lucetta's face as she dwelt upon the promise wrung from her the night before. At bottom, then, Henchard was this. How terrible a contingency for a woman who should commit herself to his care.

During the day she went out to the Ring, and to other places, not coming in till nearly dusk. As soon as she saw Elizabeth-Jane after her return indoors she told her that she had resolved to go away from home to the seaside for a few days—to Port-Bredy. Casterbridge was so gloomy.

Elizabeth seeing that she looked wan and disturbed, encouraged her in the idea, thinking a change would afford her relief. She could not help suspecting that the gloom which seemed to have come over Casterbridge in Lucetta's eyes might be partially owing to the fact that Farfrae was away from home.

Elizabeth saw her friend depart for Port-Bredy, and took charge of High-Place Hall till her return. After two or three days of solitude and incessant rain Henchard called at the house. He seemed disappointed to hear of Lucetta's absence, and though he nodded with outward indifference he went away handling his beard with a nettled mien.

The next day he called again. "Is she come now?" he asked.

"Yes. She returned this morning," replied his stepdaughter. "But she is not indoors. She has gone for a walk along the turnpike-road to Port-Bredy. She will be home by dusk."

After a few words which only served to reveal his restless impatience he left the house again.

Elizabeth saw her friend for Port-Bredy, and took

AT this hour Lucetta was bounding along the road to Port-
Bredy just as Elizabeth had announced. That she had chosen
for her afternoon walk the road along which she had returned
to Casterbridge three hours earlier in a carriage, was curious—
if anything should be called curious in concatenations of
phenomena wherein each is known to have its accounting
cause. It was the day of the chief market—Saturday—and
Farfrae for once had been missed from his corn-stand in the
dealers' room. Nevertheless it was known that he would be
home that night—"for Sunday," as Casterbridge expressed
it.

Lucetta, in continuing her walk, had at length reached the
end of the ranked trees which bordered the highway in this
and other directions out of the town. This end marked a mile;
and here she stopped.

The spot was a vale between two gentle acclivities, and the
road, still adhering to its Roman foundation, stretched onward
straight as a surveyor's line till lost to sight on the most distant
ridge. There was neither hedge nor tree in the prospect now,
the road clinging to the stubbly expanse of corn-land like a
stripe to an undulating garment. Near her was a barn—the
single building of any kind within her horizon.

She strained her eyes up the lessening road, but nothing
appeared thereon—not so much as a speck. She sighed one
word—"Donald!" and turned her face to the town for retreat.

Here the case was different. A single figure was approaching
her—Elizabeth-Jane's.

Lucetta in spite of her loneliness seemed a little vexed.
Elizabeth's face, as soon as she recognized her friend, shaped
itself into affectionate lines while yet beyond speaking
distance. "I suddenly thought I would come and meet you,"
she said smiling.

Lucetta's reply was taken from her lips by an unexpected
diversion. A bye-road on her right hand descended from the
fields into the highway at the point where she stood, and down

the track a bull was rambling uncertainly towards her and Elizabeth, who, facing the other way, did not observe him.

In the latter quarter of each year cattle were at once the mainstay and the terror of families about Casterbridge and its neighbourhood, where breeding was carried on with Abrahamic success. The head of stock driven into and out of the town at this season to be sold by the local auctioneer was very large; and all these horned beasts, in travelling to and fro, sent women and children to shelter as nothing else could do. In the main the animals would have walked along quietly enough; but the Casterbridge tradition was that to drive stock it was indispensable that hideous cries coupled with Yahoo antics and gestures should be used, large sticks flourished, stray dogs called in, and in general everything done that was likely to infuriate the viciously disposed and terrify the mild. Nothing was commoner than for a householder, on going out of his parlour, to find his hall or passage full of little children, nursemaids, aged women, or a ladies' school, who apologized for their presence by saying "A bull passing down street from the sale."

Lucetta and Elizabeth regarded the animal in doubt, he meanwhile drawing vaguely towards them. It was a large specimen of the breed, in colour rich dun, though disfigured at present by splotches of mud about his seamy sides. His horns were thick and tipped with brass; his two nostrils like the Thames Tunnel as seen in the perspective toys of yore. Between them, through the gristle of his nose, was a stout copper ring, welded on, and irremovable as Gurth's collar of brass. To the ring was attached an ash staff about a yard long, which the bull with the motions of his head flung about like a flail.

It was not till they observed this dangling stick that the young women were really alarmed; for it revealed to them that the bull was an old one too savage to be driven, which had in some way escaped, the staff being the means by which the drover controlled him and kept his horns at arm's length.

They looked round for some shelter or hiding place, and thought of the barn hard by. As long as they had kept their eyes on the bull he had shown some deference in his manner of approach; but no sooner did they turn their backs to seek the barn than he tossed his head and decided to thoroughly terrify them. This caused the two helpless girls to run wildly, whereupon the bull advanced in a deliberate charge.

The barn stood behind a green slimy pond, and it was closed save as to one of the usual pair of doors facing them, which had been propped open by a hurdle-stake, and for this opening they made. The interior had been cleared by a recent bout of threshing, except at one end where there was a stack of dry clover. Elizabeth-Jane took in the situation. "We must climb up there," she said.

But before they had even approached it they heard the bull scampering through the pond without, and in a second he dashed into the barn, knocking down the hurdle-stake in passing; the heavy door slammed behind him; and all three were imprisoned in the barn together. The mistaken creature saw them, and stalked towards the end of the barn into which they had fled. The girls doubled, so adroitly, that their pursuer was against the wall when the fugitives were already half way to the other end. By the time that his length would allow him to turn and follow them thither they had crossed over; thus the pursuit went on, the hot air from his nostrils blowing over them like a sirocco, and not a moment being attainable by Elizabeth or Lucetta in which to open the door. What might have happened had their situation continued cannot be said; but in a few moments a rattling of the door distracted their adversary's attention, and a man appeared. He ran forward towards the leading-staff, seized it, and wrenched the animal's head as if he would snap it off. The wrench was in reality so violent that the thick neck seemed to have lost its stiffness and to become half-paralysed, whilst the nose dropped blood. The premeditated human contrivance of the nose-ring was too cunning for impulsive brute force, and the creature flinched.

The man was seen in the partial gloom to be large-framed and unhesitating. He led the bull to the door, and the light revealed Henchard. He made the bull fast without and re-entered to the succour of Lucetta; for he had not perceived Elizabeth, who had climbed on to the clover-heap. Lucetta was hysterical, and Henchard took her in his arms and carried her to the door.

"You—have saved me!" she cried, as soon as she could speak.

"I have returned your kindness," he responded tenderly. "You once saved me."

"How—comes it to be you—you?" she asked, not heeding his reply.

"I came out here to look for you. I have been wanting to tell you something these two or three days; but you have been away and I could not. Perhaps you cannot talk now?"

"Oh—no. Where is Elizabeth?"

"Here am I!" cried the missing one cheerfully; and without waiting for the ladder to be placed she slid down the face of the clover stack to the floor.

Henchard supporting Lucetta on one side, and Elizabeth-Jane on the other, they went slowly along the rising road. They had reached the top and were descending again when Lucetta, now much recovered, recollected that she had dropped her muff in the barn.

"I'll run back," said Elizabeth-Jane. "I don't mind it at all, as I am not tired as you are." She thereupon hastened down again to the barn, the others pursuing their way.

Elizabeth soon found the muff, such an article being by no means small at that time. Coming out she paused to look for a moment at the bull, now rather to be pitied with his bleeding nose, having perhaps rather intended a practical joke than a murder. Henchard had secured him by jamming the staff into the hinge of the barn-door, and wedging it there with a stake. At length she turned to hasten onward after her contemplation, when she saw a green and black gig approaching from the contrary direction, the vehicle being driven by Farfrae.

His presence here seemed to explain Lucetta's walk that way. Donald saw her, drew up, and was hastily made acquainted with what had occurred. At Elizabeth-Jane mentioning how greatly Lucetta had been jeopardized he exhibited an agitation different in kind no less than in intensity from any she had seen in him before. He became so absorbed in the circumstance that he scarcely had sufficient knowledge of what he was doing to think of helping her up beside him.

"She has gone on with Mr. Henchard, you say?" he inquired at last.

"Yes. He is taking her home. They are almost there by this time."

"And you are sure she can get home?"

Elizabeth-Jane was quite sure.

"Your step-father saved her!"

"Entirely."

Farfrae checked his horse's pace; she guessed why. He was thinking that it would be best not to intrude on the other two just now. Henchard had saved Lucetta, and to provoke a possible exhibition of her deeper affection for himself was as ungenerous as it was unwise.

The immediate subject of their talk being exhausted she felt more embarrassed at sitting thus beside her past lover; but soon the two figures of the others were visible at the entrance to the town. The face of the woman was frequently turned back, but Farfrae did not whip on the horse. When these reached the town walls Henchard and his companion had disappeared down the street; Farfrae set down Elizabeth-Jane, on her expressing a particular wish to alight there, and drove round to the stables at the back of his lodgings.

On this account he entered the house through his garden, and going up to his apartments found them in a particularly disturbed state, his boxes being hauled out upon the landing, and his bookcase standing in three pieces. These phenomena, however, seemed to cause him not the least surprise. "When will everything be sent up?" he said to the mistress of the house, who was superintending.

"I am afraid not before eight sir," said she. "You see we wasn't aware till this morning that you were going to move, or we could have been forwarder."

"A-well never mind, never mind!" said Farfrae cheerily. "Eight o'clock will do well enough if it be not later. Now, don't ye be standing here talking, or it will be twelve I doubt." Thus speaking he went out by the front door and up the street.

During this interval Henchard and Lucetta had had experiences of a different kind. After Elizabeth's departure for the muff the corn-merchant opened himself frankly, holding her hand within his arm, though she would fain have withdrawn it. "Dear Lucetta, I have been very very anxious to see you these two or three days," he said; "ever since I saw you last. I have thought over the way I got your promise that night. You said to me 'If I were a man I should not insist.' That cut me deep. I felt that there was some truth in it. I don't want to make you wretched, and to marry me just now would do that as nothing else could—it is but too plain. Therefore I agree to an indefinite engagement—to put off all thought of marriage for a year or two."

"But—but—can I do nothing of a different kind?" said Lucetta. "I am full of gratitude to you—you have saved my life. And your care of me is like coals of fire on my head. I am a monied person now. Surely I can do something in return for your goodness—something practical?"

Henchard remained in thought. He had evidently not expected this. "There is one thing you might do, Lucetta," he said. "But not exactly of that kind."

"Then of what kind is it?" she asked, with renewed misgiving.

"I must tell you a secret to ask it. . . . You may have heard that I have been unlucky this year. I did what I have never done before—speculated rashly; and I lost. That's just put me in a strait."

"And you would wish me to advance some money?"

"No no!" said Henchard almost in anger. "I'm not the man to sponge on a woman, even though she may be so nearly my own as you. No Lucetta; what you can do is this; and it would save me. My great creditor is Grower, and it is at his hands I shall suffer if at anybody's; while a fortnight's forbearance on his part would be enough to allow me to pull through. This may be got out of him in one way—that you would let it be known to him that you are my intended—that we are to be quietly married in the next fortnight.— Now stop, you haven't heard all!—Let him have this story, without, of course, any prejudice to the fact that the actual engagement between us is to be a long one. Nobody else need know: you could go with me to Mr. Grower, and just let me speak to 'ee before him as if we were on such terms. We'll ask him to keep it secret. He will willingly wait then. At the fortnight's end I shall be able to face him; and I can coolly tell him all is postponed between us for a year or two. Not a soul in the town need know how you've helped me. Since you wish to be of use, there's your way."

It being now what the people called the "pinking in," of the day, that is, the quarter-hour just before dusk, he did not at first observe the result of his own words upon her. "If it were anything else," she began; and the dryness of her lips was represented in her voice.

"But it is such a little thing!" he said with a deep reproach. "Less than you have offered—just the beginning of what you have so lately promised! I could have told him as much myself, but he would not have believed me."

"It is not because I won't—it is because I absolutely can't," she said with rising distress.

"You are provoking!" he burst out. "It is enough to make me force you to carry out at once what you have promised!"

"I cannot!" she insisted desperately.

"Why? When I have only within these few minutes released you from your promise to do the thing off-hand."

"Because——he was a witness!"

"Witness—of what?"

"If I must tell you——. Don't, don't upbraid me!"

"Well—let's hear what you mean?"

"Witness of my marriage—Mr. Grower was."

"Marriage?"

"Yes. With Mr. Farfrae. O Michael, I am already his wife. We were married this week at Port-Bredy. There were reasons against our doing it here. Mr. Grower was a witness, because he happened to be at Port-Bredy at the time."

Henchard stood as if idiotized. She was so alarmed at his silence that she murmured something about lending him sufficient money to tide over the perilous fortnight.

"Married him?" said Henchard at length. "My good—what, married him whilst—bound to marry me?"

"It was like this," she explained with tears in her eyes and quavers in her voice; "Don't—don't be cruel!—I loved him so much, and I thought you might tell him of the past—and that grieved me. And then, when I had promised you, I learnt of the rumour that you had—sold your first wife at a fair, like a horse or cow. How could I keep my promise after hearing that?—I could not risk myself in your hands; it would have been letting myself down to take your name after such a scandal. But I knew I should lose Donald if I did not secure him at once—for you would carry out your threat of telling him of our former acquaintance, as long as there was a chance of keeping me for yourself by doing so. But you will not do so now, will you Michael; for it is too late to separate us?"

The notes of St. Peter's bells in full peal had been wafted to them while she spoke; and now the genial thumping of the town band, renowned for its unstinted use of the drumstick, throbbed down the street.

"Then this racket they are making is on account of it, I suppose?" said he.

"Yes—I think he has told them, or else Mr. Grower has. . . . May I leave you now? My—he was detained at Port-Bredy to-day, and sent me on a few hours before him."

"Then it is *his wife's* life I have saved this afternoon."

"Yes—and he will be for ever grateful to you."

"I am much obliged to him. . . . . . Oh you false woman!" burst from Henchard. "You promised me!"

"Yes, yes. But it was under compulsion, and I did not know all your past——"

"And now I've a mind to punish you as you deserve! One word to this bran-new husband of how you courted me, and your precious happiness is blown to atoms."

"Michael—pity me, and be generous!"

"You don't deserve pity. You did; but you don't now."

"I'll help you to pay off your debt."

"A pensioner of Farfrae's wife—not I! Don't stay with me longer—I shall say something worse. Go home."

She disappeared under the trees of the south walk as the band came round the corner, awaking the echoes of every stock and some in celebration of her happiness. Lucetta took no heed, but ran up the back street and reached her own home unperceived.

FARFRAE'S words to his landlady had referred to the removal of his boxes and other effects from his late lodgings to Lucetta's house. The work was not heavy, but it had been much hindered on account of the frequent pauses necessitated by exclamations of surprise at the event, of which the good woman had been briefly informed by letter a few hours earlier.

At the last moment of leaving Port-Bredy Farfrae, like John Gilpin, had been detained by important customers, whom, even in the exceptional circumstances, he was not the man to neglect. Moreover there was a convenience in Lucetta arriving first at her house. Nobody there as yet knew what had happened; and she was best in a position to break the news to the inmates, and give directions for her husband's accommodation. He had therefore sent on his two-days' bride in a hired brougham, whilst he went across the country to a certain group of wheat and barley ricks a few miles off, telling her the hour at which he might be expected the same evening. This accounted for her trotting out to meet him after their separation of four hours.

By a strenuous effort, after leaving Henchard, she calmed herself in readiness to receive Donald at High-Place Hall when he came on from his lodgings. One supreme fact empowered her to this, the sense that, come what would, she had secured him. Half an hour after her arrival he walked in, and she met him with a relieved gladness which a month's perilous absence could not have intensified.

"There is one thing I have not done; and yet it is important," she said earnestly when she had finished talking about the adventure with the bull. "That is, broken the news of our marriage to my dear Elizabeth-Jane."

"Ah—and you have not," he said thoughtfully. "I gave her a lift from the barn homewards; but I did not tell her either; for I thought she might have heard of it in the town, and was keeping back her congratulations from shyness, and all that."

"She can hardly have heard of it. But I'll find out—I'll go

to her now. And Donald—you don't mind her living on with me just the same as before? She is so quiet and unassuming."

"Oh no—indeed I don't," Farfrae answered with, perhaps, a faint awkwardness. "But I wonder if she would care to?"

"Oh yes," said Lucetta eagerly. "I am sure she would like to. Besides, poor thing, she has no other home."

Farfrae looked at her, and saw that she did not suspect the secret of her more reserved friend. He liked her all the better for the blindness. "Arrange as you like with her by all means," he said. "It is I who have come to your house—not you to mine."

"I'll run and speak to her," said Lucetta.

When she got upstairs to Elizabeth-Jane's room the latter had taken off her out-door things and was resting over a book. Lucetta found in a moment that she had not yet learnt the news.

"I did not come down to you, Miss Templeman," she said simply. "I was coming to ask if you had quite recovered from your fright, but I found you had a visitor. What are the bells ringing for I wonder; and the band, too, is playing? Somebody must be married; or else they are practising for Christmas."

Lucetta uttered a vague "Yes," and seating herself by the other young woman, looked musingly at her. "What a lonely creature you are," she presently said; "never knowing what's going on, or what people are talking about everywhere with keen interest. You should get out, and gossip about as other women do, and then you wouldn't be obliged to ask me a question of that kind.—Well, now, I have something to tell you."

Elizabeth-Jane said she was so glad, and made herself receptive.

"I must go rather a long way back," said Lucetta, the difficulty of explaining herself satisfactorily to the pondering one beside her growing more apparent at each syllable. "You remember that trying case of conscience I told you of some time ago—about the first lover, and the second lover." She let out in jerky phrases a leading word or two of the story she had told.

"Oh yes—I remember; the story of *your friend*," said

Elizabeth drily, regarding the irises of Lucetta's eyes as though to catch their exact shade. "The two lovers—the old and the new: how she wanted to marry the second, but felt she ought to marry the first; so that she neglected the better course to follow the evil, like the poet Ovid I've just been construing: 'Video meliora proboque, deteriora sequor.' "

"Oh, no—she didn't follow evil exactly!" said Lucetta hastily.

"But you said that she—or as I may say *you*'—answered Elizabeth, dropping the mask—"were in honour and conscience bound to marry the first?"

Lucetta's blush at being seen through came and went again before she replied anxiously, "You will never breathe this, will you, Elizabeth-Jane?"

"Certainly not, if you say not."

"Then I will tell you that the case is more complicated—worse, in fact—than it seemed in my story. I and the first man were thrown together in a strange way, and felt that we ought to be united, as the world had talked of us. He was a widower, as he supposed. He had not heard of his first wife for many years. But the wife returned, and we parted. She is now dead; and the husband comes paying me addresses again, saying, now we'll complete our purpose. But Elizabeth-Jane, all this amounts to a new courtship of me by him—I was absolved from all vows—by the return of the other woman."

"Have you not lately renewed your promise?" said the younger, with quiet surmise. She had divined man number one.

"That was wrung from me, by a threat."

"Yes—it was. But I think when anyone gets coupled up with a man in the past so unfortunately as you have done, she ought to become his wife, if she can, even if she were not the sinning party."

Lucetta's countenance lost its sparkle. "He turned out to be a man I should be afraid to marry," she pleaded. "Really afraid. And it was not till after my renewed promise that I knew it."

"Then there is only one course left to honesty. You must remain a single woman."

"But think again; do consider——"

"I am certain," interrupted her companion hardily. "I have guessed very well who the man is—my father. And I say it is him or nobody for you."

Any suspicion of impropriety was to Elizabeth-Jane like a red rag to a bull. Her craving for correctness of procedure was, indeed, almost vicious. Owing to her early troubles with regard to her mother a semblance of irregularity had terrors for her which those whose names are safeguarded from suspicion know nothing of. "You ought to marry Mr. Henchard, or nobody—certainly not—another man," she went on with a quivering lip, in whose movement two passions shared.

"I don't admit that," said Lucetta, passionately.

"Admit it or not, it is true."

Lucetta covered her eyes with her right hand, as if she could plead no more, holding out her left to Elizabeth-Jane.

"Why—you *have* married him!" cried the latter jumping up with pleasure after a glance at Lucetta's fingers. "When did you do it? Why did you not tell me, instead of teasing me like this? How very honourable of you! He did treat my mother badly once, it seems, in a moment of intoxication. And it is true that he is stern sometimes. But you will rule him entirely, I am sure, with your beauty and wealth and accomplishments. You are the woman he will adore, and we shall all three be happy together now."

"Oh, my Elizabeth-Jane!" cried Lucetta distressfully. "'Tis somebody else that I have married! I was so desperate—so afraid of being forced to anything else—so afraid of revelations that would quench his love for me that I resolved to do it off-hand, come what might, and purchase a week of happiness at any cost."

"You—have—married Mr. Farfrae!" cried Elizabeth-Jane in Nathan tones.

Lucetta bowed. She had recovered herself. "The bells are ringing on that account," she said. "My husband is downstairs. He will live here till a more suitable house is ready for us; and I have told him that I want you to stay with me just as before."

"Let me think of it—alone," the girl quickly replied, corking up the turmoil of her feeling with grand control.

"You shall. I am sure we shall be happy together."

Lucetta departed to join Donald below, a vague uneasiness floating over her joy at seeing him quite at home there. Not on account of her friend Elizabeth did she feel it; for of the bearings of Elizabeth-Jane's emotions she had not the least suspicion; but on Henchard's alone.

Now the instant decision of Susan Henchard's daughter was to dwell in that house no more. Apart from her estimate of the propriety of Lucetta's conduct, Farfrae had been so nearly her avowed lover that she felt she could not abide there.

It was still early in the evening when she hastily put on her things and went out. In a few minutes, knowing the ground, she had found a suitable lodging, and arranged to enter it that night. Returning and entering noiselessly she took off her pretty dress and arrayed herself in a plain one, packing up the other to keep as her best; for she would have to be very economical now. She wrote a note to leave for Lucetta, who was closely shut up in the drawing-room with Farfrae; and then Elizabeth-Jane called a man with a wheelbarrow; and seeing her boxes put into it she trotted off down the street to her rooms. They were in the street in which Henchard lived, and almost opposite his door.

Here she sat down and considered the means of subsistence. The little annual sum settled on her by her step-father would keep body and soul together. A wonderful skill in netting of all sorts—acquired in childhood by making seines in Newson's home—might serve her in good stead: and her studies, which were pursued unremittingly, might serve her in still better.

By this time the marriage that had taken place was known throughout Casterbridge; had been discussed noisily on kerbstones, confidentially behind counters, and jovially at the Three Mariners. Whether Farfrae would sell his business and set up for a gentleman on his wife's money, or whether he would show independence enough to stick to his trade in spite of his brilliant alliance, was a great point of interest.

XXXI

THE retort of the furmity-woman before the magistrates had
spread; and in four-and-twenty hours there was not a person
in Casterbridge who remained unacquainted with the story of
Henchard's mad freak at Weydon Priors Fair, long years
before. The amends he had made in after life were lost sight
of in the dramatic glare of the original act. Had the incident
been well-known of old and always, it might by this time have
grown to be lightly regarded, as the rather tall wild oat, but
well-nigh the single one, of a young man with whom the
steady and mature (if somewhat headstrong) burgher of to-day
had scarcely a point in common. But the act having lain as
dead and buried ever since, the interspace of years was
unperceived; and the black spot of his youth wore the aspect
of a recent crime.

Small as the police-court incident had been in itself, it
formed the edge or turn in the incline of Henchard's fortunes.
On that day—almost at that minute—he passed the ridge of
prosperity and honour, and began to descend rapidly on the
other side. It was strange how soon he sank in esteem. Socially
he had received a startling fillip downwards, and having
already lost commercial buoyancy from rash transactions, the
velocity of his descent in both aspects became accelerated
every hour.

He now gazed more at the pavements and less at the house-
fronts when he walked about; more at the feet and leggings of
men, and less into the pupils of their eyes with the blazing
regard which formerly had made them blink.

New events combined to undo him. It had been a bad year
for others besides himself, and the heavy failure of a debtor
whom he had trusted generously completed the overthrow of
his tottering credit. And now, in his desperation, he failed to
preserve that strict correspondence between bulk and sample
which is the soul of commerce in grain. For this one of his
men was mainly to blame; that worthy, in his great unwisdom,
having picked over the sample of an enormous quantity of

second-rate corn which Henchard had in hand, and removed the pinched, blasted, and smutted grains in great numbers. The produce, if honestly offered, would have created no scandal; but the blunder of misrepresentation, coming at such a moment, dragged Henchard's name into the ditch.

The details of his failure were of the ordinary kind. One day Elizabeth-Jane was passing the King's Arms, when she saw people bustling in and out more than usual when there was no market. A bystander informed her, with some surprise at her ignorance, that it was a meeting of the commissioners under Mr. Henchard's bankruptcy. She felt quite tearful, and when she heard that he was present in the hotel she wished to go in and see him, but was advised not to intrude that day.

The room in which debtor and creditors had assembled was a front one, and Henchard, looking out of the window, had caught sight of Elizabeth-Jane through the wire blind. His examination had closed, and the creditors were leaving. The appearance of Elizabeth threw him into a reverie; till, turning his face from the window, and towering above all the rest, he called their attention for a moment more. His countenance had somewhat changed from its flush of prosperity; the black hair and whiskers were the same as ever, but a film of ash was over the red.

"Gentlemen," he said, "over and above the assets that we've been talking about, and that appear on the balance-sheet, there be these. It all belongs to ye, as much as everything else I've got, and I don't wish to keep it from you, not I." Saying this he took his gold watch from his pocket, and laid it on the table; then his purse—the yellow canvas money-bag such as was carried by all farmers and dealers—untying it and shaking the money out upon the table beside the watch. The latter he drew back quickly for an instant, to remove the hair guard made and given him by Lucetta. "There—now you have all I've got in the world," he said. "And I wish for your sakes 'twas more."

The creditors, farmers almost to a man, looked at the watch, and at the money, and into the street; when Farmer James Everdene of Weatherbury spoke.

"No, no, Henchard," he said warmly. "We don't want that.

'Tis honourable in ye; but keep it. What do you say, neighbours—do ye agree?"

"Ay, sure: we don't wish it at all," said Grower, another creditor.

"Let him keep it, of course," murmured another in the background—a silent reserved young man named Boldwood; and the rest responded unanimously.

"Well," said the senior commissioner, addressing Henchard: "though the case is a desperate one, I am bound to admit that I have never met a debtor who behaved more fairly. I've proved the balance sheet to be as honestly made out as it could possibly be; we have had no trouble; there have been no evasions and no concealments. The rashness of dealing which led to this unhappy situation is obvious enough; but as far as I can see every attempt has been made to avoid wronging anybody."

Henchard was more affected by this than he cared to let them perceive, and he turned aside to the window again. A general murmur of agreement followed the commissioner's words; and the meeting dispersed. When they were gone Henchard regarded the watch they had returned to him. "'Tisn't mine by rights," he said to himself. "Why the devil didn't they take it—I don't want what don't belong to me." Moved by a recollection he took the watch to the maker's, just opposite; sold it there and then for what the tradesman offered, and went with the proceeds to one among the smaller of his creditors, a cottager of Durnover in straitened circumstances; to whom he handed the money.

When everything was ticketed that Henchard had owned, and the auctions were in progress, there was quite a sympathetic reaction in the town, which till then for some time past had done nothing but condemn him. Now that Henchard's whole career was pictured distinctly to his neighbours, and they could see how admirably he had used his one talent of energy to create a position of affluence out of absolutely nothing—which was really all he could show when he came to the town as a journeyman hay-trusser with his wimble and knife in his basket—they wondered, and regretted his fall.

Try as she might Elizabeth could never meet with him. She believed in him still, though nobody else did; and she wanted to be allowed to forgive him for his roughness to her, and to help him in his trouble.

She wrote to him: he did not reply. She then went to his house—the great house she had lived in so happily for a time—with its front of dun brick, vitrified here and there, and its heavy sash-bars—but Henchard was to be found there no more. The ex-mayor had left the home of his prosperity, and gone into Jopp's cottage by the Priory Mill—the sad purlieu to which he had wandered on the night of his discovery that she was not his daughter. Thither she went.

Elizabeth thought it odd that he had fixed on this spot to retire to, but assumed that necessity had no choice. Trees which seemed old enough to have been planted by the friars still stood around, and the back-hatch of the original mill yet formed a cascade which had raised its terrific roar for centuries. The cottage itself was built of old stones from the long-dismantled Priory, scraps of tracery, moulded window-jambs, and arch-labels, being mixed in with the rubble of the walls.

In this cottage he occupied a couple of rooms, Jopp, whom Henchard had employed, abused, cajoled, and dismissed by turns, being the householder. But even here her step-father could not be seen.

"Not by his daughter?" pleaded Elizabeth.

"By nobody—at present: that's his order," she was informed.

Afterwards she was passing by the corn-stores and hay-barns which had been the head-quarters of his business. She knew that he ruled there no longer; but it was with amazement that she regarded the familiar gateway. A smear of decisive lead-coloured paint had been laid on to obliterate Henchard's name, though its letters dimly loomed through like ships in a fog. Over these, in fresh white, spread the name of Farfrae.

Abel Whittle was edging his skeleton in at the wicket, and she said, "Mr. Farfrae is master here?"

"Yaas, Miss Henchet," he said, "Mr. Farfrae have bought the concern and all of we work-folk with it; and 'tis better for us than 'twas—though I shouldn't say that to you as a daughter-law. We work harder, but we bain't made afeard now. It was fear made my few poor hairs so thin. No busting out, no slamming of doors, no meddling with yer eternal soul and all that; and though 'tis a shilling a week less I'm the richer man; for what's all the world if yer mind is always in a larry, Miss Henchet?"

The intelligence was in a general sense true; and Henchard's stores, which had remained in a paralysed condition during the settlement of his bankruptcy, were stirred into activity again when the new tenant had possession. Thenceforward the full sacks, looped with the shining chain, went scurrying up and down under the cat-head, hairy arms were thrust out from the different door-ways, and the grain was hauled in; trusses of hay were tossed anew in and out of the barns, and the wimbles creaked; while the scales and steelyards began to be busy where guess-work had formerly been the rule.

XXXII

TWO bridges stood near the lower part of Casterbridge town.

The first, of weather-stained brick, was immediately at the end of High Street, where a diverging branch from that thoroughfare ran round to the low-lying Durnover lanes; so that the precincts of the bridge formed the merging point of respectability and indigence. The second bridge, of stone, was further out on the highway—in fact, fairly in the meadows, though still within the town boundary.

These bridges had speaking countenances. Every projection in each was worn down to obtuseness, partly by weather, more by friction from generations of loungers, whose toes and heels had from year to year made restless movements against these parapets as they had stood there meditating on the aspect of affairs. In the case of the more friable bricks and stones even the flat faces were worn into hollows by the same mixed mechanism. The masonry of the top was clamped with iron at each joint; since it had been no uncommon thing for desperate men to wrench the coping off and throw it down the river, in reckless defiance of the magistrates.

For to this pair of bridges gravitated all the failures of the town; those who had failed in business, in love, in sobriety, in crime. Why the unhappy hereabout usually chose the bridges for their meditations in preference to a railing, a gate, or a stile, was not so clear.

There was a marked difference of quality between the personages who haunted the near bridge of brick and the personages who haunted the far one of stone. Those of lowest character preferred the former, adjoining the town; they did not mind the glare of the public eye. They had been of comparatively no account during their successes; and, though they might feel dispirited, they had no particular sense of shame in their ruin. Their hands were mostly kept in their pockets; they wore a leather strap round their hips or knees, and boots that required a great deal of lacing but seemed never to get any. Instead of sighing at their adversities they spat, and instead of saying the iron had entered into their souls they said they were down on their luck. Jopp in his times of distress had often stood here; so had Mother Cuxsom, Christopher Coney, and poor Abel Whittle.

The *misérables* who would pause on the remoter bridge were of a politer stamp. They included bankrupts, hypochondriacs, persons who were what is called "out of a situation" from fault or lucklessness, the inefficient of the professional class— shabby genteel men, who did not know how to get rid of the weary time between breakfast and dinner, and the yet more weary time between dinner and dark. The eyes of this species were mostly directed over the parapet upon the running water below. A man seen there looking thus fixedly into the river was pretty sure to be one whom the world did not treat kindly for some reason or other. While one in straits on the townward bridge did not mind who saw him so, and kept his back to the parapet to survey the passersby, one in straits on this never faced the road, never turned his head at coming footsteps, but, sensitive to his own condition, watched the current whenever a stranger approached, as if some strange fish interested him, though every finned thing had been poached out of the river years before.

There and thus they would muse; if their grief were the grief of oppression they would wish themselves kings; if their grief were poverty, wish themselves millionaires; if sin, they would wish they were saints or angels; if despised love, that they were some much-courted Adonis of county fame. Some had been known to stand and think so long with this fixed gaze downward, that eventually they had allowed their poor carcases to follow that gaze; and they were discovered the next morning out of reach of their troubles, either here or in the deep pool called Blackwater, a little higher up the river.

To this bridge came Henchard as other unfortunates had come before him, his way thither being by the riverside path on the chilly edge of the town. Here he was standing one windy afternoon when Durnover church clock struck five. While the gusts were bringing the notes to his ears across the damp intervening flat a man passed behind him, and greeted Henchard by name. Henchard turned slightly and saw that the comer was Jopp, his old foreman, now employed elsewhere, to whom, though he hated him, he had gone for lodgings because Jopp was the one man in Casterbridge whose observation and opinion the fallen corn-merchant despised to the point of indifference.

Henchard returned him a scarcely perceptible nod, and Jopp stopped.

"He and she are gone into their new house to-day," said Jopp.

"Oh," said Henchard absently. "Which house is that?"

"Your old one."

"Gone into my house?" And starting up Henchard added "*My* house of all others in the town!"

"Well, as somebody was sure to live there, and you couldn't, it can do 'ee no harm that he's the man."

It was quite true: he felt that it was doing him no harm. Farfrae, who had already taken the yards and stores, had acquired possession of the house for the obvious convenience of its contiguity. And yet this act of his taking up residence within those roomy chambers while he, their former tenant, lived in a cottage, galled Henchard indescribably.

Jopp continued: "And you heard of that fellow who bought all the best furniture at your sale? He was bidding for no other than Farfrae all the while. It has never been moved out of the house, as he'd already got the lease."

"My furniture too! Surely he'll buy my body and soul likewise."

"There's no saying he won't, if you be willing to sell." And having planted these wounds in the heart of his once imperious master Jopp went on his way; while Henchard stared and stared into the racing river till the bridge seemed moving backward with him.

The low-land grew blacker, and the sky a deeper grey. When the landscape looked like a picture blotted in with ink another traveller approached the great stone bridge. He was driving a gig, his direction being also townwards. On the round of the middle arch the gig stopped. "Mr. Henchard?" came from it in the voice of Farfrae. Henchard turned his face. Finding that he had guessed rightly Farfrae told the man who accompanied him to drive home; while he alighted, and went up to his former friend.

"I have heard that you think of emigrating Mr. Henchard," he said. "Is it true? I have a real reason for asking."

Henchard withheld his answer for several instants, and then said "Yes; it is true. I am going where you were going to a few years ago, when I prevented you and got you to bide here. 'Tis turn and turn about, isn't it? Do ye mind how we stood like this in the Chalk Walk when I persuaded 'ee to stay? You then stood without a chattel to your name, and I was the master of the house in Corn Street. But now I stand without a stick or a rag, and the master of that house is you."

"Yes, yes; that's so! It's the way o' the warrld!" said Farfrae.

"Ha, ha, true!" cried Henchard, throwing himself into a mood of jocularity. "Up and down! I'm used to it. What's the odds after all!"

"Now listen to me, if it's no taking up your time," said Farfrae; "just as I listened to you. Don't go. Stay at home."

"But I can do nothing else, man," said Henchard scornfully. "The little money I have will just keep body and soul together for a few weeks, and no more. I have not felt inclined to go back to journey-work yet; but I can't stay doing nothing, and my best chance is elsewhere."

"No; but what I propose is this—if ye will listen. Come and live in your old house. We can spare some rooms very well—I am sure my wife would not mind it at all—until there's an opening for ye."

Henchard started. Probably the picture drawn by the unsuspecting Donald of himself under the same roof with Lucetta was too striking to be received with equanimity. "No, no," he said gruffly; "we should quarrel."

"You should hae a part to yourself," said Farfrae; "and nobody to interfere wi' you. It will be a deal healthier than down there by the river where you live now."

Still Henchard refused. "You don't know what you ask," he said. "However, I can do no less than thank 'ee."

They walked into the town together side by side, as they had done when Henchard persuaded the young Scotchman to remain. "Will you come in and have some supper?" said

Farfrae when they reached the middle of the town where their paths diverged right and left.

"No, no."

"By the by, I had nearly forgot. I bought a good deal of your furniture."

"So I have heard."

"Well, it was no that I wanted it so very much for myself; but I wish ye to pick out all that you care to have—such things as may be endeared to ye by associations, or particularly suited to your use. And take them to your own house—it will not be depriving me; we can do with less very well, and I will have plenty of opportunities of getting more."

"What—give it to me for nothing?" said Henchard. "But you paid the creditors for it."

"Ah, yes; but maybe it's worth more to you than it is to me."

Henchard was a little moved. "I—sometimes think I've wronged 'ee!" he said in tones which showed the disquietude that the night shades hid in his face. He shook Farfrae abruptly by the hand, and hastened away as if unwilling to betray himself further. Farfrae saw him turn through the thoroughfare into Bull Stake and vanish down towards the Priory Mill.

Meanwhile Elizabeth-Jane, in an upper room no larger than the prophet's chamber, and with the silk attire of her palmy days packed away in a box, was netting with great industry between the hours which she devoted to studying such books as she could get hold of.

Her lodgings being nearly opposite her step-father's former residence, now Farfrae's, she could see Donald and Lucetta speeding in and out of their door with all the bounding enthusiasm of their situation. She avoided looking that way as much as possible, but it was hardly in human nature to keep the eyes averted when the door slammed.

While living on thus quietly she heard the news that Henchard had caught cold and was confined to his room—possibly a result of standing about the meads in damp weather. She went off to his house at once. This time she was determined not to be denied admittance, and made her way upstairs. He was sitting up in the bed with a great-coat round him, and at first resented her intrusion. "Go away—go away," he said. "I don't like to see 'ee."

"But father."

"I don't like to see 'ee," he repeated.

However, the ice was broken, and she remained. She made the room more comfortable, gave directions to the people below, and by the time she went away had reconciled her step-father to her visiting him.

The effect, either of her ministrations or of her mere presence, was a rapid recovery. He soon was well enough to go out; and now things seemed to wear a new colour in his eyes. He no longer thought of emigration, and thought more of Elizabeth. The having nothing to do made him more dreary than any other circumstance; and one day, with better views of Farfrae than he had held for some time, and a sense that honest work was not a thing to be ashamed of, he stoically went down to Farfrae's yard and asked to be taken on as a journeyman haytrusser. He was engaged at once.

This hiring of Henchard was done through a foreman, Farfrae feeling that it was undesirable to come personally in contact with the ex-corn-factor more than was absolutely necessary. While anxious to help him he was well aware by this time of his uncertain temper, and thought reserved relations best. For the same reason his orders to Henchard to proceed to this and that country farm trussing in the usual way were always given through a third person.

For a time these arrangements worked well, it being the custom to truss in the respective stack-yards, before bringing it away, the hay bought at the different farms about the neighbourhood so that Henchard was often absent at such places the whole week long. When this was all done, and Henchard had become in a measure broken in, he came to work daily on the home premises like the rest. And thus the once flourishing merchant and mayor and what not stood as a day-labourer in the barns and granaries he formerly had owned.

"I have worked as a journeyman before now, ha'n't I?" he

would say in his defiant way; "And why shouldn't I do it again?" But he looked a far different journeyman from the one he had been in his earlier days. Then he had worn clean suitable clothes, light and cheerful in hue; leggings yellow as marigolds, corduroys immaculate as new flax, and a neckerchief like a flower-garden. Now he wore the remains of an old blue cloth suit of his gentlemanly times, a rusty silk hat, and a once black satin stock, soiled and shabby. Clad thus he went to and fro, still comparatively an active man—for he was not much over forty—and saw with the other men in the yard Donald Farfrae going in and out the green door that led to the garden, and the big house, and Lucetta.

At the beginning of the winter it was rumoured about Casterbridge that Mr. Farfrae, already in the Town Council, was to be proposed for mayor in a year or two.

"Yes; she was wise, she was wise in her generation!" said Henchard to himself when he heard of this one day on his way to Farfrae's hay barn. He thought it over as he wimbled his bonds, and the piece of news acted as a reviviscent breath to that old view of his—of Donald Farfrae as his triumphant rival who rode rough-shod over him.

"A fellow of his age going to be mayor indeed!" he murmured with a corner-drawn smile on his mouth. "But 'tis her money that floats en upward. Ha-ha—how cust odd it is! Here be I, his former master, working for him as man, and he the man standing as master, with my house and my furniture and my what-you-may-call wife all his own."

He repeated these things a hundred times a day. During the whole period of his acquaintance with Lucetta he had never wished to claim her as his own so desperately as he now regretted her loss. It was no mercenary hankering after her fortune that moved him; though that fortune had been the means of making her so much the more desired by giving her the air of independence and sauciness which attracts men of his composition. It had given her servants, house, and fine clothing—a setting that invested Lucetta with a startling novelty in the eyes of him who had known her in her narrow days.

He accordingly lapsed into moodiness, and at every allusion to the possibility of Farfrae's near election to the municipal chair his former hatred of the Scotchman returned. Concurrently with this he underwent a moral change. It resulted in his significantly saying every now and then, in tones of recklessness, "Only a fortnight more!"—"Only a dozen days!" and so forth, lessening his figures day by day.

"Why d'ye say only a dozen days?" asked Solomon Longways as he worked beside Henchard in the granary weighing oats.

"Because in twelve days I shall be released from my oath."

"What oath?"

"The oath to drink no spirituous liquid. In twelve days it will be twenty-one years since I swore it, and then I mean to enjoy myself, please God."

Elizabeth-Jane sat at her window one Sunday, and while there she heard in the street below a conversation which introduced Henchard's name. She was wondering what was the matter, when a third person who was passing by asked the question in her mind.

"Michael Henchard have busted out drinking after taking nothing for twenty-one years."

Elizabeth-Jane jumped up, put on her things, and went out.

AT this date there prevailed in Casterbridge a convivial custom—scarcely recognized as such, yet none the less established. On the afternoon of every Sunday a large contingent of the Casterbridge journeymen—steady church-goers and sedate characters—having attended service, filed from the church doors across the way to the Three Mariners Inn. The rear was usually brought up by the choir, with their bass-viols, fiddles, and flutes under their arms.

The great point, the point of honour, on these sacred occasions was for each man to strictly limit himself to half-a-pint of liquor. This scrupulosity was so well understood by the landlord, that the whole company was served in cups of that measure. They were all exactly alike—straight-sided, with two leafless lime-trees done in eel-brown on the sides—one towards the drinker's lips, the other confronting his comrade. To wonder how many of these cups the landlord possessed altogether was a favourite exercise of children in the marvellous. Forty at least might have been seen at these times in the large room, forming a ring round the margin of the great sixteen-legged oak table, like the monolithic circle at Stonehenge in its pristine days. Outside and above the forty cups came a circle of forty smoke-jets from forty clay pipes; outside the pipes the countenances of the forty church-goers, supported at the back by a circle of forty chairs.

The conversation was not the conversation of week days, but a thing altogether finer in point and higher in tone. They invariably discussed the sermon, dissecting it, weighing it, as above or below the average—the general tendency being to regard it as a scientific feat or performance which had no relation to their own lives, except as between critics and the thing criticised. The bass-viol player and the clerk usually spoke with more authority than the rest on account of their official connection with the preacher.

Now the Three Mariners was the inn chosen by Henchard as the place for closing his long term of dramless years. He

had so timed his entry as to be well-established in the large
room by the time the forty church-goers entered to their
customary cups. The flush upon his face proclaimed at once
that the vow of twenty-one years had lapsed, and the era of
recklessness begun anew. He was seated on a small table,
drawn up to the side of the massive oak board reserved for the
churchmen; a few of whom nodded to him as they took their
places, and said, "How be ye, Mr. Henchard? Quite a stranger
here."

Henchard did not take the trouble to reply for a few
moments, and his eyes rested on his stretched out legs and
boots. "Yes," he said at length; "That's true. I've been down
in spirit for weeks; some of ye know the cause. I am better
now; but not quite serene. I want you fellows of the choir to
strike up a tune; and what with that and this brew of
Stannidge's I am in hopes of getting altogether out of my
minor key."

"With all my heart," said the first fiddle. "We've let back
our strings, that's true; but we can soon pull 'em up again.
Sound A, neighbours, and give the man a stave."

"I don't care a curse what the words be," said Henchard.
"Hymns, ballets, or rantipole rubbish; the Rogue's March or
the cherubim's warble—'tis all the same to me if 'tis good
harmony, and well put out."

"Well—heh, heh—it may be we can do that, and not a man
among us that have sat in the gallery less than twenty year,"
said the leader of the band. "As 'tis Sunday, neighbours,
suppose we raise the fourth Psa'am, to Samuel Wakely's tune,
as improved by me."

"Hang Samuel Wakely's tune as improved by thee," said
Henchard. "Chuck across one of your psalters—old *Wiltshire*
is the only tune worth singing—the psalm-tune that would
make my blood ebb and flow like the sea when I was a steady
chap. I'll find some words to fit en." He took one of the
psalters and began turning over the leaves.

Chancing to look out of the window at that moment he saw
a flock of people passing by, and perceived them to be the
congregation of the upper church, now just dismissed, their
sermon having been a longer one than that the lower parish

was favoured with. Among the rest of the leading inhabitants walked Mr. Councillor Farfrae, with Lucetta upon his arm, the observed and imitated of all the smaller tradesmen's womankind. Henchard's mouth changed a little, and he continued to turn over the leaves.

"Now then," he said, "Psalm the hundred-and-ninth, to the tune of *Wiltshire*: verses ten to fifteen. I gie ye the words:

> "His seed shall orphans be, his wife
>   A widow plunged in grief;
> His vagrant children beg their bread
>   Where none can give relief.
>
> "His ill-got riches shall be made
>   To usurers a prey;
> The fruit of all his toil shall be
>   By strangers borne away.
>
> "None shall be found that to his wants
>   Their mercy will extend,
> Or to his helpless orphan seed
>   The least assistance lend.
>
> "A swift destruction soon shall seize
>   On his unhappy race;
> And the next age his hated name
>   Shall utterly deface.""

"I know the Psa'am—I know the Psa'am!" said the leader hastily; "but I would as lief not sing it. 'Twasn't made for singing. We chose it once when the gipsy stole the pa'son's mare, thinking to please him; but pa'son were quite upset. Whatever Servant David were thinking about when he made a Psalm that nobody can sing without disgracing himself, I can't fathom! Now then, the fourth Psa'am, to Samuel Wakely's tune, as improved by me."

"'Od seize your sauce—I tell ye to sing the hundred-and-ninth to *Wiltshire*, and sing it you shall!" roared Henchard. "Not a single one of all the droning crew of ye goes out of this room till that Psalm is sung!" He slipped off the table, seized the poker, and going to the door placed his back against it. "Now then, go ahead, if you don't wish to have your cust pates broke!"

"Don't 'ee, don't 'ee take on so!—As 'tis the Sabbath day, and 'tis Servant David's words and not ours, perhaps we don't mind for once, hey?" said one of the terrified choir, looking round upon the rest. So the instruments were tuned and the comminatory verses sung.

"Thank ye, thank ye," said Henchard in a softened voice, his eyes growing downcast, and his manner that of a man much moved by the strains. "Don't you blame David," he went on in low tones, shaking his head without raising his eyes. "He knew what he was about when he wrote that. If I could afford it, be hanged if I wouldn't keep a church choir at my own expense to play and sing to me at these low, dark times of my life. But the bitter thing is that when I was rich I didn't need what I could have, and now I be poor I can't have what I need!"

While they paused, Lucetta and Farfrae passed again, this time homeward, it being their custom to take, like others, a short walk out on the highway and back, between church and tea-time. "There's the man we've been singing about," said Henchard.

The players and singers turned their heads and saw his meaning.

"Heaven forbid!" said the bass-player.

"'Tis the man," repeated Henchard doggedly.

"Then if I'd known," said the performer on the clarionet solemnly, "that 'twas meant for a living man, nothing should have drawn out o' my wynd pipe the breath for that Psalm, so help me!"

"Nor from mine," said the first singer. "But, thought I, as it was made so long ago perhaps there isn't much in it, so I'll oblige a neighbour; for there's nothing to be said against the tune."

"Ah, my boys, you've sung it," said Henchard triumphantly. "As for him, it was partly by his songs that he got over me, and heaved me out. . . . I could double him up like that—and yet I don't!" He laid the poker across his knee, bent it as if it were a twig, flung it down, and came away from the door.

It was at this time that Elizabeth-Jane, having heard where

her stepfather was, entered the room with a pale and agonized countenance. The choir and the rest of the company moved off, in accordance with their half-pint regulation. Elizabeth-Jane went up to Henchard, and entreated him to accompany her home.

By this hour the volcanic fires of his nature had burnt down, and having drunk no great quantity as yet, he was inclined to acquiesce. She took his arm, and together they went on. Henchard walked blankly, like a blind man, repeating to himself the last words of the singers:

> "And the next age his hated name
> Shall utterly deface."

At length he said to her, "I am a man to my word. I have kept my oath for twenty-one years; and now I can drink with a good conscience. . . . If I don't do for him—well, I am a fearful practical joker when I choose. He has taken away everything from me, and by heavens, if I meet him, I won't answer for my deeds!"

These half-uttered words alarmed Elizabeth—all the more by reason of the still determination of Henchard's mien.

"What will you do?" she asked cautiously, while trembling with disquietude, and guessing Henchard's allusion only too well.

Henchard did not answer, and they went on till they had reached his cottage. "May I come in?" she said.

"No, no; not to-day," said Henchard; and she went away; feeling that to caution Farfrae was almost her duty, as it was certainly her strong desire.

As on the Sunday, so on the weekdays, Farfrae and Lucetta might have been seen flitting about the town like two butterflies—or rather like a bee and a butterfly in league for life. She seemed to take no pleasure in going anywhere except in her husband's company; and hence when business would not permit him to waste an afternoon she remained indoors, waiting for the time to pass till his return, her face being visible to Elizabeth-Jane from her window aloft. The latter, however, did not say to herself that Farfrae should be thankful for such devotion but, full of her reading, she cited Rosalind's exclamation: "Mistress, know yourself; down on your knees and thank heaven fasting for a good man's love."

She kept her eye upon Henchard also. One day he answered her inquiry for his health by saying that he could not endure Abel Whittle's pitying eyes upon him while they worked together in the yard. "He is such a fool," said Henchard, "that he can never get out of his mind the time when I was master there."

"I'll come and wimble for you instead of him, if you will allow me," said she.

Her motive on going to the yard was to get an opportunity of observing the general position of affairs on Farfrae's premises now that her stepfather was a workman there. Henchard's threats had alarmed her so much that she wished to see his behaviour when the two were face to face.

For two or three days after her arrival Donald did not make any appearance. Then one afternoon the green door opened, and through came, first Farfrae, and at his heels Lucetta. Donald brought his wife forward without hesitation, it being obvious that he had no suspicion whatever of any antecedents in common between her and the now journeyman hay-trusser.

Henchard did not turn his eyes toward either of the pair, keeping them fixed on the bond he twisted, as if that alone absorbed him. A feeling of delicacy, which ever prompted Farfrae to avoid anything that might seem like triumphing over a fallen rival, led him to keep away from the hay-barn where Henchard and his daughter were working, and to go on to the corn department. Meanwhile Lucetta, never having been informed that Henchard had entered her husband's service, rambled straight on to the barn, where she came suddenly upon Henchard, and gave vent to a little "Oh!"— which the happy and busy Donald was too far off to hear.

Henchard, with withering humility of demeanour, touched the brim of his hat to her as Whittle and the rest had done, to which she breathed a dead-alive "Good afternoon."

"I beg your pardon, ma'am?" said Henchard, as if he had not heard.

"I said Good afternoon," she faltered.

"Oh yes—good afternoon, ma'am," he replied, touching his

hat again. "I am glad to see you, ma'am." Lucetta looked embarrassed, and Henchard continued: "For we humble workmen here feel it a great honour that a lady should look in and take an interest in us."

She glanced at him entreatingly; the sarcasm was too bitter, too unendurable.

"Can you tell me the time, ma'am?" he asked.

"Yes," she said hastily; "half past four."

"Thank 'ee. An hour and a half longer before we are released from work. Ah, ma'am, we of the lower classes know nothing of the gay leisure that such as you enjoy."

As soon as she could do so Lucetta left him, nodded and smiled to Elizabeth-Jane, and joined her husband at the other end of the enclosure, where she could be seen leading him away by the outer gates, so as to avoid passing Henchard again. That she had been taken by surprise was obvious.

The result of this casual rencounter was that the next morning a note was put into Henchard's hand by the postman.

"Will you," said Lucetta, with as much bitterness as she could put into a small communication—"will you kindly undertake not to speak to me in the biting undertones you used to-day, if I walk through the yard at any time? I bear you no ill-will, and I am only too glad that you should have employment of my dear husband; but in common fairness treat me as his wife, and do not try to make me wretched by covert sneers. I have committed no crime, and done you no injury."

"Poor fool!" said Henchard with fond savagery, holding out the note. "To know no better than commit herself in writing like this! Why, if I were to show that to her dear husband—pooh!" He threw the letter into the fire.

Lucetta took care not to come again among the hay and corn. She would rather have died than run the risk of encountering Henchard at such close quarters a second time. The gulf between them was growing wider every day. Farfrae was always considerate to his fallen acquaintance, but it was impossible that he should not, by degrees, cease to regard the ex-corn-merchant as more than one of his other workmen. Henchard saw this, and concealed his feelings under a cover of stolidity, fortifying his heart by drinking more freely at the Three Mariners every evening.

Often did Elizabeth-Jane, in her endeavours to prevent his taking other liquor, carry tea to him in a little basket at five o'clock. Arriving one day on this errand she found her step-father was measuring up clover-seed and rape-seed in the corn-stores on the top floor, and she ascended to him. Each floor had a door opening into the air under a cat-head, from which a chain dangled for hoisting the sacks.

When Elizabeth's head rose through the trap she perceived that the upper door was open, and that her step-father and Farfrae stood just within it in conversation, Farfrae being nearest the dizzy edge, and Henchard a little way behind. Not to interrupt them she remained on the steps, without raising her head any higher. While waiting thus she saw—or fancied she saw, for she had a terror of feeling certain—her step-father slowly raise his hand to a level behind Farfrae's shoulders, a curious expression taking possession of his face. The young man was quite unconscious of the action, which was so indirect that if Farfrae had observed it he might almost have regarded it as an idle outstretching of the arm. But it would have been possible, by a comparatively light touch, to push Farfrae off his balance and send him head over heels into the air.

Elizabeth felt quite sick at heart on thinking of what this *might* have meant. As soon as they turned she mechanically took the tea to Henchard, left it, and went away. Reflecting she endeavoured to assure herself that the movement was an idle eccentricity and no more. Yet on the other hand his subordinate position in an establishment where he once had been master might be acting on him like an irritant poison; and she finally resolved to caution Donald.

XXXIV

NEXT morning, accordingly, she rose at five o'clock, and went into the street. It was not yet light; a dense fog prevailed, and the town was as silent as it was dark, except that from the rectangular avenues which framed in the borough there came a chorus of tiny rappings, caused by the fall of water-drops condensed on the boughs; now it was wafted from the West Walk, now from the South Walk; and then from both quarters simultaneously. She moved on to the bottom of Corn Street, and, knowing his time well, waited only a few minutes before she heard the familiar bang of his door, and then his quick walk towards her. She met him at the point where the last tree of the engirding avenue flanked the last house in the street.

He could hardly discern her till, glancing enquiringly he said, "What—Miss Henchard—and are ye up so airly?"

She asked him to pardon her for waylaying him at such an unseemly time. "But I am anxious to mention something," she said. "And I wished not to alarm Mrs. Farfrae by calling."

"Yes?" said he, with the cheeriness of a superior. "And what may it be? It's very kind of ye, I'm sure."

She now felt the difficulty of conveying to his mind the exact aspect of possibilities in her own. But she somehow began, and introduced Henchard's name. "I sometimes fear," she said with an effort, "that he may be betrayed into some attempt to—insult you, sir."

"But we are the best of friends."

"Or to play some practical joke upon you, sir. Remember that he has been hardly used."

"But we are quite friendly."

"Or to do something—that would injure you—hurt you—wound you." Every word cost her twice its length of pain. And she could see that Farfrae was still incredulous. Henchard, a poor man in his employ, was not, to Farfrae's view, the Henchard who had ruled him. Yet he was not only the same man, but that man with his sinister qualities formerly latent quickened into life by his buffetings.

Farfrae, happy, and thinking no evil, persisted in making light of her fears. Thus they parted, and she went homeward, journeymen now being in the street, waggoners going to the harness-maker's for articles left to be repaired, farm-horses going to the shoeing smiths, and the sons of labour showing themselves generally on the move. Elizabeth entered her lodging unhappily, thinking she had done no good, and only made herself appear foolish by her weak note of warning.

But Donald Farfrae was one of those men upon whom an incident is never absolutely lost. He revised impressions from a subsequent point of view, and the impulsive judgment of the moment was not always his permanent one. The vision of Elizabeth's earnest face in the rimy dawn came back to him several times during the day. Knowing the solidity of her character he did not treat her hints altogether as idle sounds.

But he did not desist from a kindly scheme on Henchard's account that engaged him just then; and when he met Lawyer Joyce the town-clerk later in the day he spoke of it as if nothing had occurred to damp it.

"About that little seedsman's shop," he said; "the shop overlooking the churchyard, which is to let. It is not for myself I want it; but for our unlucky fellow-townsman Henchard. It would be a new beginning for him, if a small one; and I have told the Council that I would head a private subscription among them to set him up in it—that I would be fifty pounds, if they would make up the other fifty among them."

"Yes, yes; so I've heard; and there's nothing to say against it for that matter," the town-clerk replied in his plain frank way. "But Farfrae—others see what you don't. Henchard hates 'ee—aye, hates 'ee; and 'tis right that you should know it. To my knowlege he was at the Three Mariners last night, saying in public that about you which—a man ought not to say about another."

"Is that so—ah, is that so?" said Farfrae, looking down. "Why should he do it?" added the young man bitterly. "What harm have I done him, that he should try to wrong me?"

"God only knows!" said Joyce lifting his eyebrows. "It shows much long-suffering in you to put up with him and keep him in your employ."

"But I cannet discharge a man who was once a good friend to me. How can I forget that when I came here 'twas he enabled me to make a footing for mysel'? No—no. As long as I've a day's wark to offer he shall do it if he chooses. 'Tis not I who will deny him such a little as that. But I'll drop the idea of establishing him in a shop till I can think more about it."

It grieved Farfrae much to give up this scheme. But a damp having been thrown over it by these and other voices in the air, he went and countermanded his orders. The then occupier of the shop was in it when Farfrae spoke to him, and feeling it necessary to give some explanation of his withdrawal from the negociation Donald mentioned Henchard's name, and stated that the intentions of the Council had been changed.

The occupier was much disappointed, and straightway informed Henchard, as soon as he saw him, that a scheme of the Council for setting him up in a shop had been knocked on the head by Farfrae. And thus out of error enmity grew.

When Farfrae got indoors that evening the tea-kettle was singing on the high hob of the semi-egg-shaped grate. Lucetta, light as a sylph, ran forward and seized his hands, whereupon Farfrae duly kissed her.

"Oh!" she cried playfully, turning to the window. "See— the blinds are not drawn down, and the people can look in— what a scandal!"

When the candles were lighted, the curtains drawn, and the twain sat at tea, she noticed that he looked serious. Without directly enquiring why she let her eyes linger solicitously on his face.

"Who has called?" he absently asked. "Any folk for me?"

"No," said Lucetta. "What's the matter, Donald?"

"Well—nothing worth talking of," he responded sadly.

"Then never mind it. You will get through it. Scotchmen are always lucky."

"No—not always!" he said, shaking his head gloomily as he contemplated a crumb on the table. "I know many who have not been so! There was Sandy Macfarlane, who started to America to try his fortune, and he was drowned; and Archibald Leith, he was murdered! And poor Willie Dunbleeze and Maitland Macfreeze— they fell into bad courses, and went the way of all such!"

"Why—you old goosey—I was only speaking in a general sense, of course. You are always so literal. Now when we have finished tea, sing me that funny song about high heeled shoon and siller tags, and the one-and-forty wooers."

"No, no. I couldna sing to-night! It's Henchard—he hates me; so that I may not be his friend if I would. I would understand why there should be a wee bit envy; but I cannet see a reason for the whole intensity of what he feels. Now can you, Lucetta? It is more like old-fashioned rivalry in love than just a bit of rivalry in trade."

Lucetta had grown somewhat wan. "No," she replied.

"I give him employment—I cannet refuse it. But neither can I blind myself to the fact that with a man of passions such as his there is no safeguard for conduct!"

"What have you heard—Oh Donald, dearest?" said Lucetta in alarm. The words on her lips were "anything about me?"—but she did not utter them. She could not, however, suppress her agitation, and her eyes filled with tears.

"No, no—it is not so serious as ye fancy," declared Farfrae soothingly; though he did not know its seriousness so well as she.

"I wish you would do what we have talked of," mournfully remarked Lucetta. "Give up business, and go away from here. We have plenty of money, and why should we stay?"

Farfrae seemed seriously disposed to discuss this move, and they talked thereon till a visitor was announced. Their neighbour Alderman Vatt came in.

"You've heard, I suppose, of poor Doctor Chalkfield's death? Yes—died this afternoon at five," said Mr. Vatt. Chalkfield was the councilman who had succeeded to the mayoralty in the preceding November.

Farfrae was sorry at the intelligence, and Mr. Vatt continued: "Well, we know he's been going some days, and as his family is well provided for we must take it all as it is. Now I have called to ask 'ee this—quite privately. If I should nominate 'ee to succeed him, and there should be no particular opposition, will 'ee accept the chair?"

"But there are folk whose turn is before mine; and I'm over young, and may be thought pushing?" said Farfrae after a pause.

"Not at all. I don't speak for myself only, several have named it. You won't refuse?"

"We thought of going away," interposed Lucetta, looking at Farfrae anxiously.

"It was only a fancy," Farfrae murmured. "I would na refuse if it is the wish of a respectable majority in the Council."

"Very well, then, look upon yourself as elected. We have had older men long enough."

When he was gone Farfrae said musingly, "See now how it's ourselves that are ruled by the powers above us! We plan this, but we do that. If they want to make me mayor I will stay; and Henchard must rave as he will."

From this evening onward Lucetta was very uneasy. If she had not been imprudence incarnate, she would not have acted as she did when she met Henchard by accident a day or two later. It was in the bustle of the market, when no one could readily notice their discourse.

"Michael," said she, "I must again ask you what I asked you months ago—to return me any letters or papers of mine that you may have—unless you have destroyed them. You must see how desirable it is that the time at Jersey should be blotted out, for the good of all parties."

"Why, bless the woman—I packed up every scrap of your handwriting to give you in the coach—but you never appeared."

She explained how the death of her aunt had prevented her taking the journey on that day. "And what became of the parcel then?" she asked.

He could not say—he would consider. When she was gone he recollected that he had left a heap of useless papers in his former dining-room safe—built up in the wall of his old house—now occupied by Farfrae. The letters might have been amongst them.

A grotesque grin shaped itself on Henchard's face. Had that safe been opened?

On the very evening which followed this there was a great ringing of bells in Casterbridge, and the combined brass, wood, catgut, and leather bands played round the town with more prodigality of percussion-notes than ever. Farfrae was mayor—the two-hundredth odd of a series forming an elective dynasty dating back to the days of Charles the First—and the fair Lucetta was the courted of the town. . . . But ah, that worm i' the bud—Henchard; what he could tell!

He, in the meantime, festering with indignation at some erroneous intelligence of Farfrae's opposition to the scheme for installing him in the little seed-shop, was greeted with the news of the municipal election (which by reason of Farfrae's comparative youth and his Scottish nativity—a thing unprecedented in the case—had an interest far beyond the ordinary). The bell-ringing, and the band-playing loud as Tamerlane's trumpet, goaded the downfallen Henchard indescribably: the ousting now seemed to him to be complete.

The next morning he went to the corn-yard as usual, and about eleven o'clock Donald entered through the green door, with no trace of the worshipful about him. The yet more emphatic change of places between him and Henchard which this election had established renewed a slight embarrassment in the manner of the modest younger man; but Henchard showed the front of one who had overlooked all this; and Farfrae met his amenities half-way at once.

"I was going to ask you," said Henchard, "about a packet that I may possibly have left in my old safe in the dining-room." He added particulars.

"If so, it is there now," said Farfrae. "I have never opened the safe at all as yet; for I keep ma papers at the bank, to sleep easy o' nights."

"It was not of much consequence—to me," said Henchard. "But I'll call for it this evening, if you don't mind."

It was quite late when he fulfilled his promise. He had primed himself with grog, as he did very frequently now, and a curl of sardonic humour hung on his lip as he approached the house, as though he were contemplating some terrible form of amusement. Whatever it was the incident of his entry did not diminish its force, this being his first visit to the house since he had lived there as owner. The ring of the bell spoke to him like the voice of a familiar drudge who had been bribed to forsake him; the movements of the doors were revivals of dead days.

Farfrae invited him into the dining-room, where he at once unlocked the iron safe built into the wall—*his*, Henchard's, safe, made by an ingenious locksmith under his direction. Farfrae drew thence the parcel, and other papers, with apologies for not having returned them.

"Never mind," said Henchard drily. "The fact is they are letters mostly. . . . Yes," he went on, sitting down and unfolding Lucetta's passionate bundle, "here they be. That ever I should see 'em again!—I hope Mrs. Farfrae is well after her exertions of yesterday?"

"She has felt a bit weary; and has gone to bed airly on that account."

Henchard returned to the letters, sorting them over with interest, Farfrae being seated at the other end of the dining-table. "You don't forget, of course," he resumed, "that curious chapter in the history of my past, which I told you of, and that you gave me some assistance in? These letters are, in fact, related to that unhappy business. Though, thank God, it is all over now."

"What became of the poor woman?" asked Farfrae.

"Luckily she married, and married well," said Henchard. "So that these reproaches she poured out on me do not now cause me any twinges, as they might otherwise have done. . . . Just listen to what an angry woman will say!"

Farfrae, willing to humour Henchard, though quite uninterested, and bursting with yawns, gave well-mannered attention.

" 'For me,' " Henchard read, " 'there is practically no future. A creature too unconventionally devoted to you—who feels it impossible that she can be wife of any other man; and who is yet no more to you than the first woman you meet in the street—such am I. I quite acquit you of any intention to wrong me, yet you are the door through which wrong has come to me. That in the event of your present wife's death you will place me in her position is a consolation so far as it goes—but how far does it go? Thus I sit here, forsaken by my few acquaintance, and forsaken by you.' "

"That's how she went on to me," said Henchard; "acres of words like that, when what had happened was what I could not cure."

"Yes," said Farfare absently, "it is the way wi' women." But the fact was that he knew very little of the sex; yet detecting a sort of resemblance in style between the effusions of the woman he worshipped and those of the supposed stranger, he concluded that Aphrodite ever spoke thus, whose-soever the personality she assumed.

Henchard unfolded another letter, and read it through likewise, stopping at the subscription as before. "Her name I don't give," he said blandly. "As I didn't marry her, and another man did, I can scarcely do that in fairness to her."

"Tr-rue, tr-rue," said Farfrae. "But why didn't you marry her when your wife Susan died?" Farfrae asked this, and the other questions, in the comfortably indifferent tone of one whom the matter very remotely concerned.

"Ah—well you may ask that," said Henchard, the new-moon-shaped grin adumbrating itself again upon his mouth. "In spite of all her protestations, when I came forward to do so, as in generosity bound, she was not the woman for me."

"She had already married another—maybe?"

Henchard seemed to think it would be sailing too near the wind to descend further into particulars, and he answered "Yes."

"The young lady must have had a heart that bore transplanting very readily."

"She had, she had," said Henchard emphatically.

He opened a third and fourth letter, and read. This time he approached the conclusion as if the signature were indeed coming with the rest. But again he stopped short. The truth was that, as may be divined, he had quite intended to effect a grand catastrophe at the end of this drama by reading out the name; he had come to the house with no other thought. But sitting here in cold blood he could not do it. Such a wrecking of hearts appalled even him. His quality was such that he could have annihilated them both in the heat of action; but to accomplish the deed by oral poison was beyond the nerve of his enmity.

XXXV

As Donald stated, Lucetta had retired early to her room because of fatigue. She had, however, not gone to rest, but sat in the bedside chair reading, and thinking over the events of the day. At the ringing of the door-bell by Henchard she wondered who it should be that would call at that comparatively late hour. The dining-room was almost under her bedroom; she could hear that somebody was admitted there, and presently the indistinct murmur of a person reading became audible.

The usual time for Donald's arrival upstairs came, and passed, yet still the reading and conversation went on. This was very singular. She could think of nothing but that some extraordinary crime had been committed, and that the visitor, whoever he might be, was reading an account of it from a special edition of the *Casterbridge Chronicle*. At last she left the room, and descended the stairs. The dining-room door was ajar, and in the silence of the resting household the voice and the words were recognizable before she reached the lower flight. She stood transfixed. Her own words greeted her, in Henchard's voice, like spirits from the grave.

Lucetta leant upon the bannister with her cheek against the smooth hand-rail, as if she would make a friend of it in her misery. Rigid in this position more and more words fell successively upon her ear. But what amazed her most was the tone of her husband. He spoke merely in the accents of a man who made a present of his time.

"One word," he was saying, as the crackling of paper denoted that Henchard was unfolding yet another sheet. "Is it quite fair to this young woman's memory to read at such length to a stranger what was intended for your eye alone?"

"Well yes," said Henchard. "By not giving her name I make it an example of all womankind, and not a scandal to one."

"If I were you I would destroy them," said Farfrae, giving more thought to the letters than he had hitherto done. "As another man's wife it would injure the woman, if it were known."

"No—I shall not destroy them," murmured Henchard, putting the letters away. Then he arose, and Lucetta heard no more.

She went back to her bedroom in a semi-paralysed state. For very fear she could not undress, but sat on the edge of the bed, waiting. Would Henchard let out the secret in his parting words? Her suspense was terrible. Had she confessed all to Donald in their early acquaintance he might possibly have got over it, and married her just the same—unlikely as it had once seemed; but for her or any one else to tell him now would be fatal.

The door slammed: she could hear her husband bolting it. After looking round in his customary way he came leisurely up the stairs. The spark in her eyes well-nigh went out when he appeared round the bedroom door. Her gaze hung doubtful for a moment; then to her joyous amazement she saw that he looked at her with the rallying smile of one who had just been relieved of a scene that was irksome. She could hold out no longer, and sobbed hysterically.

When he had restored her Farfrae naturally enough spoke of Henchard. "Of all men he was the least desirable as a visitor," he said. "But it is my belief that he's just a bit crazed. He has been reading to me a long lot of letters relating to his past life; and I could do no less than indulge him by listening."

This was sufficient. Henchard, then, had not told. Henchard's last words to Farfrae, in short, as he stood on the door-step had been these: "Well—I'm much obliged to 'ee for listening. I may tell 'ee more about her some day."

Finding this she was much perplexed as to Henchard's motives in opening the matter at all; for in such cases we attribute to an enemy a power of consistent action which we never find in ourselves or in our friends; and forget that abortive efforts from want of heart are as possible to revenge as to generosity.

Next morning Lucetta remained in bed, meditating how to parry this incipient attack. The bold stroke of telling Donald the truth, dimly conceived, was yet too bold; for she dreaded lest, in doing so, he, like the rest of the world, should believe that the episode was rather her fault than her misfortune.

She decided to employ persuasion—not with Donald, but with the enemy himself. It seemed the only practicable weapon left her as a woman. Having laid her plan she rose, and wrote to him who kept her on these tenterhooks:

"I overheard your interview with my husband last night—and saw the drift of your revenge. The very thought of it crushes me. Have pity on a distressed woman. If you could see me you would relent. You do not know how anxiety has told upon me lately. I will be at the Ring at the time you leave work—just before the sun goes down. Please come that way. I cannot rest till I have seen you face to face, and heard from your mouth that you will carry this horse-play no further."

To herself she said, on closing up this appeal: "If ever tears and pleadings have served the weak to fight the strong let them do so now!"

With this view she made a toilette which differed from all she had ever attempted before. To heighten her natural attractions had hitherto been the unvarying endeavour of her adult life, and one in which she was no novice. But now she neglected this, and even proceeded to impair the natural presentation. Beyond a natural reason for her slightly drawn look, she had not slept all the previous night, and this had produced upon her pretty though slightly worn features the aspect of a countenance ageing prematurely from extreme sorrow. She selected—as much from want of spirit as design—her poorest, plainest, and longest discarded attire.

To avoid the contingency of being recognized she veiled herself, and slipped out of the house quickly. The sun was resting on the hill like a drop of blood on an eyelid by the time she had got up the road opposite the Amphitheatre, which she speedily entered. The interior was shadowy, and emphatic of the absence of every living thing.

She was not disappointed in the fearful hope with which she awaited him. Henchard came over the top, descended, and Lucetta waited breathlessly. But having reached the arena she saw a change in his bearing: he stood still, at a little distance from her; she could not think why.

Nor could any one else have known. The truth was that in appointing this spot, and this hour, for the rendezvous, Lucetta had unwittingly backed up her entreaty by the strongest argument she could have used outside words, with this man of moods, glooms, and superstitions. Her figure in the midst of the huge enclosure, the unusual plainness of her dress, her attitude of hope and appeal, so strongly revived in his soul the memory of another ill-used woman who had stood there and thus in bygone days, and had now passed away into her rest, that he was unmanned, and his heart smote him for having attempted reprisals on one of a sex so weak. When he approached her, and before she had spoken a word, her point was half gained.

His manner as he had come down had been one of cynical carelessness; but he now put away his grim half-smile, and said in a kindly subdued tone, "Good night t'ye. Of course I'm glad to come if you want me."

"Oh, thank you," she said apprehensively.

"I am sorry to see 'ee looking so ill," he stammered, with unconcealed compunction.

She shook her head. "How can you be sorry?" she asked, "when you deliberately cause it?"

"What?" said Henchard uneasily. "Is it anything I have done that has pulled you down like that?"

"It is all your doing!" said she. "I have no other grief. My happiness would be secure enough but for your threats. Oh Michael, don't wreck me like this. You might think that you have done enough! When I came here I was a young woman; now I am rapidly becoming an old one. Neither my husband nor any other man will regard me with interest long."

Henchard was disarmed. His old feeling of supercilious pity for womankind in general was intensified by this suppliant appearing here as the double of the first. Moreover, that thoughtless want of foresight which had led to all her trouble remained with poor Lucetta still; she had come to meet him here in this compromising way without perceiving the risk. Such a woman was very small deer to hunt; he felt ashamed, lost all zest and desire to humiliate Lucetta there and then, and no longer envied Farfrae his bargain. He had married money, but nothing more. Henchard was anxious to wash his hands of the game.

"Well, what do you want me to do?" he said gently. "I am sure I shall be very willing. My reading of those letters was only a sort of practical joke; and I revealed nothing."

"To give me back the letters, and any papers you may have that breathe of matrimony or worse."

"So be it. Every scrap shall be yours. . . . But between you and me, Lucetta, he is sure to find out something of the matter, sooner or later."

"Ah," she said with eager tremulousness; "but not till I have proved myself a faithful and deserving wife to him, and then he may forgive me everything!"

Henchard silently looked at her: he almost envied Farfrae such love as that, even now. "H'm—I hope so," he said. "But you shall have the letters without fail. And your secret shall be kept. I swear it."

"How good you are!—how shall I get them?"

He reflected, and said he would send them the next morning. "Now don't doubt me," he added. "I can keep my word."

XXXVI

RETURNING from her appointment Lucetta saw a man waiting by the lamp nearest to her own door. When she stopped to go in he came and spoke to her. It was Jopp.

He begged her pardon for addressing her. But he had heard that Mr. Farfrae had been applied to by a neighbouring corn-merchant, to recommend a working partner; if so he wished to offer himself. He could give good security, and had stated as much to Mr. Farfrae in a letter; but he would feel much obliged if Lucetta would say a word in his favour to her husband.

"It is a thing I know nothing about," said Lucetta coldly.

"But you can testify to my trustworthiness better than anybody, ma'am," said Jopp. "I was in Jersey several years, and knew you there by sight."

"Indeed," she replied. "But I knew nothing of you."

"I think, ma'am, that a word or two from you would secure for me what I covet very much," he persisted.

She steadily refused to have anything to do with the affair, and, cutting him short because of her anxiety to get indoors before her husband should miss her left him on the pavement.

He watched her till she had vanished, and then went home. When he got there he sat down in the fireless chimney-corner looking at the iron dogs, and the wood laid across them for heating the morning kettle. A movement upstairs disturbed him, and Henchard came down from his bedroom, where he seemed to have been rummaging boxes.

"I wish," said Henchard, "you would do me a service, Jopp—now to-night, I mean, if you can. Leave this at Mrs. Farfrae's for her. I should take it myself of course, but I don't wish to be seen there."

He handed a package in brown paper, sealed. Henchard had been as good as his word. Immediately on coming indoors he had searched over his few belongings; and every scrap of Lucetta's writing that he possessed was here. Jopp indifferently expressed his willingness.

"Well—how have ye got on to-day?" his lodger asked. "Any prospect of an opening?"

"I am afraid not," said Jopp, who had not told the other of his application to Farfrae.

"There never will be in Casterbridge," declared Henchard decisively. "You must roam further afield." He said good-night to Jopp, and returned to his own part of the house.

Jopp sat on till his eyes were attracted by the shadow of the candle-snuff on the wall, and looking at the original he found that it had formed itself into a head like a red-hot cauliflower. Henchard's packet next met his gaze. He knew there had been something of the nature of wooing between Henchard and the now Mrs. Farfrae; and his vague ideas on the subject narrowed themselves down to these: Henchard had a parcel belonging to Mrs. Farfrae, and he had reasons for not returning that parcel to her in person. What could be inside it? So he went on and on till, animated by resentment at Lucetta's haughtiness as he thought it, and curiosity to learn if there were any weak sides to this transaction with Henchard, he examined the package. The pen and all its relations being awkward tools in Henchard's hands he had affixed the seals without an impression, it never occurring to him that the efficacy of such a fastening depended on this. Jopp was far less of a tyro: he lifted one of the seals with his penknife, peeped in at the end thus opened, saw that the bundle consisted of letters; and having satisfied himself thus far sealed up the end again by simply softening the wax with the candle, and went off with the parcel as requested.

His path was by the river-side at the foot of the town. Coming into the light at the bridge which stood at the end of High-Street he beheld lounging thereon Mother Cuxsom and Nance Mockridge.

"We be just going down Mixen-Lane way, to look into Peter's Finger afore creeping to bed," said Mrs. Cuxsom. "There's a fiddle and tambourine going on there. Lord, what's all the world—do ye come along too, Jopp—'twon't hinder ye five minutes."

Jopp had mostly kept himself out of this company, but present circumstances made him somewhat more reckless than usual, and without many words he decided to go to his destination that way.

Though the upper part of Durnover was mainly composed of a curious congeries of barns and farmsteads there was a less picturesque side to the parish. This was Mixen Lane, now in great part pulled down.

Mixen Lane was the Adullam of all the surrounding villages. It was the hiding-place of those who were in distress, and in debt, and trouble of every kind. Farm-labourers and other peasants, who combined a little poaching with their farming, and a little brawling and bibbing with their poaching, found themselves sooner or later in Mixen Lane. Rural mechanics too idle to mechanize, rural servants too rebellious to serve, drifted or were forced into Mixen Lane.

The lane and its surrounding thicket of thatched cottages stretched out like a spit into the moist and misty lowland. Much that was sad, much that was low, some things that were baneful, could be seen in Mixen Lane. Vice ran freely in and out certain of the doors of the neighbourhood; recklessness dwelt under the roof with the crooked chimney; shame in some bow-windows; theft (in times of privation) in the thatched and mudwalled houses by the sallows. Even slaughter had not been altogether unknown here. In a block of cottages up an alley there might have been erected an altar to disease in years gone by. Such was Mixen Lane in the times when Henchard and Farfrae were mayors.

Yet this mildewed leaf in the sturdy and flourishing Casterbridge plant lay close to the open country: not a hundred yards from a row of noble elms, and commanding a view across the moor of airy uplands and corn-fields, and mansions of the great. A brook divided the moor from the tenements, and to outward view there was no way across it—no way to the houses but roundabout by the road. But under every householder's stairs there was kept a mysterious plank nine inches wide; which plank was a secret bridge.

If you, as one of those refugee householders, came in from business after dark—and this was the business time here—you stealthily crossed the moor, approached the border of the aforesaid brook, and whistled opposite the house to which you belonged. A shape thereupon made its appearance on the other side bearing the bridge on end against the sky; it was lowered; you crossed, and a hand helped you to land yourself, together with the pheasants and hares gathered from neighbouring manors. You sold them slily the next morning, and the day after you stood before the magistrates, with the eyes of all your sympathizing neighbours concentrated on your back. You disappeared for a time: then you were again found quietly living in Mixen Lane.

Walking along the lane at dusk the stranger was struck by two or three peculiar features therein. One was an intermittent rumbling from the back premises of the inn half-way up; this meant a skittle-alley. Another was the extensive prevalence of whistling in the various domiciles—a piped note of some kind coming from nearly every open door. Another was the frequency of white aprons over dingy gowns among the women around the doorways. A white apron is a suspicious vesture in situations where spotlessness is difficult: moreover the industry and cleanliness which the white apron expressed were belied by the postures and gaits of the women who wore it—their knuckles being mostly on their hips (an attitude which lent them the aspect of two-handled mugs), and their shoulders against doorposts; while there was a curious alacrity in the turn of each honest woman's head upon her neck, and in the twirl of her honest eyes, at any noise resembling a masculine footfall along the lane.

Yet amid so much that was bad needy respectability also found a home. Under some of the roofs abode pure and virtuous souls whose presence there was due to the iron hand of necessity, and to that alone. Families from decayed villages—families of that once bulky but now nearly extinct section of village society called "liviers," or lifeholders— copyholders and others, whose roof-trees had fallen for some reason or other, compelling them to quit the rural spot that had been their home for generations—came here, unless they chose to lie under a hedge by the wayside.

The inn called Peter's Finger was the church of Mixen Lane.

It was centrally situate, as such places should be, and bore about the same social relation to the Three Mariners as the latter bore to the King's Arms. At first sight the inn was so respectable as to be puzzling. The front door was kept shut, and the step was so clean that evidently but few persons entered over its sanded surface. But at the corner of the public-house was an alley, a mere slit, dividing it from the next building. Halfway up the alley was a narrow door, shiny and paintless from the rub of infinite hands and shoulders. This was the actual entrance to the inn.

A pedestrian would be seen abstractedly passing along Mixen Lane; and then, in a moment, he would vanish, causing the gazer to blink like Ashton at the disappearance of Ravenswood. That abstracted pedestrian had edged into the slit by the adroit fillip of his person sideways; from the slit he edged into the tavern by a similar exercise of skill.

The company at the Three Mariners were persons of quality in comparison with the company which gathered here; though it must be admitted that the lowest fringe of the Mariner's party touched the crest of Peter's at points. Waifs and strays of all sorts loitered about here. The landlady was a virtuous woman who years ago had been unjustly sent to jail as an accessory to something or other after the fact. She underwent her twelvemonth, and had worn a martyr's countenance ever since, except at times of meeting the constable who apprehended her, when she winked her eye.

To this house Jopp and his acquaintances had arrived. The settles in which they sat down were thin and tall, their tops being guyed by pieces of twine to hooks in the ceiling; for when the guests grew boisterous the settles would rock and overturn without some such security. The thunder of bowls echoed from the back yard; swingels hung behind the blower of the chimney; and ex-poachers and ex-gamekeepers whom squires had persecuted without a cause sat elbowing each other—men who in past times had met in fights under the moon, till lapse of sentences on the one part, and loss of favour and expulsion from service on the other, brought them here together to a common level, where they sat calmly discussing old times.

"Dost mind how you could jerk a trout ashore with a bramble, and not ruffle the stream, Charl?" a deposed keeper was saying. "'Twas at that I caught 'ee once, if you can mind?"

"That can I. But the worst larry for me was that pheasant business at Yalbury Wood. Your wife swore false that time Joe—Oh, by Gad she did—there's no denying it."

"How was that?" asked Jopp.

"Why—Joe closed wi' me, and we rolled down together, close to his garden hedge. Hearing the noise out ran his wife with the oven-pyle, and it being dark under the trees she couldn't see which was uppermost. 'Where beest thee, Joe, under or top?' she screeched. 'Oh—under by Gad!' says he. She then began to rap down upon my skull, back, and ribs with the pyle till we'd roll over again. 'Where beest now, dear Joe, under or top?' she'd scream again. By George, 'twas through her I was took! And then when we got up in hall she sware that the cock pheasant was one of her rearing, when 'twas not your bird at all Joe; 'twas Squire Brown's bird—that's whose 'twas—one that we'd picked off as we passed his wood, an hour afore. It did hurt my feelings to be so wronged! . . . . Ah well—'tis over now."

"I might have had 'ee days afore that," said the keeper. "I was within a few yards of 'ee dozens of times, with a sight more of birds than that poor one."

"Yes—'tis not our greatest doings that the world gets wind of," said the furmity-woman, who, lately settled in this purlieu, sat among the rest. Having travelled a great deal in her time she spoke with cosmopolitan largeness of idea. It was she who presently asked Jopp what was the parcel he kept so snugly under his arm.

"Ah—therein lies a grand secret," said Jopp. "It is the passion of love. To think that a woman should love one man so well, and hate another so unmercifully."

"Who's the object of your meditation, sir?"

"One that stands high—in this town. I'd like to shame her! Upon my life 'twould be as good as a play to read her love-letters—the proud piece of silk and wax-work. For 'tis her love-letters that I've got here."

"Love-letters—then let's hear 'em good soul," said Mother Cuxsom. "Lord, do ye mind, Richard, what fools we used to be when we were younger?—getting a schoolboy to write ours for us; and giving him a penny, do ye mind, not to tell other folks what he'd put inside, do ye mind?"

By this time Jopp had pushed his finger under the seals, and unfastened the letters, tumbling them over and picking up one here and there at random, which he read aloud. These passages soon began to uncover the secret which Lucetta had so earnestly hoped to keep buried, though the epistles, being allusive only, did not make it altogether plain.

"Mrs. Farfrae wrote that!" said Nance Mockridge. "'Tis a humbling thing for us, as respectable women, that one of the same sex could do it. And now she's vowed herself to another man!"

"So much the better for her," said the aged furmity-woman. "Ah—I saved her from a real bad marriage, and she's never been the one to thank me."

"I say—what a good foundation for a skimmity-ride," said Nance.

"True," said Mrs. Cuxsom reflecting. "'Tis as good a ground for a skimmity-ride as ever I knowed; and it ought not to be wasted. The last one seen in Casterbridge must have been ten years ago, if a day."

At this moment there was a shrill whistle, and the landlady said to the man who had been called Charl: "'Tis Jim coming in. Would ye go and let down the bridge for me?"

Without replying Charl and his comrade Joe rose, and receiving a lantern from her went out at the back door and down the garden-path, which ended abruptly at the edge of the stream already mentioned. Beyond the stream was the open moor, from which a clammy breeze smote upon their faces as they advanced. Taking up the board that had lain in readiness one of them lowered it across the water, and the instant its further end touched the ground footsteps entered upon it, and there appeared from the shade a stalwart man with straps round his knees, a double-barrelled gun under his arm, and some birds slung up behind him. They asked him if he had had much luck.

"Not much," he said indifferently. "All safe inside?"

Receiving a reply in the affirmative he went on inwards, the others withdrawing the bridge and beginning to retreat in his rear. Before, however, they had entered the house a cry of "Ahoy," from the moor led them to pause.

The cry was repeated. They pushed the lantern into an outhouse, and went back to the brink of the stream.

"Ahoy—is this the way to Casterbridge?" said some one from the other side.

"Not in particular," said Charl. "There's a river afore 'ee."

"I don't care—here's for through it," said the man in the moor. "I've had travelling enough for to-day."

"Stop a minute, then," said Charl, finding that the man was no enemy. "Joe, bring the plank and lantern: here's somebody that's lost his way. You should have kept along the turnpike-road, friend, and not have strook across here."

"I should—as I see now. But I saw a light here, and says I to myself, that's an outlying house, depend on't."

The plank was now lowered; and the stranger's form shaped itself from the darkness. He was a middle-aged man, with hair and whiskers prematurely grey, and a broad and genial face. He had crossed on the plank without hesitation, and seemed to see nothing odd in the transit. He thanked them, and walked between them up the garden. "What place is this?" he asked, when they reached the door.

"A public-house."

"Ah. Perhaps it will suit me to put up at. Now then, come in, and wet your whistle at my expense for the lift over you have given me."

They followed him into the inn, where the increased light exhibited him as one who would stand higher in an estimate by the eye than in one by the ear. He was dressed with a certain clumsy richness—his coat being furred, and his head covered by a cap of sealskin, which, though the nights were chilly, must have been warm for the daytime, spring being somewhat advanced. In his hand he carried a small mahogany case, strapped, and clamped with brass.

Apparently surprised at the kind of company which confronted him through the kitchen-door, he at once abandoned his idea of putting up at the house; but taking the situation lightly, he called for glasses of the best, paid for them as he stood, in the passage, and turned to proceed on his way by the front door. This was barred, and while the landlady was unfastening it the conversation about the skimmington was continued in the sitting-room, and reached his ears.

"What do they mean by a skimmity-ride?" he asked.

"Oh, sir," said the landlady swinging her long ear-rings with deprecating modesty; "'tis old foolish thing they do in these parts, when a man's wife is—well, not too particularly his own. But as a respectable householder I don't encourage it."

"Still—are they going to do it shortly? It is a good sight to see, I suppose?"

"Well sir," she simpered. And then, bursting into naturalness, and glancing from the corner of her eye; "'Tis the funniest thing under the sun. And it costs money."

"Ah—I remember hearing of some such thing.—Now I shall be in Casterbridge for two or three weeks to come, and should not mind seeing the performance. Wait a moment." He turned back, entered the sitting-room, and said, "Here, good folks—I should like to see the old custom you are talking of, and I don't mind being something towards it—take that." He threw a sovereign on the table, and returned to the landlady at the door, of whom having inquired the way into the town he took his leave.

"There were more where that one came from," said Charl, when the sovereign had been taken up and handed to the landlady for safe keeping. "By George we ought to have got a few more while we had him here."

"No, no," answered the landlady. "This is a respectable house, thank God, and I'll have nothing done but what's honourable."

"Well," said Jopp, "now we'll consider the business begun, and will soon get it in train."

"We will," said Nance. "A good laugh warms my heart more than a cordial, and that's the truth on't."

Jopp gathered up the letters, and it being now somewhat late he did not attempt to call at Farfrae's with them that night. He reached home, sealed them up as before, and delivered the parcel at its address next morning. Within an hour its contents were reduced to ashes by Lucetta, who, poor soul, was inclined to fall down on her knees in thankfulness that at last no evidence remained of the unlucky episode with Henchard in her past. For though hers had been rather the laxity of inadvertence than of intention, that episode, if known, was not the less likely to operate fatally between herself and her husband.

XXXVII

SUCH was the state of things when the current affairs of Casterbridge were interrupted by an event of such magnitude that its influence reached to the lowest social stratum there, stirring the depths of its society simultaneously with the preparations for the skimmington. It was one of those excitements which, when they move a country-town, leave a permanent mark upon its chronicles, as a warm summer permanently marks the ring in the tree-trunk corresponding to its date.

A royal personage was about to pass through the borough, on his course further west to inaugurate an immense engineering work out that way. He had consented to halt half-an-hour or so in the town, and to receive an address from the corporation of Casterbridge, which, as a representative centre of husbandry, wished thus to express its sense of the great services he had rendered to agricultural science and economics, by his zealous promotion of designs for placing the art of farming on a more scientific footing.

Royalty had not been seen in Casterbridge since the days of the third King George, and then only by candlelight for a few minutes when that monarch, on a night-journey, had stopped to change horses at the King's Arms. The inhabitants therefore decided to make a thorough *fête carillonnée* of the unwonted occasion. Half-an-hour's pause was not long, it is true; but much might be done in it by a judicious grouping of incidents—above all, if the weather were fine.

The address was prepared on parchment, by an artist who was handy at ornamental lettering, and was laid on with the best gold leaf and colours that the sign-painter had in his shop. The Council met on the Tuesday before the appointed day, to arrange the details of the procedure.

While they were sitting, the door of the council-chamber standing open, they heard a heavy footstep coming up the stairs. It advanced along the passage, and Henchard entered the room, in clothes of frayed and threadbare shabbiness—the very clothes which he had used to wear in the primal days when he had sat among them.

"I have a feeling," he said, advancing to the table and laying his hand upon the green cloth, "that I should like to join ye in this reception of our illustrious visitor. I suppose I could walk with the rest?"

Embarrassed glances were exchanged by the council, and Grower nearly ate the end of his quill-pen off, so gnawed he it during the silence. Farfrae the young mayor, who by virtue of his office sat in the large chair, intuitively caught the sense of the meeting, and as spokesman was obliged to utter it, glad as he would have been that the duty should have fallen to another tongue.

"I hardly see that it would be proper, Mr. Henchard," said he. "The council are the council, and as ye are no longer one of the body there would be an irregularity in the proceeding. If ye were included, why not others?"

"I have a particular reason for wishing to assist at the ceremony."

Farfrae looked round. "I think I have expressed the feeling of the council?" he said.

"Yes, yes," from Dr. Bath, Lawyer Long, Alderman Tubber, and several more.

"Then I am not to be allowed to have anything to do with it officially?"

"I am afraid so, it is out of the question, indeed. But of course you can see the doings full well, such as they are to be, like the rest of the spectators."

Henchard did not reply to that very obvious suggestion, and turning on his heel went away.

It had been only a passing fancy of his, but opposition crystallized it into a determination. "I'll welcome his Royal Highness, or nobody shall!" he went about saying. "I am not going to be sat upon by Farfrae, or any of the rest of the paltry crew. You shall see."

The eventful morning was bright, a full-faced sun confronting early window-gazers eastward, and all perceived (for they were practised in weather lore) that there was permanence in the glow. Visitors soon began to flock in from county houses, villages, remote copses and lonely uplands, the latter in oiled boots and tilt-bonnets, to see the reception, or if not to see it at any rate to be near it. There was hardly a workman in the town who did not put a clean shirt on. Solomon Longways, Christopher Coney, Buzzford, and the rest of that fraternity showed their sense of the occasion by advancing their customary eleven o'clock pint to half-past ten; from which they found a difficulty in getting back to the proper hour for several days.

Henchard had determined to do no work that day. He primed himself in the morning with a glass of rum, and walking down the street met Elizabeth-Jane, whom he had not seen for a week. "It was lucky," he said to her, "my twenty-one years had expired before this came on, or I should never have had the nerve to carry it out."

"Carry out what?" said she, alarmed.

"This welcome I am going to give our Royal Visitor."

She was perplexed. "Shall we go and see it together?" she said.

"See it! I have other fish to fry. You see it. It will be worth seeing."

She could do nothing to elucidate this, and decked herself out with a heavy heart. As the appointed time drew near she got sight again of her step-father. She thought he was going to the Three Mariners; but no; he elbowed his way through the gay throng to the shop of Woolfrey the draper. She waited in the crowd without.

In a few minutes he emerged, wearing, to her surprise, a brilliant rosette, while, more surprising still, in his hand he carried a flag, of somewhat homely construction, formed by tacking one of the small union-jacks, which abounded in the town to-day, to the end of a deal wand—probably the roller from a piece of calico. Henchard rolled up his flag on the doorstep, put it under his arm, and went down the street.

Suddenly the taller members of the crowd turned their heads, and the shorter stood on tip-toe. It was said that the royal *cortège* approached. The railway had stretched out an arm towards Casterbridge at this time, but had not reached it by several miles as yet; so that the intervening distance, as well as the remainder of the journey, was to be traversed by road in the old fashion. People thus waited—the county families in their carriages, the masses on foot—and watched the far-stretching London highway to the ringing of bells, and chatter of tongues.

From the background Elizabeth-Jane watched the scene. Some seats had been arranged from which ladies could witness the spectacle, and the front seat was occupied by Lucetta, the mayor's wife, just at present. In the road under her eyes stood Henchard. She appeared so bright and pretty that, as it seemed, he was experiencing the momentary weakness of wishing for her notice. But he was far from attractive to a woman's eye, ruled as that is so largely by the superficies of things. He was not only a journeyman, unable to appear as he formerly had appeared, but he disdained to appear as well as he might. Everybody else, from the mayor to the washer-woman, shone in new vesture according to means; but Henchard had doggedly retained the fretted and weather-beaten garments of bygone years.

Hence, alas, this occurred: Lucetta's eyes slid over him to this side and to that without anchoring on his features—as gaily dressed women's eyes will too often do on such occasions. Her manner signified quite plainly that she meant to know him in public no more.

But she was never tired of watching Donald, as he stood in animated converse with his friends a few yards off, wearing round his young neck the official gold chain with great square links like that round the royal unicorn. Every trifling emotion that her husband showed as he talked had its reflex on her face and lips, which moved in little duplicates to his. She was living his part rather than her own, and cared for no one's situation but Farfrae's that day.

At length a man stationed at the furthest turn of the high-road, namely on the second bridge, of which mention has been made, gave a signal; and the corporation in their robes proceeded from the front of the Townhall to the archway erected at the entrance to the town. The carriages containing the royal visitor and his suite arrived at the spot in a cloud of dust, a procession was formed, and the whole came on to the Town hall at a walking-pace.

This spot was the centre of interest. There were a few clear yards in front of the royal carriage, sanded; and into this space a man stepped before any one could prevent him. It was Henchard. He had unrolled his private flag, and removing his hat he staggered to the side of the slowing vehicle, waving the union-jack to and fro with his left hand, while he blandly held out his right to the illustrious personage.

All the ladies said with bated breath, "Oh, look there!" and Lucetta was ready to faint. Elizabeth-Jane peeped through the shoulders of those in front, saw what it was, and was terrified; and then her interest in the spectacle as a strange phenomenon got the better of her fear.

Farfrae with mayoral authority immediately rose to the occasion. He seized Henchard by the shoulder, dragged him back, and told him roughly to be off. Henchard's eyes met his, and Farfrae observed the fierce light in them, despite his excitement and irritation. For a moment Henchard stood his ground rigidly; then by an unaccountable impulse gave way and retired. Farfrae glanced to the ladies' gallery, and saw that his Calphurnia's cheek was pale.

"Why—it is your husband's old patron!" said Mrs. Blowbody, a lady of the neighbourhood, who sat beside Lucetta.

"Patron!" said Donald's wife with quick indignation.

"Do you say the man is an acquaintance of Mr. Farfrae's?" observed Mrs. Bath, the physician's wife, a new comer to the town through her recent marriage with the doctor.

"He works for my husband," said Lucetta.

"Oh—is that all. They have been saying to me that it was through him your husband first got a footing in Casterbridge. What stories people will tell!"

"They will indeed. It was not so at all. Donald's genius would have enabled him to get a footing anywhere, without anybody's help! He would have been just the same if there had been no Henchard in the world."

It was partly Lucetta's ignorance of the circumstances of Donald's arrival which led her to speak thus; partly the sensation that everybody seemed bent on snubbing her at this triumphant time. The incident had occupied but a few moments, but it was necessarily witnessed by the royal personage, who however, with practised tact, affected not to have noticed anything unusual. He alighted, the mayor advanced, the address was read, the illustrious personage replied, then said a few words to Farfrae, and shook hands with Lucetta, as the mayor's wife. The ceremony occupied but a few minutes, and the carriages rattled heavily as Pharaoh's chariots down Corn Street and out upon the Budmouth Road, in continuation of the journey coast-ward.

In the crowd stood Coney, Buzzford, and Longways. "Some difference between him now, and when he zung at the Dree Mariners," said the first. "'Tis wonderful how he could get a lady of her quality to go snacks wi' en in such quick time."

"True. Yet how folk do worship fine clothes. Now there's a better looking woman than she that nobody notices at all, because she's akin to that hontish fellow Henchard."

"I could worship ye, Buzz, for saying that," remarked Nance Mockridge. "I do like to see the trimming pulled off such Christmas candles. I am quite unequal to the part of villain myself, or I'd gie all my small silver to see that lady toppered. . . . And perhaps I shall soon," she added significantly.

"That's not a noble passiont for a 'oman to keep up," said Longways.

Nance did not reply, but every one knew what she meant. The ideas diffused by the reading of Lucetta's letters at Peter's Finger had condensed into a scandal, which was spreading like a miasmatic fog through Mixen Lane, and thence up the back streets of Casterbridge.

This mixed assemblage of idlers known to each other presently fell apart into two bands, by a process of natural selection, the frequenters of Peter's Finger going off Mixen Lane-wards, where most of them lived, while Coney, Buzzford, Longways, and that connection remained in the street.

"You know what's brewing down there, I suppose? said Buzzford mysteriously to the others.

Coney looked at him. "Not the skimmity-ride?"

Buzzford nodded.

"I have my doubts if it will be carried out," said Longways. "If they are getting it up they are keeping it mighty close."

"I heard they were thinking of it a fortnight ago, at all events."

"If I were sure o't I'd lay information," said Longways emphatically. "'Tis too rough a joke, and apt to wake riots in towns. We know th.t the Scotchman is a right enough man, and that his lady has been a right enough 'oman since she came here, and if there was anything wrong about her afore, that's their business, not ours."

Coney reflected. Farfrae was still liked in the community; but it must be owned that, as the mayor and man of money, engrossed with affairs and ambitions, he had lost in the eyes of the poorer inhabitants something of that wondrous charm which he had had for them as a light-hearted penniless young man, who sang ditties as readily as the birds in the trees. Hence the anxiety to keep him from annoyance showed not quite the ardour that would have animated it in former days.

"Suppose we make inquiration into it, Christopher," continued Longways, "and if we find there's really anything in it, drop a letter to them most concerned, and advise 'em to keep out of the way?"

This course was decided on, and the group separated, Buzzford saying to Coney "Come, my ancient friend; let's move on. There's nothing more to see here."

These well-intentioned ones would have been surprised had they known how ripe the great jocular plot really was. "Yes—to-night," Jopp had said to the Peter's party at the corner of Mixen Lane. "As a wind-up to the royal visit the hit will be all the more pat, by reason of their great elevation to-day."

To him, at least, it was not a joke, but a retaliation.

XXXVIII

THE proceedings had been brief—too brief—to Lucetta, whom an intoxicating *Weltlust* had fairly mastered; but they had brought her a great triumph nevertheless. The shake of the royal hand still lingered in her fingers; and that chit-chat she had overheard, that her husband might possibly receive the honour of knighthood, though idle to a degree, seemed not the wildest vision; stranger things had occurred to men so good and captivating as her Scotchman was.

After the collision with the mayor Henchard had withdrawn behind the ladies' stand; and there he stood regarding with a stare of abstraction the spot on the lappel of his coat where Farfrae's hand had seized it. He put his own hand there, as if he could hardly realize such an outrage from one whom it had once been his wont to treat with ardent generosity. While pausing in this half-stupefied state the conversation of Lucetta with the other ladies reached his ears: and he distinctly heard her deny him—deny that he had assisted Donald, that he was anything more than a common journeyman.

He moved on homeward, and met Jopp in the archway to the Bull-Stake. "So you've had a snub," said Jopp.

"And what if I have?" answered Henchard sternly.

"Why I've had one too, so we are both under the same cold shade." He briefly related his attempt to win Lucetta's intercession.

Henchard merely heard his story, without taking it deeply in. His own relation to Farfrae and Lucetta overshadowed all kindred ones. He went on saying brokenly to himself, "She has supplicated to me in her time; and now her tongue won't own me nor her eyes see me! . . . And he—how angry he looked. He drove me back as if I were a bull breaking fence. . . . I took it like a lamb, for I saw it could not be settled there. He can rub brine on a green wound! . . . But he shall pay for it, and she shall be sorry. It must come to a tussle—face to face; and then we'll see how a coxcomb can front a man!"

Without further reflection the fallen merchant, bent on

some wild purpose, ate a hasty dinner, and went forth to find Farfrae. After being injured by him as a rival, and snubbed by him as a journeyman, the crowning degradation had been reserved for this day—that he should be shaken at the collar by him as a vagabond in the face of the whole town.

The crowds had dispersed. But for the green arches which still stood as they were erected Casterbridge life had resumed its ordinary shape. Henchard went down Corn Street till he came to Farfrae's house, where he knocked, and left a message that he would be glad to see his employer at the granaries as soon as he conveniently could come there. Having done this he proceeded round to the back and entered the yard.

Nobody was present, for, as he had been aware, the labourers and carters were enjoying a half-holiday on account of the events of the morning—though the carters would have to return for a short time later on, to feed and litter down the horses. He had reached the granary steps and was about to ascend, when he said to himself aloud "I'm stronger than he."

Henchard returned to a shed, where he selected a short piece of rope from several pieces that were lying about; hitching one end of this to a nail he took the other in his right hand and turned himself bodily round, while keeping his arm against his side; by this contrivance he pinioned the arm effectively. He now went up the ladders to the top floor of the corn-stores.

It was empty, except of a few sacks, and at the further end was the door often mentioned, opening under the cathead and chain that hoisted the sacks. He fixed the door open, and looked over the sill. There was a depth of thirty or forty feet to the ground; here was the spot on which he had been standing with Farfrae when Elizabeth-Jane had seen him lift his arm, with many misgivings as to what the movement portended.

He retired a few steps into the loft, and waited. From this elevated perch his eye could sweep the roofs roundabout, the upper parts of the luxurious chestnut trees, now delicate in leaves of a week's age, and the drooping boughs of the limes, Farfrae's garden; and the green door leading therefrom. In course of time—he could not say how long—that green door opened and Farfrae came through. He was dressed as if for a journey. The low light of the nearing evening caught his head and face when he emerged from the shadow of the wall, warming them to a complexion of flame-colour. Henchard watched him with his mouth firmly set, the squareness of his jaw and the verticality of his profile being unduly marked.

Farfrae came on with one hand in his pocket, and humming a tune in a way which told that the words were most in his mind. They were those of the song he had sung when he arrived years before at the Three Mariners, a poor young man, adventuring for life and fortune and scarcely knowing whitherward:

> "And here's a hand, my trusty fiere,
> And gie's a hand o' thine."

Nothing moved Henchard like an old melody. He sank back. "No: I can't do it!" he gasped. "Why does the infernal fool begin that now!"

At length Farfrae was silent, and Henchard looked out of the loft door. "Will ye come up here?" he said.

"Aye, man," said Farfrae. "I couldn't see ye. What's wrang?"

A minute later Henchard heard his feet on the lowest ladder. He heard him land on the first floor, ascend and land on the second, begin the ascent to the third. And then his head rose through the trap behind.

"What are you doing up here at this time?" he asked coming forward. "Why didn't ye take your holiday like the rest of the men?" He spoke in a tone which had just severity enough in it to show that he remembered the untoward event of the forenoon, and his conviction that Henchard had been drinking.

Henchard said nothing; but going back he closed the stair hatchway, and stamped upon it so that it went tight into its frame; he next turned to the wondering young man, who by this time observed that one of Henchard's arms was bound to his side.

"Now," said Henchard quietly, "we stand face to face—man and man. Your money and your fine wife no longer lift 'ee above me as they did but now, and my poverty does not press me down."

"What does it all mean?" asked Farfrae simply.

"Wait a bit my lad. You should ha' thought twice before you affronted to extremes a man who had nothing to lose. I've stood your rivalry, which ruined me, and your snubbing, which humbled me; but your hustling, that disgraced me, I won't stand!"

Farfrae warmed a little at this. "Ye'd no business there," he said.

"As much as any one among ye. What you forward stripling, tell a man of my age he'd no business there?" The anger-vein swelled in his forehead as he spoke.

"You insulted royalty, Henchard; and 'twas my duty, as the chief magistrate, to stop you."

"Royalty be damned," said Henchard. "I am as loyal as you, come to that."

"I am not here to argue. Wait till you cool doon, wait till you cool; and you will see things the same way as I do."

"You may be the one to cool first," said Henchard grimly. "Now this is the case. Here be we, in this four-square loft, to finish out that little wrestle you began this morning. There's the door, forty foot above ground. One of us two puts the other out by that door—the master stays inside. If he likes he may go down afterwards and give the alarm that the other has fallen out by accident—or he may tell the truth—that's his business. As the strongest man I've tied one arm to take no advantage of 'ee. D'ye understand? Then here's at 'ee!"

There was no time for Farfrae to do aught but one thing, to close with Henchard, for the latter had come on at once. It was a wrestling-match, the object of each being to give his antagonist a back fall; and on Henchard's part, unquestionably, that it should be through the door.

At the outset Henchard's hold by his only free hand, the right, was on the left side of Farfrae's collar, which he firmly grappled, the latter holding Henchard by his collar with the contrary hand. With his right he endeavoured to get hold of his antagonist's left arm, which however, he could not do, so adroitly did Henchard keep it in the rear as he gazed upon the lowered eyes of his fair and slim antagonist.

Henchard planted the first toe forward, Farfrae crossing him with his; and thus far the struggle had very much the appearance of the ordinary wrestling of those parts. Several minutes were passed by them in this attitude, the pair rocking and writhing like trees in a gale, both preserving an absolute silence. By this time their breathing could be heard. Then Farfrae tried to get hold of the other side of Henchard's collar, which was resisted by the larger man exerting all his force in a wrenching movement, and this part of the struggle ended by his forcing Farfrae down on his knees by sheer pressure of one of his muscular arms. Hampered as he was, however, he could not keep him there, and Farfrae finding his feet again the struggle proceeded as before.

By a whirl Henchard brought Donald dangerously near the precipice; seeing his position the Scotchman for the first time locked himself to his adversary, and all the efforts of that infuriated Prince of Darkness—as he might have been called from his appearance just now—were inadequate to lift or loosen Farfrae for a time. By an extraordinary effort he succeeded at last, though not until they had got far back again from the fatal door. In doing so Henchard contrived to turn Farfrae a complete somersault. Had Henchard's other arm been free it would have been all over with Farfrae then. But again he regained his feet, wrenching Henchard's arm considerably, and causing him sharp pain, as could be seen from the twitching of his face. He instantly delivered the younger man an annihilating turn by the left fore-hip, as it used to be expressed, and following up his advantage thrust him towards the door, never loosening his hold till Farfrae's fair head was hanging over the window-sill, and his arm dangling down outside the wall.

"Now," said Henchard between his gasps, "this is the end of what you began this morning. Your life is in my hands."

"Then take it, take it!" said Farfrae. "Ye've wished to long enough!"

Henchard looked down upon him in silence, and their eyes met. "O, Farfrae—that's not true!" he said bitterly. "God is my witness that no man ever loved another as I did thee at one time. . . . And now—though I came here to kill 'ee, I cannot hurt thee! Go and give me in charge—do what you will—I care nothing for what comes of me!"

He withdrew to the back part of the loft, loosened his arm, and flung himself into a corner upon some sacks, in the abandonment of remorse. Farfrae regarded him in silence; then went to the hatch and descended through it. Henchard would fain have recalled him; but his tongue failed in its task, and the young man's steps died on his ear.

Henchard took his full measure of shame and self-reproach. The scenes of his first acquaintance with Farfrae rushed back upon him—that time when the curious mixture of romance and thrift in the young man's composition so commanded his heart that Farfrae could play upon him as on an instrument. So thoroughly subdued was he that he remained on the sacks in a crouching attitude, unusual for a man, and for such a man. Its womanliness sat tragically on the figure of so stern a piece of virility. He heard a conversation below, the opening of the coach-house door, and the putting in of a horse, but took no notice.

Here he stayed till the thin shades thickened to opaque obscurity, and the loft-door became an oblong of gray light— the only visible shape around. At length he arose, shook the dust from his clothes wearily, felt his way to the hatch, and gropingly descended the steps till he stood in the yard.

"He thought highly of me once," he murmured. "Now he'll hate me, and despise me for ever!"

He became possessed by an overpowering wish to see Farfrae again that night, and by some desperate pleading to attempt the well-nigh impossible task of winning pardon for his late mad attack. But as he walked towards Farfrae's door, he recalled the unheeded doings in the yard while he had lain above in a sort of stupor. Farfrae he remembered had gone to the stable and put the horse into the gig; while doing so Whittle had brought him a letter; Farfrae had then said that he would not go towards Budmouth as he had intended—that he was unexpectedly summoned to Weatherbury, and meant to call at Mellstock on his way thither, that place lying but one or two miles out of his course.

He must have come prepared for a journey when he first arrived in the yard, unsuspecting enmity; and he must have driven off (though in a changed direction) without saying a word to any one on what had occurred between themselves. It would therefore be useless to call at Farfrae's house till very late.

There was no help for it but to wait till his return, though waiting was almost torture to his restless and self-accusing soul. He walked about the streets and outskirts of the town, lingering here and there till he reached the stone bridge of which mention has been made, an accustomed halting place with him now. Here he spent a long time, the purl of waters through the weirs meeting his ear, and the Casterbridge lights glimmering at no great distance off.

While leaning thus upon the parapet, his listless attention was awakened by sounds of an unaccustomed kind from the town quarter. They were a confusion of rhythmical noises, to which the streets added yet more confusion by encumbering them with echoes. His first incurious thought, that the clangour arose from the town band, engaged in an attempt to round off a memorable day by a burst of evening harmony, was contradicted by certain peculiarities of reverberation. But inexplicability did not rouse him to more than a cursory heed; his sense of degradation was too strong for the admission of foreign ideas; and he leant against the parapet as before.

XXXIX

WHEN Farfrae descended out of the loft, breathless from his
encounter with Henchard, he paused at the bottom to recover
himself. He arrived at the yard with the intention of putting
his horse into the gig himself (all the men having a holiday),
and driving to a village on the Budmouth Road. Despite the
fearful struggle he decided still to persevere in his journey, so
as to recover himself before going indoors and meeting the
eyes of Lucetta. He wished to consider his course in a case so
serious.

When he was just on the point of driving off Whittle arrived
with a note, badly addressed, and bearing the word "immediate"
upon the outside. On opening it he was surprised to see that
it was unsigned. It contained a brief request that he would go
to Weatherbury that evening about some business which he
was conducting there. Farfrae knew nothing that could make
it pressing; but as he was bent upon going out he yielded to
the anonymous request, particularly as he had a call to make
at Mellstock which could be included in the same tour.
Thereupon he told Whittle of his change of direction, in
words which Henchard had overheard; and set out on his way.
Farfrae had not directed his man to take the message indoors,
and Whittle had not been supposed to do so on his own
responsibility.

Now the anonymous letter was a well-intentioned but
clumsy contrivance of Longways and other of Farfrae's men,
to get him out of the way for the evening, in order that the
satirical mummery should fall flat, if it were attempted. By
giving open information they would have brought down upon
their heads the vengeance of those among their comrades who
enjoyed these boisterous old games; and therefore the plan of
sending a letter recommended itself by its indirectness.

For poor Lucetta they took no protective measure, believing
with the majority there was some truth in the scandal, which
she would have to bear as she best might.

It was about eight o'clock, and Lucetta was sitting in the

drawing-room alone. Night had set in for more than half-an-hour, but she had not had the candles lighted, for when Farfrae was away she preferred waiting for him by the firelight, and, if it were not too cold, keeping one of the window sashes a little way open that the sound of his wheels might reach her ears early. She was leaning back in her chair, in a more hopeful mood than she had enjoyed since her marriage. The day had been such a success; and the temporary uneasiness which Henchard's show of effrontery had wrought in her disappeared with the quiet disappearance of Henchard himself under her husband's reproof. The floating evidences of her absurd passion for him, and its consequences, had been destroyed, and she really seemed to have no cause for fear.

The reverie in which these and other subjects mingled was disturbed by a hubbub in the distance, that increased moment by moment. It did not greatly surprise her, the afternoon having been given up to recreation by a majority of the populace since the passage of the Royal equipages. But her attention was at once riveted to the matter by the voice of a maid-servant next door, who spoke from an upper window across the street to some other maid even more elevated than she.

"Which way be they going now?" inquired the first with interest.

"I can't be sure for a moment," said the second, "because of the malter's chimbley. Oh yes—I can see 'em. Well, I declare, I declare!"

"What, what?" from the first, more enthusiastically.

"They are coming up Corn Street after all! They sit back to back!"

"What—two of 'em—are there two figures?"

"Yes. Two images on a donkey, back to back, their elbows tied to one another's. She's facing the head, and he's facing the tail."

"Is it meant for anybody particular?"

"Well—it mid be. The man has got on a blue coat and kerseymere leggings; he has black whiskers, and a reddish face. 'Tis a stuffed figure, with a falseface."

The din was increasing now—then it lessened a little.

"There—I shan't see, after all!" cried the disappointed first maid.

"They have gone into a back street—that's all," said the one who occupied the enviable position in the attic. "There—now I have got 'em all endways nicely."

"What's the woman like? Just say, and I can tell in a moment if 'tis meant for one I've in mind."

"My—why—'tis dressed just as *she* was dressed when she sat in the front seat at the time the play-actors came to the Town-hall!"

Lucetta started to her feet; and almost at the instant the door of the room was quickly and softly opened. Elizabeth-Jane advanced into the fire-light.

"I have come to see you," she said breathlessly. "I did not stop to knock—forgive me. I see you have not shut your shutters, and the window is open."

Without waiting for Lucetta's reply she crossed quickly to the window, and pulled out one of the shutters. Lucetta glided to her side. "Let it be—hush!" she said peremptorily, in a dry voice, while she seized Elizabeth-Jane by the hand, and held up her finger. Their intercourse had been so low and hurried that not a word had been lost of the conversation without; which had thus proceeded:

"Her neck is uncovered, and her hair in bands, and her back-comb in place; she's got on a puce silk, and white stockings, and coloured shoes."

Again Elizabeth-Jane attempted to close the window; but Lucetta held her by main force.

"'Tis me," she said, with a face pale as death. "A procession—a scandal—an effigy of me, and him!"

The look of Elizabeth betrayed that the latter knew it already.

"Let us shut it out," coaxed Elizabeth-Jane, noting that the rigid wildness of Lucetta's features was growing yet more rigid and wild with the nearing of the noise and laughter. "Let us shut it out!"

"It is of no use!" she shrieked out. "He will see it, won't he? Donald will see it. He is just coming home—and it will break his heart—he will never love me any more—and oh, it will kill me—kill me!"

Elizabeth-Jane was frantic now. "Oh, can't something be done to stop it?" she cried. "Is there nobody to do it—not one?"

She relinquished Lucetta's hands, and ran to the door. Lucetta herself, saying recklessly 'I will see it!" turned to the window, threw up the sash, and went out upon the balcony. Elizabeth immediately followed her, and put her arm round her to pull her in. Lucetta's eyes were straight upon the spectacle of the uncanny revel, now advancing rapidly. The numerous lights around the two effigies threw them up into lurid distinctness: it was impossible to mistake the pair for other than the intended victims.

"Come in, come in," implored Elizabeth; "and let me shut the window!"

"She's me—she's me—even to the parasol—my green parasol!" cried Lucetta with a wild laugh as she stepped in. She stood motionless for one second—then fell heavily to the floor.

Almost at the instant of her fall the rude music of the skimmington ceased. The roars of sarcastic laughter went off in ripples, and the trampling died out like the rustle of a spent wind. Elizabeth was only indirectly conscious of this; she had rung the bell, and was bending over Lucetta, who remained convulsed on the carpet in the paroxysms of an epileptic seizure. She rang again and again, in vain; the probability being that the servants had all run out of the house to see more of the Demoniac Sabbath than they could see within.

At last Farfrae's man, who had been agape on the door-step, came up; then the cook. The shutters, hastily pushed to by Elizabeth, were quite closed, a light was obtained, Lucetta carried to her room, and the man sent off for a doctor. While Elizabeth was undressing her she recovered consciousness; but as soon as she remembered what had passed the fit returned.

The doctor arrived with unhoped-for promptitude; he had been standing at his door, like others, wondering what the uproar meant. As soon as he saw the unhappy sufferer he said, in answer to Elizabeth's mute appeal, "This is serious."

"It is a fit," Elizabeth said.

"Yes. But a fit in the present state of her health means mischief. You must send at once for Mr. Farfrae. Where is he?"

"He has driven into the country, sir," said the parlour-maid; "to some place on the Budmouth road. He's likely to be back soon."

"Never mind—he must be sent for, in case he should not hurry." The doctor returned to the bedside again. The man was dispatched, and they soon heard him clattering out of the yard at the back.

Meanwhile Mr. Benjamin Grower, that prominent burgess of whom mention has been already made, hearing the din of cleavers, tongs, tambourines, kits, crouds, humstrums, serpents, rams'-horns, and other historical kinds of music as he sat indoors in the High Street, had put on his hat and gone out to learn the cause. He came to the corner above Farfrae's, and soon guessed the nature of the proceedings; for being a native of the town he had witnessed such rough jests before. His first move was to search hither and thither for the constables; there were two in the town, shrivelled men whom he ultimately found in hiding up an alley yet more shrivelled than usual, having some not ungrounded fears that they might be roughly handled if seen.

"What can we two poor lammigers do against such a multitude!" expostulated Stubberd in answer to Mr. Grower's chiding. "'Tis tempting 'em to commit *felo de se* upon us, and that would be the death of the perpetrator; and we wouldn't be the cause of a fellow-creature's death on no account, not we."

"Get some help then. Here, I'll come with you. We'll see what a few words of authority can do. Quick now; have you got your staves?"

"We didn't want the folk to notice us as law officers, being so short-handed, sir; so we pushed our Gover'ment staves up this water-pipe."

"Out with 'em, and come along, for heaven's sake!—Ah, here's Mr. Blowbody; that's lucky." (Blowbody was the third of the three borough magistrates.)

"Well, what's the row?" said Blowbody. "Got their names—hey?"

"No. Now," said Grower to one of the constables, "you go with Mr. Blowbody round by the Old Walk, and come up the street; and I'll go with Stubberd straight forward. By this plan we shall have 'em between us. Get their names only: no attack or interruption."

Thus they started. But as Stubberd with Mr. Grower advanced into Corn Street whence the sounds had proceeded, they were surprised that no procession could be seen. They passed Farfrae's, and looked to the end of the street. The lamp-flames waved, the Walk trees soughed, a few loungers stood about with their hands in their pockets. Everything was as usual.

"Have you seen a motley crowd, making a disturbance?" Grower said magisterially to one of these in a fustian jacket, who smoked a short pipe and wore straps round his knees.

"Beg yer pardon, sir?" blandly said the person addressed, who was no other than Charl, of Peter's Finger. Mr. Grower repeated the words.

Charl shook his head to the zero of childlike ignorance. "No; we haven't seen anything; have we Joe? And you was here afore I."

Joseph was quite as blank as the other in his reply.

"H'm—that's odd," said Mr. Grower. "Ah—here's a respectable man coming that I know by sight. Have you," he inquired, addressing the nearing shape of Jopp; "have you seen any gang of fellows making a devil of a noise— skimmington-riding, or something of the sort?"

"Oh no—nothing sir," Jopp replied as if receiving the most singular news. "But I've not been far to-night, so perhaps——"

"Oh, 'twas here—just here," said the magistrate.

"Now I've noticed, come to think o't, that the wind in the Walk trees makes a peculiar poetical-like murmur to-night, sir; more than common; so perhaps 'twas that?" Jopp suggested, as he re-arranged his hand in his great-coat pocket (where it ingeniously supported a pair of kitchen tongs and a cow's horn, thrust up under his waistcoat).

"No, no, no—d'ye think I'm a fool! Constable, come this way. They must have gone into the back street."

Neither in back street nor in front street, however, could the disturbers be perceived; and Blowbody and the second constable, who came up at this time, brought similar intelligence. Effigies, donkey, lanterns, band, all had disappeared like the crew of Comus. "Now," said Mr. Grower, "there's only one thing more we can do. Get ye half a dozen helpers, and go in a body to Mixen Lane, and into Peter's Finger. I'm much mistaken if you don't find a clue to the perpetrators there."

The rusty-jointed executors of the law mustered assistance as soon as they could, and the whole party marched off to the lane of notoriety. It was no rapid matter to get there at night, not a lamp or glimmer of any sort offering itself to light the way, except an occasional pale radiance through some window curtain, or through the chink of some door which could not be closed because of the smoky chimney within. At last they entered the inn boldly, by the till then bolted front door, after a prolonged knocking of loudness commensurate with the importance of their standing.

In the settles of the large room, guyed to the ceiling by cords as usual for stability, an ordinary group sat drinking and smoking with statuesque quiet of demeanour. The landlady looked mildly at the invaders, saying in honest accents, "Good evening, gentlemen; there's plenty of room. I hope there's nothing amiss?"

They looked round the room. "Surely," said Stubberd to one of the men, "I saw you by now in Corn Street—Mr. Grower spoke to 'ee?"

The man, who was Charl, shook his head absently. "I've been here this last hour, hain't I, Nance?" he said to the woman who meditatively sipped her ale near him.

"Faith, that you have. I came in for my quiet supper-time half-pint, and you was here then, as was all the rest."

The other constable was facing the clock-case where he saw reflected in the glass a quick motion by the landlady. Turning sharply he caught her closing the oven door.

"Something curious about that oven, ma'am?" he observed advancing, opening it, and drawing out a tambourine.

"Ah," she said, apologetically; "that's what we keep here to use when there's a little quiet dancing. You see damp weather spoils it, so I put it there to keep it dry."

The constable nodded knowingly; but what he knew was nothing. Nohow could anything be elicited from this mute and inoffensive assembly. In a few minutes the investigators went out, and joining those of their auxiliaries who had been left at the door, they pursued their way elsewhither.

LONG before this time Henchard, weary of his ruminations on the bridge, had repaired towards the town. When he stood at the bottom of the street a procession burst upon his view, in the act of turning out of an alley just above him. The lanterns, horns, and multitude startled him; he saw the mounted images, and knew what it all meant.

They crossed the way, entered another street, and disappeared. He turned back a few steps and was lost in grave reflection, finally wending his way homeward by the obscure river-side path. Unable to rest there he went to his step-daughter's lodging, and was told that Elizabeth-Jane had gone to Mrs. Farfrae's. Like one acting in obedience to a charm, and with a nameless apprehension, he followed in the same direction, in the hope of meeting her, the roysterers having vanished. Disappointed in this, he gave the gentlest of pulls to the door-bell, and then learnt particulars of what had occurred, together with the doctor's imperative orders that Farfrae should be brought home, and how they had set out to meet him on the Budmouth Road.

"But he has gone to Mellstock and Weatherbury!" exclaimed Henchard, now unspeakably grieved. "Not Budmouth way at all."

But, alas! for Henchard; he had lost his good name. They would not believe him, taking his words but as the frothy utterances of recklessness. Though Lucetta's life seemed at that moment to depend upon her husband's return (she being in great mental agony lest he should never know the unexaggerated truth of her past relations with Henchard), no messenger was despatched towards Weatherbury. Henchard, in a state of bitter anxiety and contrition, determined to seek Farfrae himself.

To this end he hastened down the town, ran along the eastern road over Durnover moor, up the hill beyond, and thus onward in the moderate darkness of this spring night till he had reached a second and almost a third hill about three miles distant. In Yalbury Bottom, or Plain, at the foot of the hill, he listened. At first nothing beyond his own heart-throbs was to be heard but the slow wind making its moan among the masses of spruce and larch of Yalbury Wood which clothed the heights on either hand; but presently there came the sound of light wheels whetting their felloes against the newly stoned patches of road, accompanied by the distant glimmer of lights.

He knew it was Farfrae's gig descending the hill from an indescribable personality in its noise, the vehicle having been his own till bought by the Scotchman at the sale of his effects. Henchard thereupon retraced his steps along Yalbury Plain, the gig coming up with him as its driver slackened speed between two plantations.

It was a point in the highway near which the road to Mellstock branched off from the homeward direction. By diverging to that village as he had intended to do Farfrae might probably delay his return by a couple of hours. It soon appeared that his intention was to do so still, the light swerving towards Cuckoo Lane, the bye road aforesaid. Farfrae's off gig-lamp flashed in Henchard's face. At the same time Farfrae discerned his late antagonist.

"Farfrae—Mr. Farfrae!" cried the breathless Henchard, holding up his hand.

Farfrae allowed the horse to turn several steps into the branch lane before he pulled up. He then drew rein, and said "Yes?" over his shoulder, as one would towards a pronounced enemy.

"Come back to Casterbridge at once!" Henchard said. "There's something wrong at your house—requiring your return. I've run all the way here on purpose to tell ye!"

Farfrae was silent, and at his silence Henchard's soul sank within him. Why had he not before this thought of what was only too obvious? He who, four hours earlier, had enticed Farfrae into a deadly wrestle stood now in the darkness of late night-time on a lonely road, inviting him to come a particular way, where an assailant might have confederates, instead of going his purposed way, where there might be a better opportunity of guarding himself from attack. Henchard could almost feel this view of things in course of passage through Farfrae's mind.

"I have to go to Mellstock," said Farfrae coldly, as he loosened his rein to move on.

"But," implored Henchard, "the matter is more serious than your business at Mellstock. It is—your wife. She is ill. I can tell you particulars as we go along."

The very agitation and abruptness of Henchard increased Farfrae's suspicion that this was a ruse to decoy him on to the next wood, where might be effectually compassed what, from policy or want of nerve, Henchard had failed to do earlier in the day. He started the horse.

"I know what you think," deprecated Henchard, running after, almost bowed down with despair as he perceived the image of unscrupulous villainy that he assumed in his former friend's eyes. "But I am not what you think!" he cried hoarsely. "Believe me, Farfrae, I have come entirely on your own and your wife's account. She is in danger. I know no more, and they want you to come. Your man has gone the other way in a mistake. Oh, Farfrae, don't mistrust me—I am a wretched man, but my heart is true to you still!"

Farfrae, however, did distrust him utterly. He knew his wife was with child, but he had left her not long ago in perfect health; and Henchard's treachery was more credible than his story. He had in his time heard bitter ironies from Henchard's lips, and there might be ironies now. He quickened the horse's pace and had soon risen into the high country lying between there and Mellstock, Henchard's spasmodic run after him lending yet more substance to his thought of evil purposes.

The gig and its driver lessened against the sky in Henchard's eyes; his exertions for Farfrae's good had been in vain. Over this repentant sinner, at least, there was to be no joy in heaven. He cursed himself like a less scrupulous Job, as a vehement man will do when he loses self-respect, the last mental prop under poverty. To this he had come after a time of emotional darkness of which the adjoining woodland shade afforded inadequate illustration. Presently he began to walk back again along the way by which he had arrived. Farfrae should, at all events, have no reason for delay upon the road by seeing him there when he took his journey homeward later on.

Arriving at Casterbridge Henchard went again to Farfrae's house to make inquiries. As soon as the door opened anxious faces confronted his from the staircase, hall, and landing; and they all said in grievous disappointment "Oh—it is not he!" The man-servant, finding his mistake, had long since returned, and all hopes had been centred upon Henchard.

"But haven't you found him?" said the doctor.

"Yes. . . . I cannot tell 'ee!" Henchard replied, as he sank down on a chair within the entrance. "He can't be home for two hours."

"H'm," said the surgeon, returning upstairs.

"How is she?" asked Henchard of Elizabeth, who formed one of the group.

"In great danger, father. Her anxiety to see her husband makes her fearfully restless. Poor woman—I fear they have killed her!"

Henchard regarded the sympathetic speaker for a few instants, as if she struck him in a new light; then without further remark went out of the door and onward to his lonely cottage. So much for man's rivalry, he thought. Death was to have the oyster, and Farfrae and himself the shells. But about Elizabeth-Jane: in the midst of his gloom she seemed to him as a pin-point of light. He had liked the look of her face as she answered him from the stairs. There had been affection in it, and above all things what he desired now was affection from anything that was good and pure. She was not his own; yet for the first time he had a faint dream that he might get to like her as his own—if she would only continue to love him.

Jopp was just going to bed when Henchard got home. As the latter entered the door Jopp said "This is rather bad about Mrs. Farfrae's illness."

"Yes," said Henchard shortly, though little dreaming of Jopp's complicity in the night's harlequinade, and raising his eyes just sufficiently to observe that Jopp's face was lined with anxiety.

"Somebody has called for you," continued Jopp, when Henchard was shutting himself into his own apartment. "A kind of traveller or sea-captain of some sort."

"Oh—who could he be?"

"He seemed a well-be-doing man—had grey hair and a broadish face; but he gave no name, and no message."

"Nor do I gie him any attention." And saying this Henchard closed his door.

The divergence to Mellstock delayed Farfrae's return very nearly the two hours of Henchard's estimate. Among the other urgent reasons for his presence had been the need of his authority to send to Budmouth for a second physician; and when at length Farfrae did come back he was in a state bordering on distraction at his misconception of Henchard's motives.

A messenger was dispatched to Budmouth, late as it had grown, the night wore on, and the other doctor came in the small hours. Lucetta had been much soothed by Donald's arrival; he seldom or never left her side; and when, immediately after his entry, she had tried to lisp out to him the secret which so oppressed her, he checked her feeble words, lest talking should be dangerous, assuring her there was plenty of time to tell him everything.

Up to this time he knew nothing of the skimmington-ride. The dangerous illness and miscarriage of Mrs. Farfrae was soon rumoured through the town, and an apprehensive guess having been given as to its cause by the leaders in the exploit, compunction and fear threw a dead silence over all particulars of their orgie; while those immediately around Lucetta would not venture to add to her husband's distress by alluding to the subject.

What, and how much, Farfrae's wife ultimately explained to him of her past entanglement with Henchard, when they were alone in the solitude of that sad night, cannot be told. That she informed him of the bare facts of her peculiar intimacy with the corn-merchant became plain from Farfrae's own statements. But in respect of her subsequent conduct—her motive in coming to Casterbridge to unite herself with Henchard—her assumed justification in abandoning him when she discovered reasons for fearing him (though in truth her inconsequent passion for another man at first sight had most to do with that abandonment)—her method of reconciling to her conscience a marriage with the second when she was in a measure committed to the first: to what extent she spoke of these things remained Farfrae's secret alone.

Besides the watchman who called the hours and weather in Casterbridge that night there walked a figure up and down Corn Street hardly less frequently. It was Henchard's, whose retiring to rest had proved itself a futility as soon as attempted; and he gave it up to go hither and thither and make inquiries about the patient every now and then. He called as much on Farfrae's account as on Lucetta's, and on Elizabeth-Jane's even more than on either's. Shorn one by one of all other interests, his life seemed centering on the personality of the step-daughter whose presence but recently he could not endure. To see her on each occasion of his inquiry at Lucetta's was a comfort to him.

The last of his calls was made about four o'clock in the morning, in the steely light of dawn. Lucifer was fading into day across Durnover Moor, the sparrows were just alighting into the street, and the hens had begun to cackle from the outhouses. When within a few yards of Farfrae's he saw the door gently opened, and a servant raise her hand to the knocker, to untie the piece of cloth which had muffled it. He went across, the sparrows in his way scarcely flying up from the road-litter, so little did they believe in human aggression at so early a time.

"Why do you take off that?" said Henchard.

She turned in some surprise at his presence, and did not answer for an instant or two. Recognising him she said "Because they may knock as loud as they will: she will never hear it any more."

XLI

HENCHARD went home. The morning having now fully broke he lit his fire, and sat abstractedly beside it. He had not sat there long when a gentle footstep approached the house and entered the passage, a finger tapping lightly at the door. Henchard's face brightened, for he knew the motions to be Elizabeth's. She came into his room, looking wan and sad.

"Have you heard?" she asked. "Mrs. Farfrae? She is—dead! Yes indeed—about an hour ago."

"I know it," said Henchard. "I have but lately come in from there. It is so very good of 'ee Elizabeth, to come and tell me. You must be so tired out, too, with sitting up. Now do you bide here with me this morning. You can go and rest in the other room; and I will call 'ee when breakfast is ready."

To please him, and herself—for his recent kindliness was winning a surprised gratitude from the lonely girl—she did as he bade her, and lay down on a sort of couch which Henchard had rigged up out of a settle in the adjoining room. She could hear him moving about in his preparations; but her mind ran most strongly on Lucetta, whose death, in such fulness of life, and amid such cheerful hopes of maternity, was appallingly unexpected. Presently she fell asleep.

Meanwhile her step-father in the outer room had set the breakfast in readiness; but finding that she dozed he would not call her; he waited on, looking into the fire and keeping the kettle boiling with housewifely care, as if it were an honour to have her in his house. In truth a great change had come over him with regard to her, and he was developing the dream of a future lit by her filial presence, as though that way alone could happiness lie.

He was disturbed by another knock at the door, and rose to open it, rather deprecating a call from anybody just then. A stoutly built man stood on the doorstep, with an alien, unfamiliar air about his figure and bearing—an air which might have been called colonial by people of cosmopolitan experience. It was the man who had asked the way at Peter's Finger. Henchard nodded, and looked inquiry.

"Good morning, good morning," said the stranger with profuse heartiness. "Is it Mr. Henchard I am talking to?"

"My name is Henchard."

"Then I've caught 'ee at home—that's right. Morning's the time for business, says I. Can I have a few words with you?"

"By all means," Henchard answered, showing the way in.

"You may remember me?" said his visitor, seating himself.

Henchard observed him indifferently, and shook his head.

'Well—perhaps you may not. My name is Newson.'

Henchard's face and eyes seemed to die. The other did not notice it. "I know the name well," Henchard said at last, looking on the floor.

"I make no doubt of that. Well, the fact is I've been looking for 'ee this fortnight past. I landed at Havenpool and went through Casterbridge on my way to Falmouth, and when I got there they told me you had some years before been living at Casterbridge. Back came I again; and by long and by late I got here by coach, ten minutes ago. 'He lives down by the mill,' says they: so here I am. . . . Now—that transaction between us some twenty years agone—'tis that I've called about. 'Twas a curious business; I was younger then than I am now; and perhaps the less said about it, in one sense, the better."

"Curious business—'twas worse than curious. I cannot even allow that I'm the man you met then. I was not in my senses; and a man's senses are himself."

"We were young and thoughtless," said Newson. "However, I've come to mend matters rather than open arguments. Poor Susan—hers was a strange experience."

"It was."

"She was a warm-hearted, home-spun woman. She was not what they call shrewd or sharp at all—better she had been."

"She was not."

"As you in all likelihood know, she was simple-minded enough to think that the sale was in a way binding. She was as guiltless o' wrong-doing in that particular as a saint in the clouds."

"I know it, I know it—I found it out directly," said Henchard, still with averted eyes. "There lay the sting o't to me. If she had seen it as what it was she would never have left me—never. But how should she be expected to know? What advantages had she? None. She could write her own name, and no more."

"Well—it was not in my heart to undeceive her, when the deed was done," said the sailor of former days. "I thought, and there was not much vanity in thinking it, that she would be happier with me. She was fairly happy, and I never would have undeceived her till the day of her death. Your child died; she had another; and all went well. But a time came—mind me, a time always does come. A time came—it was some while after she and I and the child returned from America—when somebody she had confided her history to told her my claim to her was a mockery, and made a jest of her belief in my right. After that she was never happy with me. She pined and pined, and socked and sighed. She said she must leave me, and then came the question of our child. Then a man advised me how to act, and I did it, for I thought it was best. I left her at Falmouth, and went off to sea. When I got to the other side of the Atlantic there was a storm, and it was supposed that a lot of us, including myself, had been washed overboard. I got ashore at Newfoundland, and then I asked myself what I should do. Since I'm here, here I'll bide, I thought to myself; 'twill be most kindness to her, now she's taken against me, to let her believe me lost; for, I thought, while she supposes us both alive she'll be miserable; but if she thinks me dead she'll go back to him, and the child will have a home. I've never returned to this country till a month ago, and I found that, as I had supposed, she went to you, and my daughter with her. They told me in Falmouth that Susan was dead. But my Elizabeth-Jane—where is she?"

"Dead likewise," said Henchard doggedly. "Surely you learnt that too?"

The sailor started up, and took an enervated pace or two down the room. "Dead!" he said in a low voice. "Then what's the use of my money to me?"

Henchard, without answering, shook his head, as if that were rather a question for Newson himself than for him.

"Where is she buried?" the traveller inquired.

"Beside her mother," said Henchard in the same stolid tones.

"When did she die?"

"A year ago, and more," replied the other without hesitation.

The sailor continued standing. Henchard never looked up from the floor. At last Newson said: "My journey hither has been for nothing. I may as well go as I came! . . . . It has served me right. I'll trouble you no longer."

Henchard heard the retreating footsteps of Newson upon the sanded floor, the mechanical lifting of the latch, the slow opening and closing of the door that was natural to a baulked and dejected man; but he did not turn his head. Newson's shadow passed the window. He was gone.

Then Henchard, scarcely believing the evidence of his senses, rose from his seat, amazed at what he had done. It had been the impulse of a moment. The regard he had lately acquired for Elizabeth, this new-sprung hope of his loneliness that she would be to him a daughter of whom he could feel as proud as of the actual daughter she still believed herself to be, had been stimulated by the unexpected coming of Newson to a greedy exclusiveness in relation to her; so that the sudden prospect of her loss had caused him to speak mad lies like a child, in pure mockery of consequences. He had expected questions to close in round him, and unmask his fabrication in five minutes; yet such questioning had not come. But surely they would come; Newson's departure could be but momentary; he would learn all by inquiries in the town; and return to curse him, and carry his last treasure away?

He hastily put on his hat, and went out in the direction that Newson had taken. Newson's back was soon visible up the road, crossing Bull-stake. Henchard followed; and saw his visitor stop at the King's Arms, where the morning coach which had brought him waited half an hour for another coach which crossed there. The coach Newson had come by was now about to move again. Newson mounted; his luggage was put in, and in a few minutes the vehicle disappeared with him.

He had not so much as turned his head. It was an act of simple faith in Henchard's words—faith so simple as to be almost sublime. The young sailor who had taken Susan Henchard on the spur of the moment, and on the faith of a glance at her face, more than twenty years before, was still living and acting under the form of the grizzled traveller who had taken Henchard's words on trust so absolute as to shame him as he stood.

Was Elizabeth-Jane to remain his by virtue of this hardy invention of a moment? "Perhaps not for long," said he. Newson might converse with his fellow-travellers, some of whom might be Casterbridge people; and the trick would be discovered.

This probability threw Henchard into a defensive attitude, and instead of considering how best to right the wrong, and acquaint Elizabeth's father with the truth at once, he bethought himself of ways to keep the position he had accidentally won. Towards the young woman herself his affection grew more jealously strong with each new hazard to which his claim to her was exposed.

He watched the distant highway, expecting to see Newson return on foot, enlightened and indignant, to claim his child. But no figure appeared. Possibly he had spoken to nobody on the coach, but buried his grief in his own heart.

His grief—what was it, after all, to that which he, Henchard, would feel at the loss of her. Newson's affection, cooled by years, could not equal his who had been constantly in her presence. And thus his jealous soul speciously argued to excuse the separation of father and child.

He returned to the house, half expecting that she would have vanished. No: there she was—just coming out from the inner room, the marks of sleep upon her eyelids, and exhibiting a generally refreshed air.

"Oh, father," she said smiling. "I had no sooner lain down than I napped—though I did not mean to! I wonder I did not dream about poor Mrs. Farfrae, after thinking of her so; but I did not. How strange it is that we do not often dream of latest events, absorbing as they may be."

"I am glad you have been able to sleep," he said, taking her hand with anxious proprietorship—an act which gave her a pleasant surprise.

They sat down to breakfast, and Elizabeth-Jane's thoughts reverted to Lucetta. Their sadness added charm to a countenance whose beauty had ever lain in its meditative soberness.

"Father," she said, as soon as she recalled herself to the outspread meal; "it is so kind of you to get this nice breakfast with your own hands, and I idly asleep the while."

"I do it every day," he replied. "You have left me; everybody has left me: how should I live but by my own hands."

"You are very lonely, are you not?"

"Ay, child—to a degree that you know nothing of. It is my own fault. You are the only one who has been near me for weeks. And you will come no more."

"Why do you say that? Indeed I will, if you would like to see me."

Henchard signified dubiousness. Though he had so lately hoped that Elizabeth-Jane might again live in his house as daughter, he would not ask her to do so now. Newson might return at any moment, and what Elizabeth would think of him for his deception it were best to bear apart from her.

When they had breakfasted his step-daughter still lingered; till the moment arrived at which Henchard was accustomed to go to his daily work. Then she arose, and with assurances of coming again soon went up the hill in the morning sunlight.

"At this moment her heart is as warm towards me as mine is towards her; she would live with me here in this humble cottage for the asking! Yet before the evening probably he will have come; and then she will scorn me."

This reflection, constantly repeated by Henchard to himself, accompanied him everywhere through the day. His mood was no longer that of the rebellious, ironical, reckless misadventurer; but the leaden gloom of one who has lost all that can make life interesting or even tolerable. There would remain nobody for him to be proud of, nobody to fortify him; for Elizabeth-Jane would soon be but as a stranger, and worse. Susan, Farfrae, Lucetta, Elizabeth—all had gone from him one after one, either by his fault or by his misfortune. In place of them he had no interest, hobby, or desire. If he could have summoned music to his aid his existence might even now have been borne; for with Henchard music was of regal power. The merest trumpet or organ tone was enough to move him, and high harmonies transubstantiated him. But hard fate had ordained that he should be unable to call up this Divine spirit in his need. The whole land ahead of him was as darkness itself; there was nothing to come, nothing to wait for. Yet in the natural course of life he might possibly have to linger on earth another thirty or forty years—scoffed at, at best pitied.

The thought of it was unendurable.

To the east of Casterbridge lay moors and meadows, through which much water flowed. The wanderer in this direction, who should stand still for a few moments on a quiet night, might hear singular symphonies from these waters, as from a lampless orchestra, all playing in their sundry tones, from near and far parts of the moor. At a hole in a rotten weir they executed a recitative; where a tributary brook fell over a stone breastwork they trilled cheerily; under an arch they performed a metallic cymbaling; and at Durnover-Hole they hissed. The spot at which their instrumentation rose loudest was a place called Ten-Hatches, whence during high springs there proceeded a very fugue of sounds.

The river here was deep and strong at all times, and the hatches on this account were raised and lowered by cogs and a winch. A path led from the second bridge over the highway (so often mentioned) to these Hatches, crossing the stream at their head by a narrow plank-bridge. But after nightfall human beings were seldom found going that way, the path leading only to a deep reach of the stream called Blackwater, and the passage being dangerous.

Henchard however, leaving the town by the east road, proceeded to the second or stone bridge, and thence struck into this path of solitude, following its course beside the stream till the dark shapes of the ten hatches cut the sheen thrown upon the river by the weak lustre that still lingered in the west. In a second or two he stood beside the weir-hole where the water was at its deepest. He looked backwards and forwards, and no creature appeared in view. He then took off his coat and hat, and stood on the brink of the stream with his hands clasped in front of him.

While his eyes were bent on the water beneath there slowly became visible a something floating in the circular pool formed by the wash of centuries; the pool he was intending to make his death-bed. At first it was indistinct, by reason of the shadow from the bank; but it emerged thence, and took shape, which was that of a human body lying stiff and stark upon the surface of the stream.

In the circular current imparted by the central flow the form was brought forward, till it passed under his eyes; and then he perceived with a sense of horror that it was *himself*. Not a man somewhat resembling him, but one in all respects his counterpart, his actual double, was floating as if dead in Ten-Hatches-Hole.

The sense of the supernatural was strong in this unhappy man, and he turned away as one might have done in the actual presence of an appalling miracle. He covered his eyes, and bowed his head. Without looking again into the stream he took his coat and hat, and went slowly away.

Presently he found himself by the door of his own dwelling. To his surprise Elizabeth-Jane was standing there. She came forward, spoke, called him father just as before. Newson, then, had not even yet returned.

"I thought you seemed very sad this morning," she said, "so I have come again to see you. Not that I am anything but sad myself. But everybody and everything seem against you so; and I know you must be suffering."

How this woman divined things. Yet she had not divined their whole extremity.

He said to her, "Are miracles still worked, do ye think, Elizabeth? I am not a read man. I don't know so much as I could wish. I have tried to peruse and learn all my life; but the more I try to know the more ignorant I seem."

"I don't quite think there are any miracles nowadays," she said.

"No interference in the case of desperate intentions, for instance? Well, perhaps not, in a direct way. Perhaps not. But—will you come and walk with me, and I will show 'ee what I mean."

She agreed willingly, and he took her over the highway, and

by the lonely path to Ten-Hatches. He walked restlessly, as if some haunting shade, unseen of her, hovered round him and troubled his glance. She would gladly have talked of Lucetta, but feared to disturb him. When they got near the weir he stood still, and asked her to go forward and look into the pool, and tell him what she saw.

She went, and soon returned to him. "Nothing," she said.

"Go again," said Henchard, "and look narrowly."

She proceeded to the river brink a second time. On her return, after some delay, she told him that she saw something floating round and round there; but what it was she could not discern. It seemed to be a bundle of old clothes.

"Are they like mine?" asked Henchard.

"Well—they are. Dear me—I wonder if——Father, let us go away."

"Go and look once more; and then we will get home."

She went back, and he could see her stoop till her head was close to the margin of the pool. She started up; and hastened back to his side.

"Well," said Henchard; "what do you say now?"

"Let us go home."

"But tell me—do—what is it floating there?"

"The effigy," she answered hastily. "They must have thrown it into the river higher up amongst the willows at Blackwater, to get rid of it, in their alarm at discovery by the magistrates; and it must have floated down here."

"Ah—to be sure—the image o' me! But where is the other? Why that one only. . . That performance of theirs killed her, but kept me alive!"

Elizabeth-Jane thought and thought of these words, "kept me alive," as they slowly retraced their way to the town; and at length guessed their meaning. "Father—I will not leave you alone like this!" she cried. "May I live with you, and tend upon you as I used to do? I do not mind your being poor. I would have agreed to come this morning, but you did not ask me."

"May you come to me?" he cried bitterly. "Elizabeth, don't mock me! If you only would come!"

"I will," said she.

"How will you forgive all my roughness in former days? You cannot!"

"I have forgotten it. Talk of that no more."

Thus she assured him; and arranged their plans for reunion; and at length each went home. Then Henchard shaved for the first time during many days, and put on clean linen, and combed his hair; and was as a man resuscitated thenceforward.

The next morning the fact turned out to be as Elizabeth-Jane had stated: the effigy was discovered by a cow-herd, and that of Lucetta a little higher up in the same stream. But as little as possible was said of the matter, and the figures were privately destroyed.

Despite this natural solution of the mystery Henchard no less regarded it as an intervention that the figure should have been floating there. Elizabeth-Jane heard him say "Who is such a reprobate as I! And yet it seems that even I be in Somebody's hand!"

BUT the emotional conviction that he was in Somebody's hand began to die out of Henchard's breast as time slowly removed into distance the event which had given that feeling birth. The apparition of Newson haunted him. He would surely return.

Yet Newson did not arrive. Lucetta had been borne along the churchyard path; Casterbridge had for the last time turned its regard upon her, before proceeding to its work as if she had never lived. But Elizabeth remained undisturbed in the belief of her relationship to Henchard, and now shared his home. Perhaps, after all, Newson was gone for ever.

In due time the bereaved Farfrae had learnt the, at least, proximate cause of Lucetta's illness and death; and his first impulse was naturally enough to wreak vengeance in the name of the law upon the perpetrators of the mischief. He resolved to wait till the funeral was over ere he moved in the matter. The time having come he reflected. Disastrous as the result had been, it was obviously in no way foreseen or intended by the thoughtless crew who arranged the motley procession. The tempting prospect of putting to the blush people who stand at the head of affairs—that supreme and piquant enjoyment of those who writhe under the heel of the same— had alone animated them, so far as he could see; for he knew nothing of Jopp's incitements. Other considerations were also involved. Lucetta had confessed everything to him before her death, and it was not altogether desirable to make much ado about her history, alike for her sake, for Henchard's, and for his own. To regard the event as an untoward accident seemed, to Farfrae, truest consideration for the dead one's memory, as well as best philosophy.

Henchard and himself mutually forbore to meet. For Elizabeth's sake the former had fettered his pride sufficiently to accept the small seed and root business which some of the Town-Council, headed by Farfrae, had purchased, to afford him a new opening. Had he been only personally concerned

Henchard, without doubt, would have declined assistance even remotely brought about by the man whom he had so fiercely assailed. But the sympathy of the girl seemed necessary to his very existence; and on her account pride itself wore the garments of humility.

Here they settled themselves; and on each day of their lives Henchard anticipated her every wish with a watchfulness in which paternal regard was heightened by a burning, jealous dread of rivalry. Yet that Newson would ever now return to Casterbridge to claim her as a daughter there was little reason to suppose. He was a wanderer and a stranger, almost an alien; he had not seen his daughter for several years; his affection for her could not in the nature of things be keen; other interests would probably soon obscure his recollections of her, and prevent any such renewal of inquiry into the past as would lead to a discovery that she was still a creature of the present. To satisfy his conscience somewhat, Henchard repeated to himself that the lie which had retained for him the coveted treasure had not been deliberately told to that end, but had come from him as the last defiant word of a despair which took no thought of consequences. Furthermore he pleaded within himself that no Newson could love her as he loved her, or would tend her to his life's extremity as he was prepared to do cheerfully.

Thus they lived on in the shop overlooking the churchyard, and nothing occurred to mark their days during the remainder of the year. Going out but seldom, and never on a market-day, they saw Donald Farfrae only at rarest intervals, and then mostly as a transitory object in the distance of the street. Yet he was pursuing his ordinary avocations, smiling mechanically to fellow-tradesmen, and arguing with bargainers—as bereaved men do after a while.

"Time in his own grey style" taught Farfrae how to estimate his experience of Lucetta—all that it was, and all that it was not. There are men whose hearts insist upon a dogged fidelity to some image or cause, thrown by chance into their keeping, long after their judgment has pronounced it no rarity—even the reverse, indeed; and without them the band of the worthy is incomplete. But Farfrae was not of those. It was inevitable that the insight, briskness, and rapidity of his nature should take him out of the dead blank which his loss threw about him. He could not but perceive that by the death of Lucetta he had exchanged a looming misery for a simple sorrow. After that revelation of her history which must have come sooner or later in any circumstances, it was hard to believe that life with her would have been productive of further happiness.

But as a memory, notwithstanding such conditions, Lucetta's image still lived on with him, her weaknesses provoking only the gentlest criticism, and her sufferings attenuating wrath at her concealments to a momentary spark now and then.

By the end of a year Henchard's little retail seed and grain shop, not much larger than a cupboard, had developed its trade considerably, and the step-father and daughter enjoyed much serenity in the pleasant sunny corner in which it stood. The quiet bearing of one who brimmed with an inner activity characterized Elizabeth-Jane at this period. She took long walks into the country two or three times a week, mostly in the direction of Budmouth. Sometimes it occurred to him that when she sat with him in the evening after these invigorating walks she was civil rather than affectionate; and he was troubled; one more bitter regret being added to those he had already experienced at having, by his severe censorship, frozen up her precious affection when originally offered.

She had her own way in everything now. In going and coming, in buying and selling, her word was law.

"You have got a new muff, Elizabeth," he said to her one day quite humbly.

"Yes; I bought it," she said.

He looked at it again as it lay on an adjoining table. The fur was of a glossy brown, and though he was no judge of such articles he thought it seemed an unusually good one for her to possess.

"Rather costly, I suppose, my dear, was it not?" he hazarded.

"It was rather above my figure," she said quietly. "But it is not showy."

"Oh no," said the netted lion, anxious not to pique her in the least.

Some little time after, when the year had advanced into another spring, he paused opposite her empty bedroom in passing it. He thought of the time when she had cleared out of his then large and handsome house in Corn Street, in consequence of his dislike and harshness, and he had looked into her chamber in just the same way. The present room was much humbler, but what struck him about it was the abundance of books lying everywhere. Their number and quality made the meagre furniture that supported them seem absurdly disproportionate. Some, indeed many, must have been recently purchased; and though he encouraged her to buy in reason, he had no notion that she indulged her innate passion so extensively in proportion to the narrowness of their income. For the first time he felt a little hurt by what he thought her extravagance; and resolved to say a word to her about it. But before he had found the courage to speak an event happened which set his thoughts flying in quite another direction.

The busy time of the seed trade was over; and the quiet weeks that preceded the hay season had come—setting their special stamp upon Casterbridge by thronging the market with wood rakes, new waggons in yellow, green, and red, formidable scythes, and pitchforks of prong sufficient to skewer up a small family. Henchard, contrary to his wont, went out one Saturday afternoon towards the marketplace, from a curious feeling that he would like to pass a few minutes on the spot of his former triumphs. Farfrae, to whom he was still a comparative stranger, stood a few steps below the corn-exchange door—a usual position with him at this hour—and he appeared lost in thought about something he was looking at a little way off.

Henchard's eyes followed Farfrae's, and he saw that the object of his gaze was no sample-showing farmer, but his own step-daughter, who had just come out of a shop over the way. She on her part was quite unconscious of his attention, and in this was less fortunate than those young women whose very plumes, like those of Juno's bird, are set with Argus eyes whenever possible admirers are within ken.

Henchard went away, thinking that perhaps there was nothing significant, after all, in Farfrae's look at Elizabeth-Jane at that juncture. Yet he could not forget that the Scotchman had once shown a tender interest in her, of a fleeting kind. Thereupon promptly came to the surface that idiosyncrasy of Henchard's which had ruled his courses from the beginning, and had mainly made him what he was. Instead of thinking that a union between his cherished step-daughter and the energetic thriving Donald was a thing to be desired for her good and his own, he hated the very possibility.

Time had been when such instinctive opposition would have taken shape in action. But he was not now the Henchard of former days. He schooled himself to accept her will, in this as in other matters, as absolute and unquestionable. He dreaded lest an antagonistic word should lose for him such regard as he had regained from her by his devotion, feeling that to retain this under separation was better than to incur her dislike by keeping her near.

But the mere thought of such separation fevered his spirit much, and in the evening he said with the stillness of suspense: "Have you seen Mr. Farfrae to-day, Elizabeth?"

Elizabeth-Jane started at the question; and it was with some confusion that she replied "No."

"Oh—that's right—that's right. . . . It was only that I saw him in the street when we both were there." He was wondering if her embarrassment justified him in a new suspicion—that the long walks which she had latterly been taking, that the new books which had so surprised him, had anything to do with the young man. She did not enlighten him, and lest silence should allow her to shape thoughts unfavourable to their present friendly relations he diverted the discourse into another channel.

Henchard was, by original make, the last man to act stealthily, for good or for evil. But the *solicitus timor* of his love—the dependence upon Elizabeth's regard into which he had declined (or, in another sense, to which he had advanced), denaturalized him. He would often weigh and consider for hours together the meaning of such and such a deed or phrase of hers, when a blunt settling question would formerly have been his first instinct. And now, uneasy at the thought of a passion for Farfrae which should entirely displace her mild filial sympathy with himself, he observed her going and coming more narrowly.

There was nothing secret in Elizabeth-Jane's movements beyond what habitual reserve induced; and it may at once be owned on her account that she was guilty of occasional conversations with Donald when they chanced to meet. Whatever the origin of her walks on the Budmouth Road, her return from those walks was often coincident with Farfrae's emergence from Corn Street for a twenty-minutes' blow on that rather windy highway—just to winnow the seeds and chaff out of him before sitting down to tea, as he said. Henchard became aware of this by going to the Ring, and, screened by its enclosure, keeping his eye upon the road till he saw them meet. His face assumed an expression of extreme anguish.

"Of her, too, he means to rob me!" he whispered. "But he has the right. I do not wish to interfere."

The meeting, in truth, was of a very innocent kind, and matters were by no means so far advanced between the young people as Henchard's jealous grief inferred. Could he had heard such conversation as passed he would have been enlightened thus much:—

He.—"You like walking this way, Miss Henchard—and is it not so?" (uttered in his undulatory accents, and with an appraising, pondering gaze at her.)

She.—"Oh yes. I have chosen this road latterly. I have no great reason for it."

He.—"But that may make a reason for others."

She. (reddening)—"I don't know that. My reason, however, such as it is, is that I wish to to get a glimpse of the sea every day."

He.—"Is it a secret why?"

She. (reluctantly)—"Yes."

He. (with the pathos of one of his native ballads)—"Ah, I doubt there will be any good in secrets! A secret cast a deep shadow over my life. And well you know what it was."

Elizabeth admitted that she did, but she refrained from

confessing why the sea attracted her. She could not herself account for it fully, not knowing the secret possibly to be that, in addition to early marine associations, her blood was a sailor's.

"Thank you for those new books, Mr. Farfrae," she added shyly. "I wonder if I ought to accept so many!"

"Ay! why not? It gives me more pleasure to get them for you, than you to have them!"

"It cannot!"

They proceeded along the road together till they reached the town, and their paths diverged.

Henchard vowed that he would leave them to their own devices, put nothing in the way of their courses, whatever they might mean. If he were doomed to be bereft of her, so it must be. In the situation which their marriage would create, he could see no *locus standi* for himself at all. Farfrae would never recognise him more than superciliously; his poverty ensured that, no less than his past conduct. And so Elizabeth would grow to be a stranger to him, and the end of his life would be friendless solitude.

With such a possibility impending he could not help watchfulness. Indeed, within certain lines he had the right to keep an eye upon her as his charge. The meetings seemed to become matters of course with them on special days of the week.

At last full proof was given him. He was standing behind a wall close to the place at which Farfrae encountered her. He heard the young man address her as "Dearest Elizabeth-Jane," and then kiss her, the girl looking quickly round to assure herself that nobody was near.

When they were gone their way Henchard came out from the wall, and mournfully followed them to Casterbridge. The chief looming trouble in this engagement had not decreased. Both Farfrae and Elizabeth-Jane, unlike the rest of the people, must suppose Elizabeth to be his actual daughter, from his own assertion while he himself had the same belief; and though Farfrae must have so far forgiven him as to have no objection to own him as a father-in-law, intimate they could never be. Thus would the girl who was his only friend be withdrawn from him by degrees through her husband's influence; and learn to despise him.

Had she lost her heart to any other man in the world than the one he had rivalled, cursed, wrestled with for life in days before his spirit was broken, Henchard would have said "I am content." But content with the prospect as now depicted was hard to acquire.

There is an outer chamber of the brain in which thoughts unowned, unsolicited, and of noxious kind, are sometimes allowed to wander for a moment prior to being sent off whence they came. One of these thoughts sailed into Henchard's ken now.

Suppose he were to communicate to Farfrae the fact that his betrothed was not the child of Michael Henchard at all—legally, nobody's child; how would that correct and leading townsman receive the information? He might possibly forsake Elizabeth-Jane, and then she would be her step-sire's own again.

Henchard shuddered, and exclaimed "God forbid such a thing! Why should I still be subject to these visitations of the Devil, when I try so hard to keep him away!"

WHAT Henchard saw thus early was, naturally enough, seen at a little later date by other people. That Mr. Farfrae "walked with that bankrupt Henchard's step-daughter, of all women" became a common topic in the town, the simple perambulating term being used hereabout to signify a wooing; and the nineteen superior young ladies of Casterbridge, who had each looked upon herself as the only woman capable of making the merchant-Councilman happy, indignantly left off going to the church Farfrae attended, left off conscious mannerisms, left off putting him in their prayers at night amongst their blood relations; in short, reverted to their natural courses.

Perhaps the only inhabitants of the town to whom this looming choice of the Scotchman's gave unmixed satisfaction were the members of the philosophic party which included Longways, Christopher Coney, Billy Wills, Mr. Buzzford, and the like. The Three Mariners having been, years before, the house in which they had witnessed the young man and woman's first and humble appearance on the Casterbridge Stage, they took a kindly interest in their career, not unconnected, perhaps, with visions of festive treatment at their hands hereafter. Mrs. Stannidge, having rolled into the large parlour one evening, and said that it was a wonder such a man as Mr. Farfrae, "a pillow of the town," who might have chosen one of the daughters of the professional men, or private residents, should stoop so low, Coney ventured to disagree with her:

"No ma'am; no wonder at all. 'Tis she that's a stooping to he—that's my opinion. A widow-man—whose first wife was no credit to him—what is it for a young perusing woman, that's her own mistress and well-liked? But as a neat patching up of things I see much good in it. When a man have put up a tomb of best marble stone to the other one, as he've done, and weeped his fill, and thought it all over, and said to hisself, 'T'other took me in; I knowed this one first; she's a sensible piece for a partner, and there's no faithful woman in high life now';—well he may do worse than not to take her, if she's tender-inclined."

Thus they talked at the Mariners. But we must guard against a too liberal use of the conventional declaration that a great sensation was caused by the prospective event, that all the gossips' tongues were set wagging thereby, and so on, even though such a declaration might lend some *éclat* to the career of our poor only heroine. When all has been said about busy rumourers, a superficial and temporary thing is the interest of anybody in affairs which do not directly touch them. It would be a truer representation to say that Casterbridge (ever excepting the nineteen young ladies) looked up for a moment at the news, and, withdrawing its attention, went on labouring and victualling, bringing up its children and burying its dead, without caring a tittle for Farfrae's domestic plans.

Not a hint of the matter was thrown out to her step-father by Elizabeth herself, or by Farfrae, either. Reasoning on the cause of their reticence he concluded that, estimating him by his past, the throbbing pair were afraid to broach the subject, and looked upon him as an irksome obstacle whom they would be heartily glad to get out of the way. Embittered as he was against society, this moody view of himself took deeper and deeper hold of Henchard, till the daily necessity of facing mankind, and of them particularly Elizabeth-Jane, became well-nigh more than he could endure. His health declined; he became morbidly sensitive. He wished he could escape those who did not want him, and hide his head for ever.

But what if he were mistaken in his views, and there were no necessity that his own absolute separation from her should be involved in the incident of her marriage?

He proceeded to draw a picture of the alternative—himself living like a fangless lion about the back rooms of a house in which his step-daughter was mistress; an inoffensive old man, tenderly smiled on by Elizabeth, and good-naturedly tolerated by her husband. It was terrible to his pride to think of descending so low; and yet, for the girl's sake, he might put up with anything; even from Farfrae; even snubbings and masterful tongue-scourgings. The privilege of being in the house she occupied would almost outweigh the personal humiliation.

Whether this were a dim possibility or the reverse, the courtship—which it evidently now was—had an absorbing interest for him.

Elizabeth, as has been said, often took her walks on the Budmouth Road, and Farfrae as often made it convenient to create an accidental meeting with her there. Two miles out, a quarter of a mile from the highway, was the pre-historic fort called Mai Dun, of huge dimensions and many ramparts, within or upon whose enclosures a human being, as seen from the road, was but an insignificant speck. Hitherward Henchard often resorted, glass in hand, and scanned the hedgeless *Via*—for it was the original track laid out by the legions of the Empire—to a distance of two or three miles, his object being to read the progress of affairs between Farfrae and his charmer.

One day Henchard was at this spot when a masculine figure came along the road from Budmouth and lingered. Applying his telescope to his eye, Henchard expected that Farfrae's features would be disclosed as usual. But the lenses revealed that to-day the man was not Elizabeth-Jane's lover.

It was one clothed as a merchant captain; and as he turned in his scrutiny of the road he revealed his face. Henchard lived a lifetime the moment he saw it. The face was Newson's.

Henchard dropped the glass, and for some seconds made no other movement. Newson waited, and Henchard waited—if that could be called a waiting which was a transfixture. But Elizabeth-Jane did not come. Something or other had caused her to neglect her customary walk that day. Perhaps Farfrae and she had chosen another road for variety's sake. But what did that amount to? She might be here to-morrow, and in any case Newson, if bent on a private meeting and a revelation of the truth to her, would soon make his opportunity.

Then he would tell her not only of his paternity, but of the ruse by which he had been once sent away. Elizabeth's strict nature would cause her for the first time to despise her stepfather, would root out his image as that of an arch deceiver, and Newson would reign in her heart in his stead.

But Newson did not see anything of her that morning. Having stood still awhile he at last retraced his steps, and Henchard felt like a condemned man who has a few hours' respite. When he reached his own house he found her there. "Oh, father," she said innocently, "I have had a letter—a strange one—not signed. Somebody has asked me to meet him, either on the Budmouth Road at noon to-day, or in the evening at Mr. Farfrae's. He says he came to see me some time ago, but a trick was played him, so that he did not see me. I don't understand it; but between you and me I think Donald is at the bottom of the mystery, and that it is a relation of his who wants to pass an opinion on—his choice. But I did not like to go till I had seen you. Shall I go?"

Henchard replied heavily, "Yes; go."

The question of his remaining in Casterbridge was for ever disposed of by this closing in of Newson on the scene. Henchard was not the man to stand the certainty of condemnation on a matter so near his heart. And being an old hand at bearing anguish in silence, and haughty withal, he resolved to make as light as he could of his intention, while immediately taking his measures.

He surprised the young woman whom he had looked upon as his all in this world by saying to her, as if he did not care about her more: "I am going to leave Casterbridge, Elizabeth-Jane."

"Leave Casterbridge!" she cried, "and leave—me?"

"Yes, this little shop can be managed by you alone as well as by us both; I don't care about shops and streets, and folk—I would rather get into the country by myself, out of sight, and follow my own ways, and leave you to yours."

She looked down, and her tears fell silently. It seemed to her that this resolve of his had come on account of her attachment, and its probable result. She showed her devotion to Farfrae, however, by mastering her emotion and speaking out.

"I am sorry you have decided on this," she said with difficult firmness. "For I thought it probable—possible that—I might marry Mr. Farfrae some little time hence, and I did not know that you disapproved of the step!"

"I approve of anything you desire to do, Izzy," said

Henchard huskily. "If I did not approve, it would be no matter! I wish to go away. My presence might make things awkward in the future; and, in short, it is best that I go."

Nothing that her affection could urge would induce him to reconsider his determination; for she could not urge what she did not know—that when she should learn he was not related to her other than as a step-parent she would refrain from despising him, and that when she knew what he had done to keep her in ignorance she would refrain from hating him. It was his conviction that she would not so refrain; and there existed as yet neither word nor event which could argue it away.

"Then," she said at last, "you will not be able to come to my wedding, and that is not as it ought to be."

"I don't want to see it—I don't want to see it!" he exclaimed; adding more softly, "But think of me sometimes in your future life—you'll do that, Izzy?—think of me when you are living as the wife of the richest, the foremost man in the town, and don't let my sins, *when you know them all*, cause 'ee to quite forget that though I loved 'ee late I loved 'ee well."

"It is because of Donald!" she sobbed.

"I don't forbid you to marry him," said Henchard. "Promise not to quite forget me when——" He meant when Newson should come.

She promised mechanically, in her agitation; and the same evening at dusk Henchard left the town to whose development he had been one of the chief stimulants for many years.

During the day he had bought a new tool-basket, cleaned up his old hay-knife and wimble, set himself up in fresh leggings, knee-naps and corduroys, and in other ways gone back to the working-clothes of his young-manhood, discarding for ever the shabby-genteel suit of cloth and rusty silk hat that since his decline had characterized him in the Casterbridge streets as a man who had seen better days.

He went secretly and alone, not a soul of the many who had known him being aware of his departure. Elizabeth-Jane accompanied him as far as the second bridge on the highway—for the hour of her appointment with the unguessed visitor at Farfrae's had not yet arrived—and parted from him with unfeigned wonder and sorrow—keeping him back a minute or two before finally letting him go. She watched his form diminish across the moor, the yellow rush-basket at his back moving up and down with each tread, and the creases behind his knees coming and going alternately till she could no longer see them. Though she did not know it, Henchard formed at this moment much the same picture as he had presented when entering Casterbridge for the first time, nearly a quarter of a century before; except, to be sure, that the serious addition to his years had considerably lessened the spring of his stride, that his state of hopelessness had weakened him, and imparted to his shoulders, as weighted by the basket, a perceptible bend.

He went on till he came to the first milestone, which stood in the bank, halfway up a steep hill. He rested his basket on the top of the stone, placed his elbows on it, and gave way to a convulsive twitch which was worse than a sob because it was so hard and so dry.

"If I had only got her with me—if I only had!" he said. "Hard work would be nothing to me then! But that was not to be. I—Cain—go alone as I deserve—an outcast and a vagabond. But my punishment is *not* greater than I can bear!"

He sternly subdued his anguish, shouldered his basket, and went on.

Elizabeth, in the mean time, had breathed him a sigh, recovered her equanimity, and turned her face to Caster-bridge. Before she had reached the first house she was met in her walk by Donald Farfrae. This was evidently not their first meeting that day; they joined hands without ceremony, and Farfrae anxiously asked, "And is he gone—and did you tell him?—I mean of the other matter—not of ours."

"He is gone; and I told him all I knew of your friend. Donald, who is he?"

"Well, well, dearie; you will know soon about that. And Mr. Henchard will hear of it if he does not go far."

"He will go far—he's bent upon getting out of sight and sound!"

She walked beside her lover, and when they reached the Crossways, or Bow, turned with him into Corn Street instead of going straight on to her own door. At Farfrae's house they stopped and went in.

Farfrae flung open the door of the ground-floor sitting-room, saying "There he is waiting for you," and Elizabeth entered. In the arm-chair sat the broad-faced genial man who had called on Henchard on a memorable morning between one and two years before this time, and whom the latter had seen mount the coach and depart within half-an-hour of his arrival. It was Richard Newson.

The meeting with the light-hearted father from whom she had been separated half-a-dozen years, as if by death, need hardly be detailed. It was an affecting one, apart from the question of paternity. Henchard's departure was in a moment explained. When the true facts came to be handled, the difficulty of restoring her to her old belief in Newson was not so great as might have seemed likely, for Henchard's conduct itself was a proof that those facts were true. Moreover, she had grown up under Newson's paternal care; and even had Henchard been her father in nature, this father in early domiciliation might almost have carried the point against him, when the incidents of her parting with Henchard had a little worn off.

Newson's pride in what she had grown up to be was more than he could express. He kissed her again and again.

"I've saved you the trouble to come and meet me—ha-ha!" said Newson. "The fact is that Mr. Farfrae here, he said, Come up and stop with me for a day or two, Captain Newson, and I'll bring her round. Faith, says I, so I will; and here I am."

"Well, Henchard is gone," said Farfrae, shutting the door. "He has done it all voluntarily, and as I gather from Elizabeth he has been very nice with her. I was got rather uneasy, but all is as it should be, and we will have no more deefficulties at all."

"Now, that's very much as I thought,' said Newson, looking into the face of each by turns. "I said to myself aye, a hundred times, when I tried to get a peep at her unknown to herself— 'Depend upon it, 'tis best that I should live on quiet for a few days like this till something turns up for the better.' I now know you are all right, and what can I wish for more?"

"Well, Captain Newson, I will be glad to see ye here every day now, since it can do no harm," said Farfrae. "And what I've been thinking is, that the wedding may as well be kept under my own roof, the house being large, and you being in lodgings by yourself—so that a great deal of trouble and expense would be saved ye?—and 'tis a convenience when a couple's married not to hae far to go to get home?"

"With all my heart," said Captain Newson; "since, as ye say, it can do no harm, now poor Henchard's gone; though I wouldn't have done it otherwise, or put myself in his way at all; for I've already in my lifetime been an intruder into his family quite as far as politeness can be expected to put up with.—But what do the young woman say herself about it? Elizabeth, my child, come and hearken to what we be talking about, and not bide staring out o' the window as if ye didn't hear."

"Donald and you must settle it," murmured Elizabeth, still keeping up a scrutinizing gaze at some small object in the street.

"Well then," continued Newson, turning anew to Farfrae with a face expressing thorough entry into the subject; "that's how we'll have it. And Mr. Farfrae, as you provide so much, and house room, and all that, I'll do my part in the drinkables, and see to the rum and schiedam—maybe a dozen jars will be sufficient, as many of the folk will be ladies, and perhaps they won't drink hard enough to make a high average in the reckoning? But you know best. I've provided for men and shipmates times enough, but I'm as ignorant as a child how many glasses of grog a woman, that's not a drinking woman, is expected to consume at these ceremonies?"

"Oh none—we'll no want much of that—Oh no," said Farfrae, shaking his head with appalled gravity. "Do you leave all to me."

When they had gone a little further in these particulars Newson, leaning back in his chair and smiling reflectively at the ceiling, said, "I've never told ye, or have I, Mr. Farfrae, how Henchard put me off the scent that time?"

He expressed ignorance of what the Captain alluded to.

"Ah, I thought I hadn't. I resolved that I would not, I

remember, not to hurt the man's name. But now he's gone I can tell ye. Why, I came to Casterbridge nine or ten months before that day last week that I found ye out. I had been here twice before then. The first time I passed through the town on my way westward, not knowing Elizabeth lived here. Then hearing at some place—I forget where—that a man of the name of Henchard had been mayor here, I came back, and called at his house one morning. The old rascal!—he said Elizabeth-Jane had died years ago."

Elizabeth now gave earnest heed to his story.

"Now it never crossed my mind that the man was selling me a packet," continued Newson. "And, if you'll believe me, I was that upset, that I went back to the coach that had brought me, and took passage onward without lying in the town half an hour. Ha—ha—'twas a good joke, and well carried out, and I give the man credit for't!"

Elizabeth-Jane was amazed at the intelligence. "A joke?—O no!" she cried. "Then he kept you from me, father, all those months, when you might have been here?"

The father admitted that such was the case.

"He ought not to have done it!" said Farfrae.

Elizabeth sighed. "I said I would never forget him. But, oh! I think I ought to forget him now!"

Newson, like a good many rovers and sojourners among strange men and strange moralities, failed to perceive the enormity of Henchard's crime, notwithstanding that he himself had been the chief sufferer therefrom. Indeed, the attack upon the absent culprit waxing serious, he began to take Henchard's part.

"Well, 'twas not ten words that he said, after all," Newson pleaded. "And how could he know that I should be such a simpleton as to believe him? 'Twas as much my fault as his, poor fellow!"

"No," said Elizabeth-Jane firmly, in her revulsion of feeling. "He knew your disposition—you always were so trusting, father; I've heard my mother say so hundreds of times—and he did it to wrong you. After weaning me from you these five years by saying he was my father he should not have done this."

Thus they conversed; and there was nobody to set before Elizabeth any extenuation of the absent one's deceit. Even had he been present Henchard might scarce have pleaded it, so little did he value himself or his good name.

"Well, well—never mind—it is all over and past," said Newson good-naturedly. "Now about this wedding again."

Thus they conveyed; and there was nobody to set before Elizabeth any extenuation of the absent one's deceit. Even had he been present Henchard might scarce have pleaded it, so little did he value himself or his good name.

XLIV

MEANWHILE the man of their talk had pursued his solitary way eastward till weariness overtook him, and he looked about for a place of rest. His heart was so exacerbated at parting from the girl that he could not face an inn, or even a household of the most humble kind; and entering a field he lay down under a wheat-rick, feeling no want of food. The very heaviness of his soul caused him to sleep profoundly.

The bright autumn sun shining into his eyes across the stubble awoke him the next morning early. He opened his basket, and ate for his breakfast what he had packed for his supper; and in doing so overhauled the remainder of his kit. Although everything he brought necessitated carriage at his own back he had secreted among his tools a few of Elizabeth-Jane's cast off belongings, in the shape of gloves, shoes, a scrap of her handwriting and the like; and in his pocket he carried a curl of her hair. Having looked at these things he closed them up again, and went onward.

During five consecutive days Henchard's rush-basket rode along upon his shoulder between the highway hedges, the new yellow of the rushes catching the eye of an occasional field-labourer as he glanced through the quickset, together with the wayfarer's hat and head, and down-turned face, over which the twig shadows moved in endless procession. It now became apparent that the direction of his journey was Weydon Priors, which he reached on the afternoon of the sixth day.

The renowned hill, whereon the annual fair had been held for so many generations, was now bare of human beings and almost of aught besides. A few sheep grazed thereabout, but these ran off when Henchard halted upon the summit. He deposited his basket upon the turf, and looked about with sad curiosity; till he discovered the road by which his wife and himself had entered on the upland so memorable to both, five and twenty years before.

"Yes, we came up that way," he said, after ascertaining his bearings. "She was carrying the baby, and I was reading a ballet-sheet. Then we crossed about here—she so sad and weary, and I speaking to her hardly at all, because of my cursed pride, and mortification at being poor. Then we saw the tent—that must have stood more this way."—He walked to another spot; it was not really where the tent had stood, but it seemed so to him—"Here we went in, and here we sat down. I faced this way. Then I drank, and committed my crime. It must have been just on that very pixy-ring that she was standing when she said her last words to me before going off with him: I can hear their sound now, and the sound of her sobs: 'O Mike, I've lived with thee all this while, and had nothing but temper. Now I'm no more to 'ee—I'll try my luck elsewhere.' "

He experienced not only the bitterness of a man who finds, in looking back upon an ambitious course, that what he has sacrificed in sentiment was worth as much as what he has gained in substance; but the superadded bitterness of seeing his very recantation nullified. He had been sorry for all this long ago; but his attempts to replace ambition by love had been as fully foiled as his ambition itself. His wronged wife had foiled them by a fraud so grandly simple as to be almost a virtue.

It was an odd sequence that out of all this tampering with social law came that flower of nature Elizabeth. Part of his wish to wash his hands of life arose from his perception of its contrarious inconsistencies—of nature's jaunty readiness to support unorthodox social principles.

He intended to go on from this place—visited as an act of penance—into another part of the country altogether. But he could not help thinking of Elizabeth, and the quarter of the horizon in which she lived. Out of this it happened that the centrifugal tendency imparted by weariness of the world was counteracted by the centripetal influence of his love for his step-daughter. As a consequence, instead of following a straight course yet further away from Casterbridge, Henchard gradually, almost unconsciously, deflected from that right line of his first intention; till, by degrees, his wandering, like that of the Canadian woodsman, became part of a circle, of which Casterbridge formed the centre. In ascending any particular hill he ascertained the bearings as nearly as he could by means of the sun, moon, or stars, and settled in his mind the exact direction in which Casterbridge and Elizabeth-Jane lay. Sneering at himself for his weakness, he yet every hour—nay, every few minutes—conjectured her actions for the time being—her sitting down and rising up, her goings and comings, till thought of Newson's and Farfrae's counter-influence would pass like a cold blast over a pool, and efface her image. And then he would say of himself, "O you fool— All this about a daughter who is no daughter of thine!"

At length he obtained employment at his old occupation of hay-trusser, work of that sort being in demand at this autumn time. The scene of his hiring was a pastoral farm near the old western highway, whose course was the channel of all such communications as passed between the busy centres of novelty and the remote Wessex boroughs. He had chosen the neighbourhood of this artery from a sense that situated here, though at a distance of fifty miles, he was virtually nearer to her whose welfare was so dear than he would be at a roadless spot only half as remote.

And thus Henchard found himself again on the precise standing which he had occupied a quarter of a century before. Externally there was nothing to hinder his making another start on the upward slope, and by his new lights achieving higher things than his soul in its half-formed state had been able to accomplish. But the ingenious machinery contrived by the gods for reducing human possibilities of amelioration to a minimum—which arranges that wisdom to do shall come *pari passu* with the departure of zest for doing—stood in the way of all that. He had no wish to make an arena, a second time, of a world that had become a mere painted scene to him.

Very often, as his hay-knife crunched down among the sweet-smelling grassy stems, he would survey mankind and say to himself "Here and everywhere be folk dying before their time like frosted leaves though wanted by their families, the country, and the world; while I, an outcast, an encumberer of the ground, wanted by nobody, and despised by all, live on against my will!"

He often kept an eager ear upon the conversation of those

who passed along the road—not from a general curiosity by any means, but in the hope that among these travellers between Casterbridge and London some would sooner or later speak of the former place. The distance, however, was too great to lend much probability to his desire, and the highest result of his attention to wayside words was that he did indeed hear the name "Casterbridge," uttered one day by the driver of a road-waggon. Henchard ran to the gate of the field he worked in and hailed the speaker, who was a stranger.

"Yes—I've come from there, maister," he said in answer to Henchard's inquiry. "I trade up and down, ye know; though what with this travelling without horses that's getting so common my work will soon be done."

"Anything moving in the old place, mid I ask?"

"All the same as usual."

"I've heard that Mr. Farfrae, the late mayor, is thinking of getting married. Now is that true or not?"

"I couldn't say for the life o' me. Oh, no, I should think not."

"But yes John—you forget," said a woman inside the waggon-tilt. "What were them packages we carr'd there at the beginning o' the week? Surely they said a wedding was coming off soon—on Martin's Day?"

The man declared he remembered nothing about it; and the waggon went on jangling over the hill.

Henchard was convinced that the woman's memory served her well. The date was an extremely probable one, there being no reason for delay on either side. He might, for that matter, write and enquire of Elizabeth; but his instinct for sequestration had made the course difficult. Yet before he left her she had said that for him to be absent from her wedding was not as she wished it to be.

The remembrance would continually revive in him now that it was not Elizabeth and Farfrae who had driven him away from them, but his own haughty sense that his presence was no longer desired. He had assumed the return of Newson, without absolute proof that the Captain meant to return; still less that Elizabeth-Jane would welcome him; and with no proof whatever that if he did return he would stay. What if he had been mistaken in his views; if there had been no necessity that his own absolute separation from her he loved should be involved in these untoward incidents? To make one more attempt to be near her: to go back; to see her, to plead his cause before her, to ask forgiveness for his fraud, to endeavour strenuously to hold his own in her love; it was worth the risk of repulse, ay, of life itself.

But how to initiate this reversal of all his former resolves, without causing husband and wife to despise him for his inconsistency, was a question which made him tremble and brood.

He cut and cut his trusses two days more, and then he concluded his hesitancies by a sudden reckless determination to go to the wedding festivity. Neither writing nor message would be expected of him. She had regretted his decision to be absent—his unanticipated presence would fill the little unsatisfied corner that would probably have place in her just heart without him.

To intrude as little of his personality as possible upon a gay event with which that personality could show nothing in keeping, he decided not to make his appearance till evening—when stiffness would have worn off, and a gentle wish to let bygones be bygones would exercise its sway in all hearts.

He started on foot, two mornings before St. Martin's-tide, allowing himself about sixteen miles to perform for each of the three days' journey, reckoning the wedding-day as one. There were only two towns, Melchester and Shottsford, of any importance along his course, and at the latter he stopped on the second night, not only to rest, but to prepare himself for the next evening.

Possessing no clothes but the working suit he stood in—now stained and distorted by their two months of hard usage—he entered a shop to make some purchases which should put him, externally at any rate, a little in harmony with the prevailing tone of the morrow. A rough yet respectable coat and hat, a new shirt and neck-cloth, were the chief of these; and having satisfied himself that in appearance at least he would not now offend her he proceeded to the more interesting particular of buying her some present.

What should that present be? He walked up and down the street, regarding dubiously the display in the shop-windows, from a gloomy sense that what he might most like to give her would be beyond his miserable pocket. At length a caged goldfinch met his eye; the cage was a plain and small one, the shop humble; and on inquiry he concluded he could afford the modest sum asked. A sheet of newspaper was tied round the little creature's wire prison, and with the wrapped up cage in his hand Henchard sought a lodging for the night.

Next day he set out upon the last stage, and was soon within the district which had been his dealing ground in bygone years. Part of the distance he travelled by carrier, seating himself in the darkest corner at the back of that trader's van; and as the other passengers, mainly women going short journeys, mounted and alighted in front of Henchard, they talked over much local news, not the least portion of this being the wedding then in course of celebration at the town they were nearing. It appeared from their accounts that the town band had been hired for the evening party, and, lest the convivial instincts of that body should get the better of their skill, the further step had been taken of engaging the string band from Budmouth, so that there would be a reserve of harmony to fall back upon in case of need.

He heard, however, but few particulars beyond those known to him already, the incident of the deepest interest on the journey being the soft pealing of the Casterbridge bells which reached the travellers' ears while the van paused on the top of Yalbury Hill to have the drag lowered. The time was just after twelve o'clock.

Those notes were a signal that all had gone well; that there had been no slip 'twixt cup and lip in this case; that Elizabeth-Jane and Donald Farfrae were man and wife.

Henchard did not care to ride any further with his chattering companions after hearing this sound. Indeed, it quite unmanned him; and in pursuance of his plan of not showing himself in Casterbridge street till evening, lest he should mortify Farfrae and his bride, he alighted here with his bundle and bird-cage, and was soon left as a lonely figure on the broad white highway.

It was the hill near which he had waited to meet Farfrae, almost two years earlier, to tell him of the serious illness of his wife Lucetta. The place was unchanged; the same larches sighed the same notes; but Farfrae had another wife—and, as Henchard knew, a better one. He only hoped that Elizabeth-Jane had obtained a better home than had been hers at the former time.

He passed the remainder of the afternoon in a curious high-strung condition, unable to do much but think of the approaching meeting with her, and sadly satirize himself for his emotions thereon, as a Samson shorn. Such an innovation on Casterbridge customs as a flitting of bridegroom and bride from the town immediately after the ceremony was not likely, but if it should have taken place he would wait till their return. To assure himself on this point he asked a market-man when near the borough if the newly married couple had gone away and was promptly informed that they had not; they were at that hour, according to all accounts, entertaining a house-full of guests at their home in Corn Street.

Henchard dusted his boots, washed his hands at the riverside, and proceeded up the town under the feeble lamps. He need have made no inquiries beforehand, for on drawing near Farfrae's residence it was plain to the least observant that festivity prevailed within, and that Donald himself shared it, his voice being distinctly audible in the street giving strong expression to a song of his dear native country that he loved so well as never to have revisited it. Idlers were standing on the pavement in front; and wishing to escape the notice of these Henchard passed quickly on to the door.

It was wide open; the hall was lighted extravagantly, and people were going up and down the stairs. His courage failed him; to enter, footsore, laden, and poorly dressed, into the midst of such resplendency, was to bring needless humiliation upon her he loved, if not to court repulse from her husband. Accordingly he went round into the street at the back that he knew so well, entered the garden, and came quietly into the house through the kitchen, temporarily depositing the bird and cage under a bush outside to lessen the awkwardness of his arrival.

Solitude and sadness had so emolliated Henchard that he now feared circumstances he would formerly have scorned, and he began to wish that he had not taken upon himself to arrive at such a juncture. However his progress was made unexpectedly easy by his discovering alone in the kitchen an elderly woman who seemed to be acting as provisional housekeeper during the convulsions from which Farfrae's establishment was just then suffering. She was one of those people whom nothing surprises, and though to her, a total stranger, his request must have seemed odd, she willingly volunteered to go up and inform the master and mistress of the house that "a humble old friend" had come.

On second thoughts she said that he had better not wait in the kitchen, but come up into the little back parlour, which was empty. He thereupon followed her thither, and she left him. Just as she had got across the landing to the door of the best parlour a dance was struck up, and she returned to say that she would wait till that was over before announcing him—Mr. and Mrs. Farfrae having both joined in the figure.

The door of the front room had been taken off its hinges to give more space, and that of the room Henchard sat in being ajar, he could see fractional parts of the dancers whenever their gyrations brought them near the doorway, chiefly in the shape of the skirts of dresses and streaming curls of hair; together with about three-fifths of the band in profile, including the restless shadow of a fiddler's elbow and the tip of the bass-viol bow.

The gaiety jarred upon Henchard's spirits; and he could not quite understand why Farfrae, a much-sobered man and a widower, who had had his trials, should have cared for it all, notwithstanding the fact that he was quite a young man still, and quickly kindled to enthusiasm by dance and song. That the quiet Elizabeth, who had long ago appraised life at a moderate value, and who knew, in spite of her maidenhood, that marriage was as a rule no dancing matter, should have had zest for this revelry surprised him still more. However, young people could not be quite old people, he concluded, and custom was omnipotent.

With the progress of the dance the performers spread out

somewhat, and then for the first time he caught a glimpse of the once despised daughter who had mastered him and made his heart ache. She was in a dress of white silk or satin—he was not near enough to say which—snowy white, without a tinge of milk or cream; and the expression of her face was one of nervous pleasure rather than of gaiety. Presently Farfrae came round, his exuberant Scotch movement making him conspicuous in a moment. The pair were not dancing together, but Henchard could discern that whenever the changes of the figure made them the partners of a moment their emotions breathed a much subtler essence than at other times.

By degrees Henchard became aware that the measure was trod by some one who out-Farfraed Farfrae in saltatory intenseness. This was strange, and it was stranger to find that the eclipsing personage was Elizabeth-Jane's partner.

The first time that Henchard saw him he was sweeping grandly round, his head quivering, and low down, his legs in the form of an X, and his back towards the door. The next time he came round in the other direction, his white waistcoat preceding his face, and his toes preceding his white waistcoat. That happy face—Henchard's complete discomfiture lay in it. It was Newson's, who had indeed come and supplanted him.

Henchard pushed to the door, and for some seconds made no other movement. He rose to his feet, and stood like a dark ruin, obscured by "the shade from his own soul upthrown."

But he was no longer the man to stand these reverses unmoved. His agitation was great, and he would fain have been gone; but before he could leave the dance had ended, the housekeeper had informed Elizabeth-Jane of the stranger who awaited her, and she entered the room immediately.

"Oh—it is—Mr. Henchard!" she said, starting back.

"What, Elizabeth?" he cried, as he seized her hand. "What do you say?—*Mr*. Henchard? Don't, don't scourge me like that—Call me worthless old Henchard—anything; but don't 'ee be so cold as this! Oh, my maid—I see you have another—a real father in my place. Then you know all—but don't give all your thought to him! Do ye save a little room for me!"

She flushed up, and gently drew her hand away. "I could

have loved you always—I would have, gladly," said she. "But how can I when I know you have deceived me so—so bitterly deceived me. You persuaded me that my father was not my father—allowed me to live on in ignorance of the truth for years; and then, when he, my warm-hearted real father, came to find me, cruelly sent him away with a wicked invention of my death, which nearly broke his heart. Oh, how can I love as I once did a man who has served us like this!"

Henchard's lips half-parted, to begin an explanation; but he shut them up like a vice, and uttered not a sound. How should he, there and then, set before her with any effect, the palliatives of his great faults—that he had himself been deceived in her identity at first, till informed by her mother's letter that his own child had died; that, in the second accusation, his lie had been the last desperate throw of a gamester who loved her affection better than his own honour? Among the many hindrances to such a pleading not the least was this, that he did not sufficiently value himself to lessen his sufferings by strenuous appeal or elaborate argument.

Waiving therefore his privilege of self-defence he regarded only her discomposure. "Don't ye distress yourself on my account," he said with proud superiority. "I would not wish it—at such a time too, as this! I have done wrong in coming to 'ee. I see my error; but it is only for once, so forgive it. I'll never trouble 'ee again, Elizabeth-Jane—no, not to my dying day. Good-night. Good-bye!"

Then, before she could collect her thoughts, Henchard went out from her rooms, and departed from the house by the back way as he had come; and she saw him no more.

XLV

IT was about a month after the day which closed as in the last
chapter. Elizabeth-Jane had grown accustomed to the novelty
of her situation, and the only difference between Donald's
movements now and formerly was that he hastened indoors
rather more quickly after business hours than he had been in
the habit of doing for some time.

Newson had stayed in Casterbridge three days after the
wedding party (whose gaiety, as might have been surmised,
was of his making rather than of the married couple's) and was
stared at and honoured as became the returned Crusoe of the
hour. But whether or not because Casterbridge was difficult
to excite by dramatic returns and disappearances, through
having been for centuries an assize-town, in which sensational
exits from the world, antipodean absences, and such-like, were
half-yearly occurrences, the inhabitants did not altogether lose
their equanimity on his account. On the fourth morning he
was discovered disconsolately climbing a hill, in his craving to
get a glimpse of the sea from somewhere or other.

The contiguity of salt water proved to be such a necessity
of his existence that he preferred Budmouth as a place of
residence, notwithstanding the society of his daughter in the
other town. Thither he went, and settled in lodgings in a
green shuttered cottage which had a bow window, jutting out
sufficiently to afford glimpses of a vertical strip of blue sea,
to anyone opening the sash and leaning forward far enough to
look through a narrow lane of tall intervening houses.

Elizabeth-Jane was standing in the middle of her upstairs
parlour, critically surveying some rearrangement of articles
with her head to one side, when the housemaid came in with
the announcement, "Oh, please ma'am we know now how that
bird-cage came there."

In exploring her new domain during the first week of
residence—gazing with critical satisfaction on this cheerful
room and that, penetrating cautiously into dark cellars, sallying
forth with gingerly tread to the garden, now leaf-strewn by

autumn winds, and thus, like a wise field-marshal, estimating the capabilities of the site whereon she was about to open her housekeeping campaign—Mrs. Donald Farfrae had discovered, in a screened corner, a new bird-cage shrouded in newspaper, and at the bottom of the cage a little ball of feathers—the dead body of a goldfinch. Nobody could tell her how the bird and cage had come there; though that the poor little songster had been starved to death was evident. The sadness of the incident had made an impression on her. She had not been able to forget it for days, despite Farfrae's tender banter; and now when the matter had been nearly forgotten it was again revived.

"Oh, please ma'am, we know how that bird cage came there. That farmer's man who called on the evening of the wedding—he was seen wi' it in his hand as he came up the street; and 'tis thoughted that he put it down while he came in with his message, and then went away forgetting where he had left it."

This was enough to set Elizabeth thinking, and in thinking she seized hold of the idea, at one feminine bound, that the caged bird had been brought by Henchard for her as a wedding gift and token of repentance. He had not expressed to her any regrets or excuses for what he had done in the past; but it was a part of his nature to extenuate nothing, and live on as one of his own worst accusers. She went out, looked at the cage, buried the starved little singer; and from that hour her heart softened towards the self-alienated man.

When her husband came in she told him her solution of the bird-cage mystery; and begged Donald to help her in finding out, as soon as possible, whither Henchard had banished himself, that she might make her peace with him; try to do something to render his life less that of an outcast, and more tolerable to him.

Although Farfrae had never so passionately liked Henchard as Henchard had liked him, he had, on the other hand, never so passionately hated in the same direction as his former friend had done; and he was therefore not the least indisposed to assist Elizabeth-Jane in her laudable plan.

But it was by no means easy to set about discovering

Henchard. He had apparently sunk into the earth on leaving Mr. and Mrs. Farfrae's door. Elizabeth-Jane remembered what he had once attempted; and trembled.

But though she did not know it Henchard had become a changed man since then—as far, that is, as change of emotional basis can justify such a radical phrase; and she needed not to fear. In a few days Farfrae's inquiries elicited that Henchard had been seen by one who knew him, walking steadily along the Melchester highway eastward at twelve o'clock at night—in other words, retracing his steps on the road by which he had come.

This was enough; and the next morning Farfrae might have been discovered driving his gig out of Casterbridge in that direction, Elizabeth-Jane sitting beside him, wrapped in a thick flat fur—the victorine of the period—her complexion somewhat richer than formerly, and an incipient matronly dignity, which the serene Minerva eyes of one "whose gestures beamed with mind" made becoming, settling on her face. Having herself arrived at a promising haven from, at least, the grosser troubles of her life, her object was to place Henchard in some similar quietude, before he should sink into that lower stage of existence which was only too possible to him now.

After driving along the highway for a few miles they made further inquiries, and learnt of a road-mender who had been working thereabouts for weeks, that he had observed such a man at the time mentioned; he had left the Melchester coach-road at Weatherbury by a forking highway which skirted the north of Egdon Heath. Into this road they directed the horse's head, and soon were bowling across that ancient country whose surface never had been stirred to a finger's depth, save by the scratchings of rabbits, since brushed by the feet of the earliest tribes. The tumuli these had left behind, dun and shagged with heather, jutted roundly into the sky from the uplands, as though they were the full breasts of Diana Multimammia supinely extended there.

They searched Egdon, but found no Henchard. Farfrae drove onward, and by the afternoon reached the neighbourhood of some extension of the heath to the north of Anglebury, a prominent feature of which, in the form of a blasted clump of firs on the summit of a hill, they soon passed under. That the road they were following had, up to this point, been Henchard's track on foot, they were pretty certain; but the ramifications which now began to reveal themselves in the route made further progress in the right direction a matter of pure guesswork, and Donald strongly advised his wife to give up the search in person, and trust to other means for obtaining news of her step-father. They were now a score of miles at least from home, but by resting the horse for a couple of hours at a village they had just traversed it would be possible to get back to Casterbridge that same day; while to go much further afield would reduce them to the necessity of camping out for the night; "and that will make a hole in a sovereign," said Farfrae. She pondered the position, and agreed with him.

He accordingly drew rein, but before reversing their direction paused a moment, and looked vaguely round upon the wide country which the elevated position disclosed. While they looked a solitary human form came from the clump of trees, and crossed ahead of them. The person was some labourer; his gait was shambling, his regard fixed in front of him as absolutely as if he wore blinkers; and in his hand he carried a few sticks. Having crossed the road he descended into a ravine, where a cottage revealed itself, which he entered.

"If it were not so far away from Casterbridge I should say that must be poor Whittle. 'Tis just like him," observed Elizabeth-Jane.

"And it may be Whittle, for he's never been to the yard these three weeks, going away without saying any word at all; and I owing him for two days' work, without knowing who to pay it to."

The possibility led them to alight, and at least make an inquiry at the cottage. Farfrae hitched the reins to the gate-post, and they approached what was of humble dwellings surely the humblest. The walls, built of kneaded clay originally faced with a trowel, had been worn by years of rain-washings to a lumpy crumbling surface, channelled and sunken from its plane, its gray rents held together here and there by a leafy strap of ivy which could scarcely find substance enough for the purpose. The rafters were sunken, and the thatch of the roof in ragged holes. Leaves from the fence had been blown into the corners of the doorway, and lay there undisturbed. The door was ajar: Farfrae knocked; and he who stood before them was Whittle as they had conjectured.

His face showed marks of deep sadness, his eyes lighting on them with an unfocused gaze; and he still held in his hand the few sticks he had been out to gather. As soon as he recognised them he started.

"What, Abel Whittle; is it that ye are heere?" said Farfrae.

"Ay, yes, sir! You see, he was kind-like to mother when she wer here below though 'a was rough to me."

"Who are you talking of?"

"Oh sir—Mr. Henchet! Didn't ye know it? He's just gone—about half an hour ago, by the sun; for I've got no watch to my name."

"Not—dead?" faltered Elizabeth-Jane.

"Yes ma'am, he's gone! He was kind-like to mother when she wer here below, sending her the best ship-coal, and hardly any ashes from it at all; and taties, and such-like that were very needful to her. I seed en go down street on the night of your worshipful's wedding to the lady at yer side, and I thought he looked low and faltering. And I followed en over Grey's Bridge, and he turned and zeed me, and said 'You go back!' But I followed, and he turned again, and said, 'Do you hear, sir; go back!' But I zeed that he was low, and I followed on still. Then 'a said, 'Whittle, what do ye follow me for, when I've told ye to go back all these times?' And I said 'Because, sir, I see things be bad with 'ee, and ye wer kind-like to mother if ye were rough to me, and I would fain be kind-like to you.' Then he walked on, and I followed; and he never complained at me no more. We walked on like that all night; and in the blue o' the morning when 'twas hardly day I looked ahead o' me, and I zeed that he wambled, and could hardly drag along. By that time we had got past here, but I had seen that this house was empty as I went by, and I got him to come back; and I took down the boards from the windows, and helped him inside. 'What, Whittle,' he said, 'and can ye really

be such a poor fond fool as to care for such a wretch as I!'
Then I went on further, and some neighbourly woodmen lent
me a bed, and a chair, and a few other traps, and we brought
'em here, and made him as comfortable as we could. But he
didn't gain strength, for you see ma'am, he couldn't eat—no,
no appetite at all—and he got weaker; and to-day he died. One
of the neighbours have gone to get a man to measure him."

"Dear me—is that so!" said Farfrae.

As for Elizabeth, she said nothing.

"Upon the head of his bed he pinned a piece of paper, with
some writing upon it," continued Abel Whittle. "But not
being a man o' letters I can't read writing; so I don't know
what it is. I can get it and show ye?"

They stood in silence while he ran into the cottage;
returning in a moment with a crumpled scrap of paper. On it
there was pencilled as follows:

"Michael Henchard's Will.

"That Elizabeth-Jane Farfrae be not told of my death, or made to
grieve on account of me.

"& that I be not bury'd in consecrated ground.

"& that no sexton be asked to toll the bell.

"& that nobody is wished to see my dead body.

"& that no murners walk behind me at my funeral.

"& that no flours be planted on my grave.

"& that no man remember me.

"To this I put my name.

"Michael Henchard."

"What are we to do?" said Donald, when he had handed the
paper to her.

She could not answer distinctly. "Oh Donald," she said
at last through her tears. "What bitterness lies there! O I
would not have minded so much if it had not been for my
unkindness at that last parting! . . . But there's no altering—so
it must be."

What Henchard had written in the anguish of his dying was
respected as far as practicable by Elizabeth-Jane, though less
from a sense of the sacredness of last words, as such, than
from her independent knowledge that the man who wrote

them meant what he said. She knew the directions to be a piece of the same stuff that his whole life was made of, and hence were not to be tampered with to give herself a mournful pleasure, or her husband credit for large-heartedness.

All was over at last, even her regrets for having misunderstood him on his last visit, for not having searched him out sooner, though these were deep and sharp for a good while. From this time forward Elizabeth-Jane found herself in a latitude of calm weather, kindly and grateful in itself, and doubly so after the Capharnaum in which some of her preceding years had been spent. As the lively and sparkling emotions of her early married life cohered into an equable serenity, the finer movements of her nature found scope in discovering to the narrow-lived ones around her the secret (as she had once learnt it) of making limited opportunities endurable; which she deemed to consist in the cunning enlargement by a species of microscopic treatment, of those minute forms of satisfaction that offer themselves to everybody not in positive pain; which thus handled have much of the same inspiriting effect upon life as wider interests cursorily embraced.

Her teaching had a reflex action upon herself, insomuch that she thought she could perceive no great personal difference between being respected in the nether parts of Casterbridge, and glorified at the uppermost end of the social world.

Her position was indeed, to a marked degree, one that in the common phrase afforded much to be thankful for. That she was not demonstratively thankful was no fault of hers. Her experience had been of a kind to teach her, rightly or wrongly, that the doubtful honour of a brief transit through a sorry world hardly called for effusiveness, even when the path was suddenly irradiated at some half-way point by daybeams rich as hers. But her strong sense that neither she nor any human being deserved less than was given, did not blind her to the fact that there were others receiving less who had deserved much more. And in being forced to class herself among the fortunate she did not cease to wonder at the persistence of the unforeseen, when the one to whom such unbroken tranquillity had been accorded in the adult stage was she whose youth had seemed to teach that happiness was but the occasional episode in a general drama of pain.

THE END

had been accorded in the adult stage to she whose youth had seemed to teach that happiness was but the occasional episode in a general drama of pain.

THE END

EXPLANATORY NOTES

THESE notes combine textual notes and explanatory notes in one list. To save space, the textual notes use the following sigla to identify the different versions of the novel from which variants are being cited. In quotations from the MS, angled brackets enclose material deleted within the MS, and slanted lines enclose material added within the MS, usually interlinearly.

MS Manuscript (in the Dorset County Museum, Dorchester)

G *The Graphic* (weekly, 2 January–15 May 1886)

HW *Harper's Weekly* (weekly, 2 January–15 May 1886)

A1 American first edition (one volume, Henry Holt's Leisure Hour and Leisure Moment Series), 1886

E1 English first edition (2 volumes, Smith, Elder), 1886

Col Colonial Library Edition (Macmillan), 1886

87 English first one-volume edition (Sampson Low, Marston), 1887

95rc Revising copy (and possibly printer's copy) for the Osgood, McIlvaine Wessex Novels edition (a copy of Sampson Low's Half-Crown Edition, in the possession of Richard Little Purdy), n.d.

95 Wessex Novels collected edition (Osgood, McIlvaine), 1895

12 Wessex Edition (Macmillan), 1912

M Mellstock Edition (Macmillan), 1920

For help on some of these notes I thank Jana Kramer and Leon Waldoff, and for help on many of them Doug Corcoran and Simon Gatrell.

Quotations from the Bible are from the King James version. Quotations of definitions not otherwise identified are from *Webster's Third New International Dictionary* (Springfield, Mass.: G. & C. Merriam, 1961). Primary and secondary sources often cited here and in the front matter are:

Collected Letters: *The Collected Letters of Thomas Hardy*, ed. Richard Little Purdy and Michael Millgate (Oxford: Clarendon Press, 1978–88).

Life and Work: *The Life and Work of Thomas Hardy* by Thomas

Hardy, edited by Michael Millgate (London: Macmillan, 1985).
[For a brief description of this edition see 'Select Bibliography'.]

Literary Notebooks: *The Literary Notebooks of Thomas Hardy*, edited by Lennart A. Björk (London: Macmillan, 1985). Two volumes. [Partially published, Göteborg, Sweden, 1974.]

Millgate: Michael Millgate, *Thomas Hardy: His Career as a Novelist* (London: Bodley Head, 1971).

OED: *Oxford English Dictionary*.

Personal Notebooks: *The Personal Notebooks of Thomas Hardy*, edited by Richard H. Taylor (London: Macmillan, 1979).

Personal Writings: *Thomas Hardy's Personal Writings: Prefaces, Literary Opinions, Reminiscences*, edited by Harold Orel (London: Macmillan, 1966).

Purdy: Richard Little Purdy, *Thomas Hardy: A Bibliographical Study* (Oxford: Oxford University Press, 1954).

TITLE

MS: 'The Mayor of Casterbridge'; G–HW: *The Mayor of Casterbridge*; Al: *The Mayor of Casterbridge: A Novel*; El–Col: *The Mayor of Casterbridge: The Life and Death of a Man of Character*; 87–95: *The Mayor of Casterbridge: A Story of a Man of Character*; 12–M: *The Life and Death of the Mayor of Casterbridge: A Story of a Man of Character*.

PREFACE

3 *sixpenny loaf of the present date*: i.e. cheap bread which seldom fluctuates in price—unlike the gyrations in the price of bread while the Corn Laws (see below) made impractical the importation of foreign grain unless the domestic price exceeded astronomical levels (e.g. 80s./quarter for wheat in 1815). The price of a quartern loaf (4 lb. 5¼ oz.) reached 17d. in 1812, averaged 9d. to 10d. in the 1830s, and 8½d. when the Corn Laws were repealed in 1846. In 1895 (when this part of the Preface was written) the price, despite an increased demand, was only 5d.

harvest weather: Chapter XXVI (cf. pp. 184–5) reflects the historical situation. Speculators anticipating a wet season—i.e. a poor harvest—would bid up the price of grain (the delivery to take place at a later time), thus causing a rise in prices for bread.

After 1846, the possibility (and eventually the fact) of imports from India and America dampened speculation, and prices remained relatively constant.

sale of a wife: sales of wives were never a common occurrence, but dozens have been documented, mostly through newspaper accounts. Hardy himself probably took details of wife sales he had read in old copies of the *Dorset County Chronicle* (Millgate, pp. 240–2). Samuel Pyeatt Menefee in *Wives for Sale: An Ethnographic Study of British Popular Opinions* (Oxford: Basil Blackwell, 1981) traces wife-selling through English history, citing references to 387 instances, 378 of them between 1553 and 1928.

the repeal of the Corn Laws: trade in wheat, rye, and barley was for centuries restricted in England by duties on importation and penalties on exportation. Although specific stipulations varied to meet changing political and economic situations, the purpose of the laws was to protect the interests of the land-owning classes. The regulations became particularly pronounced during the Napoleonic wars and afterwards, and were increasingly resented. Sir Robert Peel, in a general shift to free trade, first made existing Corn Law duties less onerous and in 1846 succeeded in passing a law that removed the duties entirely by February 1849.

Although Hardy ignores strict historical veracity (cf., e.g., the Note to p. 262), these dates mark the obsolescence of the economic conditions that dominate the novel, so it seems reasonable that the end-date of the novel lies no later than the mid-1840s (cf. pp. 184–5).

visit of a Royal personage: Prince Albert, in 1849. See Note to p. 262.

For a discussion of changes made in the several versions of the novel, see the Note on the Text. For the reference to 'some good judges across the Atlantic' see Note to pp. 320–7.

Exhibition of Wessex life: Hardy's allusion to his career-long concentration, with several exceptions, on the ways of life and manners of 'Wessex' (the counties of Dorset, Somerset, Devon, Cornwall, Hampshire, Wiltshire, and Berkshire).

Southron: Southern.

a professor of the tongue: according to Purdy, p. 54, this is Sir George Douglas (1856–1935), author of poems and books about Scottish life and letters. Hardy had known him since 1881.

February 1895–May 1912: the Preface first appeared in the 1895 Osgood, McIlvaine edition; for the 1912 Wessex Edition there are only minor up-dating variants (as well as the addition of the last paragraph) in the Preface.

CHAPTER I

5 *Weydon-Priors*: Hardy's name for the actual town of Weyhill, in Hampshire.

Upper Wessex: added in 95rc.

fustian: a thick cotton cloth, usually dyed a dark colour.

1 *rush basket . . . aperture*: in a cancelled MS passage here Henchard has a 'two-foot rule'—identifying him as a carpenter (cf. also Note to p. 13).

rush basket: basket made from the cylindrical and often hollow stems of plants of the genera *Juncus* and *Scirpus*.

crutch of a hay-knife: a 'crutch' of a tool such as a hay-knife is a handle with a cross-bar like the head of a crutch.

wimble for hay-bonds: strictly, a gimlet, auger, or brace and bit, for boring a hole; here evidently referring to the tool that winds together several strings or twine to form a rope (or stalks of hay to form a hay-bond; cf. p. 236). Hay-bond, a hay-band: 'A rope of twisted hay used to bind up a truss or bundle of hay' (*OED*).

ballad-sheet: a broadsheet containing a song, possibly a narrative song.

6 *Nature*: compare the objective, scientific 'nature' at p. 15, l. 21 with the capitalized, personified form here.

nimbus: a luminous cloud surrounding a god or goddess when walking the earth. The word suggests an ironic attitude toward the characters. Cf. the luminous 'haloes' the drunken field-folk in *Tess of the d'Urbervilles* (Ch. X) perceive around themselves.

7 *in his van*: in front of him.

thatched hurdle: a hurdle is a rectangular frame made of cut and trimmed sticks of hazelwood that had been grown to a uniform size by pollarding (periodical cutting or pruning). Hurdles were used for various purposes such as gates, fences, or pens. Hurdles were thatched to form windbreaks for lambing ewes and their young. (See also Note to p. 206.)

8 *journeymen*: a journeyman has completed his apprenticeship to a handicraft or trade, and is an employee.

thimble-riggers: professional sharpers who with sleight of hand swindle people who try to guess under which of three thimbles is the pea.

ochreous: yellow red.

furmity: a variant of 'frumenty'. A dish made of wheat boiled in milk and seasoned with such ingredients as are named a few paragraphs later on in the novel's text.

bell-metal: an alloy of 3½ to 4 parts of copper to 1 part of tin.

off the rocks . . . into Maelstrom depths: an allusion to the myth of Scylla and Charybdis, based on the mariners' dilemma of choosing between the rocky shore of Italy and the tumultuous, whirlpool-forming waters offshore in the Strait of Messina.

12 *toper*: one who habitually drinks a great deal.

Jack Rag or Tom Straw: i.e. anyone.

She shall take the girl if she wants to: an earlier version, overwritten in the MS by the present wording, is 'She shall take one of the girls, her favourite one'.

simple as Scripture history: probably an allusion both to the common use in the Bible of 'went their ways' to mark the conclusion of an encounter and to the greater concern shown in the Bible's historical books with events than with individual motivations.

staylace: a lace or pair of laces to tie through the eyelet holes in a woman's stays or corset.

13 *my 'vation*: my salvation.

trusser: MS: '<woodman> / <sawyer> <stonemason> trusser/'.

rheumy: full of mucus; moist (cf. p. 12, l. 36: 'damp voice').

14 *Up to this moment . . . parting lips*: this paragraph is a late addition to the MS.

14, 15 *Michael, Mike*: MS names for Henchard in these two places are 'Giles' and 'Jim'. These earlier versions of Henchard's name continue to appear for about two-thirds of the MS.

15 *a couple of years*: MS: '<five> /a couple of/ years'.

'Twill be better for me and Elizabeth-Jane both: MS: '<Take care of the girl. I'll take care of this one.> /'Twill be better for me and the child both./' The 'child' is named as Elizabeth-Jane in 12.

clane: (dialect for 'clean') entirely. The word conveys the implication of guiltlessness.

16 *not till the great trumpet*: the trumpet sounds the advent of judgment day (cf. 1 Thessalonians 4: 16, also OT prophecies such as Isaiah 27: 13). At this time, according to some interpretations, husbands and wives will be reunited before being made as brothers and sisters, or as angels.

CHAPTER II

18 *felloe*: the exterior rim of a wheel supported by spokes.

Seven Sleepers: seven Christian youths concealed in a cave during the persecution of Decius (AD 250) fell asleep, awaking during the reign of Theodosius II (408–50). Shortly afterwards they fell asleep again and died like saints, after having thus demonstrated physical resurrection. The version of the myth in Chapter 18 of the Koran includes a dog stretched at the mouth of the cave to protect the sleepers.

intellect: G–HW [MS missing]: 'intellect, which was far removed from strong, though not positively weak, as that word is usually understood in this connection'.

19 *fetichistic*: irrational, superstitious reverence. This is one of Henchard's primary characteristics, and should be seen in relation to Hardy's reading of Auguste Comte, to whom fetichism is an early (and necessary) stage in humanity's growth to modern Positive thought. Many passages from Comte in Hardy's notebooks concern fetichism—cf., e.g., '*Fetichism*—universal adoration of matter' and '*Fetichism*—"Its scientific error consists in not distinguishing *life* properly so called from *spontaneous activity*" ' (*Literary Notebooks*, I, Items 641, 761; cf. also and especially I, Items 647, 722, 754, 755–62; and Björk's note to Item 754, which explains Fetichism's superiority to Theologism). These points are relevant to *The Mayor of Casterbridge* in that the novel portrays generational conflict in the context of apparent progress.

nave: the main part of a church, from the inner door to the chancel. (Cf. p. 37, l. 35.)

sacrarium: the area 'immediately surrounding the altar or communion table' (*OED*).

foot-pace: 'the step or raised platform on which an altar stands' (*OED*).

before God: added in 12.

twenty-one: G–95 [MS missing]: 'twenty'.

20 *in a far distant part of Wessex*: G–87 [MS missing]: 'more than a hundred miles off'; 95rc: 'in another part of Wessex'.

CHAPTER III

21 *woman about eighteen*: G–95 [MS missing]: 'woman of eighteen'.

withy: willow; flexible and strong.

22 *the roundabouts and highfliers*: amusement rides at fairs. A roundabout is a merry-go-round; a highflier is a balloon or swing (*OED*, which uses this passage from *A Mayor of Casterbridge* as an example).

shooting for nuts: meaning not certain, but possibly a carnival concession stand in which one shoots at a target to win a coconut or a bag of these exotic nuts.

Richard Newson . . . November: cp. p. 68, where Elizabeth-Jane tells Henchard that Newson had died 'last spring'.

23 *furmity sold here*: in what may be a slight clarification that the furmity woman is not a native (cf. p. 199 and Note), in HW her MS–G Dorset dialect pronunciation 'zold' is changed to 'sold'.

ha'p'orth: a half-penny's worth.

soi-disant: self-styled, so-called (French); literally, 'saying oneself'. A term of disparagement.

24 *cordial*: 'A comforting or stimulating drink' (*OED*).

shameless females: MS: 'nameless females'; G–Al: 'thoughtless females'.

Lord's my life: cancelled in the MS is 'God's my life'; MS–95 is 'seize my life'. At p. 25, in the MS Hardy similarly cancels 'God's my life' but substitutes 'Lord's my life'.

CHAPTER IV

26 *folly . . . wise*: echo, with ironic overtones, of Thomas Gray's 'where ignorance is bliss, / 'Tis folly to be wise' ('Ode on a Distant Prospect of Eton College').

simplicity: G–HW [MS missing]: 'almost vacuous simplicity'.

as too many rural records show: cf. Note to p. 3.

27 *Newfoundland trade*: fishing had long been Newfoundland's principal industry, with much of the catch being shipped to England. During the 1840s and later a strong government effort to broaden the economy led to increased mercantilism and vastly expanded agriculture, which of course also increased maritime trading. Newson himself may have been a fisherman, since his voyages are seasonal.

liege subjects of Labour: vassal-like or feudal allegiance, implying little freedom or leisure to travel.

needle she was filling: threading—i.e. with the weft or woof yarn or twine used in making the nets.

28 *to see, to hear, and to understand*: an echo of Isaiah 6: 9–10.

sailor, drowned or no, was probably now lost to them: MS: 'sailor was now <dead and buried> /lost to them /'; G–95: 'sailor was now lost to them'.

29 *coomb*: variant of 'combe': a short, deep valley running up from the sea-coast, also, a deep narrow valley, sometimes specifically a cleft in the flank of a hill. MS–95: 'combe'.

30 *escarpment . . . ditch . . . town*: the boundary walls and avenues of Dorchester to which Hardy refers were built in the eighteenth century atop the remnants of the Roman defences of the encampment at Durnovaria, with a ditch being dug outside the raised escarpment.

burgh and champaign: city and countryside.

dimity: 'a sheer cotton fabric of plain weave that is usually checked or striped by corded effects which are made by weaving two or more threads as one'.

barge-boards: a barge-board is 'a piece of board often elaborately ornamented that conceals roof timbers projecting over gables'.

brick-nogging: 'brickwork filled in between the timbers of a wood-framed wall or partition'.

31 *Scythes* [*et al.*] *. . . clogs*: most of these 'agricultural and pastoral' items had specific functions. A reap-hook works somewhat like a scythe; a bill-hook is a heavy knife with a hooked end used in pruning and cutting brush; a firkin is a small cask; a seed-lip is a basket in which seed that is broadcast by hand is carried by the sower; a cooper makes barrels and other wooden vessels; a horse-embrocation is liniment; a patten is 'A kind of overshoe

or sandal worn to raise the ordinary shoes out of mud or wet; consisting, since 17th c., of a wooden sole secured to the foot by a leather loop passing over the instep' (*OED*); a clog is 'a wooden-soled overshoe or sandal worn (chiefly by women) in some localities, to protect the feet from wet and dirt' (*OED*).

carts, wheel-barrows, and mill-gear: from MS to 95rc the wheel-wrights and machinists displayed 'corn-drills and winnowing-machines'—although the availability of corn-drills in Dorchester was of course contradicted by passages on pp. 167–9.

stonecrop: a yellow-flowered herb that grows on walls and rocks.

curfew: in medieval times, the ringing of the curfew bell signalled the time to extinguish all household fires. It continued to be used in many communities to signal 'various municipal or communal regulations' (*OED*).

Sicilian Mariners' Hymn: a traditional Sicilian melody, used by several writers of hymns before and after the 1840s. A hymn popular at the time of the novel's setting is attributed to John Fawcett (1740–1817). This song of closing, appropriate for the ringing of curfew bells, begins 'Lord, dismiss us with Thy blessing'.

Note at foot of page: this and the other historical footnotes first appear in 12.

32 *manna-food*: food, translated as 'bread' (Exodus 16) but probably the honey-tasting exudation from the tamarisk shrub, taken to be miraculously supplied to the Israelites during their migration from Egypt: i.e. food from heaven.

swipes: poorly brewed or thin beer.

corn-factor: a merchant who deals in corn or grain.

growed wheat: grown wheat: wheat 'That has sprouted in the ear after reaching maturity' (*OED*, which gives the passage on p. 38 of *The Mayor of Casterbridge* as an example). The condition is ordinarily caused by dampness necessitating a late harvest. Germination has begun owing to the high moisture content but the sprouts have not yet burst the hull of the kernels.

Germination within the kernel is deliberately brought about in the brewing process (see the Note to p. 277), thus the comparison of beer and bread in the lines above in the text. But if the germination has begun naturally and is not controlled, as is the case with Henchard's grain, the resulting beer is poor ('swipes').

CHAPTER V

33 *The Roast Beef of Old England*: song by Richard Leveridge, with words by Henry Fielding (*The Grub Street Opera*, III. iii).

fall: a veil that is attached to the front of a hat or bonnet.

34 *Susan Henchard's husband*: MS: '<Elizabeth Jane's father, & the elder woman's> /Susan Henchard's/ husband'.

35 *akin to a coach*: i.e. related to wealth or social standing of the sort that might justify a coat-of-arms on the family coach, or to a person who owing to his or her position would be entitled to ride in an official coach.

36 *rummers*: a rummer is a large drinking glass, used especially for wine (*OED* uses this passage from *A Mayor of Casterbridge* as an example).

grog: a mixture of a liquor (such as rum) and water. Often served hot, sometimes with lemon juice and sugar added.

banded teetotaler: possibly a member of a group 'banded' together in total opposition to drink, in contrast to the 'moderates' who rejected only strong liquors. The teetotal movement gained attention in the 1830s with the monthly *Preston Temperance Advocate*'s frequent employment of the word first used in this sense by a working man, Richard Turner, giving rise to such groups as the Band of Hope in the 1840s. Henchard, having taken his own oath in the 1820s, would be encouraged to hold to it by this sort of support, much like the modern Alcoholics Anonymous. But he does not seem to be a 'joiner', and 'banded' may be a dialect variant of 'bonded' (i.e. sworn).

as the Lord upon the jovial Jews: while Moses was on Mount Sinai receiving the commandments, the people he had led out of Egypt made a golden calf, and drank and played. Moses dissuaded the Lord from wreaking his wrath upon his followers, but upon returning to the camp he himself commanded the loyal sons of Levi to 'go in and out from gate to gate throughout the camp, and slay every man his brother, and every man his companion, and every man his neighbours'. In all, three thousand men died. (See Exodus 32.)

37 *Durnover Moor*: the flat part of Fordington Manor (cf. p. 92 n.) east of Dorchester through which flow the two rivers Frome and Cerne. Fordington, which contained Mill Street (Mixen Lane in the novel), nearly surrounded Dorchester. Part of it was brought into the Borough of Dorchester in 1835, more of it in 1894 and 1933.

G–87 [MS missing]: 'Casterbridge Moor'.

list: literally, a border or streak made of dregs. Here, the thick layer at the bottom of the loaf caused by the failure of the dough to rise.

he had outwitted: in MS–HW, a tale is narrated by Henchard here, but rather than his outwitting a sharper, he is outwitted by a competitor, and he laughs at his own gullibility. The alteration removes this aspect of detached self-observation from Henchard's personality, and sharpens the irony of the query about the bad wheat he had just dealt in.

just as the west end of a church . . . spirits in the chancel: the chancel includes the area occupied by the altar, choir, and clergy, often enclosed by a railing or lattice-work; ordinarily in the eastern end of a church. The laity sit or stand in the western end.

CHAPTER VI

39 *ruddy and of a fair countenance*: 1 Samuel 16: 12 describes David on his first appearance as 'ruddy, and withal of a beautiful countenance'; 1 Samuel 17: 42 as 'but a youth, and ruddy, and of a fair countenance'. G–95: [MS missing]: 'fair and ruddy'. The change in 12 emphasizes the biblical analogy.

41 *The corporation*: members of the town council.

42 *holland overcoat*: a good-quality overcoat made of smooth glazed or unglazed cotton or, usually, linen. The thinness attests its elegance; a holland coat would not be worn to protect one from the cold.

Elizabethan gables: Elizabethan architecture (1558–1603) marked a transition between medieval features (such as parapets, and windows that were mullioned [their panels separated by vertical posts] and hooded [protected from rain by projecting mouldings]), and Renaissance details and exterior decoration (such as bay and oriel windows). An Elizabethan gable has multicurved sides (instead of conforming precisely to the slant of the roof). The bow window is a rounded bay window.

mullioned: a mullion is 'a slender vertical usually nonstructural bar or pier forming a division between lights of windows, doors, or screens'.

yard of clay: 'A long clay tobacco-pipe' (*OED*).

four-centred Tudor arch: a pointed arch characteristic of English Perpendicular Gothic architecture of the reigns of Henry VII and VIII (1485–1547).

CHAPTER VII

45 *weal*: well-being; welfare.

settles: large chairs or benches enclosed on two sides to catch and retain heat from a fireplace. Cf. pp. 51, 256.

twelve-bushel strength: referring to the amount of barley used to make the mash, this term means that the resulting beer or ale will be of good quality.

47 *corren trade*: G–HW [MS missing]: 'corn trade'; Al: 'corrn trade'; El–Col: 'corern trade'.

advairrtisment: G [MS missing]: 'advertisement'; HW: 'advertisment'; Al: 'advarrtisement'; El–87: 'advarrtisment'; 95rc: 'advertisment'. (Of interest here is that in proofs for 95 Hardy evidently decided to try again to make a Scots-like word.)

on my way to Bristol: although Farfrae has presumably come through London on his way to the West Country, there would be little reason to take the circuitous way of Casterbridge to reach Bristol. Hardy appears to be attributing to Farfrae some curiosity to see something of England, since either Glasgow or Liverpool would have been closer to his Scottish home.

warrld: G–HW [MS missing]: 'world'.

48 *heere* (l. 2): G [MS missing], Al: 'here'.

quarters: eight bushels, a common measure of the grain trade (cf. Note to p. 3).

quag: bog or quagmire.

heere (ll. 25, 37): two of this dialect usage replaced 'here' in 95, one in 12.

seconds: next in quality to the best.

50 *warreming to the stomach*: in G–87 [MS missing], Farfrae adds '—ay, as Presbyterian cream'. ('Presbyterian cream' not identified, but probably refers to an alcoholic beverage drunk in Scotland.)

dog days: the hot and sultry time from early July to early September, so called from ancient times because during this period the rising of the sun coincides with that of the Dog Star (Sirius).

I could drink a quarter-barrel to the pitching: i.e. I could drink 9 gallons of ale (so that the sides of the cask, sealed with pitch, would be visible).

CHAPTER VIII

52 *It's hame, and it's hame . . . hame to my ain countree*: an eighteenth-century Jacobite song, of uncertain authorship.

53 *lammigers*: cripples (*OED*, which gives the passage at p. 280 of *The Mayor of Casterbridge* as an example).

slatterns: a slattern is a person, usually a woman or girl, who is negligent of slovenly appearance or surroundings; the word sometimes bears the meaning of slut or prostitute.

Buzzford's historically distorted account is based on the consequences upon the followers of the Duke of Monmouth when he declared himself king in 1685, five months after the death of his father, Charles II, who had denied his legitimacy. The reference to 'Romans' may allude to one of the reasons Monmouth thought he would be supported (James II, who succeeded Charles II, was a Roman Catholic); or it may be an ignorant conflation of Monmouth's rebellion and the resistance to the Romans' invasion of England in the first century.

During the trials for treason held in Dorchester in 1685 following the battle of Sedgemoor, Judge George Jeffreys sentenced 321 persons to death. Several dozen men were actually hanged. As a warning to future rebels, many bodies were cut into quarters and set up in public, as Buzzford describes. There are interesting analogies between Farfrae/Monmouth, and Henchard/Charles II (who had granted many honours to Monmouth, and subsequently revoked them before his death).

Gallows-Hill: in Icen Way close to its junction with the South Walk.

pigs' chaps: the pun is with 'fair faces': pig's chaps are the lower part of pigs' cheeks, used for food, often after pickling.

54 *Botany Bay*: geographically, an inlet on the east coast of Australia. Used here as the generic name for Australian convict

settlements, although owing to poor soil and water the projected penal colony prison was not established there.

Oh Nannie: English poem turned into Lowland Scottish dialect and collected by Bishop Percy in his *Reliques of Ancient English Poetry*. It queries whether 'Nanny' can happily exchange a busy social life in the city with the 'charms' of 'silent glens'.

Auld Lang Syne: Robert Burns's poem celebrating friendship is, when turned to music, generally associated with drinking, sentiment, and merriment. Its iteration in the novel establishes one of the motifs in the relationship between Henchard and Farfrae (cf. p. 271).

55 *chine*: 'The projecting rim at the heads of casks, etc., formed by the ends of the staves' (*OED*).

gaberlunzie: Scots for a wandering beggar, mendicant, or beadsman. Although gaberlunzies could be licensed and wear standard clothing and a badge, their begging tactics were reputed to be aggressive and greedy.

Arthur's Seat: a volcanic hill (823 feet) smoothed by glaciers, east of Edinburgh, a popular climb that affords excellent views.

flock: 'woollen or cotton refuse (as processing waste or old rags) reduced usually by machinery and used esp. for stuffing furniture and mattresses'.

prizes: MS: 'prizes'.

56 *toss-pots*: a toss-pot is a drunkard or sot.

As I came in by my bower door: it is not surprising that the song would disconcert a girl as determined as Elizabeth-Jane to be 'respectable'. The second stanza, given in MS–HW, reads:

> Her air sae sweet, & shape complete
> Wi' nae proportion wanting,
> The Queen o' Love did never move
> Wi' motion more enchanting.

The song 'Bonnie Peg' can be found in *Burns: Poems and Songs*, ed. James Kinsley (London: Oxford University Press, 1969), p. 726.

CHAPTER IX

58 *meads*: meadows.

60 "*bloody warriors*": *Cheiranthus cheiri*—wallflowers.

chassez-déchassez: a dance movement in which one takes an equal number of gliding steps to the right and then to the left to return to one's base line of movement.

61 *Terpsichorean*: Terpsichore is 'the muse of choral dance and song'.

Cranstoun's Goblin Page: the Goblin Page—a dwarf owned by Lord Cranstoun, 'omitting still / No opportunity of ill'—through devious actions causes riot and uproar during the wedding of his master (Walter Scott, *Lay of the Last Minstrel*, Canto VI, stanzas 7–9).

63 *studded with rusty nails . . . trained there*: cf. p. 77 and Note.

stone-staddles: foundations made of pillars, on which are set such buildings as granaries (to prevent ground dampness from spoiling the grain).

Flemish ladders: unidentified, but probably means 'short ladders': a 'Flemish account' is one in which the remittance is less than expected; and G–HW [MS missing] read: 'short Flemish ladders'.

with the air of awaiting a famine that would not come: possibly an allusion to Joseph in Egypt; cf. the Note to p. 123.

64 *Chalk Walk*: G–95rc [MS missing]: 'New Walk'.

for, hang it, Farfrae, I like thee well: added in A1.

64–5 *It's Providence*: G–87 [MS missing]: 'Surely there's destiny in it?'

CHAPTER X

66 *the quicker cripple at Bethesda*: Jewish myth interpreted a movement of the water in the pool at Bethesda (probably caused by an intermittent spring) as caused by an angel's wing; the first person to enter the water after the movement would be cured of any illness. (Jesus cures the cripple who for 38 years has been unable to move quickly enough to the pool [John 5: 2–9].) Although Jopp's rapid movement brings the phrase's implication of selfishness upon him, of course it is Henchard who here is indifferent to another's situation.

Elizabeth-Jane . . . stood before the master of the premises: MS: 'Elizabeth Jane now entered, & stood before <her father> /the master of the premises/'.

67 *rouge et noir*: (French) red and black. The colouring is Satanic, common to depictions of the devil in myth. Henchard is specifically linked to Satan as the Prince of Darkness (p. 273), and throughout the novel these colours are associated with him.

They are given a mysterious tinge at p. 66 (the red is *in* his dark pupils, the Satanic aspect emphasized by the narratorial comment 'though this could hardly be a physical fact'). Other relevant passages are p. 83, l. 8; p. 277 (the skimmington figure is also red and black).

Pembroke tables: 'A table supported on four fixed legs, having two hinged side portions or flaps, which can be spread out horizontally, and supported on legs connected with the central part by joints' (*OED*). The table is of the Georgian period.

a "Josephus": presumably a copy of the works of Flavius Josephus (AD 37–93+), Jewish soldier and scholar who changed sides after his capture by the Romans and wrote *History of the Jewish War*, *The Antiquities of the Jews*, and the autobiographical *Against Apion*. Perhaps the appositeness of Henchard's possessing Josephus' works is that both were outsiders in the societies in which they had stature.

"Whole Duty of Man": first published 1658 (anonymous, but generally attributed to Richard Allestree, as edited and rewritten by Bishop John Fell) as *The Practice of Christian Graces, or The Whole Duty of Man*, it includes prayers for 'Private [i.e. family] Devotions' and Sunday readings on such topics as wives' and husbands' duties to each other, temperance, envy, charity, and similar homiletic concerns. According to Ecclesiastes 12: 13, the 'whole duty of man' is to 'Fear God, and keep his commandments.'

That Henchard possesses such books is probably more a mark of his sense of station than of his reading. At p. 297 he says that although he is not 'a read man' he has all his life attempted to learn through books.

Chippendale and Sheraton: famous English furniture makers and designers. Thomas Chippendale (1709–79) worked in the rococo style. His *The Gentleman and Cabinet Maker's Director* (1754) offered designs of elaborate curves and carvings, fretwork, and Gothic patterns. Thomas Sheraton (1751–1806) offered neoclassic designs in *The Cabinet Maker and Upholsterer's Drawing Book* (1791), and more grotesque designs in *The Cabinet Dictionary* (1802). The chairs in Sheraton's books, and those made in Chippendale's own workshop, have curved legs; but otherwise their designs vary even within each man's work so much it is not clear whether Hardy has particular features in mind. Evidently Hardy's point here is that these chairs are unauthorized copies, the masters' patterns plagiarized and altered.

These chairs and the Pembroke table mentioned a few lines above would be commonplace English furniture – no doubt modified into the early Victorian style suggested in the phrase 'heavy mahogany'.

68 *his wife and her child*: MS: 'his wife & /her/ child'.

CHAPTER XI

70 *Ring at Casterbridge*: the Maumbury Ring on the road to Weymouth. Situated several hundred yards south of the South Walk, it was well outside of town during the time of the novel's action. Most likely originating as a neolithic earthworks or fort (enlarged and smoothed by the Romans to serve as a site for circuses and gladatorial sport), it became an artillery implacement during the Civil War in the seventeenth century. Thus it has wider associations in time and event than those Hardy drew upon. Hardy gives a fairly full account of the Rings in 'Maumbury Rings' (1908; rpt. *Personal Writings*, pp. 225–32).

fibula: 'a clasp somewhat resembling a safety pin used by the ancient Greeks and Romans.'

It was impossible to dig . . . bottle at his mouth: some of the details of this traditional burial method for Romans are given also in Hardy's report of Roman graves discovered during the excavation for Max Gate, 'Some Romano-British Relics Found at Max-Gate, Dorchester' (1884; rpt. *Personal Writings*, pp. 191–5).

Jötuns: giants in Norse mythology, the earliest beings created. This sentence entered the text in A1, with 'Föteens' instead of 'Jötuns'.

71 *in 1705 a woman . . . to the terror of them all*: Hardy gives a fuller account of the trial and execution of Mary Channing in 'Maumbury Rings' (*Personal Writings*, pp. 225–32). Mary Channing was 18 when she was executed, and extremely ill from a fever following childbirth. Her parents had forced her to marry, but her indulgent husband had given her money and allowed her lovers. Hardy questions the justice of the verdict; other students of the trial records do not.

72 *Hadrian*: Emperor of Rome 117–138. He attempted to secure Rome's position in England through constructing Hadrian's Wall in the north as a defence against the Picts and Scots. A restless traveller, he visited England in 122.

bents: stiff coarse stalks of old grass.

Æolian modulations: Aeolus is the Greek god of the winds; the term 'Æolian modulations' refers to the musical or soughing sound frequently produced by wind. (An Æolian harp is a musical instrument consisting of strings of various thicknesses stretched on a resonance box and tuned to the same note. It is placed in a window or open space so that the wind blowing across the strings produces chord-like harmonics with the same fundamental tone.) Hardy is probably remembering Shelley's *Prometheus Unbound*, IV, 185–8:

> *Ionè*: . . . What is that awful [i.e. impressive] sound?
> *Panthea*: 'Tis the deep music of the rolling world
> Kindling within the strings of the waved air
> Æolian modulations.

"I don't drink," . . . *After a minute or two he again began*: this passage, conveying that Henchard's opening apologetic declaration to Susan is that he hasn't had a drink since 'that night', is a late addition to the MS.

CHAPTER XII

76 *finnikin*: a variant of 'finicking': 'insignificant, paltry, trifling' (*OED*).

education of Achilles: the centaur Chion trained the youthful Achilles in medicine; the arts of battle, music, and poetry; and the principles of right and justice. Writing, a rare skill during the 'time' of classical mythology, is likewise one of Henchard's weak points (cf. p. 253).

77 *espaliers*: an espalier is 'a fruit tree or other plant trained to grow flat against a building, wall, railing, trellis, or other support'. Cf. p. 63, ll. 10–11.

Laocoöns: Laocoön was a Trojan priest of Apollo. As punishment for his offending the gods during the siege of Troy, his two sons were seized by two giant serpents; he came to their rescue, and all three were enwrapped by the serpents and strangled (Virgil's *Aeneid*, Book II). Hardy no doubt has in mind the famous first-century BC sculpture attributed by Pliny the Elder to Agesander, Polydorus, and Athenodorus that is in the Vatican Museum.

damn: G [MS missing]: 'hang'; HW–95rc: 'd——'.

Apollo and Diana: Apollo and Diana are twins. Apollo is the god of manly beauty, poetry, music, medicine, and prophecy (oracles); Diana (her Greek name is Artemis) is the goddess of chastity, vegetation, the moon, and the fruitfulness of women, and the protectress of wild animals. The images in the paragraph evoke both Farfrae and Henchard, in their love of music and in the competition which later develops between them.

77, 78 *nineteen years*: G–95 [MS missing]: 'eighteen years'.

78 *"Ay!"*: in MS–87, Farfrae adds: 'And it's not a small counterbalance to the immoral years that ye've done so much since!'

mostly (l. 13): added in 12.

In the nature of things, Farfrae . . . gave me birth: in MS–HW Lucetta saves Henchard's life when he falls out of a boat, and his offer of marriage is made in 'a moment of gratitude and excitement', and the couple do marry. Cf. third Note to p. 79.

Job: Job's words, early in his testing by the Lord, are: 'Let the day perish wherein I was born, and the night in which it was said, There is a man child conceived' (Job 3: 3). These words also play a large role in Hardy's *Jude the Obscure*. They form a refrain in Jude Fawley's life, and more of the passage occurs at his death. It is interesting that Job is used to express the outlook of both Hardy's most traditional and his most modern tragic heroes, and that both of them—unlike Job—bring about their own deaths, unable to bear life without the love of Elizabeth-Jane and Sue Bridehead.

79 *daughter of some harum-scarum military officer*: in MS, Lucetta is the daughter of a 'fruit merchant'; in G–HW she is a 'merchant's' daughter. *harum-scarum*: reckless, wild. Added in El.

sequestrated: seized, by a legal writ, for payment of debts.

we got naturally intimate . . . meant to marry: in the first version of Henchard and Lucetta's relationship, MS–HW, Henchard and Lucetta had married a fortnight before Susan reappeared. The version in A1–87 refers only to 'a terrible scandal' brought about by Lucetta nursing Henchard in the boarding-house during a period of depression; a sexual liaison is specifically denied by Henchard. The relationship, then, assumes final form only in 95rc.

80 *The letter to the young Jersey woman*: in MS–HW, the letter is taken by Farfrae to give it to Lucetta, who is arriving at Budmouth by ship from Jersey. She is ill owing to the crossing and takes the letter from behind her cabin door, and thus the two do not see each other.

CHAPTER XIII

82 *tumuli*: plural of tumulus: an artificial mound over an ancient grave, a barrow.

the flesh is weak: Mark 14: 38; 'Watch ye and pray, lest ye enter into temptation. The spirit truly is ready, but the flesh is weak.'

83–4 *castigate himself with the thorns*: the image may derive from Corinthians 12: 7: the apostle Paul has 'a thorn in the flesh' to prevent him becoming too elated at having had visions of paradise. Chastisement is a frequent consequence of spiritual pride; and although Henchard is scarcely elated, perhaps the suggestion of the rather indirect analogy is that Henchard selects his own chastisement for his youthful prideful acts in the hope of warding off the punishing forces about which he is superstitious.

84 *brougham*: a closed carriage drawn by one horse. The driver sits outside, in the open.

reticulated with creases: lined with a network of creases.

85 *leather breeches*: although leather breeches are long lasting, it's obvious from the context that leather breeches is a good thing to have got rid of, like a violent husband.

Agricultural Society: in the late 1830s and early 1840s county Agricultural Societies were founded to advocate the application of science and technology to farming.

wash: pig-swill, liquid food.

snuffers: devices for cutting off or trimming candle ends and burned wicks of candles, so that the candles do not burn too extravagantly; snuffers are also used to extinguish candles.

cow-barton: cow-yard.

86 *She'll wish her cake dough*: i.e. she will wish she had not taken the final step of changing her condition.

bluebeardy: reference to Bluebeard, the legendary wife-killer.

jumps: an old-fashioned bodice worn instead of stays in rural areas in the nineteenth century.

night-rail: a dressing-gown, or loose gown for private wear.

small table ninepenny: weak beer, costing only ninepence a gallon.

clammy as a cockle-snail: 'clammy' is cold and damp; a cockle-snail is the inhabitant of a cockle-shell, a marine mollusc.

CHAPTER XIV

87 *Martinmas summer*: a summer that lasts into November. St Martin's Day is on 11 November (cf. Note to p. 321).

Georgian sash windows: Georgian architecture (1702–1830) reflects classical, Renaissance, Baroque, and Palladian influences (cf. p. 141). Sash (or double-hung) windows in being opened or closed break neither the external nor internal wall lines; thus they maintain the symmetry of buildings' surfaces.

Knowledge—the result . . . had not: MS–HW: 'Knowledge, learning, accomplishments, those, alas, she had not.'

88 *to paraphrase a recent poet . . . how it came there*: Goethe; but Hardy probably took the allusion from Matthew Arnold, writing not *as* a poet but *about* a poet, Wordsworth and his views of Goethe. Arnold writes, in 'Wordsworth' (*Essays in Criticism: Second Series*): 'I remember hearing him say that "Goethe's poetry was not inevitable enough." The remark is striking and true; no line in Goethe, as Goethe said himself, but its maker knew well how it came there' (*The Complete Prose Works of Matthew Arnold*, ed. R. H. Super [Ann Arbor: University of Michigan Press, 1973], IX. 51–2. Cf. also *Literary Notebooks*, I. item 1108 and note).

unsophisticated girl: MS–HW: 'uninstructed girl'.

puffings: clothing enlarged by padding or gatherings.

coulter: a sharp disc or blade attached to the beam of a plough in front of the ploughshare and mouldboard. It cuts the sward vertically, the ploughshare cuts the soil horizontally several inches below the surface, and the mouldboard turns over the cut soil in a continuous layer. Hardy is evoking this passage from Burns's 'To a Mouse, On turning her up in her Nest, with the Plough':

> Thou saw the fields laid bare an' wast,
> An' weary Winter comin fast,
> An' cozie here, beneath the blast,
> Thou thought to dwell,

> Till crash! the cruel coulter past
> Out thro' thy cell.

We now see her: in MS–HW this paragraph is preceded by a description of Elizabeth-Jane eagerly and somewhat superciliously burning her pattens in favour of galoshes ('an article of wear just then reaching the remoter towns'), confident she will never be so 'stupid' as to again wear them (see Note to p. 144: the deletion from A1 here made the two accounts consistent).

velvet mantle or silk spencer: a mantle is 'a loose sleeveless garment worn over other clothes: an enveloping robe or cloak . . . regarded as a symbol of preeminence or authority'; a spencer is 'a woman's fitted jacket of waist length or shorter'.

89 *to which the future held the key*: added in E1.

it is her legal name: cf. also p. 124.

90 *vivâ voce*: (Latin) 'by word of mouth'; 'orally'.

91 *damn*: MS–95rc: 'd——n'.

92 *barley-mow*: a stack or heap of unthreshed barley.

Durnover: Fordington. The church is St George's. [cf. p. 37] MS–95rc: 'Dummerford'.

wheat ricks: stacks or piles of grain in the open air, customarily protected from wet with roof-shaped thatching (or with rick-cloths [cf. p. 103]).

as high as the gates of Solomon's temple: at no place in the Bible is the height of the door mentioned. The temple and porch were 20 cubits wide (1 Kings 6: 2), and the door is unclearly described as 'a fourth part of the wall' (1 Kings 6: 33), which has been taken variously to mean an opening 5 cubits wide, and a square opening. (A cubit is about 18–21 inches.)

fallow: the term applied to 'land ordinarily used for crop production when [it is] allowed to lie idle . . . during the whole or the greater portion of the growing season'.

intramural squeeze: instead of being at large in the countryside the shepherds are squeezed up in a narrow place.

flail . . . winnowing-fan: a flail is an instrument used in threshing grain, made of a heavy club that swings freely from a longer wooden club that is wielded by the workman. The flail is swung heavily into a pile of harvested and dried grain to break loose the heads of wheat, barley, etc., from the stalks. A winnowing-fan is an appliance to expose grain that has been flailed to the wind or moving air so that the chaff is blown away. It is operated with a handle (cf. p. 93).

93 *staddles*: cf. Note to p. 63.

victorine: a woman's fur cape or hood, with hanging ends.

95 *As I came down through Cannobie*: possibly a variant line in Burns's 'Bonnie Peg' (cf. p. 56 and Note), according to Richard Little Purdy and Michael Millgate, eds., *Collected Letters*, v. 90 n. (note to a letter of 5 April 1915). The metrics match; but it seems a common metric in Scots songs. In the letter Hardy says, 'I make Farfrae sing it in "The Mayor of Casterbridge." But I have not the slightest idea where I saw or heard the song, or how it got into the novel.'

CHAPTER XV

96 *Baruch*: not a prophet, but secretary and companion to the prophet Jeremiah, whose words these are (rather than, as Hardy says, Baruch's), from the Apocyphral book of Baruch, ch. 6 (otherwise known as 'The Epistle of Jeremy'), verse 9: 'And taking gold, as it were for a virgin that loveth to go gay [literally, 'fond of ornament'], they make crowns for the heads of their gods.'

An additional comment about Elizabeth-Jane is in MS (and G–E1 with slightly different wording): 'This particular virgin was just a shade too far the other way; and she paid the penalty. She was so sober, so discreet by nature, yet so hearty, that her homespun simplicity afforded none of those piquant problems which are afforded by the simplicity that is carefully constructed by art.' The passage goes on to suggest the respect felt toward Elizabeth-Jane by Casterbridge's young men even though they do not enquire about her health.

the "delicate imposition" of Rochefoucauld: François, Duc de La Rochefoucauld (1613–80), French novelist and aphorist. His maxim No. 289 from *Réflexions ou Sentences et maximes morales* (1665) is 'La simplicité affectée est une imposture délicate', which can be translated 'Simulated simplicity is a delicate imposition' but which more accurately would be translated 'Simulated simplicity is a delicate imposture.' The phrase is added in A1.

97 *unfinished girl*: MS–A1: 'ignorant girl'.

Better sell all . . . of all the philosophies: MS–HW: 'Better sell all this finery 'a b'lieve, and buy myself a copybook, and a dictionary, and a grammar of my native tongue'; A1: 'Better sell all this finery and buy myself grammar books and dictionaries and a history of my native country.'

98 *I'll mortify thy flesh for thee*: Colossians 3: 5: 'Mortify [put to death] therefore your members which are upon the earth; fornication, uncleanness, inordinate affection, evil concupiscence, and covetousness, which is idolatry.'

The context is Paul's exhortation to the Colossians to put a stricter denial of self in place of their false asceticism (which in a previous passage he has just repudiated). Given Abel Whittle's slackness, Henchard's associating him with an asceticism is of course ironic; but the more relevant analogy is between Henchard and Paul as outsiders urging their hearers to adopt a way of life that is better because it is based on principle. Henchard's ensuing humiliation of Abel is not only one of his prime violations of human dignity, but it also illustrates the nature of the 'energy' that marks his own supremacy, which is challenged by Farfrae according to a different, and appropriately superior, principle.

moment-hand: minute hand, which moves ahead a full minute at a time—i.e. a regular spasmodic twitching; it is to this that Hardy alludes.

99 *gibbered . . . terror*: MS–A1: 'replied Abel with a resigned smile': E1–95rc: 'gibbered Abel with a resigned smile'.

as a man 'ithout breeches: added in 95.

101 *fairing*: 'Cakes or sweets sold at fairs' (*OED*).

102 *sotto voce*: literally, under the voice (Italian); i.e. in an undertone or an aside.

CHAPTER XVI

103 *public rejoicing . . . national event*: the national event would appear to be something along the lines of a royal birth—possibly Princess Alice (1843) or Prince Alfred (1844). But of course Hardy's purpose is not to draw upon an event directly, but to point up yet another link between the novel's locale and the larger society of which its inhabitants form a part (cf. Note to p. 262).

rick-cloths: large, heavy waterproof coverings used to protect grain-ricks from the weather. Cf. *Far from the Madding Crowd*, Chapter XXXVI.

fine old crusted characters: Hardy gave the title 'A Few Crusted Characters' to a group of interrelated tales (originally titled 'Wessex Folks' [1891]) when the group were included in *Life's Little Ironies* (1894). 'Crusted' probably refers to the crust that forms around the edge of the bottle of old wine—suggesting a slow and easygoing maturity.

104 *just like a Scotchman*: not in MS–A1; E1–Col: 'just like him!'

105 *Æolian improvisations*: the phrase 'Æolian modulations' was added here in A1, then—Hardy probably noticing he had already used that phrase at p. 72—was altered in E1 to the present reading.

106 *reel or fling*: a reel, acc. to the *OED*, is 'a lively dance, chiefly associated with Scotland, usually danced by two couples facing each other, and describing a series of figures of eight'; a fling is 'a dance in which the arms and legs are moved with great vigour, esp. in the Highland fling'.

107 *Correggio*: Antonio Allegri (1498[?]–1534) (called Correggio after his birthplace), Italian painter of the Renaissance, whose early works present human figures of sinuous softness caught in a gentle light; his later work retains the softness but accentuates intertwining figures. His chiaroscuro, or modifying by subtle gradations tones from bright to light to darkness, is perhaps his prime technical accomplishment. Hardy's comment appended to Corregio's name in his 'Schools of Painting' notebook (*Personal Notebooks*, p. 109) is: 'great knowledge of lights and shades'. These notebooks represent his jottings about artists in a youthful self-education scheme.

mensuration: MS–HW: 'clockwork machines, and true circumference laws'; A1: 'clock-work machines, and mensuration laws'; E1–Col: 'machines, and mansuration'.

honeycombed: Henchard's meaning is not certain. One possibility is that he refers to himself as a 'honey' (a foolish and good-natured person); another is that the ground beneath him is being hollowed, i.e. his standing will be undermined.

108 *Miss M'Leod of Ayr*: in *Life and Work*, p. 19, Hardy refers to this as ' "Miss Macleod of Ayr" (an old Scotch tune to which Burns may have danced)'. As a young child, Hardy 'danced a *pas*

seul in the middle of the room' to this song while his father played it on a fiddle; it was one of the 'three or four that always moved [him] to tears'.

top sawyer: one technique for sawing large logs was with a two-handled saw, with one sawyer standing in a deep pit and a second, on the other end of the saw, atop a platform above the log. The bottom sawyer became covered with sawdust, so the phrase 'top sawyer' connotes not only a preferable position, but the domination of someone else.

CHAPTER XVII

113 *homely*: commonplace.

reign of self-control: MS: 'regime of judgment'.

114 Henchard's questioning Elizabeth-Jane and his letter to Farfrae are in a late addition to the MS.

All's well that ends well: Shakespeare's play of this name in which an unequal marriage early in the play is not accepted until late, because the male, not recognizing his wife's merits, flees the misalliance. Henchard's use of the phrase here is ironic, for it adumbrates Farfrae's and Elizabeth-Jane's eventual reconciliation. This allusion may also be one of Hardy's means of suggesting Farfrae's limitations, for Shakespeare's Bertram is by no means free of faults in character and judgement.

modus vivendi: literally, mode of living (Latin). A temporary arrangement or practical compromise about matters in dispute without a permanent settlement.

115 *finesse*: subtlety, craftiness (French).

Like Jacob in Padan-Aram: as is not unusual with Hardy's allusions, the context from which this one is drawn suggests a quality different from the narrator's ostensible purpose. Genesis 30: 25–43 and 31: 1–16 relates the stratagem by which Jacob, having already laboured fourteen years for his uncle Laban in Padan-Aram (modern-day Syria) in order to marry Leah and Rachel, proposed to take as his future wages only the speckled and spotted cattle and goats and the brown sheep that were to be born in Laban's herds and flocks following the agreement. Laban removed all existing animals of these colourations from his herds and gave them to his sons, to decrease the number of likely new births of animals of these colours which would become Jacob's. But Jacob, having anticipated such an action by Laban (who had already tricked him into marrying Leah when it was Rachel he had loved), had proposed the plan with a trick of his own in mind. When the strong animals came for water during the mating season. Jacob placed spotted sticks in front of the animals' water troughs, so that they would conceive off-colour young. He did not place the spotted sticks before the weak animals. As a result, in time Jacob came to own larger, and healthier, herds than Laban: and he took his herds and his wives and children to Canaan. By means of this allusion, Hardy casts an element of clever indirectness into Farfrae's character that is at variance with the straightforward presentations of Farfrae's financial dealings. The question before the individual reader of the novel is whether Hardy intends the ambiguity (and even self-contradictoriness) or is merely drawing upon the biblical text for its broad and powerful image of success rather than for its moral shadings.

Character is Fate, said Novalis: Novalis is the pseudonym of Friedrich Leopold, Freiherr von Hardenberg (1772–1801), a Protestant poet and novelist from Saxony whose mystical and emotional reaction to nature was influential upon Romantic literature.

The quotation is presumably drawn from *Heinrich von Ofterdingen*, Part II, written 1799–1800. Heinrich says to Sylvester: 'Je tiefer ich einsehe, dass Schicksal und Gemüt Namen Eines Begriffs sind.' ('Ever more profoundly I perceive that Fate and character are [both] names of a single idea.') *Novalis Schriften*, Volume I, ed. Paul Kluckhorn and Richard Samuel (Stuttgart: W. Kohlhammer Verlag, 1960), p. 328.

Hardy read little German, and it is almost certain that he obtained this quotation from George Eliot's *The Mill on the Floss*, Chapter 6 of Book Sixth: 'But you have known Maggie a long while, and need to be told, not her characteristics, but her history, which is a thing hardly to be predicted even from the completest knowledge of characteristics. For the tragedy of our lives is not created entirely from within. "Character," says Novalis, in one of his questionable aphorisms—"character is destiny." But not the whole of our destiny. Hamlet, Prince of Denmark, was speculative and irresolute, and we have a great tragedy in consequence. But if his father had lived to a good old age, and his uncle had died an early death, we can conceive Hamlet's having married Ophelia, and got through life with a reputation of sanity, notwithstanding many soliloquies, and some moody sarcasms towards the fair daughter of Polonius, to say nothing of the frankest incivility to his father-in-law.' (World's Classics Edition, ed. Gordon S. Haight [Oxford, 1981], pp. 401–2.)

It is possible that by so obviously paraphrasing Eliot's well-known translation Hardy intends to draw into his novel the context Eliot provides ('one of his questionable aphorisms'), and thereby qualify the assertion made so directly in the novel. None the less, this assertion about the dominance of character bears authorial commitment, in opposition to the novel's contrasting viewpoint at Chapter XXXIV, where it is Farfrae who says 'it's ourselves that are ruled by the powers above us'. In context Farfrae obviously is rationalizing his wish to stay in Casterbridge to be mayor despite Lucetta's urging that he retire so they can live elsewhere.

Part of the MS is missing here, and this and the next three paragraphs are not in HW–A1.

as Faust has been described: Hardy is quoting directly from Thomas Carlyle's 'Goethe's Helena' (1828). Goethe's poem and Christopher Marlowe's play about Faust are the most famous portrayals of this prototypical figure willing to exchange his soul for such benefits as power or knowledge or love in his current existence. The appropriateness of alluding to Faust would appear to turn upon Henchard's willingness to challenge customary social 'laws' such as marriage bonds, taboos against nakedness (in the case of exposing Abel Whittle), and blood bonds (in telling the returned Newson that Elizabeth-Jane is dead). Carlyle's further comment on Faust certainly is relevant to Henchard: 'He is still [having abandoned 'the sympathies, the common interests and persuasions by which the mass of mortals . . . are held together'] but a slave; the slave of impulses, which are stronger, not truer or better, and the more unsafe that they are solitary.'

116 *no Romeo part*: Shakespeare's Romeo, in defiance of the feud between his family the Montagues and the Capulets, woos and weds the Capulet Juliet, with disastrous results. Farfrae consciously avoids putting love ahead of all other considerations.

dirk against the cudgel: a dirk is 'a long straight-bladed dagger formerly carried esp. by the Scottish highlanders'; a cudgel is 'a short heavy stick'. In MS, it is a 'rapier' against a 'bludgeon'.

Bellerophon . . . cankered in soul: with divine aid, Bellerophon overcame great obstacles to win successes; but when he attempted to fly Pegasus to the abode of the gods they turned against him. Two of his children died and he was flung from Pegasus and lamed or blinded (depending on the version); thereafter he shunned mankind and wandered grief-stricken and bitter. The parallels, early and late, with Henchard's life are obvious.

CHAPTER XVIII

117 *box passenger*: a passenger on a coach who sits outside alongside the driver above the 'box' (usually containing materials and tools to service the coach and horses). He would have a view of ruts across the road of water-courses worn into the road-bed.

acquaintance: MS–HW: 'marriage, hasty as it was'.

fifteen or sixteen years: MS–95: 'eighteen years'.

118 *Poor thing—better you had not known me*: MS: 'Poor thing—<six years of shilly shallying with me—engagement as she calls it!> / better <she> //you// had <seen> //saved// the devil <than me> //'s life than mine!//' A revision for A1 brought the passage to its present form.

In MS–HW, Henchard gives the letters to Elizabeth-Jane to deliver to the coach; Elizabeth-Jane in turn gives them to Farfrae, who has noted it is 'tedious' for her to wait in the chilly weather for the tardy coach. Lucetta does not appear, and Farfrae's efforts to return the letters to Henchard coincides with Mrs Henchard's death so he retains them. (This, then, is Hardy's first stratagem for Farfrae's being in possession of Lucetta's letters in Chapter XXXIV.) (See also Note to p. 148.)

119 *toss-pot*: cf. Note to p. 56.

the subtle-souled girl: MS–HW: 'Elizabeth Jane'.

120 *ounce pennies*: pennies were placed on a dead person's eyes to ensure their remaining closed, for a folk belief was that a corpse's open eyes were looking for the next person to die. (See p.134 and Note for another superstitious use of coins at death.)

121 *harm in it*: MS–HW continue: 'Baint we all handfuls [G–HW: 'lumps'] of one mixture, the dead and the living—say?'; the MS then has this further sentence: 'Why, folks go to dust, & they grow & grow up in the shape of ivy-thrum & such-like, & climb the church tower that they climbed in the flesh, & so there's no such terrible difference.'

To respect the dead . . . throats get dry: added in G.

doxology: 'praise to the Deity'.

varnished for natomies: refers to the practice of robbing graves and selling their contents to medical students and lecture-halls.

CHAPTER XIX

122 *pier-glass*: a tall mirror fitted between windows.

   entablature: the part of the mirror frame above the side columns.

123 *like the brethren at the avowal of Joseph*: Genesis 42–5 presents the core of the Joseph story; the passage in the novel draws especially from 45: 1–4. Joseph's brethren are troubled by his presence not only because of guilt for having sold him into slavery years earlier but because in the meantime he has become the most powerful man in Egypt while they, having come to Egypt to buy grain during a great famine, are in his power. Numerous parallels and instructive contrasts exist between Henchard's and the Joseph story: both men are outsiders in the societies in which they have gained pre-eminence; both had spent years in gaining this pre-eminence; both see themselves as fulfilling the will of larger forces (Genesis 45: 5, 8; *Mayor* XLI). Unlike Henchard, who takes for granted Newson's death, Joseph repeatedly asks his brothers whether their father (Jacob) is still alive; again unlike Henchard, who avows his identity to Elizabeth-Jane on an irresistible impulse, Joseph has patiently and cannily tested his brothers' feelings and fears, and in their presence has repeatedly restrained himself, going aside to weep in order to release his emotions. None of these parallels and contrasts pertains to Elizabeth-Jane, of course; the allusion evokes primarily the uncertainty and fear at the discovery of a previously unsuspected relationship with someone in power.

125 *though more patient than her husband*: not in G–HW [MS missing]; A1–95rc: 'though better educated than her husband'.

126 *He remained unnerved and purposeless . . . suddenly said*: added in A1.

127 *Prester John . . . harpies*: Prester John was a legendary Christian ruler from the East, in some versions Tartary, in others Ethiopia. The version Hardy draws on is that in Canto XXXIII of Ariosto's *Orlando Furioso*. Ariosto's Prester John had in his

youth searched for Adam and Eve's terrestial paradise. For this presumption God made him blind; worse, whenever he attempted to eat, harpies (hungry mythological monsters with a woman's head and vulture's body and claws) would steal his food and defecate on the table and food. Henchard would probably not have known of Prester John or Ariosto (although it's hard to know just how well or poorly read he is [see the Note to p. 67]); but the terms in which his superstitiousness is expressed (cf. p. 126, ll. 37–8) make the allusion clearly relevant.

Schwarzwasser: literally, black water (German). The name of Dorchester derives from 'Dwyr', meaning dark, or *dwr*, meaning water, both in reference to the river that flows near by. Cf. also p. 224 and p. 296 which appear to give the name more specifically to a pool upstream beyond Ten Hatches Weir.

Franciscan priory: this priory was one of those dissolved by Henry VIII in 1538–43. It is near what is now Priory Lane.

weir: 'a dam in a stream to raise the water level or divert its flow'.

128 *back lane into the town*: following this in MS–HW [a sheet of MS containing part of the passage is missing] are two paragraphs indicating that Henchard's emotions reject Elizabeth-Jane even though his will asserts that 'he would cherish her as his own'. 'Henchard was a man of strong feeling, deprived of objects for its indulgence, though always seeking them; and it hit him hard that this child of his, as he had deemed her, upon whose ultimate attachment to himself as her father he had, as a final throw, staked all the sunshine of his future, should be revealed as spurious.'

129 *dust and ashes*: an expression of worthlessness (Genesis 18: 27), especially as a measure of contrast with one's previous state (Job 30: 19).

CHAPTER XX

130 *girl*: G–HW [MS missing]: 'sensible unselfish girl'.

marks of the beast: i.e. associated with commercial or working class standing. Cf. Revelation 13: 17: 'And that no one might buy or sell, save he that had the mark, the name of the beast, or the number of his name.'

131 *Minerva*: Roman goddess of wisdom, handicrafts, and war. Pallas Athena is the Greek form.

Princess Ida: the heroine of Tennyson's *The Princess* (1847), who has formed a university solely for women. The lines Hardy quotes describe the penmanship not of Princess Ida herself but of a man who, disguised as a woman in order to gain entrance to the university, is writing to Princess Ida in what he assumes to be a female's hand.

chain-shot: a cannon load, formed by connecting two balls or half balls with a short chain, used in naval warfare to cut a ship's masts, rigging, and sails. Elizabeth-Jane is writing in what she later calls 'round hand' (p. 139).

132 *wimbling hay-bonds*: cf. Note to p. 5.

133 *glide down her peachy cheeks*: MS–A1: 'come'.

many of these educational works: MS: '<almost all> /many of these/ educational works <to the self-teaching student>'.

134 *men who held in their mouths coins of Hadrian, Posthumus, and the Constantines*: Roman rulers of Britain: Hadrian (Emperor 117–38), Posthumus (usurper governor of Britain 258–68), the Constantines (three Emperors ruling 306–37, 337–40, and 407–11). The coins were to pay Charon for the trip across the river Styx.

Karnac: a village forming part of ancient Thebes in central Egypt where were located many great temples, now ruins of immense archaeological value.

wraith: an apparition of a living being.

135 *stranger. And this . . . was simply pretty*: MS–HW: 'stranger, leaving her a plain human shell'.

Northern Lights: the Aurora Borealis, an atmospheric luminosity over the North Pole, visible at times from much of the northern hemisphere.

cameo: 'a gem carved in relief; *esp*: a small piece of sculpture on a stone (as onyx or sardonyx) or on a shell having layers of different colours, the figure being cut in relief in one layer and another serving as background'.

136 *Austerlitz*: on 2 December 1805 Napoleon defeated a superior force of Russians and Austrians. It was his greatest military success, and other successes and alliances followed. But the total defeat of his naval forces at Trafalgar a few weeks before Austerlitz (21 October 1805) meant that his true gains would be limited: without a fleet he was unable to invade England to complete his domination of existing governments. Thus, in

classical tragic fashion, Napoleon's triumph at Austerlitz coincided with the turn of his fortunes. In similar fashion, if the banquet forms Henchard's high point, it occurs shortly after the discovery that he has sold sprouted grain, which is the first significant mar upon his name in Casterbridge.

leery: empty, i.e. hungry (*OED*, which gives this passage in *The Mayor of Casterbridge* as an example). (Also spelled 'larry'.)

137 *I wish I was dead*: The MS is missing here, but G–HW have a sentence preceding Elizabeth-Jane's wish to be dead: 'Why should I be called low, when my lowness is of other people's making?' There are other nearby deletions for A1 of references to Elizabeth-Jane as 'low'.

138 *Not? But I can't help using rural words*: MS, HW: 'Not?—will it do if one can't /kerp &/ talk the up-country way? It makes me sorry, but I can't help using work-folk words'; G: 'Not? Will it do if one can't help talking in the up-country way? It makes me sorry; but I can't help using work-folk words.'

CHAPTER XXI

140 *High-Place Hall*: MS: '<Little-Park & Little-Park House> /High-Street Hall/'; G–87: 'High Street Hall'; 95rc: 'High Place Hall'.

façade: face (from the French); the front of a building, usually a building that is distinguished by special architectural treatment or details.

motes: minute particles.

141 *studious girl's mind*: G–A1 [MS missing]: 'simple girl's mind'.

Palladian: influenced by late-Renaissance architect Andrea Palladio (1508–80), esp. his *I quattro libri dell'architettura*, a study of antique Roman buildings. The Palladian style, a dominant architectural style in England 1715–60, is noted for symmetry, openness, and academic adherence to classical forms.

Gothic age: the Gothic Age lasted from the middle of the twelfth century to the advent of the Renaissance in the sixteenth century. Gothic architecture is characterized by pointed arches, flying buttresses, ribbed vaults, the use of stained glass (esp. in large window areas subdivided by tracery), and rich detail (which John Ruskin credited to the sincere feeling, artistry, and freedom of the individual craftsman). Despite these readily identifiable features, Gothic architecture evaded fixed canons, and Gothic cathedrals were decades and even centuries in their construction, their original plans usually undergoing evolution and modification.

keystone of the arch: the centre stone at the apex of the arch.

142 *the old bull-stake, the old cock-pit*: referring to the sports of bull-baiting and cock-fighting; i.e. the alley opens on to the more raucous and rowdy part of Casterbridge.

pier: one of two square pillars for a gate, door, or archway.

143 *It had better be done properly . . . off his hands by this arrangement*: Henchard's offering Elizabeth-Jane an annuity (as a means of making her an allowance) is a late addition to the MS.

144 *where her pattens had hung*: while writing the novel, Hardy forgot he earlier (in MS–HW) had had Elizabeth-Jane burn her pattens (see Note to p. 88: the contradictory passage there was not corrected until A1).

apotheosis: transformation into a higher state (literally, into that of a god or goddess).

Thus mounted: see Note to p. 31 for an explanation of pattens.

145 *tailing*: inferior quality grain or refuse that remains after milling.

146 *fly*: a one-horse covered carriage for hire, such as a cab or hansom.

CHAPTER XXII

148 *mon ami*: (French) my friend. MS: '<Giles> /James/'; HW–A1: 'Michael'.

imbecile: MS–HW continue: 'I spoke to her once in passing through the town'. This meeting, observed by Henchard, was deleted as part of his reduction for A1 of sensational but irrelevant events aimed to please the magazine readers. The meeting is described in the passage spanned by the Note to p. 118 (but for clarity not discussed there).

I ought to endeavour . . . promise to me: MS–HW: 'we ought to repair our former mistake as soon as we decently could'.

étourderie: careless blunder. Added during a revision for A1.

150 *fiasco*: 'an utter and often ridiculous failure esp. of an ambitious or pretentious undertaking' (derives from Italian for 'bottle of wine', probably through events in theatrical history).

given her time and heart to him: this reads, in a cancelled passage of the MS, 'given the freshest years of her life to him'; in MS–HW, 'given herself to him' (cf. third Note to p. 79); in A1–95, 'given her time and attention to him'.

151 *And considering what we—*: added in 95rc.

clue line: variant of 'clew-line': 'A tackle connecting the clew [corner] of a sail to the upper yard or the mast, by which it is drawn up in furling' (*OED*); in Scots, 'clew-line' might mean an extended thread from a ball of yarn.

of unmistakably French extraction on one side or the other: added in A1.

152 *well-known conception of Titian's*: Tiziano Vecellio (1485–1576), Venetian painter, several of whose sensuous and erotic paintings of a reclining or semi-reclining woman portray her with her right hand raised, sometimes placed behind her head as a sort of pillow (e.g. 'Jupiter and Antiope', 'The Andrians', 'Sleeping Ariadne and Revellers'), sometimes the forearm masking the face ('Diane and Actaeon'). Titian's paintings were much imitated.

mistress of a large house and fortune . . . wretched bit of Latin yet: in MS–HW, Lucetta's account is of a trip to Paris where she is arranged and pinned and stitched and padded and thereby acquires the looks of a 'lady'.

153 *weak Apostle . . . "Thy speech bewrayeth thee"*: Peter had twice simply denied he was a companion of the arrested Jesus, but when confronted by a third accuser with this linguistic circumstantial evidence of guilty association he 'began to curse and to swear' (Matthew 26: 73). Lucetta fears that her use of French will associate her with the locality where she had had an affair with Henchard.

The sentence that includes this expression, and the sentence preceding, entered the text at A1, where 'bewrayeth' was spelled 'betrayed' (it becomes 'bewrayeth' in E1). The phrase at p. 151, ll. 27–8, which refers to Lucetta's French background, was also added at A1, probably to emphasize for Hardy's American readers why Lucetta's having been resident on Jersey might be recognized through her speech, even though p. 153, ll. 1–7 already might have been thought sufficient.

Both 'betray' and 'bewray' can mean 'to exhibit incidentally'; 'to reveal . . . unintentionally, and usually what it is intended to conceal' (*OED*). The common modern equivalent of 'bewray' is 'expose'.

netting: delicate network, done with needles (*OED*).

154 *carrefour*: square or crossroads (French). (*Webster's Third International Dictionary* illustrates the term with this sentence from *The Mayor of Casterbridge*.)

gibbous: rounded, protuberant or humpbacked; i.e. the farmers have wads of money on their persons. (*Webster's Third International Dictionary* illustrates this term with this sentence from *The Mayor of Casterbridge*.)

155 *why their marriage should take place*: in MS–HW this read: 'why their marriage should no longer continue void' (cf. third Note to p. 79).

Candlemas: the feast to celebrate the Purification of the Virgin. Now 2 February, but according to Millgate, p. 245 and n. 26 on pp. 397–8, Hardy always uses the Old Style dating for Candlemas, 14 February; and as late as 1873 Dorchester's Candlemas Hiring Fair took place on 14 February (Millgate, p. 99). MS: '<spring> /Candlemas/'.

157 *cyma-recta*: a double curve, the upper part concave and the lower convex.

temporary parting from her in Jersey: MS–HW: 'temporary parting from her after their few days of union' (cf. third Note to p. 79).

CHAPTER XXIII

158 *under a black velveteen coat*: MS: 'and cloth coat': G–95rc: 'and black velveteen coat'.

silver-topped switch: MS–A1: 'switch'.

Hyperborean: pertaining to an extreme northern region with the connotation of frigid or frozen. But here it also, and probably specifically, is intended to evoke Farfrae's Scots characteristics.

160 *kerseymere*: a fine woollen fabric, with fancy twill weaves. Because of kerseymere's fineness and because it retains moisture, this would be a peculiar fabric for a Dorset farmer to wear to market. Hardy probably made the common error of confusing this with 'kersey,' a coarse ribbed cloth made from long wool.

161 *chief hiring-fair*: i.e. that held on Candlemas Day (cf. Note to p. 155). Periods of employment actually began on Lady Day (cf. p. 162 and Note).

whitey-brown crowd flecked with white: that is, the labourers would be wearing their smockfrocks, to announce their availability for hire for the coming year.

long bonnets: from MS to 95rc this was 'wing-bonnets', but Hardy evidently thought this was redundant with the description of them as resembling waggon-tilts.

waggon-tilts: a tilt is a coarse cloth or canvas canopy or awning, as for a cart or stall.

carters: teamsters; carriers.

smockfrocks: loose-fitting over-garments of coarse linen worn by farm-labourers and other workers in place of a coat.

stood an old shepherd: many phrases and details of the old shepherd's situation and of hiring fairs appear also in Hardy's 'The Dorsetshire Labourer' (1883; rpt. in *Personal Writings*, pp. 174–5).

162 *Lady Day*: 6 April (Old Style); 25 March (New Style): Feast of the Annunciation.

thirty-five mile: MS–95: 'seventy mile'.

Dan Cupid's magnet: a punning reference to the force that attracts lovers.

164 *ark*: a word of multiple references, all implying protection and safety, but primarily a reference to the boat of Noah, to which the dove returned when it could not find dry land (Genesis 8: 9).

CHAPTER XXIV

166 *malignant star*: based on the astrological idea that one's fate is determined by the relationship of heavenly bodies at one's birth; cf. p. 187 and its final Note.

Open Place in spectacular dramas: the action of Greek drama customarily takes place in an open or public area, outside palaces or city walls, and frequently adjoining thoroughfares which bring messengers, travellers, and seekers into the community which is to be affected by the confluence of incidents, personalities, and knowledge.

hawkers: costermongers; itinerant retailers.

node of all orbits: a node is a central point in a system.

167 *horse-drill*: a horse-drawn planting machine, which makes a small furrow in the soil, drops seeds into the furrow, and then covers the seed. (The *OED* gives this passage from *The Mayor*

of Casterbridge as an example.) The machine consists of a series of pairs of discs whose convex sides face each other at a slight angle to spread the soil to form furrows, a seed-box and a mechanism described at p. 168, ll. 10–13 which places seeds at a regular interval into a long gullet-like tube to fall into the furrows just before the soil falls back to cover them. The discs cause the 'series of circling irradiations'; and the arrangement of the housing containing the mechanism and the gullet-like tubes make this part of the instrument resemble at once insects and 'an upright musical instrument with the front gone'. Jethro Tull invented the horse-drill at his farm at Howberry, near Wallingford, in 1701. The new methods of husbandry did not gain quick acceptance anywhere, but it is none the less noteworthy that a full century passed before the horse-drill was introduced into the isolated Casterbridge area (cf. p. 169, ll. 33–4). (But cf. the MS–95rc reading at p. 31, which suggests Hardy wasn't certain when the machine came to Wessex. As with the coming of the railroad to Dorchester and Prince Albert's visit [cf. Note to p. 262], Hardy could be altering fact in order to heighten dramatic effect, here of course Farfrae's and Henchard's symbolically representing generational conflict.)

seed-lip: cf. Note to p. 31.

Heptarchy: the confederation of seven Angle and Saxon kingdoms held to have existed from the sixth and ninth centuries. Each kingdom had its own law, but ordinarily one of the seven rulers was accepted as king. The kingdoms were Northumbria, Mercia, East Anglia, Essex, Kent, Sussex, and Wessex.

168 *pitchforked on*: thrown on; the comparison is with throwing shocks of grain or hay on to a wagon.

jackanapes: a fop (dialect); a general derogatory term. Henchard appears to be calling Farfrae a rascal who has come from nowhere to take upon himself more than is his due or right.

169 *'Lass of Gowrie'*: a Scottish song by Lady Nairne (1766–1845).

No more sowers . . . among thorns: cf. Mark 4: 3–20; Matthew 13: 4–7. In 95rc, a hand other than Hardy's (probably Sir George Douglas's [see Note to p. 4]) revised the first clause to read 'No more sowing your seed about broadcast'. But Hardy ignored this, as he did other markings in this hand, and retained his own phrasing. Other variants, however, indicate Hardy's respect for Douglas's advice.

'*He that observeth the wind shall not sow,*'—so the Preacher said: Ecclesiastes 11: 4, within a passage counselling that one get on with necessary work without waiting for ideal conditions. The purpose of the horse-drill (cf. Note to p. 167) is to increase the efficacy of human action in the face of the inevitable vagaries of weather and other conditions of husbandry, and may be anti-romantic in this sense, but it clearly is in keeping with the pragmatism of the biblical passage.

170 *enfilading*: sweeping from end to end, lengthwise.

171 *in her first excitement*: G–HW [MS missing]: 'in her first excitement after the discovery that their hasty marriage was void, and his method of rewarding her for saving his life by wedding her had proved itself to be a generosity altogether delusive. The only evidences of that marriage in existence were two—the register, and the letters alluding to the event.' A1 omits all of this, including the reference to 'excitement'. E1 in restoring the reference to excitement brings this passage to its final form.

172 *They were intimate—rather*: added in 95.

CHAPTER XXV

175 *civilly*: all printed versions have 'curtly'; but although this reading adds a bit of spininess to Farfrae, distracted from contemplation of Lucetta by Elizabeth-Jane's 'wise little remarks', the word is most likely the result of a compositor misreading Hardy's penmanship in the MS.

Protean: Proteus is a sea god in the service of Poseidon who had the power of assuming any shape he wished.

177 *"Not at all!" . . . consequent dismissal*: in MS–HW Henchard claims he and Lucetta are married ('If going to church [G–HW: 'registry'] don't make us so, I should like to know what it does make us'), while Lucetta says their marriage was voided by Susan's return.

179 *Yet having decided . . . fate offered*: not in G–HW [MS missing].

"meaner beauties of the night": Sir Henry Wotton (1568–1639), 'On his Mistress, the Queen of Bohemia', first and fourth stanzas:

> You meaner beauties of the night,
>   That poorly satisfy our eyes

> More by your number than your light;
>   You common people of the skies,
> What are you when the moon shall rise?

> . . . .

> So, when my Mistress shall be seen
>   In form and beauty of her mind,
> By virtue first, then choice, a Queen,
>   Tell me, if she were not designed
>   The eclipse and glory of her kind?

CHAPTER XXVI

181 *refluent*: 'flowing back, [as] of the sea, waves, rivers' (*OED*).

    gazebo: a structure that serves as a look-out, commanding an extensive prospect.

    between gentle and simple: between gentility and low social rank.

182 *like some Tuscan painting of the two disciples supping at Emmaus*: Luke 24: 13–35 gives the story of the two men walking from Jerusalem to Emmaus two days after the crucifixion, meeting a third (Jesus, though they are prevented from recognizing him), and inviting him to sup with them. Hardy's fondness for the inversion of biblical contexts leads him to identify Lucetta, a timorous woman of only temporal concerns, directly with the resurrected Jesus—an identification made specific in G, which expands the MS 'third' to 'third and chief,' a phrase altered to 'third and haloed' in 12. [A1 has the MS reading.]

    The paintings of this event I have seen do not have a halo (e.g. neither of the paintings titled *Supper at Emmaus* by Michelangelo Merisi da Caravaggio [1573–1610]); what Hardy appears to allude to are the pre-Renaissance Tuscan (Florentine) painters who do use haloes. In 12, he also adds the phrase 'like the evangelist who had to write it down': presumably to account for Elizabeth-Jane being present in a scene that in the biblical account includes only three persons.

183 *Mixen Lane*: mixen: 'A place where dung and refuse is laid' (*OED*).

    pis aller: a last resource or makeshift (French; literally, 'to go worse').

184 *before foreign competition*: cf. Notes to p. 3.

185 *Alastor*: 'a relentless or avenging spirit; a Nemesis' (*OED*).

lackey: servant, man-in-waiting.

bell-board: probably the board on which the bells were hung in a Victorian house in order to summon the servants.

reap-hooks: see Note to p. 31.

water-tights: 'watertight boots' (*OED*, which gives this passage from *The Mayor of Casterbridge* as an example).

186 *springes*: snares or traps; derived from the meaning 'a noose fastened to an elastic body and drawn close with a sudden spring to catch a bird or other animal'.

"Wide-oh": a variant of 'wido' ('wide-awake') or 'wide' (alert, well-informed); it also draws upon the slang term 'wide boy', meaning a sharp, streetwise, intelligent operator, perhaps even a swindler. The term verges on criminal cant (Eric Partridge, *A Dictionary of Slang and Unconventional English*, 8th edn., ed. Paul Beale [New York: Macmillan, 1984], p. 1337).

187 *Henchard felt like Saul at his reception by Samuel*: Saul encounters Samuel in two contexts relevant to Henchard's reception by the weather prophet, and Hardy employs details from both. In 1 Samuel 9, the youthful Saul is in search of his father's asses, and goes to Samuel, who as a man of God has the power of foresight. Samuel had been told by the Lord that the future king of Israel would be coming to him, and Samuel has set aside food for him. Samuel tells Saul he 'will tell thee all that is in thine heart' (verse 19). By the 28th chapter of 1 Samuel, Saul has had all his successes, has been abandoned by God, and is now beset by a Philistine army. Samuel has died, after having anointed Saul's successor as king, David. Saul goes in disguise to a woman of Endor known to have a 'familiar spirit'. She addresses him by name, as the weather prophet does Henchard. She calls up the spirit of Samuel, whose prophecy of Saul's death on the morrow is as accurate as Fall's weather prediction. Enervated by Samuel's prediction, and having eaten nothing all day, Saul is persuaded to eat by the woman of Endor. This allusion to Samuel was added in A1.

Cure the evil: scrofula (tubercular swelling of the neck's lymph glands); also called 'the King's evil' because it was supposed that kings had the power to cure it with a simple touch. Fall is not a witch, but a conjuror, one with second sight and the ability to counteract the curses of witches.

toad-bag: cf. *Life and Work*, p. 115: ' "Toad Fair". An old man, a wizard, used to brings toads' legs in little bags to Bagber Bridge [close to where Hardy was living], where he was met by crowds of people who came in vehicles and on foot, and bought them as charms to cure scrofula by wearing them round the neck. These legs were supposed to twitch occasionally in the bag, and probably did, when it gave the wearer's blood a "turn", and changed the course of the disease.' Ruth Firor, *Folkways in Thomas Hardy* (Philadelphia, 1931), pp. 117–18, cites other sources that the bag bore a live toad.

dung-mixen: dung and refuse from cow-stalls.

like living in Revelations: the book of Revelations forecasts far more in the way of droughts than of heavy rainfall; but possibly the principal word is 'tempest', evoking the sense so prevalent throughout Revelations of plagues and climatic disturbances (esp. Chs. VII–XVI).

scheme: astrological drawing, to justify a prediction based on the relative positions of heavenly bodies, real and imaginary.

188 *welkin*: the vault of heaven above our heads, the abode of the gods. Hardy's word-choice reinforces the sense that Henchard's opponents are divine (*and* natural).

CHAPTER XXVII

190 *turn of the scales*: from MS–95rc it is specified as the 'third turn of the scales'.

somebody has been roasting a waxen image of me, or stirring an unholy brew to confound me: Henchard's superstitiousness accepts both that supernatural powers oppose him and that these powers can be manipulated by witchcraft. The most famous instance in Hardy of the destruction of a wax image is in *The Return of the Native*, where Susan Nunsuch makes and burns an image of Eustacia shortly before Eustacia drowns (Book Fifth, Chs. VII–IX).

191 *Capitol*: the *Capitolium* or temple of Jupiter on the Capitoline Hill in Rome. Defeated enemies of Rome were paraded in triumphal processions concluding at the Capitol, after which they were usually sent into slavery.

shambles: slaughter-house.

one laden . . . one was: in MS–95rc both wagons are full at this passage. The change at 95 make this passage consistent with p. 192, where MS–12 have Farfrae's wagon as empty.

You can hear my horses' bells half a mile such a night as this: cf. *The Woodlanders*, Chapter XIII, which has a similar contretemps involving carters' bells.

gawkhammer way: a gawkhammer is 'a silly gaping fellow' (William Barnes, *A Glossary of the Dorset Dialect* [1886; rpt. St Peter Port, Guernsey: Toucan Press, 1970], p. 65).

192 *thill horse*: a horse that is placed between the shafts by which a wagon or cart is drawn and attached to these shafts by a harness.

giddying worm into a sheep's brain: reference to a disease of sheep called 'gid' or 'turnsick' or 'sturdy', caused by the hydatid *Coenurus cerebralis*. (*OED* gives this passage from *A Mayor of Casterbridge* as an example.)

193 *pot-house*: alehouse or tavern.

194 *"stitches" or shocks*: a pile of sheaves of grain in a harvested field, set upright, leaning against each other at the top but separated at the bottom—leaving an open area such as the one Henchard sits in—to further the drying of the grain and straw before being threshed or flailed. One or two sheaves may be placed on the top for protection against the weather, which would enhance the shocks' resemblance to tents.

196 *proposed to marry me . . . I thought I ought to marry you*: in MS–HW Lucetta's comments refer to Henchard's motives for marrying her in Jersey (cf. third Note to p. 79) rather than to his reasons for proposing marriage after Susan's death.

CHAPTER XXVIII

199 *petty sessions*: 'the sessions of magistrates or justices that require no jury and that are held in exercise of summary jurisdiction and similar minor matters'. Hardy himself served as magistrate for petty sessions.

Shallow and Silence: two justices in Shakespeare's *Henry IV, Part 2*. Justice Shallow in his youth had been called 'lusty Shallow' (III.ii) and had swashbuckled with Jack Falstaff; he is mocked by Falstaff for his inability to conduct himself in a professional manner. Silence becomes inebriated and is carried to bed.

ashlar: stone masonry smoothed to make an even facing to be set in mortar; the outer face may be rough or smooth.

the country of the Psalmist where the clouds drop fatness: Psalm 65 praises the bountifulness of the Lord. Line 11 reads: 'Thou crownest the year with thy goodness; and thy paths drop fatness.' The country is Palestine of 400–200 BC; Hardy's allusion presumably is intended to suggest the age of the clothing and its original high quality. Like her clothing, the furmity-woman has seen better days. (A less speculative reading of this passage is that the bonnet has fat spattered on it, and that Hardy has adapted or misremembered the Psalm.)

apron that had been white: cf. p. 8, l. 36. White apparel represents an effort to appear respectable on the part of a law-defying person, or someone of low class. Cf. also p. 255.

steeped aspect: Hardy's implication with 'steeped' is not entirely clear. Most obviously it suggests 'soaked' or drunk, immersed in liquid (imaged in the greasy condition of the woman's clothing); but it is evident from the common-sense awareness that drunkenness and tatterdemalion attire occur in both city and country that Hardy's full intention is to convey something more than the furmity woman's disreputable state. Several slang or dialect usages of 'steeped' turn on the idea of elevation and precipitousness, such as ambitious, brilliant, extravagant: i.e. Hardy appears to be suggesting that the woman bears herself more assertively than a country person would, a suggestion quite in keeping with the way he portrays her calm demeanour during the legal proceedings. For additional cause to think 'steeped' carries this suggestion, see p. 257—'she spoke with cosmopolitan largeness of idea'—and the Note to p. 23.

200 *Henchard being no note-taker himself*: not in MS–HW (see Note to p. 67).

eleven, b.m., on the night of the fifth instinct, Hannah Dominy: i.e. 11 p.m. on the fifth of this month (instant), in the year of our Lord (Anno Domini).

201 *land-smuggler*: receiver and distributor of goods smuggled by sea from the Continent to evade high duties. Hardy's grandfather stored smuggled rum at Higher Bockhampton from about 1801 to 1805 (*Personal Notebooks*, pp. 8–9).

202 *'Tis as true as the light*: cf. John 1: 8–9; Christ is 'the true Light, which lighteth every man that cometh into the world'.

The sensation in the court was indescribably great: added in A1.

larry: excitement, commotion.

CHAPTER XXIX

205 *Abrahamic success*: Abraham, whose name means 'the father of many nations' (Genesis 17: 4), is the ancestor of the Hebrews and a patriarch of the faiths of Judaism, Christianity, and Islam. The Lord promises Abraham that his descendants will be as numerous as the 'dust of the earth' (Genesis 13: 16). Abraham was also 'very rich in cattle' (Genesis 13: 2); but husbandry is more stressed with his son Isaac (Genesis 26: 12–14) and especially with his grandson Jacob, who combined selective breeding and primitive magic to great advantage (see Note to p. 115). This allusion was added to the novel in A1.

Yahoo: the human beings satirized as uncouth, excitable, ignorant, cowardly, and cruel by Jonathan Swift in Book 4 of *Gulliver's Travels*.

dun: 'a variable colour averaging a nearly neutral slightly brownish dark grey and ranging from red to yellow in hue'.

seamy sides: wrinkled, greasy (*OED*)—probably means damp with sweat.

Thames Tunnel: a double archway tunnel under the Thames from Rotherhithe to Wapping, designed by Marc Brunel (1769–1849), opened in 1843.

perspective toys: toys that create three-dimensional effects and the impression of receding distances.

Gurth's collar of brass: the brass collar worn by Gurth, a swineherd in Walter Scott's *Ivanhoe*, contains the name of his owner. It is welded on, and unremovable, because Gurth is a slave.

206 *hurdle-stake*: a short stake about 36 inches long, cut to form one of the vertical posts of a hurdle (cf. p. 7 and Note).

sirocco: a hot wind, specifically one blowing from the deserts across the northern Mediterranean, where it can become moist and oppressive.

What might have happened. . . . He ran forward: MS–HW contain a lengthy scene in the barn, during which Elizabeth-Jane heroically grabs the bull's leading-staff and is dragged on the floor, but manages to climb a ladder to the stack of clover. In these versions Lucetta alone is being threatened by the bull when Henchard enters.

207 *floor*: MS–HW: 'floor. "I thought you were up there!" she said.

"But thank God, 'tis all right now. He always protects us when we don't expect him [G–HW: 'Him'] to." '

gig: a light carriage with one pair of wheels, drawn by one horse; a chaise.

208 *forwarder*: more prompt, further along in the job.

209 *coals of fire on my head*: cf. Proverbs 25: 22.

211 *A pensioner of Farfrae's wife*: actually, Henchard's indebtedness would in practicality be to Farfrae himself. Before the Married Women's Property Acts of 1870 and 1882 effective control of Lucetta's wealth would have devolved upon her husband (unless it was previously controlled by the will of her aunt). Cf. also p. 197: Henchard tells Lucetta, 'I am quite willing that every penny of your property shall remain to your personal use'—i.e. he knows that legally the income from her property would ordinarily be his to control upon marriage (as it is with Farfrae when he marries Lucetta). (See Lee Holcombe, *Wives and Property: Reform of the Married Women's Property Law in Nineteenth-Century England* [Toronto: University of Toronto Press, 1983].)

CHAPTER XXX

213 *John Gilpin*: in 'The Diverting History of John Gilpin' (1782), by William Cowper (1731–1800), the title character delays accompanying his wife, who has already left with friends to celebrate their twentieth wedding anniversary, in order to tend to three just-arrived customers.

215 *Ovid*: Roman poet (43 BC–AD 17), whose portrayal of love as restlessness, a kind of illness, applies with particular force to Hardy's heroines, whose lots in life are seldom improved when they fall in love. The famous passage Elizabeth-Jane quotes to Lucetta may be translated 'I see better things and approve them; I follow the worse' (*Metamorphoses*, VII. 20–1). Medea is rationalizing her desperate love for Jason, which goes against her own judgement, by claiming she must be under the influence of a god. (She is: Venus is helping Jason gain the golden fleece.)

In all versions previous to 12, Elizabeth-Jane paraphrases Romans 7: 19: 'so that the good she would have done she did not, and the evil that she would not, that she did—exactly like the apostle Paul'. Clearly Hardy at this point wants to convey the grounds for Elizabeth-Jane's judgement on Lucetta's defiance of conventionality in marrying Farfrae (Elizabeth-Jane does not know when she cites the passage that Lucetta *has* followed the 'evil' course). As is often the case with Hardy's revisions, changing Elizabeth-Jane's authority from the Bible to Ovid substantially enriches the novel. It displays Elizabeth-Jane's audodidacticism without altering the basic impression that she is a prig; her learning has not diminished her obsession with respectability. As the novel proceeds it becomes clear that in contrast to Lucetta, Elizabeth-Jane is able to 'construe' Ovid. Her own love decisions follow the guidance of modest expectations; in Ovid's terms, she not only sees, but follows, the best course open to her.

were thrown together . . . talked of us: in MS–HW Lucetta's story is of her and Henchard's marriage (cf. third Note p. 79).

216 *not—another man*: MS: 'not <Mr Farfrae> /—another man/'.

Nathan tones: King David impregnated Bathsheba, the wife of Uriah. Because he had been consecrated for battle Uriah would not have intercourse with Bathsheba, so in order to prevent discovery of the adultery, David had Uriah placed in the thick of the fighting, where he was killed. David and Bathsheba married and a child was born. The prophet Nathan, by posing to David a hypothetical case of a wealthy man taking a poor man's only lamb, led David into pronouncing judgement against the doer of such a heinous deed. 'Thou art the man,' said Nathan (in a presumably condemnatory and stern tone), and proceeded to deliver God's curse against the house of David, including the death of the infant (2 Samuel 12: 7–14).

CHAPTER XXXI

218 *fillip*: a sharp, smart blow; more specifically, a blow formed by pressing the nail of a finger against the thumb and suddenly releasing it. The connotation of Hardy's word-choice is that Henchard is being flicked aside, like an insect, as if by a god's fingernail.

trusted generously: MS–95rc: 'trusted implicitly'.

219 *pinched, blasted, and smutted grains*: pinched (grains not filled in the ear before maturing, thus shrivelled upon drying); blasted (grains infected with a blight); smutted (grains infected with a black powdery fungus).

219–20 Hardy's account of the bankrupt who offered his watch and was praised for his care in preparing the records is historical; cf. Millgate, pp. 238–9, quoting the *Dorset County Chronicle* of 17 April 1826.

219 *I've got in the world*: added in 95.

of Weatherbury: added in 12.

221 *vitrified*: glazed by exposure to heat.

sash-bars: cf. p. 87: 'Georgian sash windows'.

purlieu: 'a place of resort'; 'a locality . . . just beyond or sometimes just within given bounds: an outlying or adjacent district'.

window-jambs: side-posts of a window frame.

arch-labels: lintels, the moulding at the top of a window-frame.

222 *larry*: cf. Note to p. 202.

cat-head: a piece of timber or iron projecting on the outside of a building, on to which was fastened a pulley. The chains of a tackle running on the pulley were used to lift heavy objects up to different levels of the building. See also pp. 238, 270.

wimbles: see Note for p. 5. Here, 'wimble' seems to be part of the mechanism for lifting hay to the loft.

steelyards: a steelyard is 'a portable balance for weighing designed to be suspended (as from a hook or the free hand of the user) when in operation—called also *lever scales*'. Since this is itself a scale, the phrase 'scales and steelyards' must be intended to convey Farfrae's precision: he weighs small as well as large amounts of produce in transactions.

CHAPTER XXXII

223 *friable*: crumbly.

coping: a protective covering course or capping of a wall, frequently of stone or tile and usually sloping or curved to carry off water.

stile: steps or bars to allow a person to cross easily a fence which encloses livestock.

224 *the iron had entered into their souls*: cf. Psalms 105: 18: 'Whose feet they hurt with fetters: he was laid in iron'; the Book of Common Prayer renders this passage: 'Whose feet they hurt in the stocks: the iron entered into his soul.' Literally, in Hebrew,

'his soul came into iron'. The person named is Joseph, and the scene describes what happened to him when he was taken into Egypt; the context in the novel suggests that people who do not suffer intensely do not use heroic phrases.

misérables: unhappy wretches (French).

Adonis: in Graeco-Roman mythology, a beautiful youth loved by Aphrodite and Persephone. In more ancient times, Adonis was a vegetation god, whose effigy was used in ceremonies and afterwards flung into water—an interesting parallel with Henchard's effigy.

either here or . . . up the river: added in 12.

Blackwater: cf. p. 127 and Note.

226 *chattel*: tangible possession other than real estate or freehold.

227 *prophet's chamber*: a woman of Shunem and her husband built for Elisha a 'little chamber' on the roof of their house, where he could live when his travels took him to their locality. The room held 'a bed, and a table, and a stool, and a candlestick' (2 Kings 4: 10).

228 *and a sense that honest work was not a thing to be ashamed of*: added in A1.

stack-yards: 'a yard or field containing straw or grain in stacks'.

229 *stock*: 'a kind of stiff close-fitting neckcloth' (*OED*).

she was wise in her generation: Henchard acknowledges Lucetta's prudence in marrying Farfrae in defiance of the contemporary morality which would have mandated that she marry the man who had been her illicit lover. The allusion is to the master's (or Jesus': the translation is disputed) commendation of the steward who, threatened with discharge, falsifies accounts of his master's debtors in order to gain their future hospitality: 'for the children of this world are in their generation wiser than the children of light' (Luke 16: 8). This is one of the most controversial of all of Jesus' parables, in its apparent condonation of expedient self-serving and (in the following verse) its advocacy of contributing ill-gotten money to God's causes in order to gain personal salvation.

reviviscent: 'causing renewed life' (*OED*, which gives this passage in *The Mayor of Casterbridge* as the example).

230 *twenty-one years*: G–95 [MS missing]: 'twenty years'. Cf. Note to p. 235.

CHAPTER XXXIII

231 *the choir*: Hardy's father and grandfather played in a similar church band in Stinsford parish. *Under the Greenwood Tree* portrays the replacement of the choir by the harmonium. Cf. also below: the 'bass-viol player' has an 'official connection with the preacher'.

Stonehenge: near Salisbury, in Wiltshire, comprising primarily a circular formation, and within that a horseshoe formation, both of large sarsen stones standing on end. Probably intended as a place of worship, it was built in several phases from 2800 to 1100 BC.

232 *let back our strings*: except when the instrument is being played, strings are kept loose so as not to bend, over time, the wood in the bow and instrument.

stave: technically, a staff of five parallel lines on which the notes of music are written, but here meaning a passage of music.

ballets . . . rantipole rubbish . . . Rogue's March . . . cherubim's warble: Henchard is contrasting extremes in music. A 'ballet' may be either a dialect variant of 'ballad' (cf. p. 54), or a medieval lyric, or a polyphonic, unaccompanied vocal piece, or a madrigal. A 'rantipole' is 'characterized by a wild unruly manner or attitude: rakish'. The Rogue's March is played while a soldier is being discharged from the service in disgrace (cf. *Life and Work*, p. 127); in this context, the song of a cherubim (one of the order of angels known especially for knowledge and justice) would underscore a moment of earned salvation or a song of praise of the deity.

fourth Psa'am, to Samuel Wakely's tune: Psalm 4 expresses confidence in the Lord as a counterbalance to the despairing lament 'O ye sons of men, how long will ye turn my glory into shame?' The singer's specific troubles are not named, but traditionally the occasion is laid to Absalom's revolt. Although the Psalm has relevance for Henchard's situation, clearly its last line does not reflect his mood: 'I will both lay me down in peace, and sleep: for thou, Lord, only makest me dwell in safety.' (Samuel Wakely has not been identified.)

old Wiltshire *is the only tune worth singing*: *Wiltshire*, by George T. Smart (1776–1867), is a Common Metre tune to which were sung many hymns and psalms, especially Psalm 34—a familiar hymn of praise of God whose evocation by the tune would form a particularly sharp contrast for the spirit of Psalm 109.

233 *Servant David*: David is traditionally credited with writing many of the Psalms. He is referred to as God's 'servant David' (2 Samuel 7: 8) and when addressing God he calls himself 'thy servant'. He is referred to as 'his servant David' in the *Benedictus* (Luke 1: 69) in the Morning Prayer (Book of Common Prayer).

234 *comminatory*: denunciatory.

235 *twenty-one years*: MS–95: 'twenty years'. Cf. Note to p. 230.

235–6 *Rosalind's exclamation*: *"Mistress, know yourself; down on your knees and thank heaven fasting for a good man's love"*: from Shakespeare's *As You Like It*, III. v. 57–8. Rosalind is speaking to Phoebe, who has been rejecting Silvius' devotion. Rosalind's next lines also bear upon Elizabeth-Jane's knowledge of Lucetta's past: 'For I must tell you friendly in your ear, /Sell when you can, you are not for all markets.'

236 *I'll come and wimble for you*: for 'wimble' see p. 5 and Note.

238 *rape-seed*: seed for *Brassica napus*, a plant related to turnips grown as food for sheep.

CHAPTER XXXIV

240 *rimy*: frosty (rime = hoar-frost).

241 *sylph*: one of the race of imaginary beings that inhabit the air.

242 *funny song about high heeled shoon and siller tags, and the one-and-forty wooers*: the song is unidentified. ('Shoon' is 'shoes'; 'siller' is 'silver'.)

243 *'Why, bless the woman . . . safe been opened?*: MS–HW [part of MS missing] explain how Lucetta's letters failed to be returned, in a manner consistent with the account given in the Note to p. 118.

244 *Charles the First*: reigned 1625–49.

worm i' the bud: the worm in the bud is concealment; cf. Shakespeare's *Twelfth Night*, II. iv. 110–12; 'she never told her love, / But let concealment like a worm i' th' bud / Feed on her damask cheek.'

Tamerlane: the Anglicized name of Timur Lenk (1336–1405), the Turkic, Islamic conqueror of the area from Mongolia to the Mediterranean. His armies carried large trumpets; Hardy may also be alluding to the appearance of trumpets in Handel's opera *Tamerlane* (1724) and to Nicholas Rowe's *Tamerlane* (1702).

245 *there is practically no future . . . forsaken by you*: in G–HW [MS missing], Lucetta's letter refers to her marriage with Henchard (cf. third Note to p. 79).

246 *Aphrodite*: the goddess of sexual love and beauty.

CHAPTER XXXV

249 *she dreaded . . . than her misfortune*: added in A1, the first version of this passage ended with Lucetta's fear that the rest of the world should believe 'appearances, and not her story'. In 95rc is pencilled 'that the episode had been rather her fault than her misfortune'. With a subsquent change in tense, the passage took its final form in 95.

Beyond a natural reason for her slightly drawn look: added in 12. (Cf. Note to p. 286.)

She selected . . . discarded attire: in MS–HW Lucetta's preparation to meet Henchard was a lengthy exercise involving 'disfiguring ointments' to acquire which required 'three or four' visits that day to the chemist's.

250 *in his bearing: he stood still . . . grim half-smile*: MS–HW: 'He was evidently shocked, put away his cynical half-smile.' The passage relating Henchard's reaction to noting the similarities in his meetings in the amphitheatre with Susan and Lucetta was added in A1; the passage lower on p. 250 ('double of the first') also was added in A1.

251 *zest and desire to humiliate Lucetta*: MS–HW: 'zest and desire for Lucetta'.

I can keep my word: continuing after this in MS–HW, and concluding the chapter, is a lengthy scene in which Farfrae, in search for Henchard to tell him he has purchased the seed business for him, comes across Henchard and Lucetta in the amphitheatre; but he does not recognize Lucetta. Both its irrelevance for the plot and its deletion for the first book edition indicate this is one of the scenes intended to create incidents for the serial instalments.

CHAPTER XXXVI

252 *iron dogs*: (dialect) andirons, in the shape of sitting dogs, used to support burning wood in a fireplace.

253 *candle-snuff*: burned wick of a candle.

tyro: 'one familiar with the rudiments of a subject but lacking in practical experience: novice'.

Mixen-Lane way . . . Peter's Finger: for 'Mixen Lane' see Note to p. 183. 'Peter's Finger' is the name of an inn at Lytchett Minster, a corruption of the name of a church, St Peter-ad-Vincula (St Peter in Chains). Cf. p. 255: 'The inn called Peter's Finger was the church of Mixen Lane.'

254 *congeries*: a collection of things heaped together.

Adullam: near the fortified Canaanite city of the same name is this cave, in which David took refuge from Saul. Hardy's next sentence paraphrases 1 Samuel 22: 2: 'And every one that was in distress, and everyone that was in debt, and every one that was discontented, gathered themselves unto him.'

bibbing: drinking, of a habitual nature (cf. bibulous).

sallows: willows, chiefly of low-growing or scrubby species.

255 *skittle-alley*: skittles = the game of ninepins.

"liviers," or lifeholders: a lifehold is a lease held for the duration of specific persons' lives, usually members of one family or of three generations of a single family, sometimes simply three persons. A lifehold is a tenuous holding. The best-known lifeholds in Hardy novels are that which lapses on the death of Mr Durbeyfield, causing the expulsion of Tess and the remainder of her family and leading to her eventual return to Alec (*Tess of the d'Urbervilles*); and that which lapses on the self-induced death of Mr South, causing Giles Winterborne to lose the cottages that had come to him through his mother, who had been a South (*The Woodlanders*).

copyholders: a court-roll is a record of rents and holdings on a manor, 'a copy of which constitutes the tenant's title to his holding' (*OED*). Such a tenant is known as a 'copyholder'. Although technically held at the will of the lord of the manor, such tenancy—controlled by customary practice in the neighbourhood and not subject to arbitrary decisions by the landowner—amounted to securely held property. (Copyhold and other residual feudal forms of tenure ownership were abolished in 1925, and replaced by the single concept of 'soçage'—that is, 'ownership', or fee simple.)

roof-trees: a roof-tree is the main beam in the ridge of a roof. The bearing of this passage is as literal as it is analogous. A frequent means of losing one's copyhold was to give up to the lord of the manor this permanent tenure for the limited lifehold tenure, in exchange for cash or for repairs to the residences which the copyholders could not afford otherwise. The reference to roof-trees first appears in G.

256 *causing the gazer to blink like Ashton at the disappearance of Ravenswood*: Ravenswood, riding furiously along the seashore to keep an appointment to fight a duel with Colonel Ashton, disappears suddenly in quicksand. Ashton 'rubbed his eyes, as if he had witnessed an apparition' (Walter Scott, *The Bride of Lammermoor*, Chapter XXXV).

fillip: here (cp. p. 218 and Note), the word seems to mean to move quickly, as if propelled by a smart blow.

swingels: swingle: either a cudgel; 'the striking part or swipple of a flail' (cf. Note to p. 92); or a form of flail, specifically 'a wooden instrument resembling a sword' used to beat and scrape flax or hemp (*OED*). Given the nature of Peter's Finger and of its customers, any one or all of these types of swingles could be on the premises.

blower of the chimney: a sheet of metal (or cloth—see *Tess of the d'Urbervilles*, Chapter XXX) that improves the draught of a fire, by increasing the movement of air up the chimney.

257 *oven-pyle*: a variant of 'oven-peel': 'a pole with a broad flat disc at the end for thrusting loaves, pies, etc., into the oven and withdrawing them from it' (*OED*).

258 *skimmity-ride*: alternate for 'skimmington' (cf. p. 260): 'A ludicrous procession, formerly common in villages and country districts, usually intended to bring ridicule or odium upon a woman or her husband in cases where the one was unfaithful to, or ill-treated, the other' (*OED*, which uses passages in Chapters XXXIX and XL of *The Mayor of Casterbridge* as examples). At p. 260, in the MS the landlady of Peter's Finger defines the practice as aimed at a wife who is 'a scold, or a bad bargain in any way'; from G to 95rc at a wife who is 'a bad bargain in any way'. The solely sexual emphasis enters the text at 95. The name evidently derives from the frequent practice of representing the woman wielding a milk-skimming ladle against the man.

261 *no evidence remained*: MS–HW: 'no evidence, beyond the simple entry in a remote parish register, remained' (cf. Notes to p. 79 and p. 171).

CHAPTER XXXVII

262 *royal personage . . . engineering work*: Prince Albert passed through Dorchester in late July 1849 on his way to Weymouth to lay the foundation stone of the Portland Breakwater. Hardy may have witnessed the event as a child; but he also in later years could have read an account of the Prince's visit in the 26 July 1849 issue of the *Dorset County Chronicle* (Millgate, pp. 242–3). The Prince travelled by railroad, which had reached Dorchester in 1847; but—presumably to stress the plot's occurrence in a traditional world previous to the rapid change in rural customs and economics brought about by the spread of the railroad—Hardy has the event, and the entire novel, take place before the appearance of the railroad in Casterbridge (cf. p. 321 and Note) as well as before the repeal of the Corn Laws (cf. p. 3 and Note). See also Note to p. 103.

the third King George: George III (reigned 1760–1820) frequently summered in Weymouth, passing through Dorchester (Casterbridge) on his way thence.

fête carillonnée: high festival, marked by bell ringing.

264 *tilt-bonnets*: cf. p. 161 and Note.

deal wand: pine or fir stick.

calico: cotton cloth.

cortège: a train of attendants, as at a court (French).

265 *royal unicorn*: in the Royal coat of arms, the unicorn wears a chain.

266 *staggered*: MS–95: 'advanced'.

with mayoral authority: added in 95rc.

Calphurnia's cheek was pale: Brutus thus describes Caesar's third wife, coming with Caesar and their retinue from the games, at which Caesar had three times refused the crown (*Julius Caesar*, I. ii. 185). It is the elevation of Caesar that brings about Brutus' willingness to take part in his assassination, and in a similar manner Farfrae's elevation and Lucetta's social status are referred to by supporters of the skimmington (see pp. 267, 268).

267 *rattled heavily as Pharaoh's chariots*: that is, as if they were not in good working order. In Exodus 16: 24–5, the Egyptian army is pursuing the Israelites between the two walls of the water that had been divided by the Lord to assist the Israelites' flight: 'And the lord . . . took off [clogged] their chariot wheels, that they

drave them heavily: so that the Egyptians said, Let us flee from the face of Israel; for the Lord fighteth for them against the Egyptians.' This allusion first appears in A1.

hontish: haughty or boorish (dialect). In MS–95rc this was 'mandy', another dialect word, meaning 'saucy'.

CHAPTER XXXVIII

269 *Weltlust*: pleasure in things of the world. The clause 'whom an intoxicating *Weltlust* had fairly mastered' was added in A1.

He can rub brine on a green wound: bathing a fresh wound with salt water can be a means of controlling infection and regulating the growth of the reparative scar tissue; but it is very painful, and no doubt it is the pain, not the medical benefits, that Henchard has in mind. Francis Bacon says, in 'Of Revenge', 'A man that studieth revenge keeps his own wound green'. The basis in revenge has bearing upon the passage in the novel.

coxcomb: 'a foolish, conceited, showy person, vain of his accomplishments, appearance, or dress; a fop' (*OED*).

271 *And here's a hand . . . hand o' thine*: these lines are from the last stanza of Burns' 'Auld Lang Syne', the famous song of renewal of old friendship (cf. Note to p. 54). ('fiere' = friend.)

273 *Prince of Darkness*: cf. Note to p. 67.

274 *one or two miles*: G–95rc [MS missing]: 'three or four miles'.

CHAPTER XXXIX

276 *mummery*: pantomime; ridiculous or hypocritical ceremony.

277 *malter's chimbley*: a malter or maltster is a maker of malt, an ingredient used in brewing made of barley or another grain. The grain is brought to germination in warm water in order to develop certain enzymes; and then the germination is halted by drying and curing the malt with hot air—thus both parts of the method require a chimney. The resulting malt externally looks like the original barley but is brittle and has a flavour. (Heat is also required in subsequent steps of brewing.)

kerseymere leggings: cf. Note to p. 160.

278 *puce*: dark red.

280 *tongs*: kitchen tongs: what Jopp carries (p. 281). Added in 95rc.

kits: three-stringed pocket fiddles, about 15–20 inches long, used by dancing masters of seventeenth–early nineteenth centuries.

crouds: also termed crouths, crowds, cruits; the usual name is crwths, a six-stringed ancient Celtic or Welsh lyre, still in use in Wales in the nineteenth century.

humstrums: hurdy-gurdies; ancient multi-stringed instruments sounded by a rosined wheel (turned by a crank with the right hand) rubbing the strings while the left hand presses keys connected to rods that alter the pitch of several strings. Usually two or more bass strings play single pitches continuously, forming a drone harmony like that of a bagpipe.

serpents: 'An obsolete bass wind instrument of deep tone, about 8 feet long, made of wood and covered with leather and formed with three U-shaped turns' (*OED*); used in church and military bands until the middle of the nineteenth century.

rams'-horns: resembling shofars (traditional Jewish synagogue horns), harsh-sounding wind instruments made of goat or ram horns. They sound only two notes.

lammigers: cf. Note to p. 53.

felo de se: (from Latin, meaning 'felon of oneself'); ' "one who deliberately puts an end to his own existence, or commits any unlawful malicious act, the consequence of which is his own death" (Blackstone)' (*OED*).

Gover'ment staves: long polished sticks with official markings (described in Hardy's 'The Three Strangers'). Before the creation of a standardized constabulary (beginning with Sir Robert Peel's London 'bobbies' in 1829), the staves would be all that would mark the local constables as enforcers of the law.

281 *soughed*: to make a sighing or moaning sound, as by wind or water. Hardy's care with word-choice is again seen here: 'sough' has several relevant meanings in Scots: 'to breathe one's last: die'; 'to preach or pray in a whining tone'; 'the whiz of a missile or the hiss of a swung sword or club'—all of which reinforce the significance of the evening's skimmington for the wife of the story's Scotsman.

shook his head to the zero of childlike ignorance: broadly moved his head up and down and left and right simultaneously.

282 *crew of Comus*: Milton's *Comus* (1634) contains a 'rout of Monsters headed like sundry sorts of wilde beasts, but otherwise like Men and Women,' who make 'a riotous and unruly noise,

with Torches in their hands'. When Comus hears a chaste maiden approach he orders them to 'Break off' and 'Run to your shrouds, within these Brakes and Trees' (ll. 93, 145–7).

CHAPTER XL

285 *Yalbury Bottom . . . Cuckoo Lane*: these place-names first appear in 95rc.

off gig-lamp: the one on the right side of the vehicle. For 'gig', see Note to p. 207.

286 *He knew his wife was with child*: added in 95rc. This amplifies the doctor's remark about the state of Lucetta's health (p. 280) and a less direct indication of pregnancy (p. 290). During the revision for 12, Hardy inserted yet another indication of pregnancy (cf. Note to p. 249).

Over this repentant sinner, at least, there was to be no joy in heaven: Luke 15: 7 states that heaven rejoices over one repentant sinner more than over ninety-nine just persons. Here, then, Henchard is stressing his outcast condition as being beyond retrieval.

He cursed himself like a less scrupulous Job: even after his three advisers had counselled him to examine himself for the sin that must account for all of the woes that had befallen him, Job refused to see the blame in himself, being 'righteous in his own eyes' (Job 32: 1). (However, after the exhortation by Elihu and the statement by God delivered 'out of the whirlwind' [Job 38: 1] Job retracted his questioning of God's inexplicable actions, saying, 'I abhor myself, and repent in dust and ashes' [Job 42: 6].) The suggestion appears to be that Henchard is too ready to curse himself, without an attempt at self-justification or a criticism of the universe.

288 *and miscarriage*: added in 95rc.

bare facts of her peculiar intimacy with: MS–HW: 'bare facts of her void marriage with'; A1: 'bare facts of her early attachment to' (cf. third Note to p. 79).

289 *Lucifer*: Venus, as the morning star.

CHAPTER XLI

291 *It was the man who had asked the way at Peter's Finger*: added in G.

292 *She could write her own name, and no more*: this of course is
contradicted by Susan's revelatory letter to Henchard about
Elizabeth-Jane's true parentage. An addition to explain her
writing skill, and then a revision in which the explanation is
deleted (see the Note to p. 125), suggest that Hardy may have
realized the contradiction, tried to alleviate it, and then had to
accept that there was no way to reconcile his need at one point
in the plot for an illiterate dependent woman and at another for
a revelation from the dead Susan.

socked: 'socked' is south-west English dialect for 'sighed' (*OED*
gives this passage from *The Mayor of Casterbridge* as an
example); i.e. 'socked' is redundant in the phrase, but Hardy
may also be relating 'socked' to 'soughed', a kind of whine (p.
281). (Cf. 'The Ruined Maid': 'And you'd sigh, and you'd
sock'.)

293 *A year ago, and more*: MS–A1: 'Two years ago next twenty-
fourth of March'; earlier (cancelled) readings in MS are: 'The
twenty-fourth of March' and then 'Three years ago next twenty-
fourth of March'.

295–6 *In place of them . . . in his need*: these lines emphasizing the
importance of music to Henchard are a late addition to the MS
(which contains the phrase 'auxiliary spirit' instead of 'Divine
spirit').

296 *high harmonies*: exalted, intense, rich music.

transubstantiated: changed into another substance, usually from
a lower (physical) to a higher (spiritual).

recitative: a manner of speaking in musical performances (such
as dialogue in operas) that falls between singing and speech.

fugue: 'a contrapuntal musical composition in which one or two
melodic themes are repeated or imitated by the successively
entering voices and developed in a continuous interweaving of
the voice parts into a well-defined single structure'.

only to a deep . . . called Blackwater: MS–95rc: 'to no place in
particular' (the passage, from 'the path leading' to 'being
dangerous', is absent from HW–A1). For 'Blackwater' cf. p. 127
and Note.

CHAPTER XLII

301 *Time in his own grey style*: according to Shelley's *Epipsychidion*,
it is 'Young Love' that is doing the teaching ('Young Love

should teach Time, in his own gray style, / All that thou [basically, Ideal Love] art' [ll. 55–6]). But Farfrae's response to knowledge of Lucetta's life is a pragmatic, more shallow redaction of Shelley's speaker's efforts to accept the evolutions of an Ideal Love. The principal difference is that while Shelley's speaker cannot find words to express transcendent love, Farfrae ceases to feel intense love.

303 *netted*: ensnared by stratagem or wile; or simply caged.

Juno's bird . . . Argus eyes: an evocation of spying and self-consciousness. Zeus had fallen in love with Io, and barely prevented discovery by his wife Juno (Hera) by turning Io into a heifer. To make certain Io is not returned to human shape, Juno sets Argus—some of whose hundred eyes are always open—to watch her. Mercury (Hermes), at Zeus's order, sings to Argus and puts all hundred eyes to sleep, whereupon he kills Argus. Juno then puts Argus' eyes on to the tail feathers of her sacred bird, the peacock, which has become the image of preening vanity. (Io also has a parallel with Elizabeth-Jane, for after other trials she regains human form and has thereafter a happy life, bearing by Zeus a son, one of whose descendants is Hercules.)

ken: sight; range of vision; knowledge.

304 *solicitus timor*: anxious fear (Latin).

305 *with an appraising, pondering gaze at her*: MS–A1: 'with a Scotchman's pondering, world-not-realized gaze at her'.

306 *"Thank you for those new books . . . "It cannot!"*: that Farfrae has been giving books to Elizabeth-Jane is first made explicit in 95rc—cf. Note to p. 314.

locus standi: (Latin) literally, a 'place to stand'; a recognized position, or right to appear in court. Hardy's word-choice evokes both the common saying 'there's no place for me here' and Henchard's characteristic application to himself of a merciless legalistic standard of behaviour.

behind a wall . . . and then kiss her: the oddness of this image—although Henchard is behind a wall he sees that Elizabeth-Jane looks around before she and Farfrae kiss—was created during Hardy's revisions for E1 and 95. In MS–A1 there are two meetings between the lovers. Henchard is behind the wall during one of them; and the kiss occurs during the second, south of Casterbridge, which Henchard observes through an eye-glass as he lies hidden in the huge earthwork outside Casterbridge.

For E1 Hardy moved the description of Henchard's spying so that it is the returned Newson he sees in his telescope (cf. Note to pp. 309–11). Then, while reading proofs for 95 he restored Farfrae's and Elizabeth-Jane's kiss, but placed it here, with the passage 'and then kiss her, the girl looking quickly round to assure herself that nobody was near'.

CHAPTER XLIII

309 *éclat*: brilliance (French).

tittle: an extremely small or the smallest amount.

His health declined; he became morbidly sensitive: added in E1.

310–11 Henchard's resorting to the earthen fort to spy upon Elizabeth-Jane is taken from an earlier passage in MS–A1 (cf. Note to p. 306); but E1 adds the appearance of Newson and Elizabeth-Jane's mentioning to Henchard the strange letter she has received. (In MS–A1, Elizabeth-Jane had been meeting Newson surreptitiously for some time—cf. Note to p. 314.)

310 *Via*: road (Latin).

transfixture: 'The condition of being transfixed or fixed to the spot with some feeling' (*OED*, which gives this passage from *The Mayor of Casterbridge* as its example).

312 *for she could not urge . . . refrain from hating him*: MS–A1: 'and it must be confessed that there was a leaven of half-heartedness in her deprecations, which after-events explained' (cf. Note to p. 314).

when you know them all: added in E1.

knee-naps: leather covers worn over the knees by thatchers.

313 *that his state of hopelessness had weakened him*: added in E1.

Cain: Cain, the first-born son of Adam and Eve, killed his brother Abel (Genesis 4). He protests to God that his punishment, to be 'a fugitive and a vagabond . . . in the earth . . . is greater than I can bear' (verses 12–13). Henchard like Cain is an outcast for having violated basic human ties, but unlike Cain he does not protest the severity of his punishment nor his inadequacy to meet it.

314 *The meeting with the light-hearted father . . . what can I wish for more?"*: in MS–A1, Newson's reappearance is no surprise to Elizabeth-Jane. The two have been meeting several times a

week. Newson is quite content with this arrangement, as is consistent with his character in all the novel's versions; but Elizabeth-Jane's complicity is not consistent with her otherwise straightforward non-ironic approach to life nor with her evolving through Hardy's several revisions away from her initial simple and acquiescent personality. In E1–87, it is Newson who furnished the money so Elizabeth-Jane could purchase books, sending her money without revealing his identity but pledging her secrecy. This, too, of course, violates the characterization of Elizabeth-Jane, and also make necessary the change described in the Note to p. 306.

315 *schiedam*: a strong gin, named after the city of its origin in south-western Netherlands.

316 *nine or ten months before that day last week*: MS: '<a year or more> /nine or ten months/ before that day'; 'last week' was added on proofs for 95. The contradiction in time-span (the narrator has just given it as 'between one or two years' [p. 314]) is owing to the plot change discussed in another Note to p.314, in which Newson and Elizabeth-Jane had been meeting for some time.

Elizabeth sighed . . . ought to forget him now!": MS–A1: '"I never heard of such a thing!" said Elizabeth-Jane. "That's enough. He's a bad man. I can forget him now." '

CHAPTER XLIV

318 *quickset*: a hedge, usually of English hawthorn or whitethorn, for ornamentation or boundary marker.

five and twenty years before: MS–95: 'two or three and twenty years before'.

319 *pixy-ring*: 'A circular band of grass differing in colour from the grass around it, a phenomenon supposed by popular belief to be produced by fairies dancing: really caused by the growth of certain fungi' (*OED*). The fungus is the *Marasmius oreades*, which 'is unable to grow twice in the same place and so, when once established, grows relentlessly year by year in an ever-widening ring' (Geoffrey Keynes, *Times Literary Supplement*, 14 September 1984, p. 1021).

the Canadian woodsman: 'Cruising in the woods of Canada—Without a compass the best woodsman cannot keep a straight line. Walks in circles, occupying him from ½ hour to 2 hrs. &

an unobservant person will circumnavigate the same 100 acres
of wood all day long' (John Rowan, *The Emigrant and Sportsman
in Canada* [London, 1876], p. 273; recorded by Hardy in
Literary Notebooks, I, item 976 and note).

320 *pari passu*: at an equal pace (Latin).

nobody . . . will: MS–87: 'nobody, live on, and can't die if I try'.
(The pages containing this passage are crossed out in 95rc, and
the printer's copy which Hardy sent to Osgood, McIlvaine's
printers restoring this part of the novel [see the following note]
has not survived.)

320–7 *He often kept an eager ear . . . [end of Ch. XLIV]*: E1–87
have—instead of Henchard's abortive and nearly directly fatal
return to Casterbridge for Elizabeth-Jane's marriage—a comparatively brief description of the wedding-dance (cf. Note to 327).
An American admirer, Rebekah Owen, noticed that an English
edition she read (87) did not contain Henchard's return, which
she had read in A1. At her urging, which was backed up by her
sister Catherine and by Mary Drisher of New York, Hardy
restored this account in 95 (see Carl J. Weber, *Hardy and the Lady
from Madison Square* [Waterville, Maine: Colby College Press,
1952], pp. 64–5, 86), also making several minor but clarifying
alterations as well as adding Henchard's explicit acknowledgement
(p. 322, ll. 3–7) that in making one more effort to secure the
affection of Elizabeth-Jane he was risking his very life.

321 *what with this travelling without horses that's getting so common*:
an allusion to the impingement upon Wessex of the railroad (cf.
Note to p. 262).

Martin's Day: St Martin's Day, 11 November.

sequestration: in this context (cp. p. 79 and Note), separation or
isolation.

322 *a gentle wish . . . hearts*: this passage replaces in 95 the former
[MS–A1]: 'the question who was or was not present had
become a matter of indifference'. As with p. 322, ll. 3–7, this
alteration increases the sense of the emotional blow upon
Henchard of Elizabeth-Jane's rejection.

only two towns . . . at the latter: in MS-A1 there is only one
sizeable town along Henchard's route; the passage is absent in
E1–87 (see Note to p. 320–7); in 95 the town is named as
Shottsford; the second town, Melchester, appears in 12. It seems
that Henchard is working somewhere between Weydon Prior
(Weyhill) and Melchester (Salisbury).

323 *drag*: 'A device for retarding the rotation of the wheels of a vehicle when descending a hill; *esp.* an iron shoe to receive the wheel and cause friction on the ground' (*OED*).

lest he should mortify Farfrae and his bride: not in MS–A1.

324 *a Samson shorn*: Judges 16: 17: ' . . . he told her [Delilah] . . . if I be shaven, then my strength will go from me, and I shall become weak, and be like any other man.' By opening his secrets to Delilah, Samson brings about his own destruction; in like manner Henchard's uncharacteristic 'weakness' concerning Elizabeth-Jane makes *him* like 'any other man'.

that he loved so well as never to have revisited it: added in 95.

325 *emolliated*: 'to make weak, ineffective, or effeminate'.

a humble old friend: added in 95 (MS–A1: 'he').

326 *saltatory*: 'of or relating to dancing'; 'characterized by movement in leaps and bounds'; 'proceeding by leaps rather than by gradual transitions: discontinuous'.

who had indeed come and supplanted him: added in 95.

and stood like a dark ruin, obscured by "the shade from his own soul upthrown": this image of Henchard conflates two lines from Shelley's *Revolt of Islam*. Canto VII, stanza xxxvii: 'Such are the thoughts which, like the fires that flare / In storm-encompassed isles, we cherish yet / In this dark ruin . . . '. Shelley's speaker, who is encompassed by 'this dark ruin,' cherishes the possibility of 'some recompense' (stanza xxxvi).

The context of the second part of this image (Canto VIII, stanza vi) is a series of queries and answers regarding the source of one's fate. The speaker in Shelley's poem, like Hardy's narrator here, seems to suggest that one's deeds, and his or her reaction to the consequences of those deeds, stem from the individual's internal qualities.

> What is that Power? Some moon-struck sophist stood
> Watching the shade from his own soul upthrown
> Fill Heaven and darken Earth, and in such mood
> The Form he saw and worshipped was his own,
> His likeness in the world's vast mirror shown;
> And 'twere an innocent dream, but that a faith
> Nursed by fear's dew of poison, grows thereon,
> On all who scorn its laws, to wreak immortal wrath.

From G–A1 the first part of the image reads 'in dark despair' rather than 'like a dark ruin'. When Hardy dropped this section of the novel from E1–87, he retained the Shelleyan image for Henchard, moving it to the scene where Henchard sees Newson in his telescope (cf. Note to pp. 309–11), in the sentence 'He stood in dark despair, obscured by "the shade from his own soul upthrown" '. Thus, the full MS image was not printed until 95.

327 *how can I love . . . like this*: Hardy's concern to attain the wanted shadings with Elizabeth-Jane's character is nowhere more evident than in frequent small but pointed changes from several earlier versions of this statement—MS: 'how can I <love> do anything but hate a man who has served me like this'; G–A1: 'how can I do anything but *hate* a man . . . '; E1–87 [not in: see Note to pp. 320–7]; 95: 'how can I love, or do anything more for, a man who has served us like this'. Also, in the lines immediately above in this same speech, 'my warm-hearted real father' is added in 95; and also in 95 'a wicked invention of my death' replaces the neutral 'an account of my death'.

palliatives . . . elaborate argument: in E1–87, which lack Henchard's appearance at Elizabeth-Jane's wedding, much of this passage is retained, at the penultimate paragraph of Ch. XLIII (p. 317). *palliatives*: to palliate is 'to cover with excuses: conceal or disguise the enormity of by excuses and apologies'; 'to moderate the intensity of: lessen . . . *obs*: [to] moderate, compromise'.

CHAPTER XLV

328 *Crusoe*: Robinson Crusoe, in the book (1718) by Daniel Defoe, lived alone on an island for years after being shipwrecked, and several years further with a native companion before being rescued and returning home.

assize-town: as the county town, Casterbridge would be the site of periodical sessions of assizes (judge-and-jury courts, the highest local courts) for civil and criminal cases.

sensational exits: attending executions was a popular spectator sport until the authorities began to conduct them inside prison walls, away from public view.

antipodean: at the diametrically opposite side of the world—i.e. Australia. The passage is probably an allusion to criminals being transported to Australia (cf. Note to p. 54: 'Botany Bay').

329 *had discovered, in a screened corner . . . gift and token of repentance*:

in E1–87, Elizabeth-Jane is made to think of Henchard, and thus to go in search of him, by being reminded of him while living in his former house.

extenuate nothing: just before he stabs himself Othello says (*Othello*, v. ii. 340–3):

> I pray you, in your letters,
> When you shall these unlucky deeds relate,
> Speak of me as I am; nothing extenuate.
> Nor set down aught in malice.

330 *the victorine of the period*: cf. p. 93 and Note.

Minerva eyes: cf. p. 131.

whose gestures beamed with mind: from *The Revolt of Islam*, Canto I, stanza liv, describing females in an immortal Senate.

Diana Multimammia: many-breasted Diana (Latin), referring particularly to her temple at Ephesus where as goddess of fruitfulness she was depicted with many breasts. For 'tumuli' see Note to p. 82.

331 *"and that will make a hole in a sovereign," said Farfrae*: added in 87.

332 *ship-coal*: imported coal, perhaps brought on ship from Newcastle, thus expensive and probably of good quality.

I seed en go down street . . . I thought: E1–87: 'I couldn't forget him, and traipsed out here to look for him, about the time of your worshipful's wedding to the lady at yer side, and I seed him walking along in the rain, and I thought.' The phrase 'and I seed him walking along in the rain' remains in 95rc but was deleted in proof for 95.

332–3 *What, Whittle! . . . wretch as I*: added in E1.

333 *& that no man remember me*: added in MS interlinearly.

O I would not have minded . . . that last parting: 'my unkindness at' is added in 12; and the sentence is of course not in E1–87 (cf. Note to pp. 320–7).

334 *for having misunderstood him on his last visit*: not in E1–87.

for not having searched him out sooner: added in E1.

Capharnaum: Capernaum, on the north-western shore of the Sea of Galilee, important for military and government activities, and the site of several of Jesus' miracles as well as his headquarters for a time. The parallel is of course with Casterbridge, with

Henchard analogous to Jesus in causing the unwonted disturbance in the even keel of life which Elizabeth-Jane prefers.

treatment, of those: MS–95rc: 'treatment, even to the magnitude of positive pleasure, those'.

DIALECT GLOSSARY

as lief not, rather not, prefer not (233)

ballet, ballad (54)

be jowned, euphemism for 'be damned'; perhaps comes from 'be drowned' (131)

bruckle, unsteady and 'shaky' (*OED*); i.e. unreliable (53)

clane, (clean), i.e. entirely (15)

gawkhammer, 'a silly gaping fellow' (191)

hag-rid, colloquialism for 'out of sorts'; the term's original folk meaning is 'cursed' (i.e. ridden by a hag, or witch) (130)

hontish, haughty, unmannerly, boorish (267)

iron dogs, andirons (252)

jacknapes, a fop (168)

jumped-up, conceited, arrogant (168)

keacorn, windpipe or gullet (16)

larry, excitement, commotion (202)

leery, empty, i.e. hungry (136)

mid, may or might (277)

Od send, God send; i.e. God curse me, may I be damned (16)

plim, swell—in this case, inflated by intestinal gas (32)

rantipole, rakish, wild, unruly (232)

should have minded, bear in mind: would have been reminded, i.e. remembered (24)

sniff and snaff, trifles and foolish talk; the Victorian equivalent of a little light flirtation (114)

socked, sighed (292)

stunpoll, stonehead, blockhead (107)

taties, potatoes (53)

turmit-head, turnip-head (200)

twanking, complaining (86)

varden, farden; i.e. farthing (114)

voot, foot (113)

wambling, wandering about aimlessly (200)

'Wide-oh', see Explanatory Note (186)

zwailing, swaying or swaggering from side to side (191)

JANE AUSTEN	**Emma**
	Persuasion
	Pride and Prejudice
	Sense and Sensibility
ANNE BRONTË	**The Tenant of Wildfell Hall**
CHARLOTTE BRONTË	**Jane Eyre**
EMILY BRONTË	**Wuthering Heights**
WILKIE COLLINS	**The Woman in White**
JOSEPH CONRAD	**Heart of Darkness**
	Nostromo
CHARLES DARWIN	**The Origin of Species**
CHARLES DICKENS	**Bleak House**
	David Copperfield
	Great Expectations
	Hard Times
GEORGE ELIOT	**Middlemarch**
	The Mill on the Floss
ELIZABETH GASKELL	**Cranford**
THOMAS HARDY	**Jude the Obscure**
WALTER SCOTT	**Ivanhoe**
MARY SHELLEY	**Frankenstein**
ROBERT LOUIS STEVENSON	**Treasure Island**
BRAM STOKER	**Dracula**
WILLIAM MAKEPEACE THACKERAY	**Vanity Fair**
OSCAR WILDE	**The Picture of Dorian Gray**

THE OXFORD SHERLOCK HOLMES

American Literature

British and Irish Literature

Children's Literature

Classics and Ancient Literature

Colonial Literature

Eastern Literature

European Literature

History

Medieval Literature

Oxford English Drama

Poetry

Philosophy

Politics

Religion

The Oxford Shakespeare

A complete list of Oxford Paperbacks, including Oxford World's Classics, OPUS, Past Masters, Oxford Authors, Oxford Shakespeare, Oxford Drama, and Oxford Paperback Reference, is available in the UK from the Academic Division Publicity Department, Oxford University Press, Great Clarendon Street, Oxford OX2 6DP.

In the USA, complete lists are available from the Paperbacks Marketing Manager, Oxford University Press, 198 Madison Avenue, New York, NY 10016.

Oxford Paperbacks are available from all good bookshops. In case of difficulty, customers in the UK can order direct from Oxford University Press Bookshop, Freepost, 116 High Street, Oxford OX1 4BR, enclosing full payment. Please add 10 per cent of published price for postage and packing.